Connected Mathematics™

Stretching and Shrinking

Similarity

Teacher's Guide

Glenda Lappan
James T. Fey
William M. Fitzgerald
Susan N. Friel
Elizabeth Difanis Phillips

Needham, Massachusetts
Upper Saddle River, New Jersey

The Connected Mathematics™ Project was developed at Michigan State University with financial support from the Michigan State University Office of the Provost, Computing and Technology, and the College of Natural Science.

This material is based upon work supported by the National Science Foundation under Grant No. MDR 9150217.

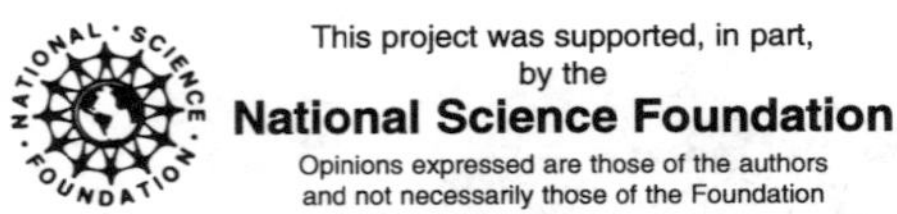

The Michigan State University authors and administration have agreed that all MSU royalties arising from this publication will be devoted to purposes supported by the Department of Mathematics and the MSU Mathematics Education Enrichment Fund.

Photo Acknowledgements: 14 © Superstock, Inc.; 21 © Barbara Alper/Stock, Boston; 25 © G. Ricatto/Superstock, Inc.; 30 © Mark M. Boulton, from National Audubon Society/Photo Researchers, Inc.; 37 © Nita Winter/The Image Works; 45 © Peter Menzel/Stock, Boston; 55 © J. Mahoney/The Image Works; 70 © Ira Kirschenbaum/Stock, Boston; 72 © N. Rowan/The Image Works

ISBN 0-13-180790-0
3 4 5 6 7 8 9 10 07 06 05 04

The Connected Mathematics Project Staff

Project Directors

James T. Fey
University of Maryland

William M. Fitzgerald
Michigan State University

Susan N. Friel
University of North Carolina at Chapel Hill

Glenda Lappan
Michigan State University

Elizabeth Difanis Phillips
Michigan State University

Project Manager

Kathy Burgis
Michigan State University

Technical Coordinator

Judith Martus Miller
Michigan State University

Collaborating Teachers/Writers

Mary K. Bouck
Portland, Michigan

Jacqueline Stewart
Okemos, Michigan

Curriculum Development Consultants

David Ben-Chaim
Weizmann Institute

Alex Friedlander
Weizmann Institute

Eleanor Geiger
University of Maryland

Jane Mitchell
University of North Carolina at Chapel Hill

Anthony D. Rickard
Alma College

Evaluation Team

Mark Hoover
Michigan State University

Diane V. Lambdin
Indiana University

Sandra K. Wilcox
Michigan State University

Judith S. Zawojewski
National-Louis University

Graduate Assistants

Scott J. Baldridge
Michigan State University

Angie S. Eshelman
Michigan State University

M. Faaiz Gierdien
Michigan State University

Jane M. Keiser
Indiana University

Angela S. Krebs
Michigan State University

James M. Larson
Michigan State University

Ronald Preston
Indiana University

Tat Ming Sze
Michigan State University

Sarah Theule-Lubienski
Michigan State University

Jeffrey J. Wanko
Michigan State University

Field Test Production Team

Katherine Oesterle
Michigan State University

Stacey L. Otto
University of North Carolina at Chapel Hill

Teacher/Assessment Team

Kathy Booth
Waverly, Michigan

Anita Clark
Marshall, Michigan

Julie Faulkner
Traverse City, Michigan

Theodore Gardella
Bloomfield Hills, Michigan

Yvonne Grant
Portland, Michigan

Linda R. Lobue
Vista, California

Suzanne McGrath
Chula Vista, California

Nancy McIntyre
Troy, Michigan

Mary Beth Schmitt
Traverse City, Michigan

Linda Walker
Tallahassee, Florida

Software Developer

Richard Burgis
East Lansing, Michigan

Development Center Directors

Nicholas Branca
San Diego State University

Dianne Briars
Pittsburgh Public Schools

Frances R. Curcio
New York University

Perry Lanier
Michigan State University

J. Michael Shaughnessy
Portland State University

Charles Vonder Embse
Central Michigan University

Field Test Coordinators

Michelle Bohan
Queens, New York

Melanie Branca
San Diego, California

Alecia Devantier
Shepherd, Michigan

Jenny Jorgensen
Flint, Michigan

Sandra Kralovec
Portland, Oregon

Sonia Marsalis
Flint, Michigan

William Schaeffer
Pittsburgh, Pennsylvania

Karma Vince
Toledo, Ohio

Virginia Wolf
Pittsburgh, Pennsylvania

Shirel Yaloz
Queens, New York

Student Assistants

Laura Hammond
David Roche
Courtney Stoner
Jovan Trpovski
Julie Valicenti
Michigan State University

Advisory Board

Joseph Adney
Michigan State University (Emeritus)

Charles Allan
Michigan Department of Education

Mary K. Bouck
Portland Public Schools
Portland, Michigan

C. Stuart Brewster
Palo Alto, California

Anita Clark
Marshall Public Schools
Marshall, Michigan

David Doherty
GMI Engineering and Management Institute
Flint, Michigan

Kay Gilliland
EQUALS
Berkeley, California

David Green
GMI Engineering and Management Institute
Flint, Michigan

Henry Heikkinen
University of Northern Colorado
Greeley, Colorado

Anita Johnston
Jackson Community College
Jackson, Michigan

Elizabeth M. Jones
Lansing School District
Lansing, Michigan

Jim Landwehr
AT&T Bell Laboratories
Murray Hill, New Jersey

Peter Lappan
Michigan State University

Steven Leinwand
Connecticut Department of Education

Nancy McIntyre
Troy Public Schools
Troy, Michigan

Valerie Mills
Ypsilanti Public Schools
Ypsilanti, Michigan

David S. Moore
Purdue University
West Lafayette, Indiana

Ralph Oliva
Texas Instruments
Dallas, Texas

Richard Phillips
Michigan State University

Jacob Plotkin
Michigan State University

Dawn Pysarchik
Michigan State University

Rheta N. Rubenstein
University of Windsor
Windsor, Ontario, Canada

Susan Jo Russell
TERC
Cambridge, Massachusetts

Marjorie Senechal
Smith College
Northampton, Massachusetts

Sharon Senk
Michigan State University

Jacqueline Stewart
Okemos School District
Okemos, Michigan

Uri Treisman
University of Texas
Austin, Texas

Irvin E. Vance
Michigan State University

Linda Walker
Tallahassee Public Schools
Tallahassee, Florida

Gail Weeks
Northville Public Schools
Northville, Michigan

Pilot Teachers

California

National City

Laura Chavez
National City Middle School

Ruth Ann Duncan
National City Middle School

Sonia Nolla
National City Middle School

San Diego

James Ciolli
Los Altos Elementary School

Chula Vista

Agatha Graney
Hilltop Middle School

Suzanne McGrath
Eastlake Elementary School

Toni Miller
Hilltop Middle School

Lakeside

Eva Hollister
Tierra del Sol Middle School

Vista

Linda LoBue
Washington Middle School

Illinois

Evanston

Marlene Robinson
Baker Demonstration School

Michigan

Bloomfield Hills

Roxanne Cleveland
Bloomfield Hills Middle School

Constance Kelly
Bloomfield Hills Middle School

Tim Loula
Bloomfield Hills Middle School

Audrey Marsalese
Bloomfield Hills Middle School

Kara Reid
Bloomfield Hills Middle School

Joann Schultz
Bloomfield Hills Middle School

Flint

Joshua Coty
Holmes Middle School

Brenda Duckett-Jones
Brownell Elementary School

Lisa Earl
Holmes Middle School

Anne Heidel
Holmes Middle School

Chad Meyers
Brownell Elementary School

Greg Mickelson
Holmes Middle School

Rebecca Ray
Holmes Middle School

Patricia Wagner
Holmes Middle School

Greg Williams
Gundry Elementary School

Lansing

Susan Bissonette
Waverly Middle School

Kathy Booth
Waverly East Intermediate School

Carole Campbell
Waverly East Intermediate School

Gary Gillespie
Waverly East Intermediate School

Denise Kehren
Waverly Middle School

Virginia Larson
Waverly East Intermediate School

Kelly Martin
Waverly Middle School

Laurie Metevier
Waverly East Intermediate School

Craig Paksi
Waverly East Intermediate School

Tony Pecoraro
Waverly Middle School

Helene Rewa
Waverly East Intermediate School

Arnold Stiefel
Waverly Middle School

Portland

Bill Carlton
Portland Middle School

Kathy Dole
Portland Middle School

Debby Flate
Portland Middle School

Yvonne Grant
Portland Middle School

Terry Keusch
Portland Middle School

John Manzini
Portland Middle School

Mary Parker
Portland Middle School

Scott Sandborn
Portland Middle School

Shepherd

Steve Brant
Shepherd Middle School

Marty Brock
Shepherd Middle School

Cathy Church
Shepherd Middle School

Ginny Crandall
Shepherd Middle School

Craig Ericksen
Shepherd Middle School

Natalie Hackney
Shepherd Middle School

Bill Hamilton
Shepherd Middle School

Julie Salisbury
Shepherd Middle School

Sturgis

Sandra Allen
Eastwood Elementary School

Margaret Baker
Eastwood Elementary School

Steven Baker
Eastwood Elementary School

Keith Barnes
Sturgis Middle School

Wilodean Beckwith
Eastwood Elementary School

Darcy Bird
Eastwood Elementary School

Bill Dickey
Sturgis Middle School

Ellen Eisele
Sturgis Middle School

James Hoelscher
Sturgis Middle School

Richard Nolan
Sturgis Middle School

J. Hunter Raiford
Sturgis Middle School

Cindy Sprowl
Eastwood Elementary School

Leslie Stewart
Eastwood Elementary School

Connie Sutton
Eastwood Elementary School

Traverse City

Maureen Bauer
Interlochen Elementary School

Ivanka Berskshire
East Junior High School

Sarah Boehm
Courtade Elementary School

Marilyn Conklin
Interlochen Elementary School

Nancy Crandall
Blair Elementary School

Fran Cullen
Courtade Elementary School

Eric Dreier
Old Mission Elementary School

Lisa Dzierwa
Cherry Knoll Elementary School

Ray Fouch
West Junior High School

Ed Hargis
Willow Hill Elementary School

Richard Henry
West Junior High School

Dessie Hughes
Cherry Knoll Elementary School

Ruthanne Kladder
Oak Park Elementary School

Bonnie Knapp
West Junior High School

Sue Laisure
Sabin Elementary School

Stan Malaski
Oak Park Elementary School

Jody Meyers
Sabin Elementary School

Marsha Myles
East Junior High School

Mary Beth O'Neil
Traverse Heights Elementary School

Jan Palkowski
East Junior High School

Karen Richardson
Old Mission Elementary School

Kristin Sak
Bertha Vos Elementary School

Mary Beth Schmitt
East Junior High School

Mike Schrotenboer
Norris Elementary School

Gail Smith
Willow Hill Elementary School

Karrie Tufts
Eastern Elementary School

Mike Wilson
East Junior High School

Tom Wilson
West Junior High School

Minnesota

Minneapolis

Betsy Ford
Northeast Middle School

New York

East Elmhurst

Allison Clark
Louis Armstrong Middle School

Dorothy Hershey
Louis Armstrong Middle School

J. Lewis McNeece
Louis Armstrong Middle School

Rossana Perez
Louis Armstrong Middle School

Merna Porter
Louis Armstrong Middle School

Marie Turini
Louis Armstrong Middle School

North Carolina

Durham

Everly Broadway
Durham Public Schools

Thomas Carson
Duke School for Children

Mary Hebrank
Duke School for Children

Bill O'Connor
Duke School for Children

Ruth Pershing
Duke School for Children

Peter Reichert
Duke School for Children

Elizabeth City

Rita Banks
Elizabeth City Middle School

Beth Chaundry
Elizabeth City Middle School

Amy Cuthbertson
Elizabeth City Middle School

Deni Dennison
Elizabeth City Middle School

Jean Gray
Elizabeth City Middle School

John McMenamin
Elizabeth City Middle School

Nicollette Nixon
Elizabeth City Middle School

Malinda Norfleet
Elizabeth City Middle School

Joyce O'Neal
Elizabeth City Middle School

Clevie Sawyer
Elizabeth City Middle School

Juanita Shannon
Elizabeth City Middle School

Terry Thorne
Elizabeth City Middle School

Rebecca Wardour
Elizabeth City Middle School

Leora Winslow
Elizabeth City Middle School

Franklinton

Susan Haywood
Franklinton Elementary School

Clyde Melton
Franklinton Elementary School

Louisburg

Lisa Anderson
Terrell Lane Middle School

Jackie Frazier
Terrell Lane Middle School

Pam Harris
Terrell Lane Middle School

Ohio

Toledo

Bonnie Bias
Hawkins Elementary School

Marsha Jackish
Hawkins Elementary School

Lee Jagodzinski
DeVeaux Junior High School

Norma J. King
Old Orchard Elementary School

Margaret McCready
Old Orchard Elementary School

Carmella Morton
DeVeaux Junior High School

Karen C. Rohrs
Hawkins Elementary School

Marie Sahloff
DeVeaux Junior High School

L. Michael Vince
McTigue Junior High School

Brenda D. Watkins
Old Orchard Elementary School

Oregon

Canby

Sandra Kralovec
Ackerman Middle School

Portland

Roberta Cohen
Catlin Gabel School

David Ellenberg
Catlin Gabel School

Sara Normington
Catlin Gabel School

Karen Scholte-Arce
Catlin Gabel School

West Linn

Marge Burack
Wood Middle School

Tracy Wygant
Athey Creek Middle School

Pennsylvania

Pittsburgh

Sheryl Adams
Reizenstein Middle School

Sue Barie
Frick International Studies Academy

Suzie Berry
Frick International Studies Academy

Richard Delgrosso
Frick International Studies Academy

Janet Falkowski
Frick International Studies Academy

Joanne George
Reizenstein Middle School

Harriet Hopper
Reizenstein Middle School

Chuck Jessen
Reizenstein Middle School

Ken Labuskes
Reizenstein Middle School

Barbara Lewis
Reizenstein Middle School

Sharon Mihalich
Reizenstein Middle School

Marianne O'Connor
Frick International Studies Academy

Mark Sammartino
Reizenstein Middle School

Washington

Seattle

Chris Johnson
University Preparatory Academy

Rick Purn
University Preparatory Academy

Contents

Overview

A knowledge of the concept of similarity is important to the development of children's understanding of the geometry in their environment. In their immediate environment and in their studies of natural and social sciences, students frequently encounter phenomena that require familiarity with the ideas of enlargement, scale factors, area growth, indirect measurement, and other similarity-related concepts. Similarity is an instance of proportionality. Piaget considered proportional reasoning one of the six abilities that characterize formal-operational thinking.

Students in the middle grades often experience difficulty with ideas of scale. They confuse *adding* situations with *multiplying* situations. Situations requiring comparison by addition or subtraction come first in students' experience with mathematics and often dominate their thinking about any comparison situation, even those in which *scale* is the fundamental issue. When considering the dimensions of a rectangle that began as 3 units by 5 units and was enlarged to a similar rectangle with a short side of 6 units, many students will say the long side is now 8 units rather than 10 units; they add 3 units to the 5 units rather than multiply the 5 by 2. These students may struggle to build a useful conception that will help them distinguish between situations that call for addition and situations that call for scaling up or down, which are multiplicative.

The problems in this unit are designed to help students begin to accumulate the knowledge and experiences necessary to make these kinds of distinctions and to reason about scaling in geometry situations. The next unit, *Comparing and Scaling,* continues to develop these ideas in scaling situations that are more numerical.

The investigations in this unit are new to the middle grades curriculum: they are geometric, and they require the students' active involvement. Students cannot be expected to absorb everything in a single experience, so important concepts and ideas are repeated in new contexts throughout the unit.

The Mathematics in *Stretching and Shrinking*

The activities in the beginning of the unit elicit students' first notion about similarity as two figures with the same shape. Students may have difficulty with the concept of similarity because of the way the word is used in everyday language—family members are "similar," houses are "similar." Through the activities in *Stretching and Shrinking,* students will grow to understand that the everyday use of a word and its mathematical use may be different. For us to determine definitively whether two figures are similar, ***similarity*** must have a precise mathematical definition.

Tests for Similarity

Two figures are similar if (1) the measures of their corresponding angles are equal and (2) the lengths of their corresponding sides increase by the same factor, called the *scale factor.*

For rectangles, since all angles are right angles, we need only check the ratios of the lengths of corresponding sides. For example, rectangles A and B are similar, but neither is similar to rectangle C.

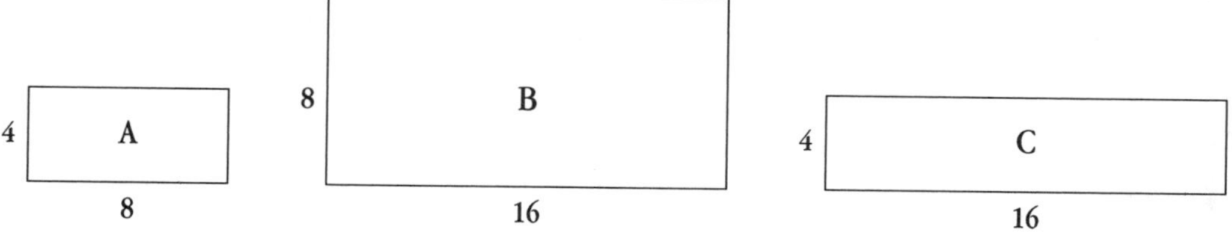

The scale factor from rectangle A to rectangle B is 2 because the length of each side of rectangle A multiplied by 2 gives the length of the corresponding side of rectangle B. The scale factor from rectangle B to rectangle A is $\frac{1}{2}$ because the length of each side of rectangle B multiplied by $\frac{1}{2}$ gives the length of the corresponding side of rectangle A. Rectangle C is not similar to rectangle A, because the lengths of corresponding sides do not increase by the same factor.

The perimeter from rectangle A to rectangle B also increases by a scale factor of 2, but the area increases by the square of the scale factor, or 4. This can be seen by dividing rectangle B into four rectangles congruent to rectangle A.

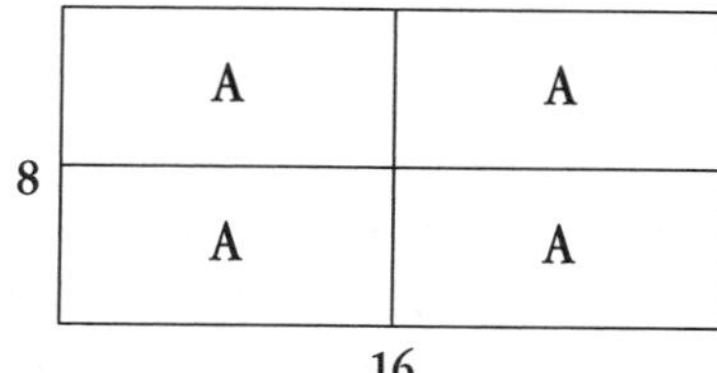

For triangles to be similar, the measures of corresponding angles must be equal and the lengths of corresponding sides must increase by the same factor. Through their experiments with rep-tiles in Investigation 3, students discover a special property of triangles: angles are what determine a triangle's shape, and we only have to check the angles to determine whether two triangles are similar. The ratio of corresponding sides will be equal if corresponding angles are equal.

For polygons other than rectangles and triangles, we must make sure that corresponding angles are congruent and that lengths of corresponding sides increase by the same scale factor.

Equivalent Ratios

In similar figures, there are several equivalent ratios. Some are formed by comparing lengths within a figure. Others are formed by comparing lengths between two figures. For example, for the rectangles on page 1b, the ratio of length to width is $\frac{4}{8}$ or $\frac{1}{2}$ for rectangle A and $\frac{8}{16}$ or $\frac{1}{2}$ for rectangle B. We could also look at the ratios of corresponding sides: width to width and length to length are $\frac{8}{16}$ and $\frac{4}{8}$, respectively, which are equivalent ratios.

Equivalent ratios can be used to solve interesting problems. For example, shadows made by the sun can be thought of as sides of similar triangles, because the sunlight hits the objects at the same angle. Shown below is a building of unknown height and a meterstick, both of which are casting a shadow. To find the height of the building, we can use the scale factor between the lengths of the shadows. Since going from 0.25 to 10 involves a scale factor of 40, we multiply the height of the meterstick by 40 to obtain the height of the building, or 40 meters. We could also think of this as $\frac{x}{10} = \frac{1}{0.25}$ and use equivalent fractions to find the value of x that would make the ratios equivalent.

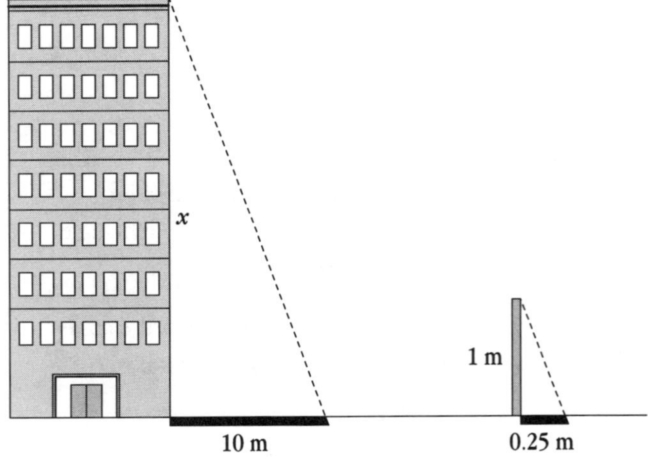

Similarity Transformations

The rubber-band stretcher introduced in Investigation 1 is a tool for physically producing a similarity transformation. It does not give precise results, but it is an effective way to introduce students to similarity transformations. More precision is gained in transformations governed by algebraic rules that specify how coordinates are to be changed.

In this unit, students will create figures on a coordinate system and use algebraic rules to transform them into similar figures. For example, if the coordinates of a figure are multiplied by 2, the algebraic transformation is from (x, y) to $(2x, 2y)$. In general, if the coordinates of a figure are (x, y), algebraic rules of the form $(nx + a, ny + b)$ will transform it into a similar figure with a scale factor of n. These algebraic rules are called *similarity transformations.*

Mathematical and Problem-Solving Goals

Stretching and Shrinking **was created to help students**

- Enlarge figures using rubber-band stretchers and coordinate plotting
- Informally visualize similar and distorted transformations
- Identify similar figures visually and by comparing sides and angles
- Recognize that lengths between similar figures change by a constant scale factor
- Build larger, similar shapes from copies of a basic shape
- Divide a shape into smaller, similar shapes
- Recognize the relationship between similarity and equivalent fractions
- Learn the effect of scale factor on length ratios and area ratios
- Discover that areas of similar figures are related by the square of the scale factor
- Observe and visualize ratios of lengths and areas
- Recognize that triangles with equal corresponding sides are similar
- Recognize that rectangles with equivalent ratios of corresponding sides are similar
- Determine and use scale factors to find unknown lengths
- Collect examples of figures and search for patterns in the examples
- Use the concept of similarity to solve real-world problems
- Draw or construct counterexamples to explore similarity transformations
- Make connections between algebra and geometry
- Use geometry software to explore similarity transformations

The overall goal of the Connected Mathematics curriculum is to help students develop sound mathematical habits. Through their work in this and other geometry units, students learn important questions to ask themselves about any situation that can be represented and modeled mathematically, such as: *How does the mathematical idea of "similar" differ from the everyday use of the word? In similar figures, what is exactly the same? What is different? How is it different? How can we find a way to describe the sizes of two similar figures? When figures are similar, what relationship can we find in their areas? In their perimeters? Where can we apply these similarity concepts in the everyday world? Can the coordinate system help us understand similarity? To understand ratios? How do ideas of stretching and shrinking tie algebra and geometry together?*

Summary of Investigations

Investigation 1: Enlarging Figures

Similarity is introduced at an informal level, and students use their intuition about enlargements to answer questions about how simple figures grow. Students make drawings of similar figures by using a pair of rubber bands, then compare side lengths, perimeters, and areas of the original and enlarged figures.

Investigation 2: Similar Figures

Students build a good working definition of *similar* in mathematical terms, and they begin to see connections between geometry and algebra. Using the coordinate system, they draw several geometric figures, some that are similar to one another and others that are distorted. They explore algebraic rules that cause images to change size and to move about the coordinate plane, and they compare angle measures and lengths of corresponding sides informally as they investigate transformations. For the first time, students find that for two figures to be similar, corresponding angles must be congruent and corresponding sides must grow by the same factor.

Investigation 3: Patterns of Similar Figures

Students deepen their understanding of what it means for two figures to be similar. In addition, they explore the relationship between the areas of similar figures. The idea that area does not grow at the same rate as side length when a figure is enlarged so that its shape is preserved is quite difficult to grasp. Through experiments with rep-tiles—shapes of which copies can be put together to make larger, similar shapes—students explore what it takes for figures to be similar and discover how triangles are special. These experiences help them build mental images to support their evolving ideas about the relationship between scale factor and area.

Investigation 4: Using Similarity

Students discover the usefulness of their new knowledge of similarity and scale factors by solving real-world problems. Each problem focuses on the concept of similar rectangles, and determining the scale factor is the key to its solution.

Investigation 5: Similar Triangles

Students apply their new knowledge about similarity of triangles to real-world problems. They use the shadow and mirror methods to find the height of a tall object, and they compare their data to decide which method gives more consistent results. They also use similar triangles to find the distance across a physical feature, such as a pond. In each problem, they employ the special feature of triangles—that they are similar if their corresponding angles are equal.

Investigation 6: Stretching and Shrinking with a Computer

Students use the Logo programming language to investigate the effects of changes in scale. Because the *Turtle Math* software dynamically demonstrates the effects of changing scale, it is particularly useful for building students' conceptual understanding of negative scale factors. This investigation requires *Turtle Math* software and only one or two days of computer access.

Connections to Other Units

The ideas in *Stretching and Shrinking* build on and connect to several big ideas in other Connected Mathematics units.

Big Idea	Prior Work	Future Work
enlarging and shrinking plane figures	finding angle measures, lengths, and areas of plane geometric figures (*Shapes and Designs*; *Covering and Surrounding*)	scaling quantities, objects, and shapes up and down (*Comparing and Scaling*; *Filling and Wrapping*; *Data Around Us*)
identifying the corresponding parts of similar figures	developing and applying concepts of vertex, angle, angle measure, side, and side length (*Shapes and Designs*; *Covering and Surrounding*)	analyzing how two-dimensional shapes are affected by different isometries; generating isometric transformations (*Kaleidoscopes, Hubcaps, and Mirrors*)
describing and producing transformations of plane figures	developing computer programs to construct two-dimensional shapes (*Shapes and Designs*); developing strategies for representing three-dimensional objects in two dimensions (*Ruins of Montarek*); using symbols to communicate operations (*Variables and Patterns*)	finding the equation of a line (*Moving Straight Ahead*); expressing linear relationships with symbols; determining whether linear expressions are equivalent (*Say It with Symbols*); writing directions for isometries in two dimensions (*Kaleidoscopes, Hubcaps, and Mirrors*)
analyzing scale factors between figures; applying scale factors to solve two-dimensional geometric problems	using factors and multiples (*Prime Time*); measuring two-dimensional figures (*Covering and Surrounding*); using ratios in fraction form (*Bits and Pieces I*; *Bits and Pieces II*); using maps (*Variables and Patterns*)	scaling and comparing figures and quantities (*Comparing and Scaling*; *Data Around Us*); using slope to solve problems involving linear relationships (*Moving Straight Ahead*)
applying properties of similar figures	exploring properties of two-dimensional shapes; finding areas, perimeters, and side lengths of shapes (*Shapes and Designs*; *Covering and Surrounding*)	exploring ratios and proportional relationships (*Comparing and Scaling*); developing the concept of slope (*Moving Straight Ahead*)
using the computer program *Turtle Math* to generate similar figures and to apply properties of similar figures	writing Logo programs to produce geometric shapes with specified properties (*Shapes and Designs*)	using a graphing calculator to apply mathematical models to problem situations (*Thinking with Mathematical Models*)

Materials

For students

- Labsheets
- Graphing calculators
- Shapes A, B, C, D, G, I, J, K, L, O, P, R, and T from the ShapeSet™ or 4 copies of each cut from Labsheet 3.2 (1 set per student; see "Manipulatives" on the next page)
- No. 16 (3 inch) rubber bands (2 per student)
- State or local maps (optional)
- Mirrors (1 per student or group)
- Centimeter and half-centimeter grid paper (provided as blackline masters)
- Dot paper (optional; provided as a blackline master)
- Transparent centimeter and half-centimeter grids (optional; copy the grids onto transparency film)
- Macintosh computer with *Turtle Math* software (optional; 1 for every 2–4 students; see "Technology" on the next page)
- Angle rulers (1 per 2–4 students)
- Masking tape
- Scissors (optional)
- Rulers and metersticks (1 per student or group)
- Tools for measuring longer distances, such as tape measures, string, or sticks cut to 1 meter
- Blank sheets of transparency film (optional)
- Blank sheets of paper

For the teacher

- Transparencies and transparency markers (optional)
- ShapeSet or transparencies of shapes A, B, C, D, G, I, J, K, L, O, P, R, and T from Labsheet 3.2 (copy the labsheet onto transparency film)
- $8\frac{1}{2}$" by 11", 11" by 14", and 11" by 17" sheets of paper (optional; 1 of each)
- Transparencies of Labsheet 3.3 (optional)
- Transparent centimeter and half-centimeter grids (optional; copy the grids onto transparency film)
- Chart paper (optional)
- Macintosh computer with *Turtle Math* software (optional)

Manipulatives

Investigation 3 and the optional Unit Project use shapes from the ShapeSet, which is available through Dale Seymour Publications®. The ShapeSet is a set of polygons that students can use to explore similarity and scale. If you do not have ShapeSets, you can make the shapes needed in Investigation 3 by copying the labsheet provided and cutting out the shapes. Or, make complete ShapeSets (needed for the optional Unit Project) from the blackline masters provided. A ShapeSet consists of 16 copies of shapes A and B and 8 copies of the remaining polygons.

Technology

We expect that students will use calculators freely to perform arithmetic computations so that their focus can be on analyzing the problems and searching for patterns. Connected Mathematics was developed with the belief that calculators should always be available and that students should decide when to use them. For this reason, we do not designate specific problems as "calculator problems."

Investigation 6 was written for use with *Turtle Math,* a version of the Logo computer language. *Turtle Math* runs on a Macintosh computer (system requirements: model LC or better, System 7 or later, minimum of 4 MB RAM). Ideally, Investigation 6 should be done with one computer per two to four students. However, because the learning payoff of the investigation is significant, it is recommended that even if you have only one computer, you do this investigation as a demonstration.

Pacing Chart

This pacing chart gives estimates of the class time required for each investigation and assessment piece. Shaded rows indicate opportunities for assessment.

Investigations and Assessments	Class Time
1 Enlarging Figures	2 days
2 Similar Figures	4 days
Check-Up	$\frac{1}{2}$ day
3 Patterns of Similar Figures	3 days
Quiz A	1 day
4 Using Similarity	4 days
Quiz B	1 day
5 Similar Triangles	3 days
6 Stretching and Shrinking with a Computer	2 days
Unit Test	1 day
Self-Assessment	Take home
Unit Project (optional)	1 day

Stretching and Shrinking Vocabulary

The following words and concepts are used in *Stretching and Shrinking.* Concepts in the left column are those essential for student understanding of this and future units. The Descriptive Glossary gives descriptions of many of these words.

Essential terms developed in this unit	**Terms developed in previous units**	**Nonessential terms**
compare	angle	coordinate graphing
corresponds, corresponding	angle measure	midpoint
image	area	rep-tile
ratio	congruent	transform, transformation
scale, scale factor	coordinate graphing	image
similar	coordinates	
	diameter	
	dimensions	
	line plot	
	line segment	
	parallel	
	perimeter	
	perpendicular	
	vertex	

Assessment Summary

Embedded Assessment

Opportunities for informal assessment of student progress are embedded throughout *Stretching and Shrinking* in the problems, the ACE questions, and the Mathematical Reflections. Suggestions for observing as students explore and discover mathematical ideas, for probing to guide their progress in developing concepts and skills, and for questioning to determine their level of understanding can be found in the Launch, Explore, or Summarize sections of all investigation problems. Some examples:

- Investigation 5, Problem 5.1 *Launch* (page 74a) suggests how you can help your students understand the theory behind the technique of measuring shadows to estimate an object's height and then assess their grasp of the concept.
- Investigation 4, Problem 4.4 *Explore* (page 58e) suggests questions you can ask to assess students' understanding of the scale on a map and how it relates to measurements of area.
- Investigation 3, Problem 3.2 *Summarize* (page 40c) suggests an activity you can use to help students discover what makes triangles special in the context of similarity: if their angles are equal, two triangles are automatically similar.

ACE Assignments

An ACE (Applications–Connections–Extensions) section appears at the end of each investigation. To help you assign ACE questions, a list of assignment choices is given in the margin next to the reduced student page for each problem. Each list indicates the ACE questions that students should be able to answer after they complete the problem. Many of the ACE questions in this unit ask students to decide whether two or more shapes are similar. With these types of questions, grid paper, transparent grids, and dot paper can be very helpful. We recommend that students have access to these throughout their work in this unit.

Partner Quiz

Two quizzes, which may be given after Investigations 3 and 4, are provided with *Stretching and Shrinking.* These quizzes are designed to be completed by pairs of students with the opportunity for revision based on teacher feedback. You will find the quizzes and their answers in the Assessment Resources section. As an alternative to the quizzes provided, you can construct your own quizzes by combining questions from these quizzes, the Question Bank, and unassigned ACE questions.

Check-Ups

One check-up, which may be given after Investigation 2, is provided for use as a quick quiz or warm-up activity. The check-up is designed for students to complete individually. You will find the check-up and its answer key in the Assessment Resources section.

Question Bank

A Question Bank provides questions you can use for homework, reviews, or quizzes. You will find the Question Bank and its answer key in the Assessment Resources section.

Notebook/Journal

Students should have notebooks to record and organize their work. Notebooks should include student journals and sections for vocabulary, homework, and quizzes and check-ups. In their journals, students can take notes, solve investigation problems, write down ideas for their projects, and record their ideas about Mathematical Reflections questions. Journals should be assessed for completeness rather than correctness; they should be seen as "safe" places where students can try out their thinking. A Notebook Checklist and a Self-Assessment are provided in the Assessment Resources section. The Notebook Checklist helps students organize their notebooks. The Self-Assessment guides students as they review their notebooks to determine which ideas they have mastered and which they still need to work on.

Unit Test

The final assessment in *Stretching and Shrinking* is a unit test with in-class and take-home portions. The in-class test focuses on similarity concepts and their use in real-world situations. The take-home project gives students an opportunity to demonstrate their understanding of the concepts studied in the unit in a creative way. Students select an image, enlarge or shrink it by plotting coordinates on a grid, and prepare a display and write a report on their work, including an analysis of how the image changed and how it remained the same.

The Optional Unit Project: All-Similar Shapes

The All-Similar Shapes Project is an opportunity for students to investigate more shapes and further develop their understanding of similarity. Students sort a set of shapes into groups of shapes that are similar to all others of that type. A shortened explanation of the project appears at the end of the student text.

Introducing Your Students to *Stretching and Shrinking*

One way to introduce this unit is by discussing the questions on the opening page of the student edition, which are designed to start students thinking about the concept of similarity and the ways in which it can be used. Allow students to share their ideas.

Talk with the class about the meaning of the word *similarity* as it is used in everyday conversation. You may want to show photographs or pictures from magazines, which represent objects that are often many times larger than the image in the photograph but have the same shape. Most students are familiar with scale models of airplanes, cars, and trains. Keep the conversation focused on eliciting what students think the word *similar* means rather than on trying to define the word mathematically. When students propose situations in which they think similarity is used, ask how they could judge whether two objects are similar.

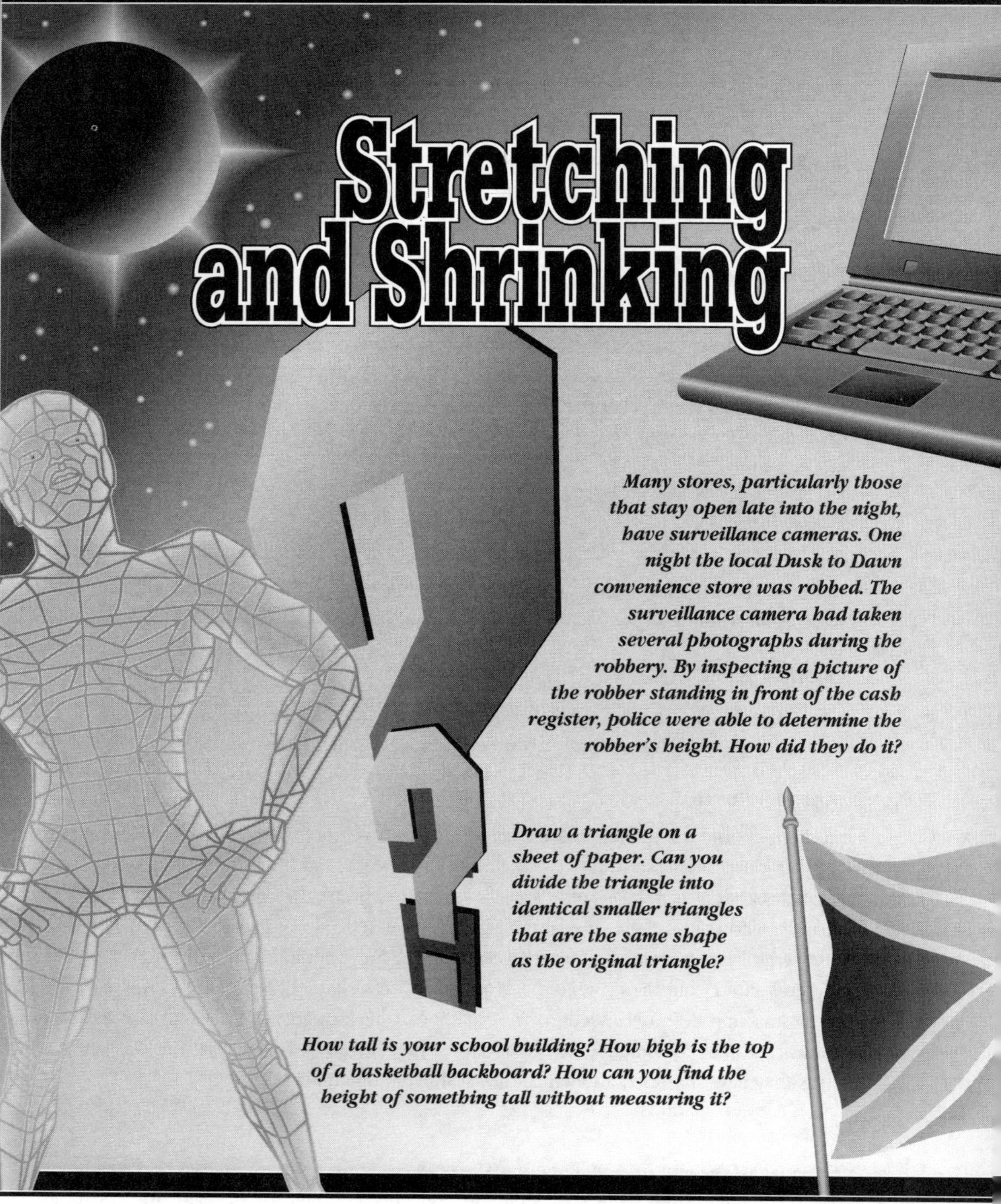

Stretching and Shrinking
Many stores, particularly those that stay open late into the night, have surveillance cameras. One night the local Dusk to Dawn convenience store was robbed. The surveillance camera had taken several photographs during the robbery. By inspecting a picture of the robber standing in front of the cash register, police were able to determine the robber's height. How did they do it?
Draw a triangle on a sheet of paper. Can you divide the triangle into identical smaller triangles that are the same shape as the original triangle?
How tall is your school building? How high is the top of a basketball backboard? How can you find the height of something tall without measuring it?

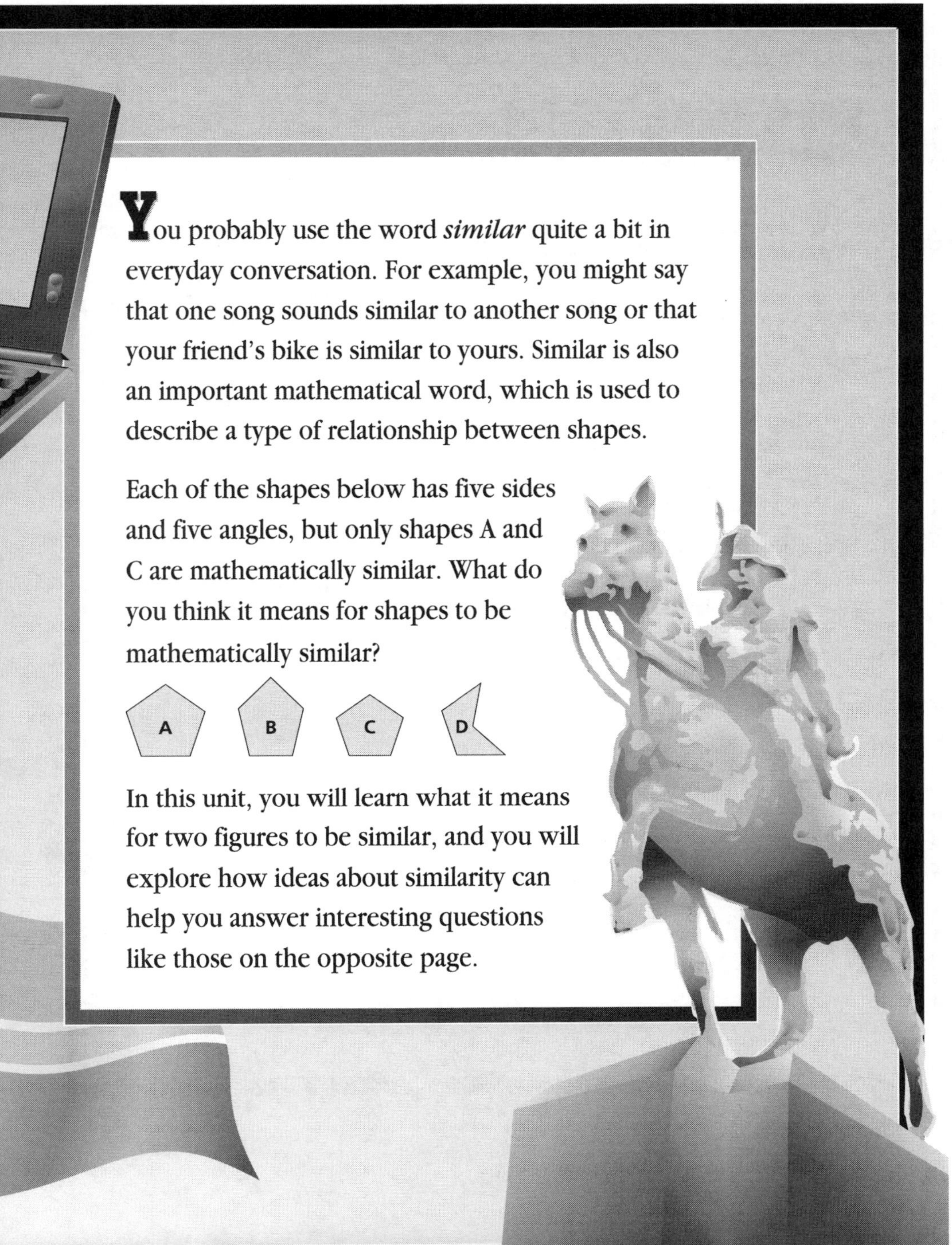

You probably use the word *similar* quite a bit in everyday conversation. For example, you might say that one song sounds similar to another song or that your friend's bike is similar to yours. Similar is also an important mathematical word, which is used to describe a type of relationship between shapes.

Each of the shapes below has five sides and five angles, but only shapes A and C are mathematically similar. What do you think it means for shapes to be mathematically similar?

In this unit, you will learn what it means for two figures to be similar, and you will explore how ideas about similarity can help you answer interesting questions like those on the opposite page.

Mathematical Highlights

The Mathematical Highlights page provides information for students and for parents and other family members. It gives students a preview of the activities and problems in *Stretching and Shrinking*. As they work through the unit, students can refer back to the Mathematical Highlights page to review what they have learned and to preview what is still to come. This page also tells students' families what mathematical ideas and activities will be covered as the class works through *Stretching and Shrinking*.

Mathematical Highlights

In *Stretching and Shrinking* you will explore the geometry concept of similarity. The unit should help you to:

- Recognize similar figures visually and identify that figures are similar by comparing sides and angles;
- Understand and use the equivalence of ratios of sides to examine similar figures and find unknown lengths;
- Understand the relationship between measures of lengths in figures and the scale factor relating two similar figures;
- Use the scale factor between figures to scale a figure up or down and to predict the lengths of corresponding edges and areas; and
- Use the concept of similarity to solve everyday problems.

As you work the problems in this unit, make it a habit to ask yourself questions about situations that involve similar figures: *What is the same and what is different about two similar figures? What determines whether two shapes are similar? When figures are similar, how are the lengths, areas, and scale factor related?*

Using This Teacher's Edition

The Investigations

The teaching materials for each investigation consist of three parts: an overview, student pages with teaching outlines, and detailed notes for teaching the investigation.

The overview of each investigation includes brief descriptions of the problems, the mathematical and problem-solving goals of the investigation, and a list of necessary materials.

Essential information for teaching the investigation is provided in the margins around the student pages. The "At a Glance" overviews are brief outlines of the Launch, Explore, and Summarize phases of each problem for reference as you work with the class. To help you assign homework, a list of "Assignment Choices" is provided next to each problem. Wherever space permits, answers to problems, follow-ups, ACE questions, and Mathematical Reflections appear next to the appropriate student pages.

The Teaching the Investigation section follows the student pages and is the heart of the Connected Mathematics curriculum. This section describes in detail the Launch, Explore, and Summarize phases for each problem. It includes all the information needed for teaching, along with suggestions for what you might say at key points in the teaching. Use this section to prepare lessons and as a guide for teaching investigations.

Assessment Resources

The Assessment Resources section contains blackline masters and answer keys for the quizzes, the check-up, the Question Bank, and the Unit Test. It also provides guidelines for assigning the optional unit project. A sample of a student's work, along with a teacher's comments about how the work was assessed, will help you to evaluate your students' efforts on the Unit Test Take-Home Project. Blackline masters for the Notebook Checklist and the Self-Assessment are given. These instruments support student self-evaluation, an important aspect of assessment in the Connected Mathematics curriculum. Samples of three students' responses to the Self-Assessment are shown, along with a teacher's evaluation.

Blackline Masters

The Blackline Masters section includes masters for all labsheets and transparencies. Blackline masters of half-centimeter grid paper, centimeter grid paper, dot paper, and the ShapeSet are also provided.

Additional Practice

Practice pages for each investigation offer additional problems for students who need more practice with the basic concepts developed in the investigations as well as some continual review of earlier concepts.

Descriptive Glossary

The Descriptive Glossary provides descriptions and examples of the key concepts in *Stretching and Shrinking*. These descriptions are not intended to be formal definitions, but are meant to give you an idea of how students might make sense of these important concepts.

INVESTIGATION 1

Enlarging Figures

In this investigation, students approach the concept of similarity from their intuition about what similarity means. Using the rubber-band "stretcher" described in the investigation, students are able to produce drawings similar to existing drawings. They begin with simple figures so that they will be more likely to be successful with the task; starting with more complicated shapes, students might get frustrated with their poor drawings and miss the important mathematical ideas.

In Problem 1.1, Stretching a Figure, students make a stretcher by tying two rubber bands together. They use the stretcher to enlarge three figures, and they compare how line lengths, areas, and angles were affected. Students then make and test predictions about how a drawing would be affected if they were to change the anchor point of the stretcher. While these rubber-band drawings are not exact, they do focus students' attention on shape and preserving shape. The questions asked raise issues about what causes shape to be preserved.

Mathematical and Problem-Solving Goals

- *To make enlargements of simple figures with a rubber-band stretcher*
- *To describe in an intuitive way what the word* similar *means*
- *To consider relationships between lengths and between areas in simple, similar figures*

Materials

Problem	For students	For the teacher
1.1	Graphing calculators, Labsheet 1.1A or 1.1B (1 per student), Labsheet 1.2A or 1.2B (1 per student), transparent centimeter and half-centimeter grids (optional; copy the grids onto transparency film), No. 16 (3 inch) rubber bands (2 per student), masking tape, blank sheets of paper (1 per student)	Transparencies 1.1A and 1.1B (optional), chart paper (optional), 2 rubber bands

Student Pages 5–13 | Teaching the Investigation 13a–13e

INVESTIGATION 1

Enlarging Figures

In this investigation, you will use rubber bands to make enlargements of drawings. Although this is not a precise way to enlarge drawings, it's fun—and you can see some interesting relationships between a figure and its enlarged image.

Think about this!

As you work on this investigation, think about these questions:

- When a figure is enlarged, which of its features remain the same?
- When a figure is enlarged, which of its features change?

1.1 Stretching a Figure

Michelle, Daphne, and Mukesh are the officers of their school's Mystery Book Club. Mukesh designed a flyer inviting new members to attend the club's next meeting.

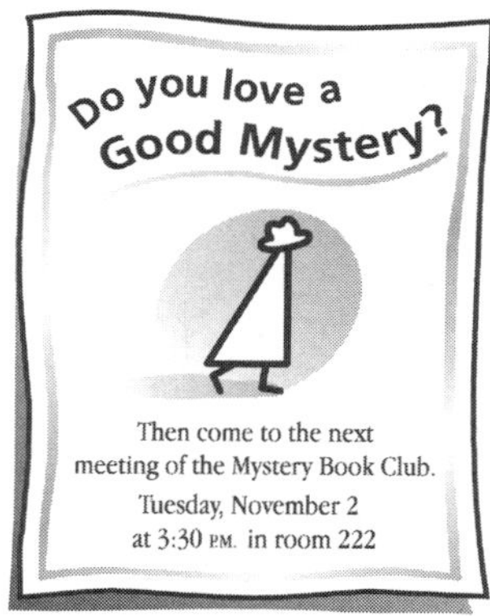

Do you love a Good Mystery?
Then come to the next meeting of the Mystery Book Club.
Tuesday, November 2
at 3:30 P.M. in room 222

1.1

Stretching a Figure

At a Glance

Grouping: individuals

Launch

- Demonstrate how to make an enlargement of a figure using a stretcher.
- Ask students to compare the two figures.
- Have students make their stretchers.

Explore

- As students work, remind them to follow the figure with the knot.
- Distribute Labsheet 1.2 as students finish with Labsheet 1.1.

Summarize

- As a class, talk about relationships between the original figure and its image.
- Discuss the follow-up questions.

Assignment Choices

ACE questions 1–7 (7 requires 3 rubber bands and Labsheet 1.1; 6 involves the formula for the area of a circle)

Daphne thought it would be a good idea to make a large poster announcing the meeting. She wanted to use the detective figure from the flyer, but at a larger size. Michelle showed her a clever way to enlarge the figure by using rubber bands.

Instructions for stretching a figure

1. Make a "two-band stretcher" by tying the ends of two identical rubber bands together. Bands about 3 inches long work well.
2. Tape the sheet with the picture you want to enlarge to your desk next to a blank sheet of paper. If you are right-handed, put the figure on the left. If you are left-handed, put it on the right.

Right-handed Setup

Left-handed Setup

3. With your finger, hold down one end of the stretcher on point *P*. Point *P* is called the *anchor point.*
4. Put a pencil in the other end of the stretcher. Stretch the rubber bands with your pencil until the knot is on the outline of your picture.
5. Guide the knot around the original picture, while your pencil traces out a new picture. (Don't allow any slack in the rubber bands.) This new drawing is the **image** of the original drawing.

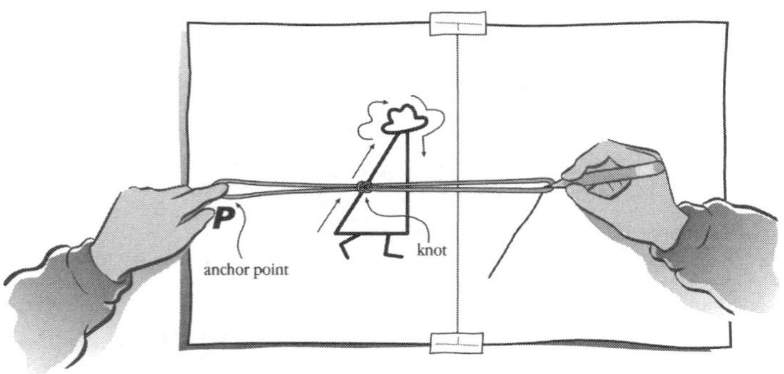

Problem 1.1

A. Use the method described on the previous page to enlarge the figures on Labsheets 1.1 and 1.2.

B. *Compare* is an important word in mathematics. When you **compare** two figures, you look at what is the *same* and what is *different* about them. Compare each original figure to the enlarged image you made. Make a detailed list about what is the same and what is different about them. Be sure to consider

- the lengths of the line segments
- the areas
- the angles (for figures with angles)
- the general shape of the figure

Explain each comparison you make in detail. For example, rather than just saying that two lengths are different, tell exactly which lengths you are comparing and explain how they differ.

Problem 1.1 Follow-Up

Michelle used her stretcher to enlarge triangle *ABC.* She labeled the vertices of the image *A′*, *B′*, and *C′* (read, "A prime, B prime, and C prime") to show that they *correspond* to the vertices *A, B,* and *C* of triangle *ABC.*

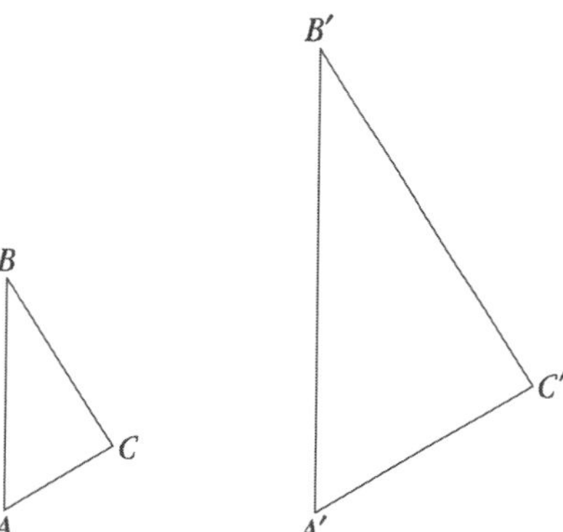

In mathematics, we use the word **corresponding** to describe how parts of a figure are related to parts of an enlargement or reduction of the figure. In the triangles above, $\angle BAC$ and $\angle B'A'C'$ are corresponding angles, and side *AB* and side *A′B′* are corresponding sides.

Answers to Problem 1.1

B. Here are some of the things students should notice:

- The lengths double. For example, on the enlargement of rectangle *ABCD*, the length of the new line segment *AB* is twice the length of the original line segment *AB*.
- The areas quadruple. For example, approximately four of the original rectangle *ABCD* could fit into the enlarged rectangle. If students say that the areas are three or four times as large, this is fine at this stage.
- The angles and the general shape of the figures are the same.

1. Name each pair of corresponding sides and each pair of corresponding angles in triangles *ABC* and *A′B′C′*.

2. a. Copy triangle *ABC* onto a sheet of paper. Choose an anchor point, and enlarge the triangle with your stretcher.
   b. Predict what would happen if you moved the anchor point up or down and further away from triangle *ABC* and then used your stretcher to enlarge it. Test your prediction by choosing a new anchor point and enlarging the triangle. Is your prediction correct?
   c. Predict what would happen if you moved the anchor point up or down and closer to triangle *ABC* and then used your stretcher to enlarge it. Test your prediction. Is it correct?

Answers to Problem 1.1 Follow-Up

1. Corresponding sides: *BC* and B′C′, *AB* and *A′B′*, *AC* and *A′C′*. Corresponding angles: ∠*ABC* and ∠*A′B′C′*, ∠*ACB* and ∠*A′C′B′*, ∠*BAC* and ∠*B′A′C′*. (Some students may refer to the angles with only the vertex label, such as ∠*A*. This is fine, but they eventually will need to be able to read the more common notation.)
2. The location of the anchor point (as long as the stretch of the band is not too great) will not affect the size of the image. A two-band stretcher used carefully will produce an image with side lengths about twice as long as the original figure's side lengths.

Applications • Connections • Extensions

As you work on these ACE questions, use your calculator whenever you need it.

Applications

1. Triangle *PQR* is an enlargement of triangle *STU*. Name all the pairs of corresponding sides and all the pairs of corresponding angles between the triangles.

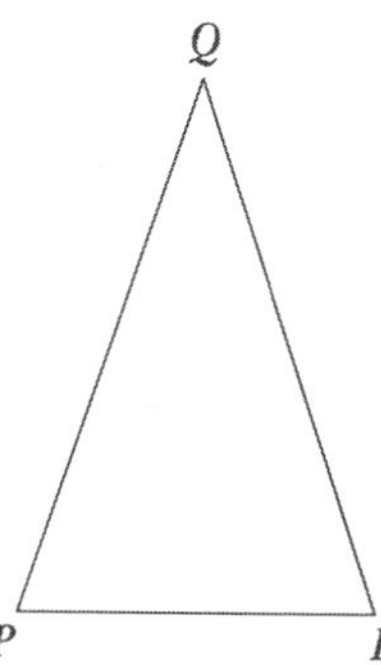

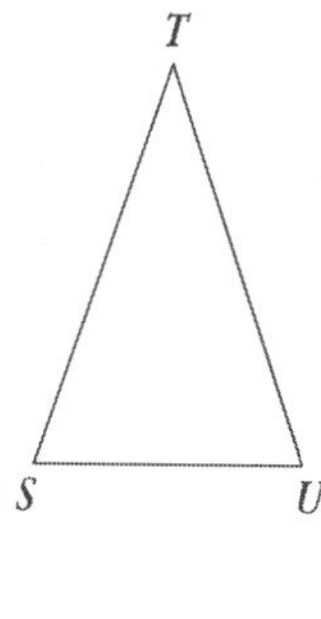

2. Copy square *WXYZ* and anchor point *P* onto a sheet of paper. Enlarge the square with your two-band stretcher. Label the image *W′X′Y′Z′* so that vertex *W′* corresponds to vertex *W*, vertex *X′* corresponds to vertex *X*, and so on.

P

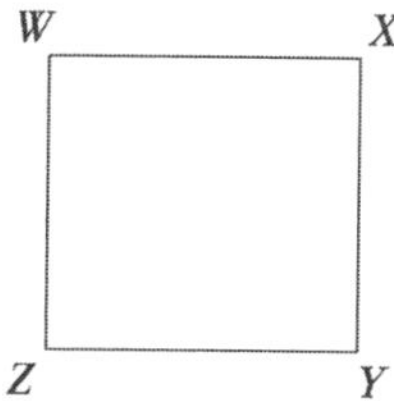

a. How does the length of side *W′X′* compare to the length of side *WX*?

b. How does the perimeter of square *WXYZ* compare to the perimeter of square *W′X′Y′Z′*?

c. How many copies of square *WXYZ* can fit inside square *W′X′Y′Z′*? (In other words, how do their areas compare?)

2.

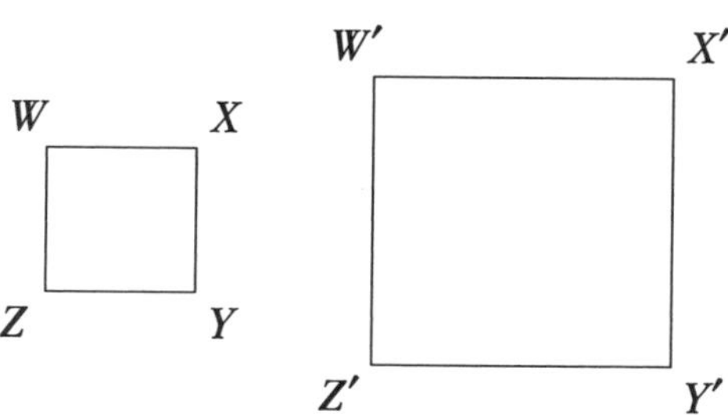

Answers

Applications

1. Corresponding sides are *PQ* and *ST*, *QR* and *TU*, *PR* and *SU*. Corresponding angles are ∠*PQR* and ∠*STU*, ∠*QRP* and ∠*TUS*, ∠*QPR* and ∠*TSU*.

2. See below left.

2a. Side *W′X′* is about twice the length of side *WX*.

2b. The perimeter of square *WXYZ* is about half the perimeter of square *W′X′Y′Z′*.

2c. About four copies of square *WXYZ* will fit into square *W′X′Y′Z′*, so square *W′X′Y′Z′* has four times the area of square *WXYZ*.

3. See below right.

3a. The side lengths of parallelogram $A'B'C'D'$ are twice the corresponding side lengths of parallelogram $ABCD$.

3b. Four copies of parallelogram $ABCD$ will fit into parallelogram $A'B'C'D'$, so the larger parallelogram has four times the area of the smaller.

Connections

4. See page 13e.

3. Copy parallelogram $ABCD$ and anchor point P onto a sheet of paper. Enlarge the parallelogram with your two-band stretcher. Label the image $A'B'C'D'$ so that vertex A' corresponds to vertex A, vertex B' corresponds to vertex B, and so on.

P

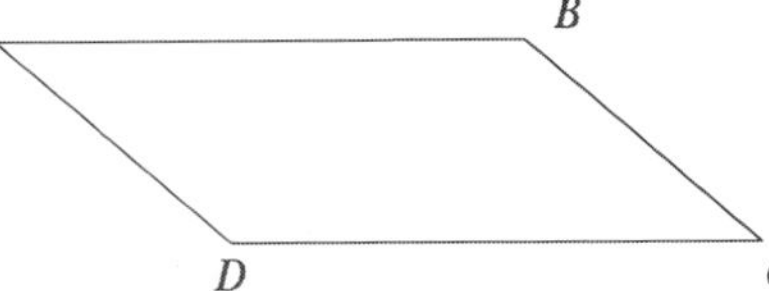

a. How do the side lengths of parallelogram $A'B'C'D'$ compare to the side lengths of parallelogram $ABCD$?

b. How many copies of parallelogram $ABCD$ can fit inside parallelogram $A'B'C'D'$? (In other words, how do their areas compare?)

Connections

4. Copy circle C and anchor point P onto a sheet of paper. Make an enlargement of the circle using your two-band stretcher.

P

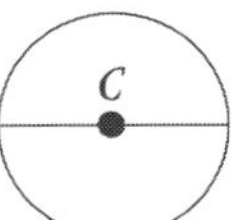

a. How do the diameters of the circles compare?

b. How do the areas of the circles compare? Explain your reasoning.

3.

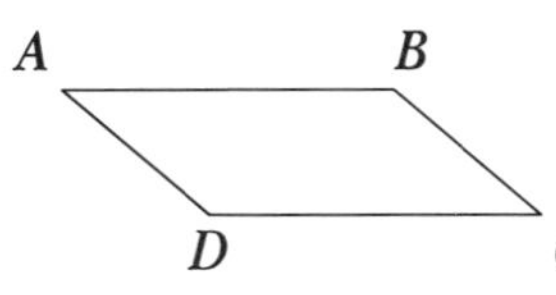

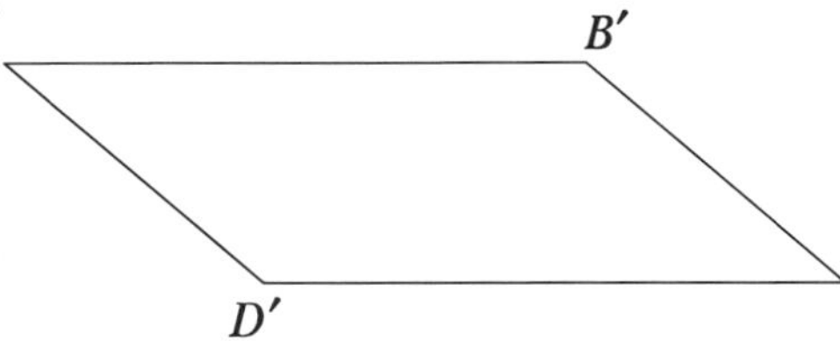

Extensions

5. Circle A' is an enlargement of a smaller circle A made by using a two-band stretcher. Circle A is not shown.

a. How does the diameter of circle A' compare to the diameter of circle A?

b. How does the area of circle A' compare to the area of circle A?

6. a. Suppose each of the small circles below has a diameter of 8 centimeters, and the large circle has a diameter of 16 centimeters. What is the combined area of the two small circles?

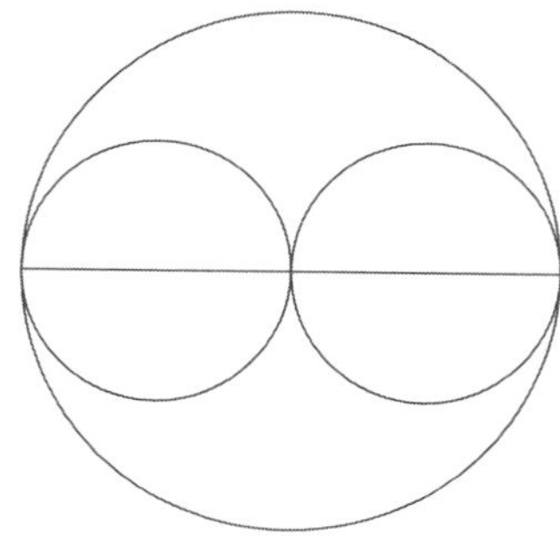

b. What is the area inside the large circle and above the two small circles?

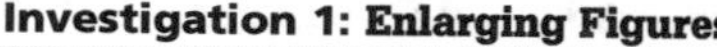

Extensions

5. Note: Due to the difficulty of tracing the path of the knot, students are not asked to draw the original circle from which circle A' was made. Students can, however, draw circle A if they want to by realizing that its radius must be half the radius of circle A' or by enlisting the help of a friend in using a stretcher to trace the path of the knot as the pencil is taken around circle A'. See illustration below left.

5a. The diameter of circle A' is twice the diameter of circle A.

5b. The area of circle A' is four times the area of circle A.

6a. Each small circle has a radius of 4 cm and thus an area of 16π cm^2. Together, the two copies have an area of 32π cm^2. See illustration below left.

6b. The large circle has a radius of 8 cm and thus an area of 64π cm^2. The area outside the small circles is $(64\pi - 32\pi)$ cm^2 = 32π cm^2.

5.

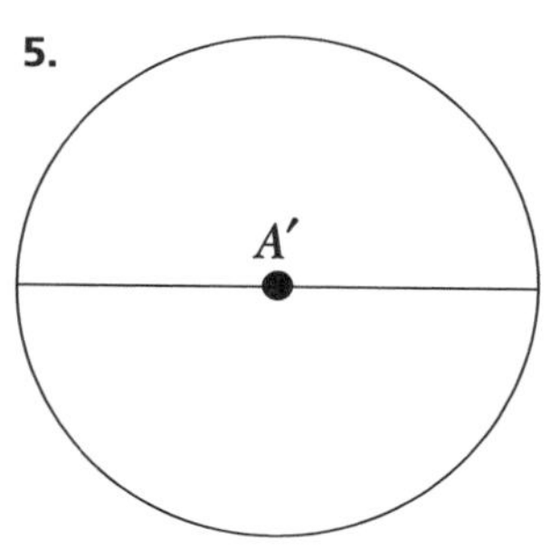

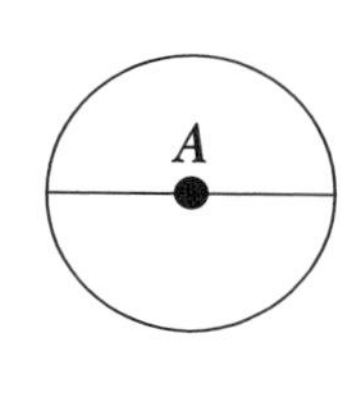

6a.

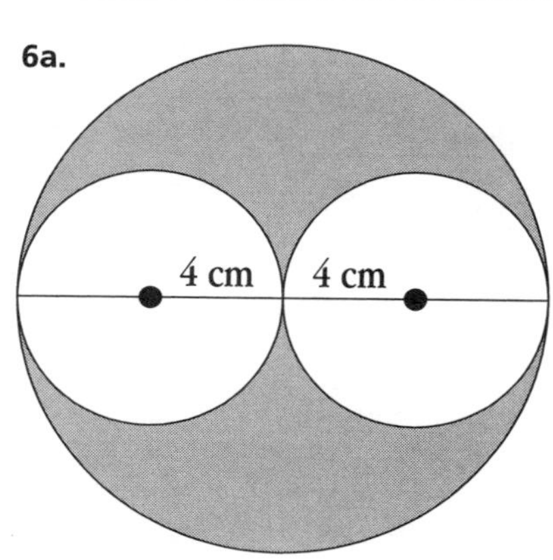

7a. The image is about three times as large as the original, but it has the same shape.

7b. The lengths of the line segments in the image are about three times the lengths of those in the original.

7c. The area of the image is about nine times the area of the original. (Note: This is because area increases as the *square* of the scale factor.)

7. Make a three-band stretcher by tying three identical rubber bands together. Use this stretcher to enlarge the drawing on Labsheet 1.1.

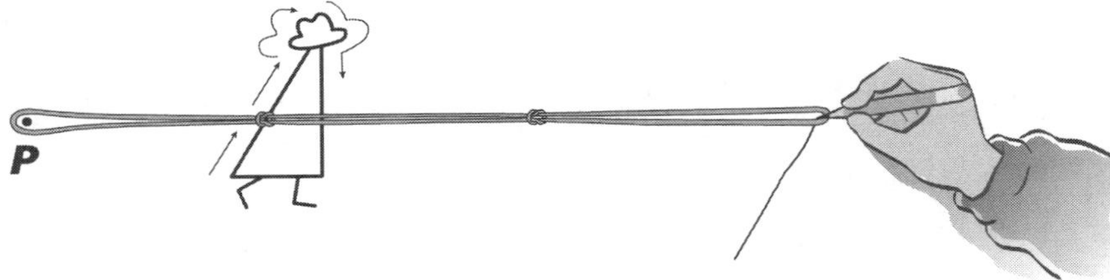

a. How does the shape of the image compare to the shape of the original figure?

b. How do the lengths of the line segments in the two figures compare?

c. How do the areas of the two figures compare?

Mathematical Reflections

In this investigation, you learned how to use a stretcher to enlarge figures. These questions will help you summarize what you have learned:

1. Suppose you used your two-band stretcher to enlarge the rectangle below.

   a. How would the side lengths of the enlarged rectangle compare to the side lengths of the original rectangle?

   b. How would the perimeter of the enlarged rectangle compare to the perimeter of the original rectangle?

   c. How would the area of the enlarged rectangle compare to the area of the original rectangle?

2. How does the location of the anchor point affect the image drawn with a stretcher?

Think about your answers to these questions, discuss your ideas with other students and your teacher, and then write a summary of your findings in your journal.

Possible Answers

1a. The side lengths would be about twice as long as those in the original.

1b. The perimeter would be about twice the original perimeter.

1c. The area would be about four times the original area. To show how the area increases, we could subdivide the new rectangle into four congruent rectangles that are similar to the original rectangle.

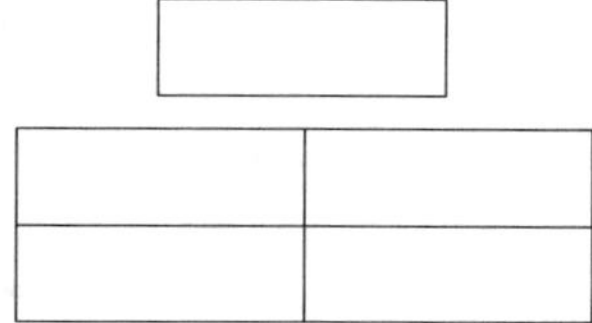

2. The location of the anchor point does not affect the size of the image. It only affects the location of the image on the page.

Tips for the Linguistically Diverse Classroom

Diagram Code The Diagram Code technique is described in detail in *Getting to Know Connected Mathematics*. Students use a minimal number of words and drawings, diagrams, or symbols to respond to questions that require writing. Example: Question 1c—A student might answer this question by writing *4 × Area 1*. Below this, the student might draw a rectangle labeled *Area 1* and the new rectangle, divided into four = congruent rectangles similar to the original.

TEACHING THE INVESTIGATION

1.1 • Stretching a Figure

In this problem, students use rubber bands to enlarge a figure. They then compare the original to the enlargement to determine which features have changed and which have remained the same.

Launch

Transparent grids may be a helpful visual aid to some students in comparing figures; you may want to have them available throughout this unit.

To get students started, you will need to demonstrate how to draw a figure with a rubber-band stretcher, either using chalk on the chalkboard or a marker on chart paper taped to the board. Test your setup before class so you know everything fits. Place the anchor point so that the enlarged drawing will not overlap the original.

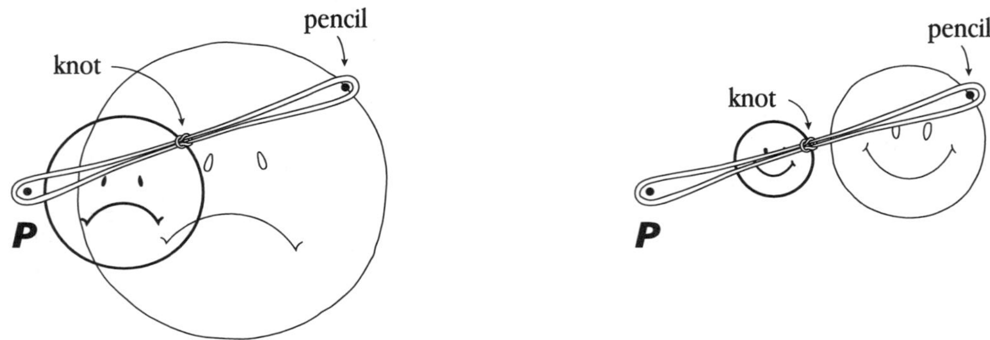

Have some fun with the setup; choose a figure to enlarge that your students will find interesting, such as a popular cartoon character, a logo, a smiley face, or a ghost.

> I have a super machine called a stretcher that will help me draw an interesting copy of this figure. My machine has two parts. Watch me carefully while I make a stretcher before your very eyes!

Tie the two rubber bands together by passing one band through the other and back through itself. Pull on the two ends, moving the knot to the center of the bands. You may need to pull on the knot so that both bands form half of the knot.

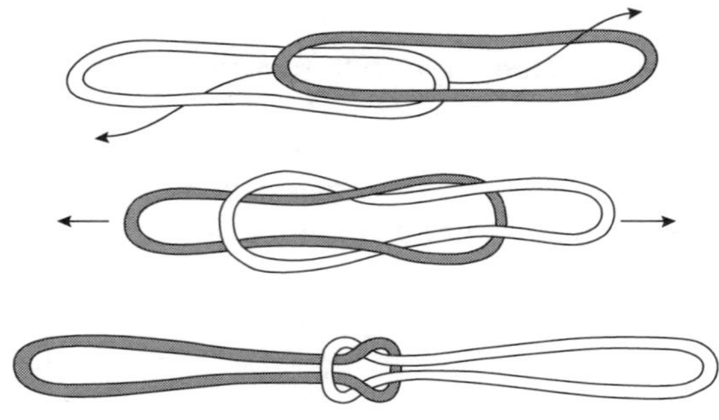

Hold your finished stretcher in the air and demonstrate its stretch. Then, use it to draw a copy of the figure as you describe the process.

> Notice that I put one end of my stretcher on a point, called the *anchor point,* and hold it down securely without covering up any more of the band than necessary. I put the marker (chalk) through the other end and stretch the bands until the knot is just above part of my figure. I move my marker as I trace the figure with the knot. I try to keep the knot directly over the original figure as my marker draws the new figure. The more carefully the knot traces the original, the better my drawing will be.

Finish the drawing, then ask students to describe what happened. They will probably say the two figures look alike but that the new one is larger. Until they have made their own drawings, you do not need to press for more specific observations or relationships.

Distribute two rubber bands, a blank sheet of paper, and Labsheet 1.1A (for right-handed students) or 1.1B (for left-handed students) to each student. Have students affix the two sheets to their desks using masking tape as shown in the student edition. Left-handed students will have the anchor point to their right and the blank sheet of paper to their left.

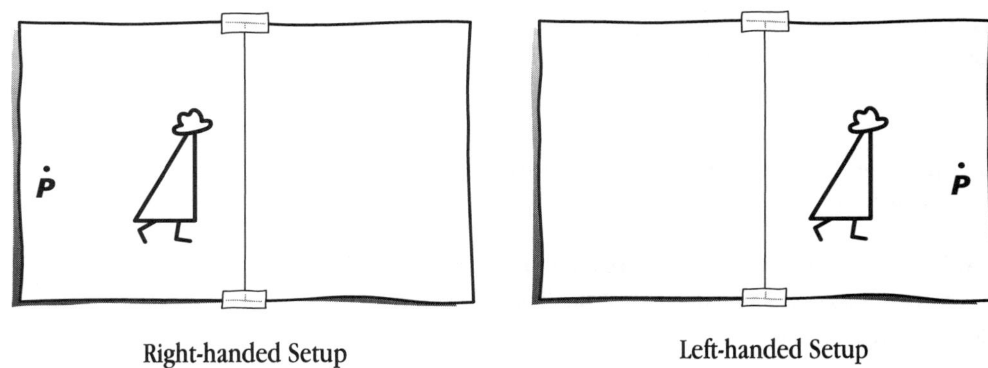

Right-handed Setup   Left-handed Setup

Let the students make their stretchers. Some students will have a hard time tying the bands together and will need assistance. You may want to be sure everyone has made a stretcher before the class begins drawing.

Explore

As students work, you may want to mention that their drawings will be more accurate if they hold the pencil vertically and keep the rubber bands as close to the point of the pencil as possible.

As students finish their first drawing, distribute Labsheet 1.2A or 1.2B. They can use the reverse of the plain sheets of paper for the second drawing. Remind students to trace the figure they are trying to copy with the knot, as they may be tempted to draw the object freehand. Accuracy is not the issue here, but students can get better drawings by being careful with the placement of the rubber bands on the pencil and the path of the knot on the figure.

A stretcher made from two rubber bands gives a figure enlarged by a factor of 2. This means the length measures are twice as long. Students may guess different factors for the growth of the lengths, which is fine at this stage.

Summarize

Ask students to describe what they noticed about the figures they drew. Explain that the word *image* will be used to refer to a drawing made with a stretcher. Students should recognize that the two figures look alike and that the image is larger.

What is the relationship between the side lengths of the original figure and the side lengths of the image?

Students may mention things other than that the side lengths have doubled; don't be too concerned about the exactness of their observations at this stage, as long as their answers are reasonable for their drawings.

How do the features of the original rectangle *ABCD* compare to its image?

This question is meant to focus students' attention on lengths, perimeter, area, and angles—all features that we want to investigate in this unit about similar figures. If students say only that the image is larger, ask more specific questions.

How do the lengths of the sides compare? How do the perimeters compare? The areas? The angles?

Throughout this unit, students will be asked to compare figures to their enlargements. Use this first instance to set a precedent for focusing on certain elements of the figures and forming complete and thoughtful answers to these kinds of questions.

The follow-up raises the important issue of developing ways to think and communicate about corresponding parts of figures. It then focuses attention on the issue of whether the location of the anchor point (within the stretch of the rubber bands) affects the size of the image. Most students assume that the further away the anchor point is, the larger the image will be. In fact, given that the two rubber bands are alike in stretch, the location of the anchor point does not affect the size of the image at all—though it does affect its location. This interesting and important idea will surprise most students.

For the Teacher: Rubber Band Stretchers

Notice that the two rubber bands stretch so that the image of each point on the figure is twice as far from the anchor point as the original point. It is this preserving of the 2 to 1 ratio that makes the figure twice as large. No matter where you move the anchor point, the points on the image are still twice as far from the anchor point as the points on the original figure are from the anchor point. With three rubber bands and the first knot tracing the figure, the image will be three times as large as the original because its distance from the anchor point is three times as far. This is a ratio of 3 to 1.

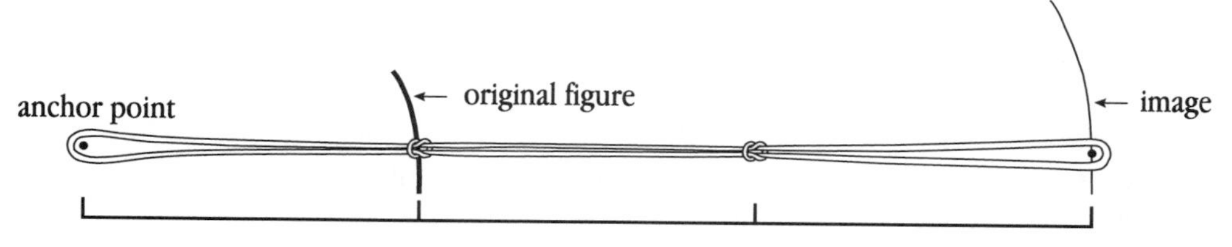

You may want to use ACE question 2 in class to review the use of the stretcher and to emphasize the questions about side lengths, perimeters, areas, and angles one would ask to compare an original figure to its image. As students work through the investigations in the unit, it is important to ask them repeatedly what they think *similarity* means.

The pairs of figures we got from using the stretcher are similar to each other. What do you think it means for two figures to be similar? *(They look alike. They have the same shape.)*

ACE questions 2 and 3 introduce the idea that a parallelogram can be subdivided into four congruent shapes similar to the original; while the sides grow by a factor of 2, the area grows by a factor of 4. Students will not see this very clearly in this informal setting, but the questions will focus their attention on what happens to lengths and areas as figures are enlarged. Do not push for conclusions as these key ideas are introduced; they will be revisited often in the succeeding investigations.

In this investigation, students have just begun to think about how similar figures are related. Two rubber bands will produce a figure whose sides are about twice the length of the corresponding sides of the original figure.

What happens if we make a stretcher using *three* rubber bands?

After students have made some conjectures, you may assign ACE question 7 so they can explore their ideas. The image will have lengths about three times those of the original and an area nine times that of the original.

Additional Answers

ACE Answers

Connections

4.

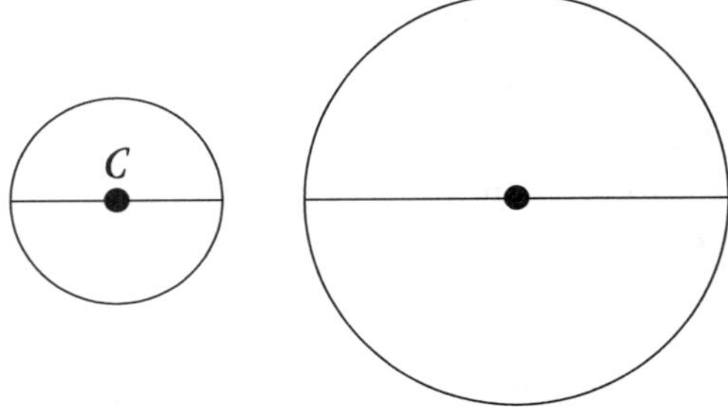

4a. The diameter of the small circle is about half the diameter of the large circle.

4b. The area of the large circle is about four times the area of the small circle. Possible explanation: This makes sense, as the radius is twice as long. (If r is the radius of the small circle, then the formula for the area of the circle is πr^2. The large circle has a radius that's twice as long ($2r$), so it's area is $\pi(2r)^2$ or $4\pi r^2$, 4 times the area of the small circle. Some students may have forgotten the formula for the area of a circle and may need to use grid paper to compare the areas.)

INVESTIGATION 2

Similar Figures

In this investigation, students create similar and nonsimilar shapes using a coordinate system. The use of numbers to locate points in a plane is a useful and important idea in mathematics. We will begin to form a more precise mathematical definition of *similar.* Students will use the idea of same shape, or similarity, to discover that similar figures have *corresponding angles that are equal* and *corresponding sides that grow by the same factor.* We call this factor the *scale factor,* because it tells us the scale of enlargement (stretching or shrinking) between the figures. The scale factor applies only to similar figures. In nonsimilar figures, all pairs of corresponding side lengths will not be in the same ratio.

In Problem 2.1, Drawing Wumps, students graph members of a fictitious family, plus other figures that claim to be in the Wump family. Members of the Wump family are similar to one another; the impostors are not similar, but distorted—one vertically and one horizontally. Students compare the shapes, side lengths, and angles of the figures they have drawn. In Problem 2.2, Nosing Around, students continue to work with the Wump family as they investigate side lengths, angles, and perimeters of similar rectangles and are introduced to the idea of a scale factor. In Problem 2.3, Making Wump Hats, they investigate the effect that altering the rule for making a shape on a coordinate grid has on the shape.

Mathematical and Problem-Solving Goals

- *To review locating points in a coordinate system*
- *To graph figures using algebraic rules*
- *To predict how figures on a coordinate system are affected by a given rule*
- *To learn that corresponding angles of similar figures are equal and that corresponding sides grow by the same factor*
- *To compare lengths and angles in similar and nonsimilar figures informally*
- *To experiment with examples and counterexamples of similar shapes*

Materials

Problem	For students	For the teacher
All	Graphing calculators, angle rulers (optional; 1 per student)	Transparencies 2.1A to 2.3B (optional)
2.1	Labsheet 2.1A (1 per student), Labsheet 2.1B (3 per student)	Transparent half-centimeter grid (optional; copy the grid onto transparency film)
2.2	Grid paper (optional; provided as a blackline master)	
2.3	Labsheet 2.3A and 2.3B (1 per student)	
ACE	Centimeter grid paper, transparent grids (optional)	

Student Pages 14–27 | **Teaching the Investigation 27a–27m**

INVESTIGATION 2

Similar Figures

Zack and Marta wanted to design a computer game that involved several animated characters. Marta asked her uncle Carlos, a programmer for a video game company, about computer animation. Carlos explained that the computer screen can be thought of as a grid made up of thousands of tiny points called *pixels.* To animate figures, you need to enter the coordinates of key points on the figure. The computer uses these points to draw the figure in different positions.

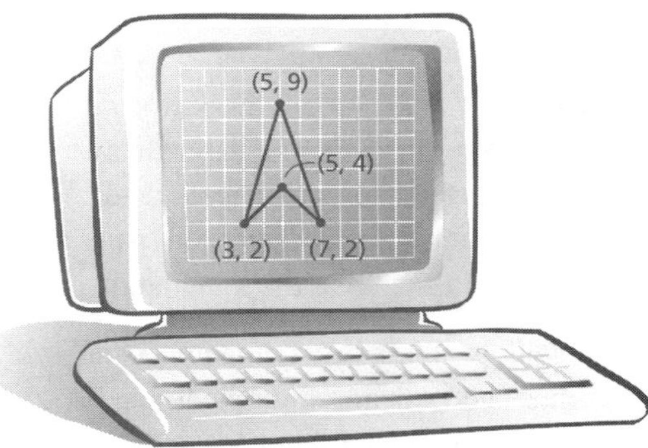

Marta told her uncle that sometimes the figures in their game would need to change size. Her uncle explained that a computer can make figures larger and smaller if you give it a rule for finding the key points in the new figure from key points in the original figure.

Did you know?

With a computer graphics program, you can create images and then rotate, stretch, and copy them. There are two basic kinds of graphics programs. *Paint programs* make images out of *pixels* (which is a short way of saying "picture elements"). *Draw programs* make images out of lines that are drawn from mathematical equations.

The images you create in a graphics program are displayed on the computer screen. The images on your screen may be created by a beam of electrons that activates a chemical in the screen called phosphor. If you have a laptop computer, the images on the screen are probably made by an electric current acting on a material in the screen called liquid crystal.

2.1 Drawing Wumps

Zack and Marta's computer game involves a family called the Wumps. The members of the Wump family are various sizes, but they all have the same shape. Mug Wump is the game's main character. By enlarging or reducing Mug, a player can transform him into other Wump family members.

Zack and Marta experimented on paper with enlarging and reducing figures on a coordinate grid. First, Zack drew Mug Wump on dot paper. Then, he labeled the key points from *A* to *Z* and from *AA* to *FF* and listed the coordinates for each point. Marta described the rules that would transform Mug into different sizes to create other members of the Wump family.

2.1 Drawing Wumps

At a Glance

Grouping: individuals

Launch

- Introduce students to plotting points on a grid. *(optional)*
- Tell the story of the Wump family.
- Help the class understand how to follow the four sets of points to draw Mug Wump.
- Talk about how rules specify the points for the other characters.

Explore

- Have students draw the figures and compare them.

Summarize

- As a class, compare the five figures, including angles and side lengths.

Assignment Choices

ACE questions 1, 3, 11–13 (11 requires centimeter grid paper), and unassigned choices from earlier problems

2.1

Problem 2.1

Lurking among the members of the Wump family are some impostors who, at first glance, look like the Wumps but are actually quite different.

A. Use the instructions below to draw Mug Wump on the dot paper grid on Labsheet 2.1B. Describe Mug's shape.

B. Use Labsheet 2.1A and two more copies of Labsheet 2.1B to make Bug, Lug, Thug, and Zug. After drawing the characters, compare them to Mug. Which characters are the impostors?

C. Compare Mug to the other characters. What things are the same about Mug and Zug? Mug and Lug? Mug and Bug? Mug and Thug? What things are different? Think about the general shape, the lengths of sides, and the angles of each figure.

Instructions for drawing Wumps

1. To draw Mug, use the sets of coordinate pairs given in the chart on the next page. Plot the points from the "Mug Wump" column on Labsheet 2.1B. Connect the points with line segments as follows:
   - For Set 1, connect the points in order, and then connect the last point to the first point.
   - For Set 2, connect the points in order (don't connect the last point to the first point).
   - For Set 3, connect the points in order, and then connect the last point to the first point.
   - For Set 4, make a dot at each point (don't connect the dots).
2. To draw Zug, Lug, Bug, and Thug, use the given rule to find the coordinates of each point. For example, the rule for finding the points for Zug is $(2x, 2y)$. This means that you multiply each of Mug's coordinates by 2. Point A on Mug is (2, 0), so the corresponding point A on Zug is (4, 0). Point B on Mug is (2, 4), so the corresponding point B on Zug is (4, 8).
3. Plot the points for Zug, Lug, Bug, and Thug, and connect them according to the directions in step 2.

Answers to Problem 2.1

A. Possible answer: Mug looks like a cat with straight arms and legs.

B. Bug and Zug are big versions of Mug, so they are the other Wumps. Lug and Thug look like Mug too—they have a rectangular nose, two ears, and a smile—but Lug is too wide and Thug is too tall. They are the impostors.

C. From Mug to Zug and Bug, the angles and the general shape stayed the same, but the lengths grew. From Mug to Zug the lengths doubled, and from Mug to Bug they tripled. From Mug to Lug and Thug, corresponding lengths did not grow the same. Thug and Lug are the same type of creature as Mug—the number of eyes, ears, arms, and legs are the same, and the body parts are in the same places—but they look distorted. Lug is the same height as Mug but three times as wide. Thug is the same width as Mug but three times as tall. Many of their angles are different from Mug's angles.

Rule	Mug Wump (x, y)	Zug (2x, 2y)	Lug (3x, y)	Bug (3x, 3y)	Thug (x, 3y)
Point	**Set 1**	**Set 1**	**Set 1**	**Set 1**	**Set 1**
A	(2, 0)	(4, 0)			
B	(2, 4)	(4, 8)			
C	(0, 4)				
D	(0, 5)				
E	(2, 5)				
F	(0, 8)				
G	(0, 12)				
H	(1, 15)				
I	(2, 12)				
J	(5, 12)				
K	(6, 15)				
L	(7, 12)				
M	(7, 8)				
N	(5, 5)				
O	(7, 5)				
P	(7, 4)				
Q	(5, 4)				
R	(5, 0)				
S	(4, 0)				
T	(4, 3)				
U	(3, 3)				
V	(3, 0) (connect *V* to *A*)				
	Set 2 (start over)	**Set 2**	**Set 2**	**Set 2**	**Set 2**
W	(1, 8)				
X	(2, 7)				
Y	(5, 7)				
Z	(6, 8)				
	Set 3 (start over)	**Set 3**	**Set 3**	**Set 3**	**Set 3**
AA	(3, 8)				
BB	(4, 8)				
CC	(4, 10)				
DD	(3, 10) (connect *DD* to *AA*)				
	Set 4 (start over)	**Set 4**	**Set 4**	**Set 4**	**Set 4**
EE	(2, 11) (make a dot)				
FF	(5, 11) (make a dot)				

Nosing Around

At a Glance

Grouping:* *pairs

Launch

- Display the noses of Mug, Zug, Bug, Lug, and Thug.
- Discuss what information would be needed to determine which noses are similar.

Explore

- Help students agree which measurement to call width and which to call length.
- Assist students with finding the ratios and interpreting what they mean.

Summarize

- Discuss the patterns students see in the chart.
- Help students further explore the relationships between similar figures.

Problem 2.1 Follow-Up

1. In mathematics, we say that figures like Mug and Zug (but not Mug and Lug) are **similar.** What do you think it means for two figures to be mathematically similar?
2. The members of the Wump family are all similar. How do their corresponding sides compare? How do their corresponding angles compare?

2.2 Nosing Around

All the members of the Wump family have the same angle measures. Is having the same angle measures enough to make two figures similar? All rectangles have four right angles. Are all rectangles similar? What about these two rectangles?

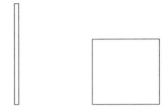

These rectangles are not similar, because they don't have the same shape—one is tall and skinny, and the other looks like a square. To be similar, it is not enough for figures to have the same angle measures.

In this problem, you will investigate rectangles more closely to try to figure out what else is necessary for two rectangles to be similar. You will compare side lengths, angle measures, and perimeters.

One way to compare two quantities is to form a **ratio**. For example, Mug Wump's nose is 1 unit wide and 2 units long. To compare the width to the length, we can use the ratio *1 to 2,* which can also be written as the fraction $\frac{1}{2}$.

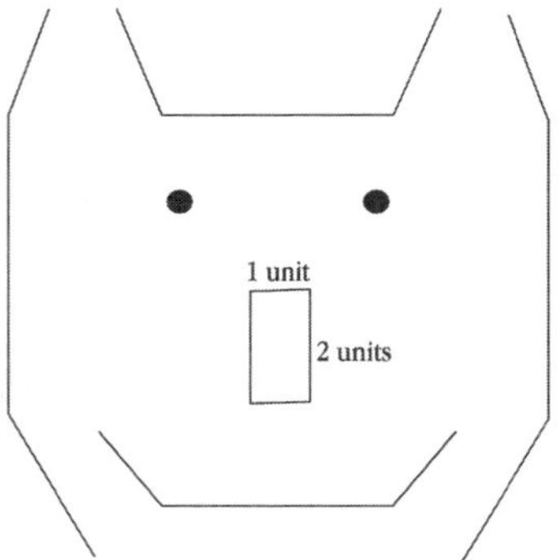

Assignment Choices

ACE questions 2, 4, 5, and unassigned choices from earlier problems

Answers to Problem 2.1 Follow-Up

1. Similar means they have the same shape—you could enlarge Mug to get Zug (and to get Bug). They have the same angles, and the sides of Zug are triple those of Mug.
2. The corresponding sides of Zug are double those of Mug. The corresponding sides of Bug are triple those of Mug. Their corresponding angles among all three Wumps are equal.

Problem 2.2

Copy the chart below. The Wumps in the chart are numbered according to their size. Mug is Wump 1. Since the segments that make up Zug are twice as long as the segments that make up Mug, Zug is Wump 2. Since the segments that make up Bug are three times as long as the segments that make up Mug, Bug is Wump 3. Since Lug and Thug are not similar to the Wumps, they are at the bottom of the chart.

A. Look carefully at the noses of Mug, Zug, Bug, Lug, and Thug. In your table, record the dimensions, the ratio of width to length ($\frac{\text{width}}{\text{length}}$), and the perimeter of each nose.

B. Look at the data you recorded for Mug, Zug, and Bug. What patterns do you see? Explain how the values in each column change as the Wumps get bigger. Look for relationships between the values in the different columns.

C. The rule for making Wump 4 is $(4x, 4y)$. The rule for making Wump 5 is $(5x, 5y)$. Add data to the chart for Wumps 4 and 5. Do their noses fit the patterns you noticed in part B?

D. Use the patterns you found to add data for Wumps 10, 20, and 100 to the chart. Explain your reasoning.

E. Do Lug's nose and Thug's nose seem to fit the patterns you found for the Wumps? If not, what makes them different?

The Wump Noses (Plus Lug and Thug)

Wump	Width of nose	Length of nose	$\frac{\text{Width}}{\text{Length}}$	Perimeter
Wump 1 (Mug)	1	2	$\frac{1}{2}$	
Wump 2 (Zug)	2			
Wump 3 (Bug)	3			
Wump 4				
Wump 5				
⋮				
Wump 10				
Wump 20				
Wump 100				
Lug				
Thug				

Answers to Problem 2.2

A. See page 27j.

B. See page 27j.

C. Yes, Wumps 4 and 5 fit the patterns.

D. The data for Wumps 10, 20, and 100 fit the patterns.

E. Lug's and Thug's noses do not fit the patterns. For example, the width of Lug's nose increases, but the length does not.

Problem 2.2 Follow-Up

To find the length, width, and perimeter of Zug's nose, we can multiply the length, width, and perimeter of Mug's nose by 2. The number 2 is called the *scale factor* from Mug's nose to Zug's nose. The **scale factor** is the number that we multiply the dimensions of an original figure by to get the dimensions of an enlarged or reduced figure.

The scale factor from Mug to Bug is 3. You can multiply the side lengths of Mug's nose by 3 to find the side lengths of Bug's nose. We can also say that the side lengths and the perimeters *grow by a scale factor of 3.*

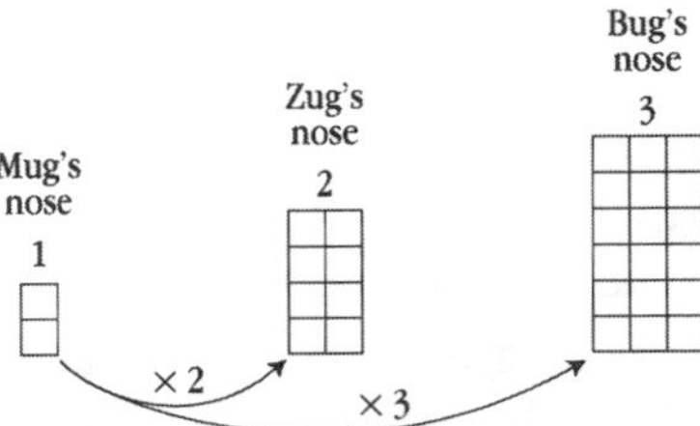

1. Is there a scale factor from Mug's nose to Wump 4's nose? Why or why not?

2. Is there a scale factor from Mug's nose to Thug's nose? Why or why not?

3. The dimensions of Bug's nose are 3×6. Suppose this nose is enlarged by a scale factor of 3.
   a. What are the dimensions of the new nose?
   b. What is the perimeter of the new nose?

4. a. What is the scale factor from Wump 2 to Wump 10?
   b. What is the scale factor from Wump 10 to Wump 2?

Answers to Problem 2.2 Follow-Up

1. yes; The scale factor is 4 because we multiply the length and width of Mug's nose by 4 to get the new dimensions.
2. no; One dimension increases by a factor of 3 and the other does not.
3. a. 9×18
   b. 54 units
4. a. 5
   b. $\frac{1}{5}$

2.3 Making Wump Hats

Zack and Marta experimented with multiplying each of Mug's coordinates by different whole numbers to create other similar figures. Marta wondered how multiplying the coordinates by a decimal, or adding numbers to or subtracting numbers from each coordinate, would affect Mug's shape. When she asked her uncle about this, he gave her the coordinates for a new shape—a hat for Mug to wear—and some rules to try on the shape.

	Hat 1	Hat 2	Hat 3	Hat 4	Hat 5	Hat 6
Point	(x, y)	$(x + 2, y + 2)$	$(x + 3, y - 1)$	$(2x, y + 2)$	$(2x, 3y)$	$(0.5x, 0.5y)$
A	(0, 4)	(2, 6)	(3, 3)	(0, 6)	(0, 12)	(0, 2)
B	(0, 1)					
C	(6, 1)					
D	(4, 2)					
E	(4, 4)					
F	(3, 5)					
G	(1, 5)					
H	(0, 4)					

Problem 2.3

Use the table and dot paper grids on Labsheets 2.3A and 2.3B.

- To make Mug's hat, plot points *A–H* from the Hat 1 column on the grid labeled Hat 1, connecting the points as you go.
- For Hats 2–6, use the rules in the table to fill in the coordinates for each column. Then, plot each hat on the appropriate grid, connecting the points as you go.

Problem 2.3 Follow-Up

1. What rule would make a hat with line segments $\frac{1}{3}$ the length of Hat 1's line segments?
2. What happens to a figure on a coordinate grid when you add to or subtract from its coordinates?
3. What rule would make a hat the same size as Hat 1 but moved up 2 units on the grid?
4. What rule would make a hat with line segments twice as long as Hat 1's line segments and moved 8 units to the right?

2.3 Making Wump Hats

At a Glance

***Grouping:* individuals**

Launch

- Distribute Labsheets 2.3A and 2.3B.
- Introduce the idea of analyzing what effect changes in the rule will have on the hats.

Explore

- Circulate as students fill in the table and draw the hats.
- For students who catch on quickly, ask questions to extend their thinking about the effect of changes in the rule.

Summarize

- As a class, examine the figures and discuss how changes in the rule affected them.
- Go through the follow-up questions carefully.

Answers to Problem 2.3

See page 27j.

Answers to Problem 2.3 Follow-Up

1. $(\frac{1}{3}x, \frac{1}{3}y)$
2. If you add to the *x*-coordinate, the figure moves to the right. If you subtract from the *x*-coordinate, it moves to the left. If you add to the *y*-coordinate, the figure moves up. If you subtract from the *y*-coordinate, it moves down.
3. $(x, y + 2)$
4. $(2x + 8, 2y)$

Assignment Choices

ACE questions 6–10, 14, and unassigned choices from earlier problems

Assessment

It is appropriate to use the check-up after this problem.

Answers

Applications

1a. *JK* and *HG*, *KL* and *GF*, *JL* and *HF*

1b. $\angle JKL$ and $\angle HGF$, $\angle KLJ$ and $\angle GFH$, $\angle KJL$ and $\angle GHF$

2. For Chug, you multiply the coordinates by 4, so the rule is (4*x*, 4*y*). For Hug, the rule is (5*x*, 5*y*). Chug's lengths are 4 times the corresponding lengths of Mug. Hug's lengths are 5 times the corresponding lengths of Mug. For both grandparents, corresponding angles are equal.

3. The angles would be the same, and the side lengths would be 6 times longer than the corresponding side lengths of Mug.

4. The angles would be the same, and the side lengths would be only 0.5 (or $\frac{1}{2}$) the length of the corresponding side lengths of Mug.

Applications • Connections • Extensions

As you work on these ACE questions, use your calculator whenever you need it.

Applications

1. The triangles below are similar.

a. Name the pairs of corresponding sides.

b. Name the pairs of corresponding angles.

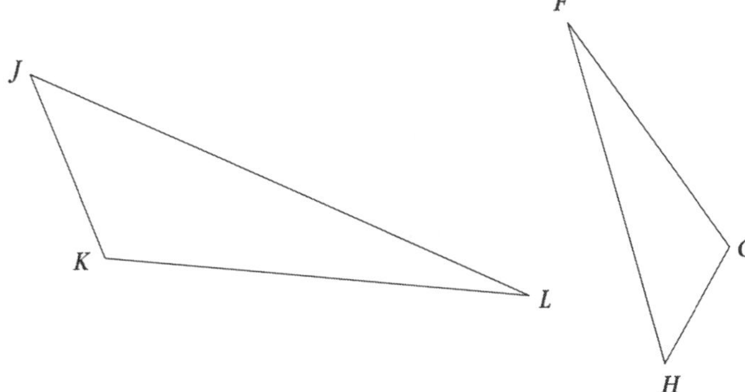

2. Mug's grandparents, Chug and Hug, are the fourth and fifth members of the Wump family (in the table for Problem 2.2, Chug is Wump 4 and Hug is Wump 5). How do the side lengths and angle measures of Mug's grandparents compare to the side lengths and angle measures of Mug? You may use the table from Problem 2.2 to help you answer this question.

3. If you used the rule (6*x*, 6*y*) to transform Mug into a new figure, how would the angles of the new figure compare to Mug's angles? How would the side lengths of the new figure compare to Mug's side lengths?

4. If you used the rule (0.5*x*, 0.5*y*) to transform Mug into a new figure, how would the angles of the new figure compare to Mug's angles? How would the side lengths of the new figure compare to Mug's side lengths?

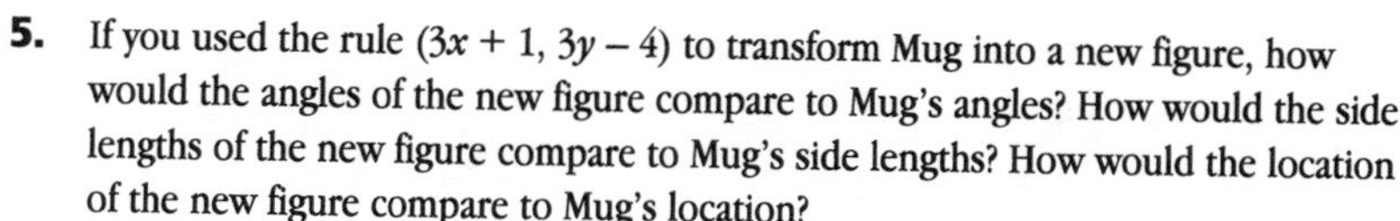

5. If you used the rule $(3x + 1, 3y - 4)$ to transform Mug into a new figure, how would the angles of the new figure compare to Mug's angles? How would the side lengths of the new figure compare to Mug's side lengths? How would the location of the new figure compare to Mug's location?

6. a. Draw a triangle *ABC* with vertices *A* (0, 0), *B* (3, 0), and *C* (0, 4).

   b. Draw a triangle *A′B′C′* by applying the rule $(2.5x, 2.5y)$ to the vertices of triangle *ABC*.

   c. How do the lengths of the sides of triangle *A′B′C′* compare to the lengths of the corresponding sides of triangle *ABC*?

   d. How do the measures of the angles of triangle *A′B′C′* compare to the measures of the corresponding angles of triangle *ABC*?

   e. Are triangles *ABC* and *A′B′C′* similar? Explain.

7. a. Draw a triangle *XYZ* with vertices *X* (5, 8), *Y* (0, 5), and *Z* (10, 2).

   b. Apply a rule to triangle *XYZ* to get a similar triangle, *X′Y′Z′*, with a scale factor of 1. What rule did you use? How do the lengths of the sides of triangle *X′Y′Z′* compare to the lengths of the corresponding sides of triangle *XYZ*?

   c. Apply a rule to triangle *XYZ* to get a similar triangle, *X″Y″Z″*, with a scale factor of $\frac{1}{5}$. What rule did you use? How do the lengths of the sides of triangle *X″Y″Z″* compare to the lengths of the corresponding sides of triangle *XYZ*?

8. a. Use triangle *ABC* from question 6 and the rule $(3x, y)$ to draw a new triangle.

   b. How do the measures of the angles of the new triangle compare to the measures of the corresponding angles of triangle *ABC*?

   c. Are the two triangles similar? Explain.

5. The angles would be the same, and the side lengths would be 3 times longer. Also, the figure would be moved 1 unit to the right and 4 units down.

6a. See page 27l.

6b. See page 27l.

6c. The side lengths are now 7.5, 10, and 12.5; they have each been multiplied by 2.5.

6d. The angle measures all remained the same.

6e. The triangles are similar, because the angles are the same and their side lengths have increased by the same scale factor.

7a. See page 27l.

7b. See page 27l.

7c. See page 27m.

8a. See below left.

8b. Two of the angles are not the same. Only the right angle remained the same.

8c. The triangles are not similar, because there is no scale factor that could be used to transform one triangle into the other, and all corresponding angles do not have the same measure.

8a.

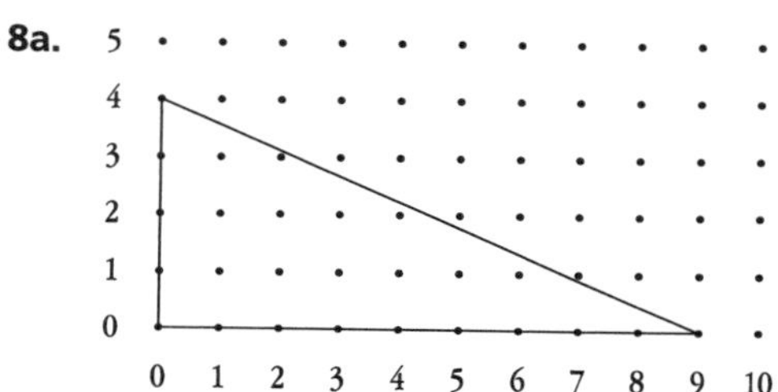

9a. See page 27m.

9b. See page 27m.

9c. See page 27m.

9d. The lengths of rectangle $A'B'C'D'$ are 1.5 those of rectangle $ABCD$. The lengths of rectangle $A''B''C''D''$ are 0.25 those of rectangle $ABCD$.

9e. Yes, rectangles $A'B'C'D'$ and $A''B''C''D''$ are similar, with a scale factor of 6 from the small to the large rectangle and $\frac{1}{6}$ from the large to the small rectangle.

9f. No, adding a constant amount to each side is different from multiplying each side by a constant scale factor. Multiplying by the scale factor enlarges or shrinks the figure. Adding a constant amount will distort the figure.

10. See page 27m.

Connections

11a. Rectangles will vary, but all should have an area of 14 cm^2. Some possible dimensions for the rectangle are 1×14, 2×7, and 4×3.5

11b. Possible answer: $(2x, 2y)$. Students may give any rule of the form $(2x + a, 2y + b)$, where a and b can be any numbers.

11c. Answers will vary. Actual perimeters may vary depending on the dimensions chosen for rectangle $ABCD$, but in comparing the two rectangles, the perimeter of $A'B'C'D'$ should be twice the perimeter of $ABCD$.

9. **a.** Copy rectangle $ABCD$ onto a piece of grid paper.

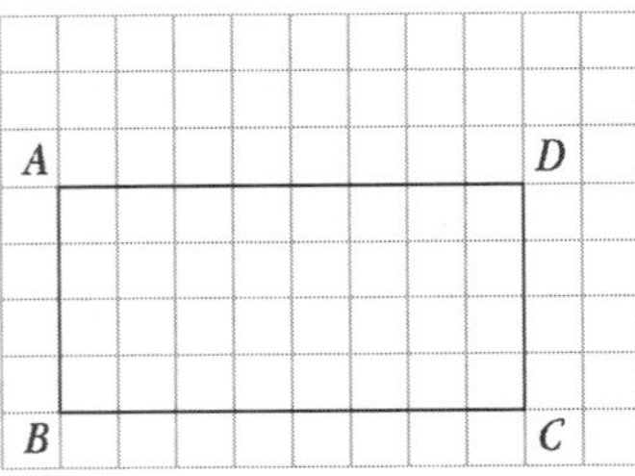

b. Make a similar rectangle by applying a scale factor of 1.5 to rectangle $ABCD$. Label the new rectangle $A'B'C'D'$.

c. Make another similar rectangle by applying a scale factor of 0.25 to rectangle $ABCD$. Label the new rectangle $A''B''C''D''$.

d. Tell how the lengths of the sides of each new rectangle compare to the lengths of the corresponding sides of rectangle $ABCD$.

e. Are rectangles $A'B'C'D'$ and $A''B''C''D''$ similar to each other? If so, what is the scale factor from rectangle $A'B'C'D'$ to rectangle $A''B''C''D''$? What is the scale factor from rectangle $A''B''C''D''$ to rectangle $A'B'C'D'$?

f. If you make a rectangle by adding 3 units to each side of rectangle $ABCD$, will it be similar to rectangle $ABCD$? Explain your reasoning.

10. Redraw Hat 1 (from Problem 2.3). Draw a new hat by applying the rule $(2x + 1, 2y + 2)$ to Hat 1. How does the new hat compare to Hat 1? Are they similar? Explain your reasoning.

Connections

11. **a.** On centimeter grid paper, draw a rectangle with an area of 14 square centimeters. Label it $ABCD$.

b. Use a rule to transform rectangle $ABCD$ into a rectangle that is twice as long and twice as wide. Label the rectangle $A'B'C'D'$. What rule did you use to make rectangle $A'B'C'D'$?

c. What is the perimeter of rectangle $A'B'C'D'$? How does it compare to the perimeter of rectangle $ABCD$?

12. You can think of a map as a reduced copy of a real country, state, or city. A map is similar to the place it represents. Below is a map of South Africa. The scale for the map is 1 centimeter = 240 kilometers. This means that 1 centimeter on the map represents 240 kilometers in the real world. Using this scale and a ruler, estimate these distances:

Cape Town, South Africa

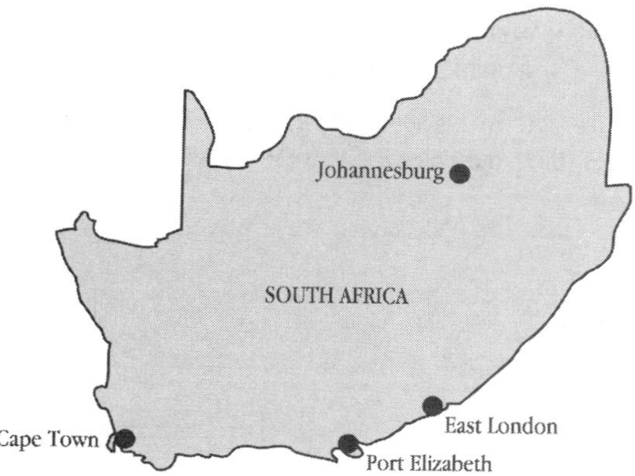

a. Cape Town to Port Elizabeth

b. Johannesburg to East London

12a. about 744 km

12b. about 792 km

Extensions

13. Drawings will vary. (**Teaching Tip**: In ACE 13, you may encourage some students to place the origin of the grid somewhere within the figure. Although students have not yet been exposed to graphing in all four quadrants, this situation can make them think about graphing below the x-axis and to the left of the y-axis.)

14a. Possible answer: Using the rule $(x + 5, y - 1)$, C will be at (6, 0).

14b. Possible answer: Using the rule $(2x, 2y - 1)$, C'' will be at (2, 1).

14c. Possible answer: Using the rule $(x + 4, 2y - 1)$, C''' will be at (5, 1).

Extensions

13. Select a drawing of a comic strip character from a newspaper or magazine. Draw a grid over the figure, or tape a transparent grid on top of the figure. Identify key points on the figure and then enlarge the figure by applying the rule $(2x, 2y)$ to the points.

14. Point A has coordinates (2, 4), point B has coordinates (6, 1), and point C has coordinates (1, 1).

- **a.** A rule is appled to A, B, and C to get A', B', and C'. Point A' is at (7, 3) and point B' is at (11, 0). Where is point C' located?
- **b.** A different rule is applied to A, B, and C to get A'', B'', and C''. Point A'' is at (4, 7) and point B'' is at (12, 1). Where is point C'' located?
- **c.** A different rule is applied to A, B, and C to get A''', B''', and C'''. Point A''' is at (6, 7) and point B''' is at (10, 1). Where is point C''' located?

Mathematical Reflections

In this investigation, you made a character named Mug Wump on a coordinate grid. Then, you used rules—such as $(2x, 2y)$ and $(2x, y)$—to transform Mug into other characters. Some of the characters you made were similar to Mug Wump, and some weren't. These questions will help you summarize what you have learned:

1. How did you decide which characters were similar to Mug Wump?
2. What types of rules produced figures similar to Mug Wump? What types of rules did not? Explain your answers.
3. If two figures are similar, describe the relationships between their
   - **a.** general shapes
   - **b.** angle measures
   - **c.** side lengths

Think about your answers to these questions, discuss your ideas with other students and your teacher, and then write a summary of your findings in your journal.

Tips for the Linguistically Diverse Classroom

Original Rebus The Original Rebus technique is described in detail in *Getting to Know Connected Mathematics*. Students make a copy of the text before it is discussed. During the discussion, they generate their own rebuses for words they do not understand; the words are made comprehensible through pictures, objects, or demonstrations. Example: Question 3—key words for which students might make rebuses are *figures are similar* (two similar triangles), *relationships* ($2 \times ?$, $4 \times ?$), *general shapes* (triangles), *angles measures* (arrows drawn to the corresponding angles of the two triangles), *side lengths* (arrows drawn to the corresponding sides of the two triangles).

Possible Answers

1. Answers will vary, but essentially, similar figures have the same shape. Students might talk about angles being the same or side lengths all doubling or tripling. They might mention that Thug and Lug were distorted, and therefore not similar to Mug, because each changed in only one direction.

2. Rules of the form $(2x, 2y)$ and $(3x, 3y)$ produced figures that were similar to Mug. In these rules, x and y are multiplied by the same number, stretching the new figure by the same factor in both directions. Rules such as $(3x, y)$ and $(x, 3y)$ did not produce similar figures. These rules stretch the figure in only one direction, which makes it fatter or thinner than the original. Rules of the form $(nx + a, ny + b)$ also produce figures similar to the original, but the image is moved a units horizontally and b units vertically. For example, $(2x + 7, 2y - 4)$ creates a figure similar to but twice as large as the original and moved to the right 7 units and down 4 units.

3a. Their shapes are the same.

3b. Their corresponding angles are the same.

3c. Their corresponding side lengths are related by the same scale factor.

TEACHING THE INVESTIGATION

2.1 • Drawing Wumps

In this problem, students draw a character named Mug Wump by connecting points on a coordinate grid. By applying transformations to this character they create other characters. Students then determine which characters are members of the Wump family—that is, which characters have the same shape as Mug—and which characters are imposters. As students work, they begin to develop a sense of what it means for figures to be similar.

Launch

If your students don't know how to locate points on a coordinate grid, you might introduce them to the process by playing a game of tic-tac-toe on a 4 by 4 grid on which marks are made on intersection points rather than in squares.

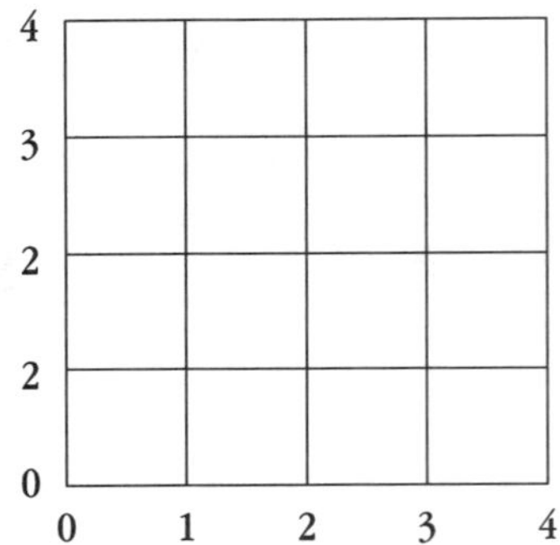

Explain that players will take turns telling you two numbers that designate the location of the *intersection point* for their X or O, and that the winner is the first person who gets four marks in a row—horizontally, vertically, or diagonally.

> We'll play the left side of the class against the right side. The left side can go first by giving me two numbers.

The first player states an ordered pair of numbers. If both numbers are between 0 and 4, the point they designate will be on the 4 by 4 grid; if a point is not on the board, the team loses its turn. For example, if a student says (5, 1), count along the horizontal axis until you get to 4 and then say, "Sorry, your point fell off the board!" Students will quickly learn to use the correct numbers and recognize that the order of the numbers is important. The first number tells how many spaces to the right (along the horizontal axis) of 0 we count, and the second number tells how high (along the vertical axis) we count. In the future, you may want to present variations of the game—for example, moving the origin, including negative numbers, or using fractions.

When students know their way around the coordinate plane, introduce the story of Zack and Marta's computer game, whose star characters are the Wump family.

Distribute Labsheets 2.1A and 2.1B. Students may need help understanding how to plot and connect the points in the four sets for drawing Mug Wump. Draw this basic figure as a class to make sure everyone understands how to locate and connect the four sets of points, including how to start over to draw the mouth, nose, and eyes.

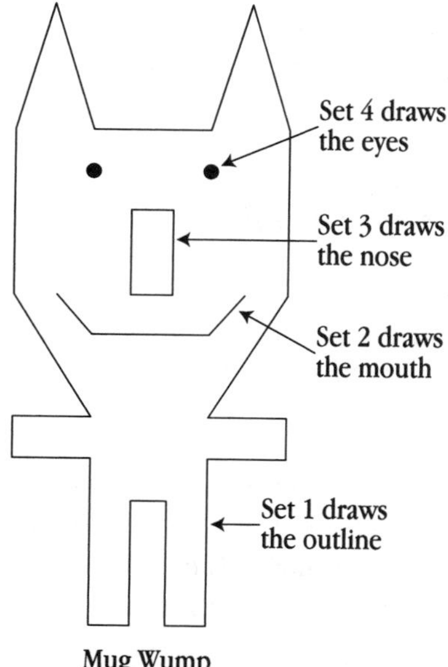

Mug Wump

Students will also need assistance with interpreting the symbolic rules for determining the points for the other four characters.

The points for Zug are found from the points for Mug. The rule is (2*x*, 2*y*). What do you think this rule tells us to do to a point for Mug to get a point for Zug? *(Multiply each coordinate by 2, or double the numbers for the coordinates.)*

What do the rules for Lug, Bug, and Thug tell us to do? *(For Lug, we multiply the x-coordinate by 3 and use the same y-coordinate. For Bug, we multiply each coordinate by 3. For Thug, we keep x the same and multiply the y-coordinate by 3.)*

When you feel that students are ready, launch the challenge of drawing the remaining four characters.

Explore

Have students work individually but check their work within a group. You may want to use Transparency 2.1D to help check students' points on Labsheet 2.1A.

Once students have drawn all the characters, ask them to compare them and to think about which belong to the Wump family and why. Ask students to look at how the characters' shapes, side lengths, and angles compare.

Summarize

As a class, compare the five figures.

How would you describe to a friend the figures that you drew? How do they compare?

Which figures seem to belong to the Wump family, and which don't? *(Mug, Zug, and Bug do, because they have the same shape. Lug and Thug are distorted.)*

Which figures are similar to each other? *(Mug, Zug, and Bug)* Are Lug and Thug related? Are they similar? *(No, Lug is wide and short, while Thug is narrow and tall.)*

In earlier units, we learned that angles and side lengths are important to determining the shape of a figure. How do the corresponding angles of these five figures compare?

You may want to use the figures on Transparency 2.1C to help the class compare the corresponding angles of the five figures. Superimpose the images to compare angles. If you don't have a projector, cut out a set of figures that you can hold up and compare angles. Cutting the figures from different colors of paper will help make the comparisons clearer. This technique will also reinforce the idea that what we measure in angles is the *amount of turn between the sides,* not the side lengths. In Mug, Zug, and Bug, corresponding angles are equal. Corresponding angles between Mug and Lug (or Mug and Thug) are not equal.

For the Teacher: Comparing Angles

Another interesting demonstration is to use the overhead projector to compare Mug and Bug. Tape a picture of Bug to the projection screen or to a clear wall, then project the image of Mug onto the picture of Bug. Move the projector closer to or farther away from the picture of Bug, until Mug's image corresponds exactly with Bug's. Do the same for Mug and Thug. (Try this on your own before doing it with the class.)

Now let's look at corresponding side lengths in the five figures. How are the lengths related? Are some of them related and others not?

Compare some of the lengths to establish that in Mug, Zug, and Bug, corresponding lengths grow in the same way (are multiplied by the same number).You may also want to superimpose a transparent half-centimeter grid over the figures on Transparency 2.1C. Students will begin to notice that if the coefficients of the x- and y-coordinates of the rule are equal, the figure will be similar to the original. If the coefficients are different, the figure will change more in one direction than the other and thus will be distorted. One special case to point out is when x and y are both multiplied by 1 to get a new figure. The figures will be similar, but even more, they will be congruent: they will have exactly the same size and shape.

Summarize what students have discovered.

Based on what you know so far, what do you think it means for two figures to be similar?

Students will probably now mention that the figures will have equal angles as well as having the same shape.

For the Teacher: Similarity Transformations

Algebraic rules of the form (nx, ny) are called *similarity transformations*, because they *transform* a figure in the plane into a similar figure in the plane. In Problem 2.2, students will see that adding a number to x or y moves the figure around on the grid but does not affect its size. A more general form of similarity transformations of this sort is $(nx + a, ny + b)$. Rules in which the coefficient of both x and y is 1—for example, $(x + 3, y - 2)$—move the figure around, but the figure retains its shape and size; it is congruent to the original. Other transformations in the plane, such as flips and turns, also preserve congruence; these are studied in the Grade 8 *Kaleidoscopes, Hubcaps, and Mirrors* unit.

2.2 • Nosing Around

In this problem, students focus on the properties of similar figures.

Launch

Show the top half of Transparency 2.2B, or draw the noses of the Wump family and the impostors on a transparent grid. Explain that you have copied *only* the noses from the five figures students drew in the last problem. Ask questions to help students begin to compare the five rectangles.

How does Zug's nose compare with Mug's nose? *(Zug's is larger.)* How many of Mug's noses can you put in Zug's nose? *(4)*

How do the perimeters of Mug's and Zug's noses compare? *(The perimeter of Zug's nose is twice that of Mug's nose.)* Does this relationship apply to Mug and Bug? *(The perimeter of Bug's nose is three times that of Mug's nose.)* to Mug and Thug? *(no)* to Mug and Lug? *(no)*

The noses are all rectangles, but they are not all similar. How can we tell if two rectangles are similar? What information do we need to help us answer this question?

Students will probably suggest gathering information on the width, length, and perimeter of the noses, but not the ratio of width to length. Read Problem 2.2 with the class, which suggests that students think about this ratio. Discuss the meaning of the ratio $\frac{\text{width}}{\text{length}}$ with the class. If students mention area, you can add it to the chart. However, they will look specifically at area in a later problem.

If students do not mention it, ask whether they need to look at the angle measures. They should respond no, since all the angles of every rectangle are right angles.

Explore

Have students work in pairs to fill in the chart and to answer the questions. Establish an agreement that the class will call the vertical measurement the length and the horizontal measurement the width so students can compare their work.

If students still have trouble determining which sides to call length and which to call width, help them sort this out by indicating the first two rows of the chart.

You will need to help some students find and interpret the ratios. Ask what they think each ratio means. Help them understand that a ratio of $\frac{1}{2} = \frac{\text{width}}{\text{length}}$ means that the length is twice the width (or that the width is half the length).

Students who only understand the part-whole meaning of fractions may need a lot of assistance here, as we are using fractions to compare two measures that are not parts of a whole. Ask students what the ratio means. What does it tell about how the sides of the rectangles compare? Using precise language to interpret the ratios in the context of the problem will help students to understand what ratios mean.

As shown in the follow-up question, the scale factor from Mug to Zug is 2 and from Mug to Bug is 3. This means that all linear measures of the figures, such as side lengths or perimeter, are multiples of the corresponding measures in the original figure.

For the Teacher: Area Growth

Some students will raise the issue of area, but don't press for an understanding of area growth here. One of the difficult and surprising things for students to grasp is that even though the lengths increase or decrease by the same factor, the areas are enlarged by the square of this factor. So Zug's nose is $2^2 = 4$ times the area of Mug's nose, and Bug's nose is $3^2 = 9$ times the area of Mug's nose. We do not focus on developing these concepts fully until a later problem. Though we do not consider volume in this unit, for completeness you may want to remember that the pattern continues; volume grows by the cube of the scale factor between the edges. In the *Filling and Wrapping* unit, students explore similar three-dimensional figures.

Summarize

Complete and review the chart for Wumps 1 through 5 with the class, perhaps using the table on Transparency 2.2B. Ask what patterns students notice. Ask how they found the dimensions for Wumps 4 and 5. They will probably mention that the width grows by 1 and the length grows by 2 for each step in the table, that all the ratios of width to length are $\frac{1}{2}$ for the Wumps (but not for Lug or Thug), and that the perimeter increases by 6 for each step. The chart gives you an opportunity to help students describe growth in a different way: we can say that the widths are multiples of 1, the lengths are multiples of 2, and the perimeters are multiples of 6.

Are the noses of Wumps 1 through 5 similar? *(Yes; they have the same shape, the same angles, and the same ratios.)*

Ask questions about Wump noses not listed in the table.

I want to grow a new Wump from Wump 1 (Mug). The scale factor is 9. What are the dimensions and perimeter of Wump 9's nose? *(The nose is 9 by 18 and has a perimeter of 54.)* How did you find these values?

What if the scale factor is 75—what are the measurements of the new nose? *(It is 75 by 150 with a perimeter of 450.)*

Move into a discussion of the rules that could be written to describe the changes.

Why are the dimensions 75 by 150? What rule would produce this figure?

The scale factor tells what to multiply the old sides by to get the new sides. Since Mug's nose is 1 by 2, the new nose is 1×75 by 2×75, or 75 by 150. The rule is $(75x, 75y)$.

In a rectangle, why does the perimeter grow at the same rate as the side lengths?

Students should be able to explain that the perimeter behaves like the width and length because it is a linear measurement also. Some might recognize that since perimeter $= 2(L + W)$ and if the scale factor is 2, the new perimeter $= 2(2L + 2W)$, which is just double the original perimeter. A few students might see that in the expression $2(2L + 2W)$, which can be taken from the table, the factor $(2L + 2W)$ is the perimeter of the original rectangle.

What is the rule for Wump 100? for Wump *n*?

The rules are $(100x, 100y)$ and (nx, ny), respectively.

How can you tell what the scale factor will be between two similar figures if all you know is the rule you are to use to draw the new figure from the original?

Help the class understand that since all rules that give a similar figure have the same coefficient for x and y, this coefficient tells the factor by which the sides of the figure will grow. You only have to read the coefficient of x and y (which must be the same) to know the scale factor.

Describe rules that will give a similar but smaller figure than the original. *(rules with a coefficient of x and y that is less than 1)*

Describe rules that will give a figure that is similar to and larger than the original. *(rules with a coefficient of x and y that is greater than 1)*

What happens if the coefficient of x and y is exactly 1?

If both coefficients are 1, the new figure will be the same size as the original. Explain to the class that we call such figures *congruent*. Congruence is a special case of similarity: the corresponding angles are equal, and the corresponding sides are equal and, therefore, have a ratio of 1.

> Let's go in the reverse direction. How can you find the scale factor from the original to the image if all you know are the dimensions of two similar figures? *(We need to find the ratio of the corresponding sides or the ratio of sides in the image to sides in the original.)*

These questions connect back to the work in the *Variables and Patterns* unit; students are looking for a general rule to express Wump family noses.

Once you feel students have some understanding that similar figures have the same shape and sides that grow or shrink by the same rate, expand their thinking by asking some of the above questions in reverse.

> If the perimeter of the nose of a new Wump family member is 150, what is the length and width of the nose? What scale factor was used to grow this new Wump from Mug 1?

Students might reason as follows: The perimeter is 150. I must find a number that, when multiplied by the original perimeter, gives the product 150. That is, $6 \times ? = 150$, so the scale factor is 25. Therefore the length is $2 \times 25 = 50$, and the width is $1 \times 25 = 25$.

> If the length of the nose of a new Wump is 180, what is the width and perimeter of the nose? What scale factor was used?

Students might reason that the width is half the length, or 90. This means that the perimeter is 540. The scale factor must be 90.

If your class is ready, ask what scale factor is needed to produce a rectangle with a perimeter of 3. This requires students to shrink the original rectangle (Mug's nose) by a scale factor of $\frac{1}{2}$.

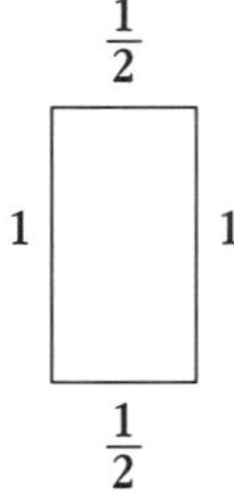

You might want to extend the idea of similar rectangles to similar quadrilaterals.

> On grid paper, draw a quadrilateral that is not a rectangle. Make a similar quadrilateral using a scale factor of 2. Compare the measures of the corresponding lengths and the corresponding angles of the two figures. How can you decide whether two quadrilaterals are similar?

2.3 • Making Wump Hats

In this problem, students investigate what effect adding to or subtracting from the x- and y-coordinates, or multiplying the coordinates by a number, will have on the image. The figure students will be transforming is simple enough to allow them to concentrate on what is happening as they manipulate the rule.

Launch

Distribute Labsheets 2.3A and 2.3B, and look at the table and grids as a class.

> This problem is similar to what we did when we drew the Wump family and the impostors. Look at the rules for drawing the hats. As you draw each hat, think about how the rule for each hat changes the image compared to hat 1.
>
> After you have drawn the six hats, look back over them and think about how adding or multiplying in the rule affects the new figure. How can you predict what will happen to a figure just by analyzing what is happening in the rule?

Explore

You may need to help students understand that points A and H are identical so that the line segments will connect at the end to finish the drawing of the hat.

As students fill in the table and draw the hats, ask extension questions of students who catch on quickly. Challenge them to make up a rule to fit constraints you supply (such as "three times bigger than hat 1 and moved up"), or to make up a rule that would send the image into another quadrant. Though they may not have formally studied negative numbers or had much experience with all four quadrants of a coordinate system, many students will be able to figure out how to move a figure around by manipulating the rule.

Summarize

This is another opportunity to superimpose the images and the original (using Transparency 2.3B) to help students examine what happens to the corresponding angles.

> Is each image similar to the original? Why or why not?
>
> How can you tell, by looking at the figures, which are similar? How do the ratios of the sides compare?

The images made by the rules $(x + 2, y + 2)$, $(x + 3, y - 1)$, and $(0.5x, 0.5y)$ are similar to the original. The images made by $(2x, y + 2)$ and $(2x, 3y)$ do not retain the same shape.

> How do the rules affect what happens to the image?

Multiplying both coordinates by the same number preserves shape, but if the factors are different, the hat stretches or shrinks unevenly. Adding or subtracting just moves the figures up or down or to the right or left.

How did we get a hat that kept its shape? This means the original grew at the same rate in both directions. *(by multiplying coordinates by the same number)*

For the Teacher: Positive or Negative

This is not exactly correct, but it is what students will be able to say from their experiences so far. In the unit *Accentuate the Negative*, students will return to this question and see that it is the coefficient *without regard to its sign* that makes the difference. So, if the x is multiplied by –2 and the y by 2, we still get a similar figure.

How did we get a hat that grew or shrunk more in one direction than the other? *(by multiplying the coordinates by different numbers)*

So, what does the factor we multiply by seem to do? *(It tells how the figures grow or shrink.)*

Now, let's see if we can sort out what adding or subtracting a number does. Do we have any hats that did not grow or shrink? *(yes)* What seems to have happened to them? *(they moved on the grid)*

Let's be more specific. What would the rule $(x + 2, y)$ do? If you don't know, plot the points and see. *(It would shift the figure to the right 2 units.)*

What about $(x, y + 2)$? *(It shifts the figure up 2 units.)*

What if I do both, $(x + 2, y + 2)$? *(The figure would be shifted up and to the right.)*

Go through the follow-up questions carefully. After you discuss question 4, offer some new rules for students to predict what would happen.

What effect would the rule $(5x - 5, 5y + 5)$ have on the original? *(The figure will be similar; its sides will be 5 times as long and it will be moved to the left 5 and up 5.)*

What about the rule $(\frac{1}{4}x, 4y - \frac{5}{6})$? *(This rule would not give a similar figure; the figure will be shrunk in one direction and stretched in the other. It will be moved down $\frac{5}{6}$ of a unit.)*

Make up a rule that will shrink the figure, keep it similar, and move it to the right and up. *[One possibility is $(\frac{2}{3}x + 2, \frac{2}{3}y + 1)$.]*

Additional Answers

Answers to Problem 2.2

A. Here is the completed chart:

Wump	Width of nose	Length of nose	$\frac{\text{Width}}{\text{Length}}$	Perimeter
Wump 1 (Mug)	1	2	$\frac{1}{2}$	6
Wump 2 (Zug)	2	4	$\frac{2}{4}$	12
Wump 3 (Bug)	3	6	$\frac{3}{6}$	18
Wump 4	4	8	$\frac{4}{8}$	24
Wump 5	5	10	$\frac{5}{10}$	30
⋮				
Wump 10	10	20	$\frac{10}{20}$	60
Wump 20	20	40	$\frac{20}{40}$	120
Wump 100	100	200	$\frac{100}{200}$	600
Lug	3	2	$\frac{3}{2}$	10
Thug	1	6	$\frac{1}{6}$	14

B. Answers will vary. Students should see at least the following patterns:

- The width and length can be found by multiplying the original (Mug's) width and length by the Wump family member's number.
- For Wumps, the ratio of width to length is always the same ($\frac{1}{2}$) when it is expressed in simplest form.
- The perimeter of any Wump's nose is Mug's perimeter multiplied by that Wump's number. From one Wump to the next, the perimeter increases by 6.

Answers to Problem 2.3

	Hat 1	Hat 2	Hat 3	Hat 4	Hat 5	Hat 6
Point	(x, y)	$(x + 2, y + 2)$	$(x + 3, y - 1)$	$(2x, y + 2)$	$(2x, 3y)$	$(0.5x, 0.5y)$
A	(0, 4)	(2, 6)	(3, 3)	(0, 6)	(0, 12)	(0, 2)
B	(0, 1)	(2, 3)	(3, 0)	(0, 3)	(0, 3)	(0, 0.5)
C	(6, 1)	(8, 3)	(9, 0)	(12, 3)	(12, 3)	(3, 0.5)
D	(4, 2)	(6, 4)	(7, 1)	(8, 4)	(8, 6)	(2, 1)
E	(4, 4)	(6, 6)	(7, 3)	(8, 6)	(8, 12)	(2, 2)
F	(3, 5)	(5, 7)	(6, 4)	(6, 7)	(6, 15)	(1.5, 2.5)
G	(1, 5)	(3, 7)	(4, 4)	(2, 7)	(2, 15)	(0.5, 2.5)
H	(0, 4)	(2, 6)	(3, 3)	(0, 6)	(0, 12)	(0, 2)

See drawings on the next page.

Hat 1

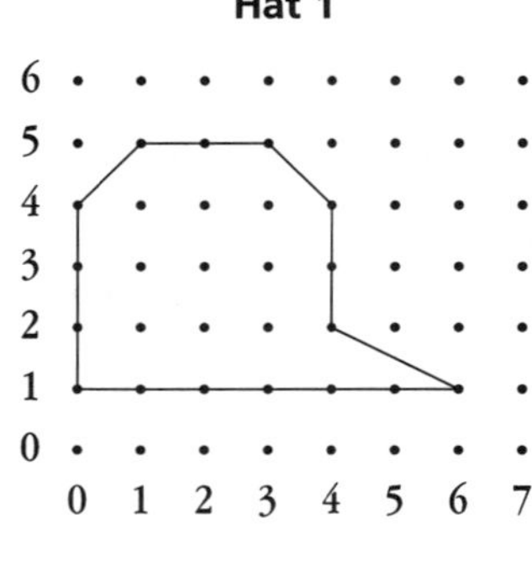

Hat 2

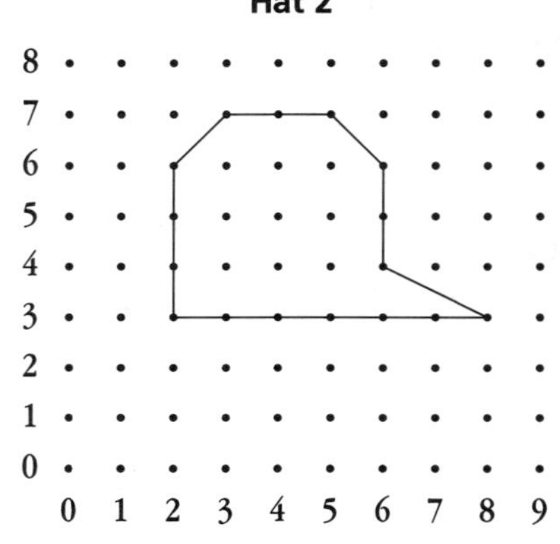

Hat 3

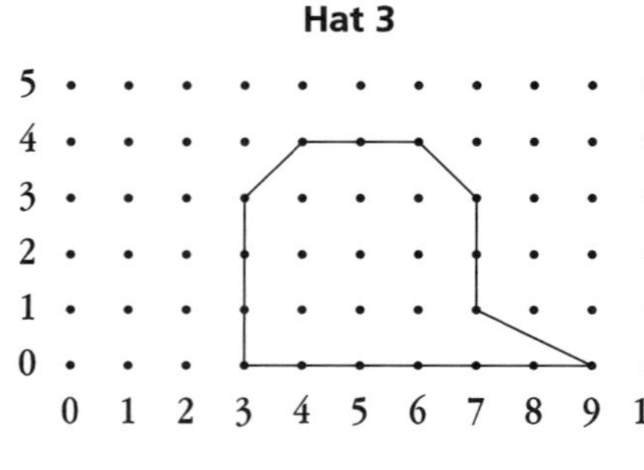

Hat 4

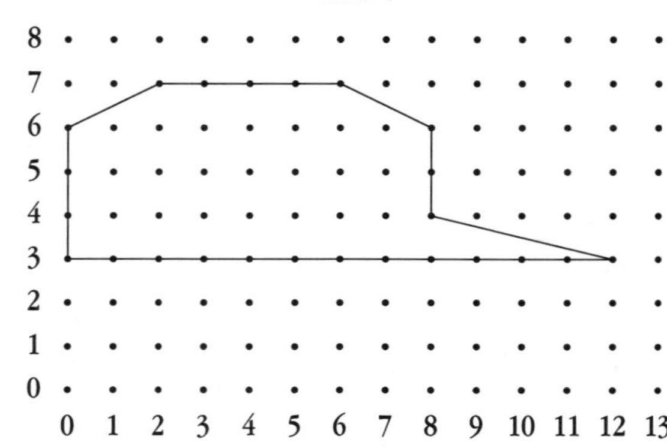

Hat 5

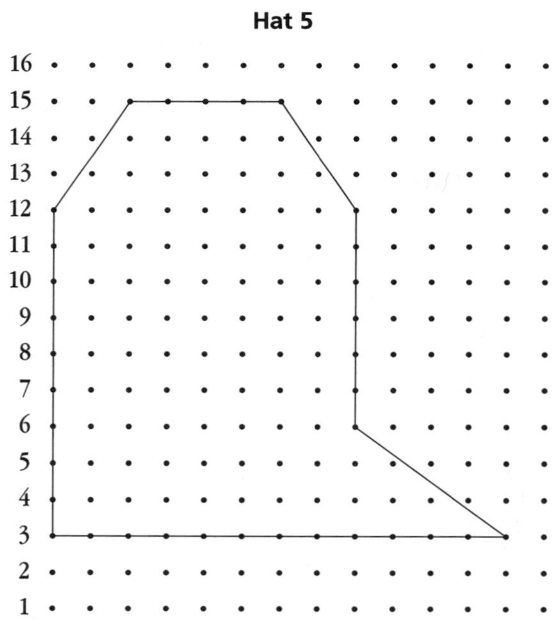

Hat 6

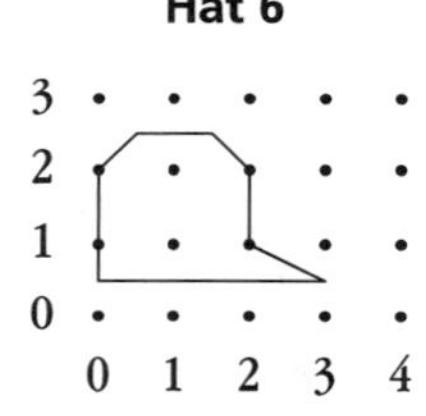

ACE Answers

Applications

6a.

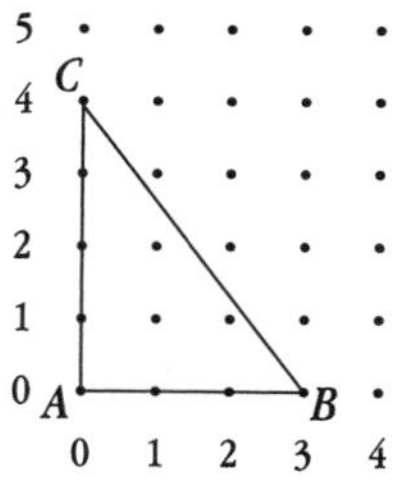

6b.

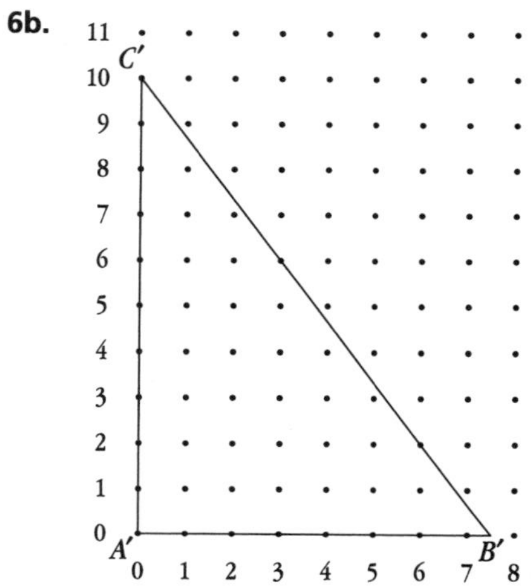

7a.

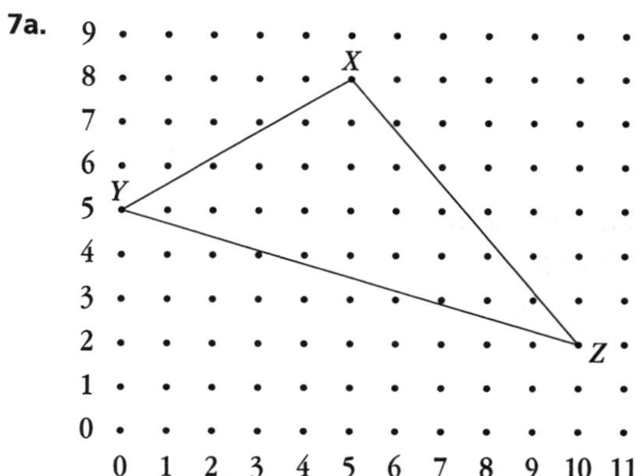

7b. Possible rule: (*x*, *y*); The sides of triangle *X′Y′Z′* are the same length as those of triangle *XYZ*.

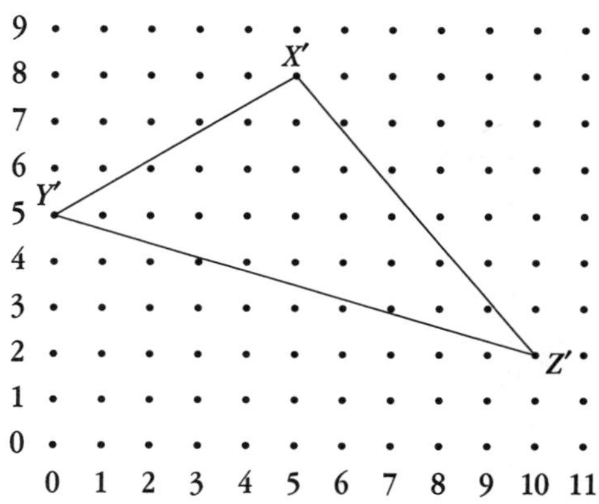

7c. Possible rule: $(0.2x, 0.2y)$; The sides of triangle $X''Y''Z''$ are $\frac{1}{5}$ the length of those of triangle XYZ.

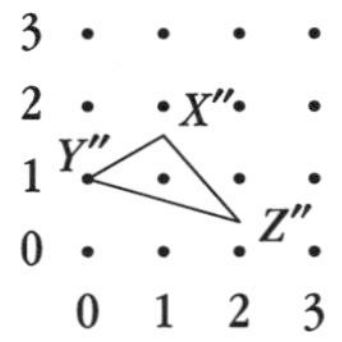

9a.

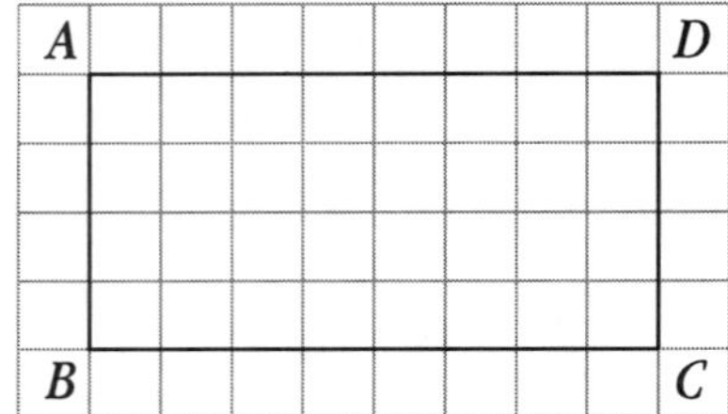

9b.

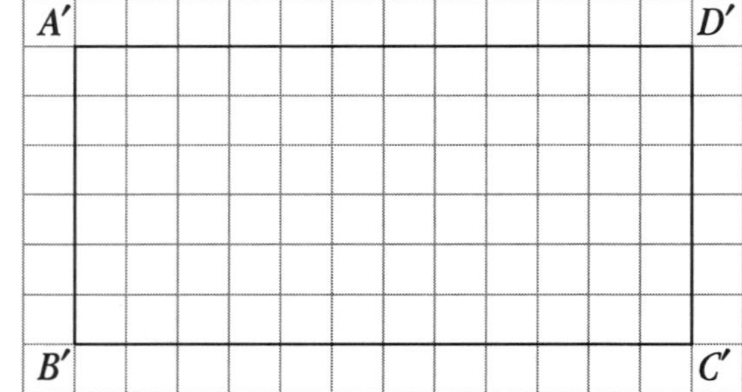

9c.

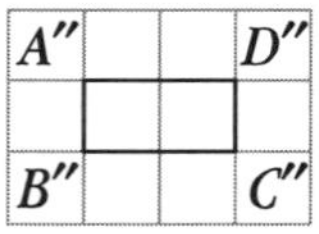

10. The new hat is similar to Hat 1, because the angles are the same and the lengths of the new hat are all twice those of Hat 1. The new hat has also been shifted up.

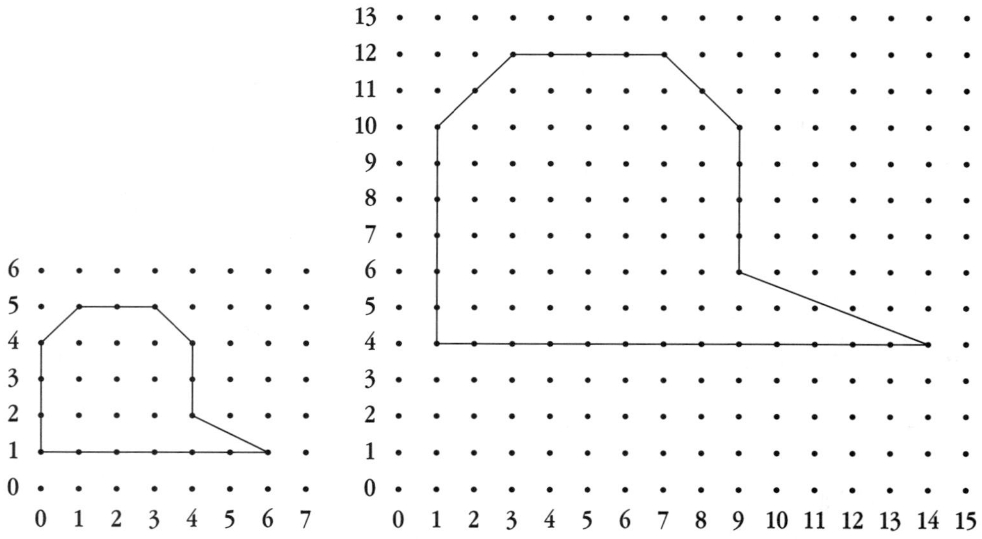

Patterns of Similar Figures

In this investigation, students will analyze groups of figures to test their ideas about which are similar and why. They are challenged to use their definition of *similarity* and to find the scale factor between pairs of similar figures. In addition, students will explore what the scale factor between two similar figures reveals about how their areas compare. If two figures are similar and the scale factor from the small to the large figure is s, the area of the large figure is s^2 times the area of the small figure. As this is often a difficult concept for students, the problems first focus on length measures between similar figures and allow students to become comfortable with these ideas before they tackle the area relationship.

In Problem 3.1, Identifying Similar Figures, students apply their knowledge of similarity to sets of polygons. Problems 3.2 and 3.3, Building with Rep-tiles and Subdividing to Find Rep-tiles, challenge students to put copies of a basic shape (a rep-tile or "repeating tile") together to make a larger, similar shape. Then, they subdivide large shapes into smaller, similar shapes. Their work with rep-tiles raises the issue of area relationships naturally.

Mathematical and Problem-Solving Goals

- *To recognize similar figures and to be able to tell why they are similar*
- *To understand that any two similar figures are related by a scale factor, which is the ratio of their corresponding size*
- *To build a larger, similar shape from copies of a basic shape (a rep-tile)*
- *To find rep-tiles by dividing a large shape into smaller, similar shapes*
- *To understand that the sides and perimeters of similar figures grow by a scale factor and that the areas grow by the square of the scale factor*
- *To find a missing measurement in a pair of similar figures*
- *To recognize that triangles with equal corresponding angles are similar*

Materials		
Problem	**For students**	**For the teacher**
All	Graphing calculators, angle rulers (optional; 1 per group), rulers (optional; 1 per group)	Transparencies 3.1A to 3.ACE (optional)
3.1	Labsheet 3.1 (1 per student), transparent centimeter and half centimeter grids (optional; copy grids onto transparency film), transparency markers (optional)	
3.2	Figures A, B, C, D, G, I, K, L, O, P, R, and T from the ShapeSet or 4 copies of each cut from Labsheet 3.2 (1 per student)	ShapeSet or transparencies of the shapes needed for Problem 3.2 (optional; copy Labsheet 3.2 onto transparency film)
3.3	Labsheet 3.3 (1 per student), scissors (optional)	Transparency of Labsheet 3.3 (optional)

Student Pages 28–40 | **Teaching the Investigation 40a–40j**

3.1

Identifying Similar Figures

At a Glance

Grouping: small groups

Launch

- As a class, examine one of the sets of polygons.
- Talk about what similar means and how we can decide whether two figures are similar.

Explore

- Let small groups work with the polygons on Labsheet 3.1.
- Give each group a transparent grid for measuring lengths and copying and comparing angles. *(optional)*

Summarize

- Talk about how students determined which shapes were similar.
- Review the relationships between corresponding angles and side lengths of similar figures.
- Have groups investigate the areas of the similar shapes. *(optional)*

Patterns of Similar Figures

In the last investigation, you met the Wump family. You found that Mug, Bug, and Zug are similar—they have exactly the same shape. You also discovered that, to make a figure that is similar to a given figure, you keep the same angles and multiply each length of the original figure by the same number. For example, to go from Mug to Zug, you use the same angles and multiply each length by 2. To make a smaller member of the Wump family, you could shrink Mug by keeping the same angles and multiplying each length by a number less than 1, such as 0.5.

3.1 Identifying Similar Figures

How good are you at spotting changes in a figure's shape? Can you look at two figures and decide whether they are similar? In the last investigation, you learned some mathematical ideas about what makes figures similar. Here, you will use your visual perception to predict which figures might be similar, and then use mathematics to check your predictions.

Problem 3.1

Examine the four sets of polygons on Labsheet 3.1. Two shapes in each set are similar, and the other is an impostor.

In each set, which polygons are similar? Explain your answers. You may cut out the polygons if it helps you think about the question.

Problem 3.1 Follow-Up

1. For each pair of similar figures on Labsheet 3.1, tell what number the side lengths of the small figure must be multiplied by to get the side lengths of the large figure. (You learned that this number is the scale factor from the small figure to the large figure.)
2. For each pair of similar figures on Labsheet 3.1, tell what number the side lengths of the large figure must be multiplied by to get the side lengths of the small figure. (This number is the scale factor from the large figure to the small figure.)
3. How are the scale factors in parts 1 and 2 related?

Assignment Choices

ACE questions 1–7, 16, 17, and unassigned choices from earlier problems

Answers to Problem 3.1

Rectangles A and C are similar, parallelograms B and C are similar, decagons A and C are similar, and stars A and B are similar.

Answers to Problem 3.1 Follow-Up

1. The scale factor from rectangle A to rectangle C is 4, the scale factor from parallelogram B to parallelogram C is 2, the scale factor from decagon A to decagon C is 3, and the scale factor from star A to star B is 3.
2. The scale factor from rectangle C to rectangle A is $\frac{1}{4}$, the scale factor from parallelogram C to parallelogram B is $\frac{1}{2}$, the scale factor from decagon C to decagon A is $\frac{1}{3}$, and the scale factor from star B to star A is $\frac{1}{3}$.
3. One scale factor is the inverse of the other.

Rectangle set

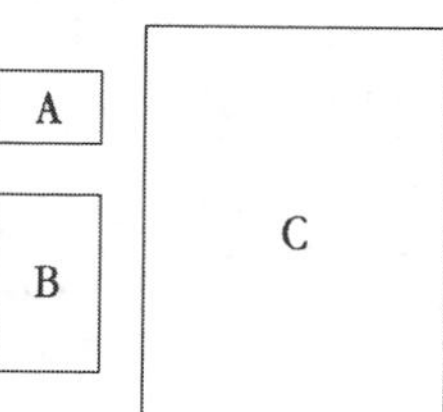

Parallelogram set

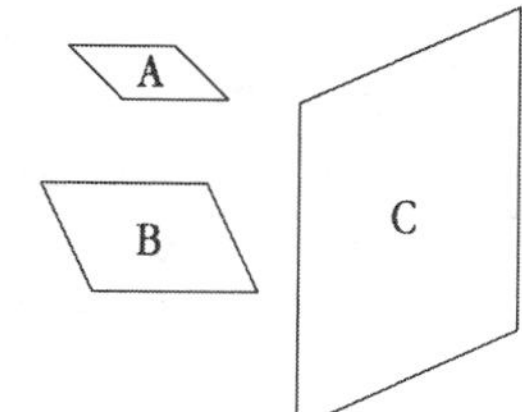

Decagon set

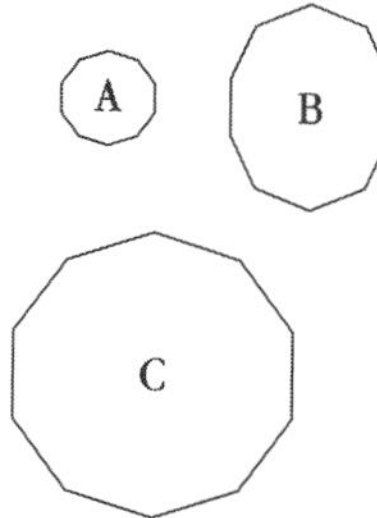

Star set

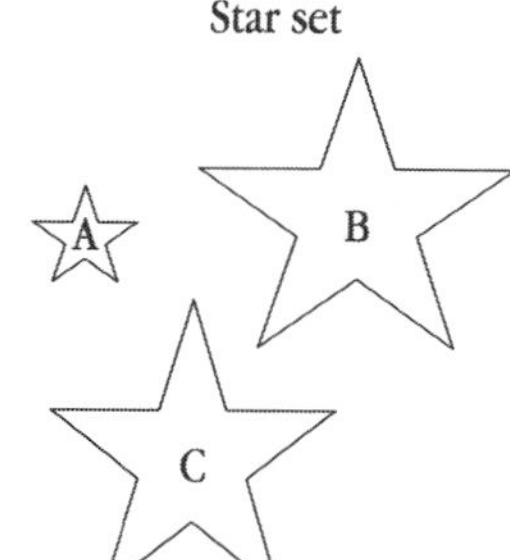

3.2 Building with Rep-tiles

A **rep-tile** is a shape whose copies can be put together to make a larger, similar shape. The small triangle below is a rep-tile. The two large triangles are formed from copies of this rep-tile. Can you explain why each large triangle is similar to the small triangle?

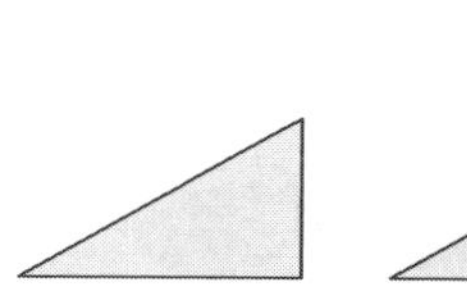

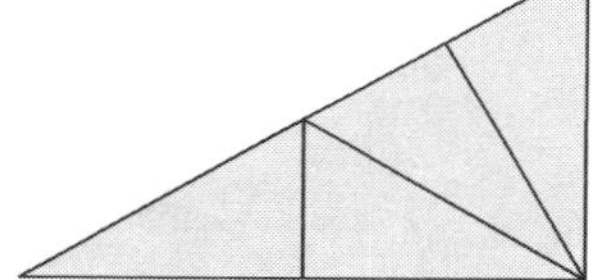

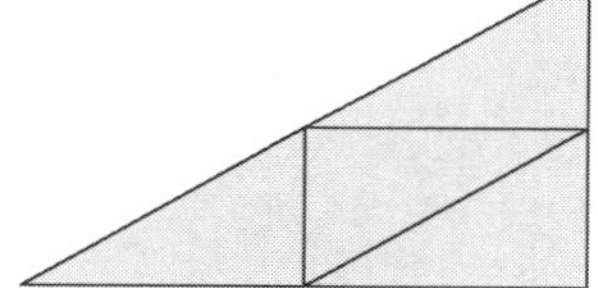

3.2 Building with Rep-tiles

At a Glance

Grouping: individuals, then small groups

Launch

- Use a demonstration to help the class discover what a rep-tile is.
- Help students set up a table for keeping track of their findings.

Explore

- For students who are struggling, suggest ways they might simplify their search.
- Have groups of four combine their shapes to explore part C.

Summarize

- As a class, record the findings in a table.
- Discuss the relationship between scale factor and area.
- Review the special attributes of triangles and rectangles in relation to similarity.

Assignment Choices

ACE questions 11–14, 18, 19, and unassigned choices from earlier problems

This reptile is *not* a rep-tile.

In this problem, your challenge is to figure out which of the shapes below are rep-tiles.

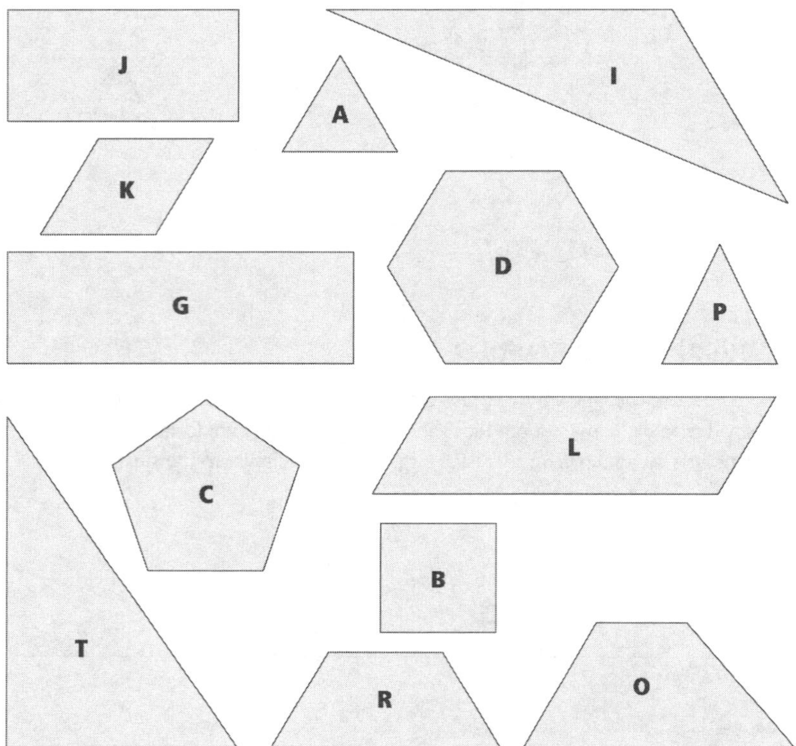

Subdividing to Find Rep-tiles

At a Glance

Grouping: individuals, then pairs

Launch

- Make sure students understand that the challenge is to subdivide shapes into smaller, similar shapes.

Explore

- Ask some students to copy their shapes onto a transparency for sharing in the summary. *(optional)*

Summarize

- Have the class share ideas, focusing on the scale factor and its relationship to area.
- Review the follow-up questions.

Problem 3.2

Use the shapes shown on page 30 from your ShapeSet™, or cut out copies of the shapes from Labsheet 3.2.

A. Start with four copies of one of the shapes. Try to find a way to put the four copies together—with no overlap and no holes—to make a larger, similar shape. If you are successful, make a sketch showing how the four shapes (rep-tiles) fit together, and give the scale factor from the original shape to the new shape. Repeat this process with each shape.

B. For each rep-tile you found in part A, try to find a different way to arrange the copies to get a similar shape. Sketch each new arrangement. How does the scale factor for each new arrangement compare to the scale factor for the first arrangement?

C. Start with one of the rep-tiles you found in part A. Try to add copies of the rep-tile to this shape to make the next-largest similar shape. If you are successful, make a sketch showing how the copies fit together. Repeat this process with each rep-tile you found in part A.

Problem 3.2 Follow-Up

1. Examine your work from Problem 3.2 carefully. What is the relationship between the scale factor and the number of copies of an original shape needed to make a larger, similar shape?
2. Is the number of copies of an original shape used to make a new shape related to the side lengths or the area of the new shape?

3.3 Subdividing to Find Rep-tiles

In Problem 3.2, you arranged rep-tiles to form larger, similar shapes. In this problem, you reverse the process. You start with a large shape and try to divide it into smaller, congruent shapes that are similar to the original shape. (Two shapes are *congruent* if they are exactly the same size and shape.) An example is shown at right.

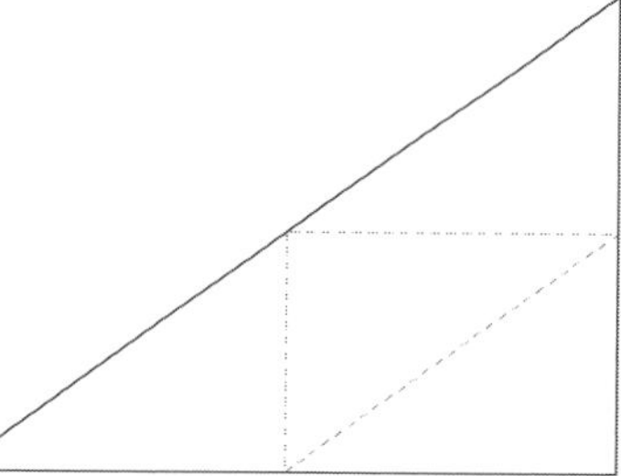

Answers to Problem 3.2

A. Shapes A, B, G, I, J, K, L, P, R, and T are rep-tiles. It takes four copies of each to make a larger, similar figure with a scale factor of 2.

B. See page 40g.

C. See page 40g.

Answers to Problem 3.2 Follow-Up

1. The scale factor squared gives the number of copies of a small shape needed to make a larger shape.
2. See page 40i.

Assignment Choices

ACE questions 8–10, 15, 20, and unassigned choices from earlier problems

Assessment

It is appropriate to use Quiz A after this problem.

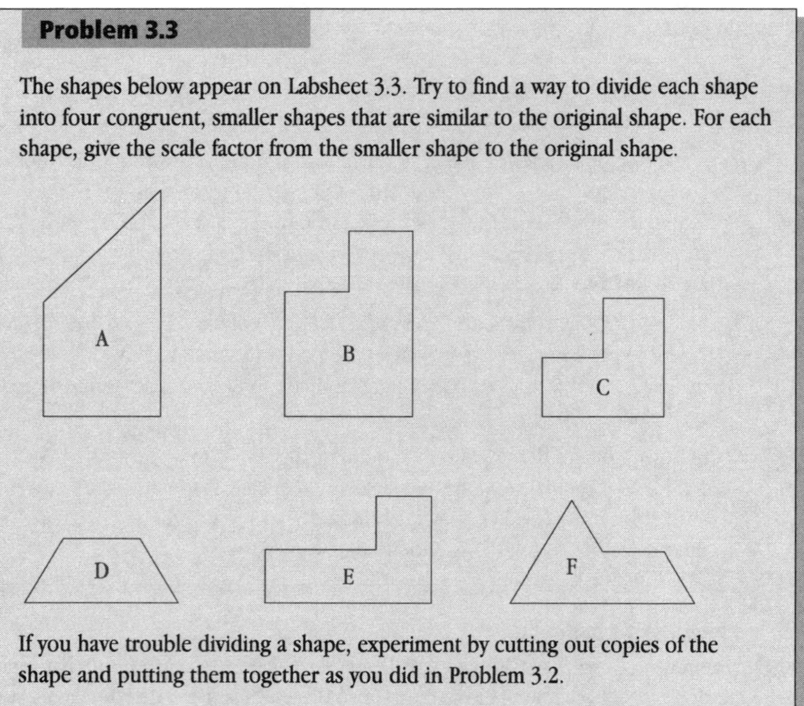

Problem 3.3

The shapes below appear on Labsheet 3.3. Try to find a way to divide each shape into four congruent, smaller shapes that are similar to the original shape. For each shape, give the scale factor from the smaller shape to the original shape.

If you have trouble dividing a shape, experiment by cutting out copies of the shape and putting them together as you did in Problem 3.2.

Problem 3.3 Follow-Up

1. Choose one of the shapes on Labsheet 3.3. Divide each small figure within the shape in the same way you divided the original shape. How many of these new shapes does it take to cover the original shape?

2. For the shape you subdivided in question 1, what is the scale factor from the smallest shape to the original shape?

3. How does the scale factor from question 2 relate to the number of the smallest shapes it takes to cover the original shape? What is the relationship between the scale factor and the areas of the large and small figures?

Answers to Problem 3.3

See page 40i.

Answers to Problem 3.3 Follow-Up

1. If we divide each small shape inside any of the original shapes, we now have 4×4 or 16 very small shapes.
2. The scale factor from the smallest shape to the original shape is 4.
3. Since the scale factor from the smallest shape to the original shape is 4, the area of the large shape is 4^2, or 16, times the area of the smallest shape. 16 is the number of the smallest shapes needed to cover the large shape. The square of the scale factor tells how the areas relate.

Applications • Connections • Extensions

As you work on these ACE questions, use your calculator whenever you need it.

Applications

1. The sides that form the right angle of a right triangle are called the *legs* of the triangle. This right triangle has legs of length 2 centimeters and 3 centimeters. Draw three triangles that are similar to this triangle.

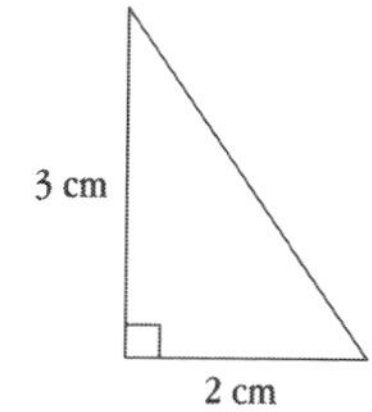

In 2–5, a pair of similar triangles is given. Find the missing measurement.

2.

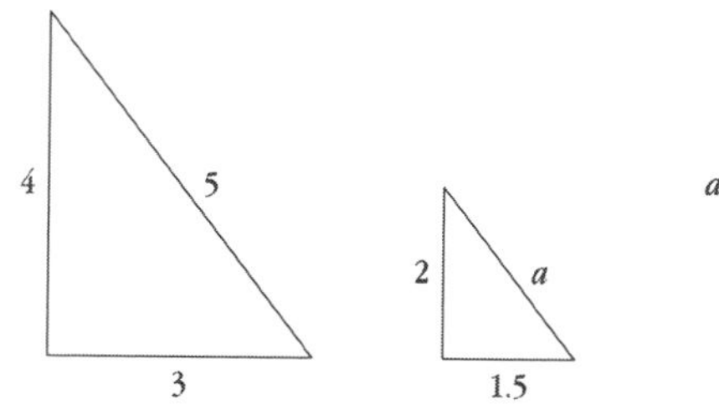

$a = ?$

3.

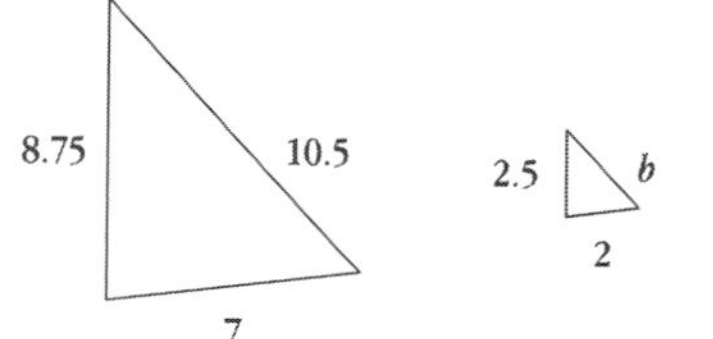

$b = ?$

4.

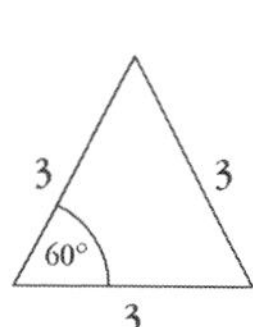

4 4 c 4

$c = ?$

Answers

Applications

1. See below left.
2. $a = 2.5$
3. $b = 3$
4. $c = 60°$

1. Possible answer:

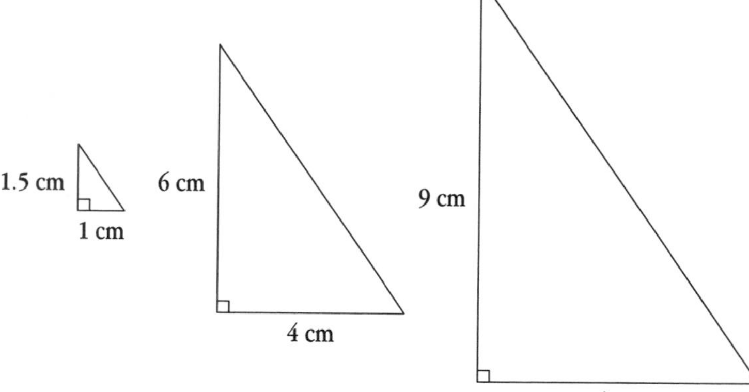

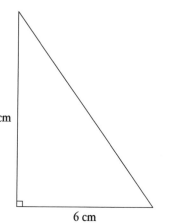

ACE

5. $d = 16\frac{2}{3}$

6. **(Teaching Tip:** You may want to use Transparency 3.ACE for a class discussion of ACE questions 6 and 7. The shapes can be cut out and superimposed to compare angles and will make it easier to see which shape is an enlargement of another.) Shapes A and C are similar. The corresponding angles are the same in all three shapes, but the sides of shape A have not grown by the same factor to form the corresponding sides of shape B.

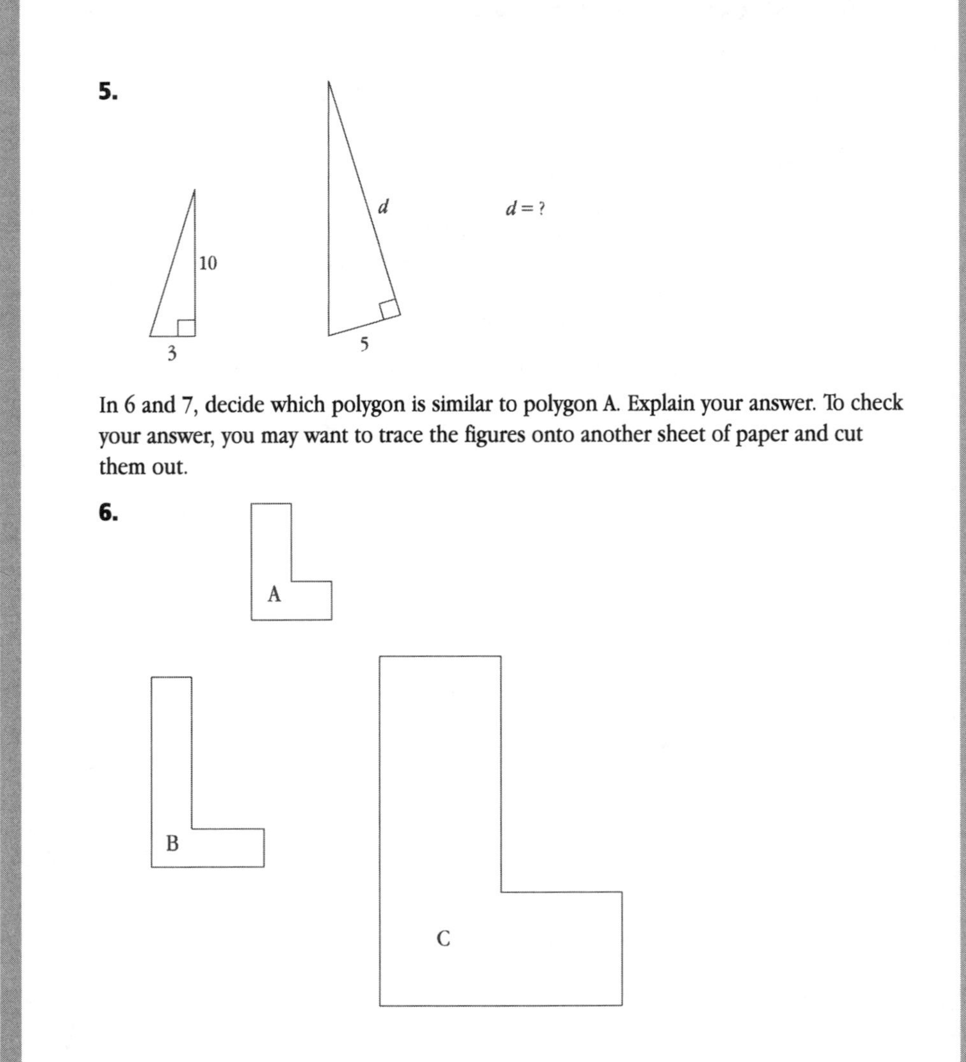
5.
10
3
d
5
d = ?
In 6 and 7, decide which polygon is similar to polygon A. Explain your answer. To check your answer, you may want to trace the figures onto another sheet of paper and cut them out.
6.
A
B
C

ACE

7.

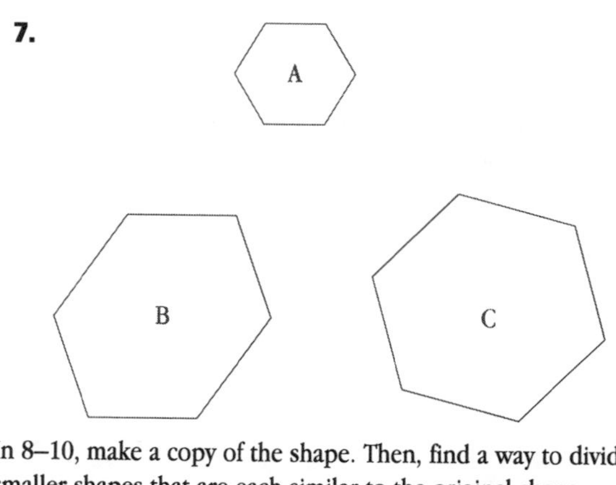

In 8–10, make a copy of the shape. Then, find a way to divide it into four identical, smaller shapes that are each similar to the original shape.

8.

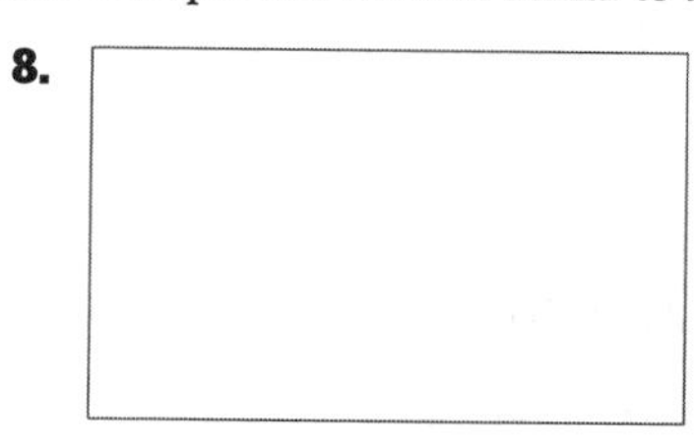

9.

10.

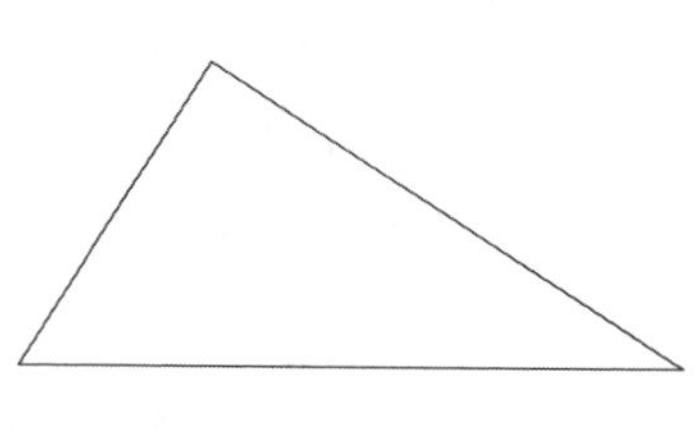

7. (See the Teaching Tip on p. 34.) Shapes A and C are similar. The angles of shape A are not congruent to the angles of shape B, even though corresponding sides have grown by the same factor.

8.

9. See below left.

10. See below left.

9.

10.

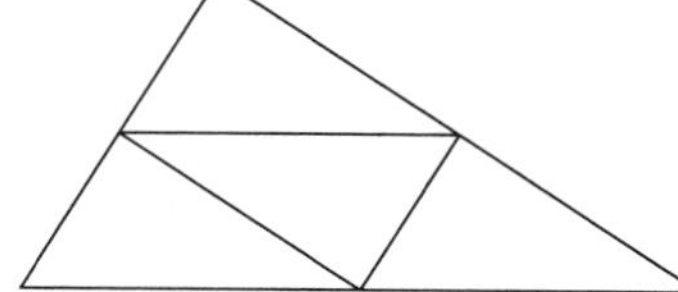

Connections

11a. 10 cm^2

11b. 15 cm^2 (Note: One way to find this is to break the hexagon into a rectangle, with an area of 10 cm^2, and two triangles, each with an area of $2\frac{1}{2}$ cm^2.)

12a. 16,000 m^2 (Note: This scale can also be thought of as 1 cm = 4000 cm, so the scale factor is 4000. The area would increase by the square of the scale factor, so $10 \times 4000 \times 4000 = 160{,}000{,}000$ cm^2, or 16,000 m^2. Students might also solve this by first finding the dimensions of the building, or by multiplying the 10 cm^2 area of the scale drawing by the scale for area, which is 40 m × 40 m, giving $10 \times 1600 = 16{,}000$ m^2.)

12b. $15 \times 4000 \times 4000 = 240{,}000{,}000$ cm^2 or 24,000 m^2

13. The area of the model and the building would both increase by a factor of 2 × 2 or 4, which gives $10 \times 4 = 40$ cm^2 for the model and $4 \times 16{,}000 = 64{,}000$ m^2 for the building.

14. (Note: This scale can also be thought of as 1 cm = 500 cm, so the scale factor is 500.)

14a. The fence will be $75 \times 500 = 37{,}500$ cm or 375 m long.

14b. $7\frac{1}{2} \times 500 \times 500 = 1{,}875{,}000$ cm^2 or 187.5 m^2

Connections

In 11–14, use this information: The Rosavilla School District wants to build a new middle school building. They asked architects to make scale drawings of some possible layouts for the building. After much discussion, the district narrowed the possibilities to these two:

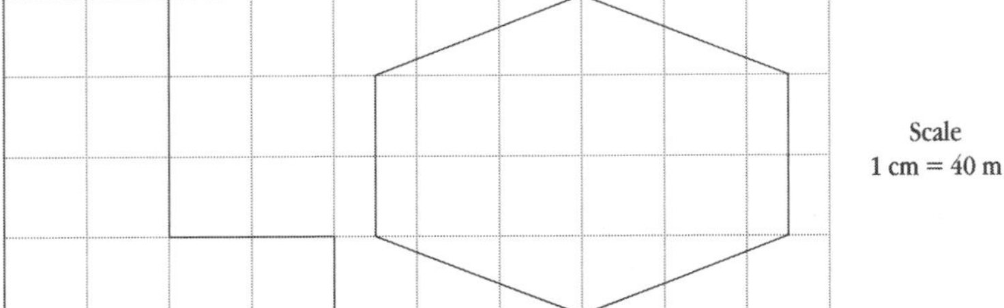

11. **a.** What is the area of the L-shaped scale drawing?

b. What is the area of the hexagonal scale drawing?

12. **a.** What would be the area of the L-shaped building?

b. What would be the area of the hexagonal building?

13. The school board likes the L-shaped layout but wants a building with more space. If they increase the L-shaped model by a scale factor of 2, how would the area of the scale drawing change? How would the area of the building change?

14. After more discussion, the architects made a detailed drawing of the final plans for the building and the school grounds using the scale 1 centimeter = 5 meters.

a. In the drawing, the fence around the football field is 75 centimeters long. How long will the fence around the actual field be?

b. In the drawing, the gymnasium floor has an area of $7\frac{1}{2}$ square centimeters. How much floor covering will be needed to build the gym?

c. The music teacher is excited about her new music room! It will be a rectangular room that is 20 meters long and has a floor area of 300 square meters. What are the dimensions of the music room in the scale drawing?

Extensions

15. A **midpoint** is a point that divides a line segment into two equal parts. Each part is one half the length of the original line segment. Draw a figure on grid paper by following these steps:

Step 1 Draw an 8-by-8 square.
Step 2 Mark the midpoint of each side.
Step 3 Connect the midpoints in order with four line segments to form a new figure. (The line segments should not intersect inside the square.)
Step 4 Repeat steps 2 and 3 three more times, each time working with the newest figure.

a. What kind of figure is formed when the midpoints of the sides of a square are connected?

b. Find the area of the original square.

c. Find the area of the new figure that is formed at each step.

d. How do the areas change between successive figures? Look at your drawing. Why does your answer make sense?

e. Are there any similar figures in your drawing? Explain.

14c. The dimensions of the room must be 20 m by 15 m, so the dimensions in the scale drawing must be 4 cm by 3 cm.

Extensions

15.

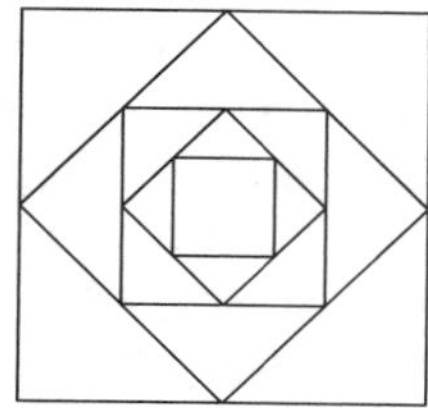

15a. You always get another square. (Note: This can be demonstrated on the overhead projector with a square of wax paper.)

15b. $8 \times 8 = 64$ square units

15c. The areas are 32, 16, 8, and 4 square units.

15d. The area is cut in half each time. Possible explanation: The "left-over" triangles could be put together to fill half the original square. [Note: The squares will converge on a point at the center of the squares, called the *centroid.* The area of the nth square drawn inside the original is $64 \times (\frac{1}{2})^n$.]

15e. There are similar squares and similar triangles in the drawing.

16. Rectangle A is similar to rectangle B and also similar to rectangle C. Can you conclude that rectangle B is similar to rectangle C? Explain your answer. Use drawings and examples to illustrate your answer.

17. Are all squares similar? Explain your answer.

18. **a.** Which shapes below are similar? How do you know?

b. State a scale factor for each pair of similar shapes you found in part a. Be specific about the direction of the scale factor. For example, if you found that A and B are similar, state whether the scale factor you give is from A to B or from B to A.

c. For each pair of similar shapes you found, predict how the two areas compare.

19. **a.** Which shapes below are similar? How do you know?

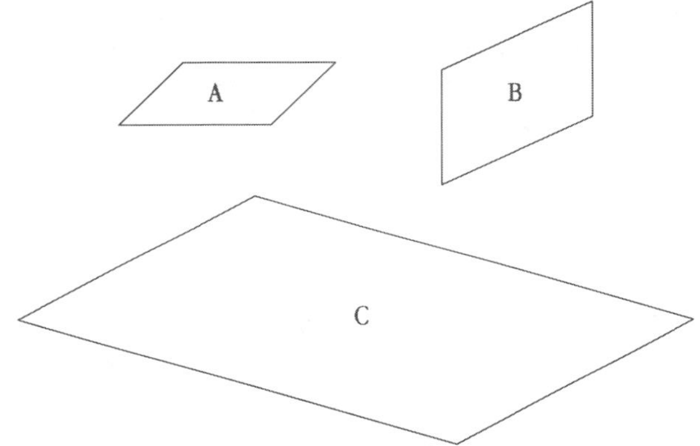

16. See page 40j.

17. Yes. All squares have four congruent sides, which guarantees that once a scale factor is used to determine one side, the other three sides will use the same scale. In addition, unlike rhombuses, which can have different angles, corresponding angles of two different squares are always 90° and therefore always congruent.

18a. Shapes A and C are similar. Shape A has side lengths of 28 mm and 22 mm with angles of 55° and 125°, and shape C has side lengths of 14 mm and 11 mm with the same angles.

18b. The scale factor from shape A to C is $\frac{1}{2}$. The scale factor from shape C to A is 2.

18c. By dividing shape A into four congruent regions, you can see that shape A has an area 4 times that of shape C.

19a. Shapes A and C are similar. Shape A has side lengths of 22 mm and 13 mm with angles of 45° and 135°, and shape C has side lengths of 66 mm and 39 mm with the same angles.

b. State a scale factor for each pair of similar shapes you found in part a. Be specific about the direction of the scale factor. For example, if you found that A and B are similar, state whether the scale factor you give is from A to B or from B to A.

c. For each pair of similar shapes you found, predict how the two areas compare.

20. a. Copy the large shape below, and subdivide it into nine copies of the small shape.

b. What is the scale factor from the small shape to the large shape?

c. How does the area of the large shape compare to the area of the small shape?

d. If two shapes are similar, how can you use the scale factor from the smaller shape to the larger shape to predict how the areas of the shapes compare?

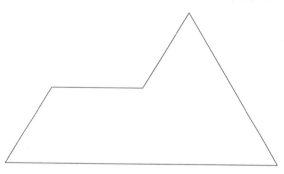

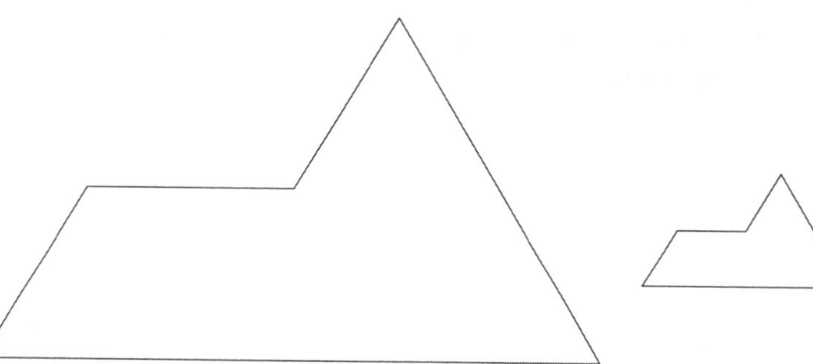

20a. Possible answer:

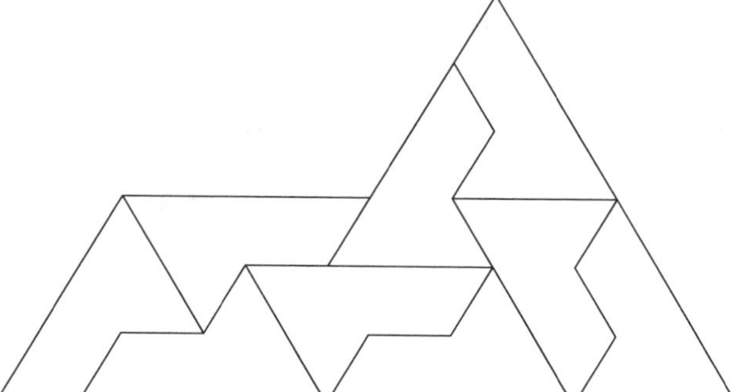

19b. The scale factor from shape A to C is 3. The scale factor from shape C to A is $\frac{1}{3}$.

19c. By dividing shape C into nine congruent regions, you can see that shape C has an area 9 times that of shape A.

20a. See below left.

20b. 3

20c. The large shape has an area 9 times that of the small shape.

20d. The areas of two similar shapes compare as the square of the scale factor between them. In this case, the scale factor is 3, and the area of the large shape is $3^2 = 9$ times that of the small shape.

Mathematical Reflections

In this investigation, you determined whether shapes were similar by comparing corresponding parts. You also explored rep-tiles, shapes whose copies can be put together to make larger, similar shapes. These questions will help you summarize what you have learned:

1. How can you decide whether two figures are similar?
2. What does a scale factor between two similar figures tell you?
3. Explain how you can find a scale factor between two similar figures. Use an example to explain your thinking.
4. Explain how you can use the scale factor to determine how the area of an enlarged figure compares to the area of the original figure.

Think about your answers to these questions, discuss your ideas with other students and your teacher, and then write a summary of your findings in your journal.

Possible Answers

1. Two figures are similar if their corresponding angles are equal and if the ratios between their corresponding sides are the same, so corresponding angles can be compared and the ratios of corresponding sides can be computed to determine whether two figures are similar.

2. The scale factor tells what factor a side—or any other length measure, such as perimeter—of the original figure must be multiplied by to find the length of the corresponding side in the other figure.

3. You can compute the ratio of corresponding sides to find the scale factor between two similar figures (divide a side of one figure by its corresponding side in the other figure). Possible example:

1
3

2
6

In these similar rectangles, the scale factor from the small rectangle to the large is $6 \div 3 = 2$.

4. If the scale factor between two similar figures is 4, the area of the larger figure is 4×4 times the area of the smaller figure. It takes 16 of the small figures to cover the same area as the large figure. In general, if the scale factor between two similar figures is s, the area of the larger figure is s^2 times the area of the smaller figure.

Tips for the Linguistically Diverse Classroom

Diagram Code The Diagram Code technique is described in detail in *Getting to Know Connected Mathematics*. Students use a minimal number of words and drawings, diagrams, or symbols to respond to questions that require writing. Example: Question 3—A student might answer this question by drawing a rectangle with dimensions of 3 by 6 units and another with dimensions of 9 by 18 units. Below these, the student might write *Scale factor = 18 ÷ 6 = 3* and draw an arrow to the corresponding sides of 18 and 6.

TEACHING THE INVESTIGATION

3.1 • Identifying Similar Figures

This investigation provides another opportunity to discuss what it means for two figures to be similar and how two figures can be checked to verify that they are similar.

Launch

Display Transparencies 3.1A and 3.1B, or refer to the polygon sets pictured in the student edition. Indicate one of the sets of polygons, and ask the class which two figures in the set are similar. Let them offer conjectures.

Explore

Let students examine the polygon sets on Labsheet 3.1 in small groups. You may want to give each group a transparent centimeter or half-centimeter grid (a half sheet is sufficient) and transparency markers, which can be used to measure lengths and to copy angles for making comparisons. Students could also make their comparisons with rulers and angle rulers.

As you work with individual groups, ask questions that will prepare students to summarize what they know about similarity in mathematical terms.

> What can you say about the angles of similar figures? What about the side lengths of similar figures—how are they related?

Summarize

Discuss which figures in each set are similar, which are not, and how the students reasoned about them. You may want to cut out the figures in each polygon set from Transparencies 3.1A and 3.1B and superimpose them to check corresponding angles and compare corresponding sides.

You want students to leave this problem with the ability to talk about similarity from a mathematical perspective. They need to understand that for two figures to be similar, they must have the same shape. This involves both angles and side lengths. Specifically:

- In similar figures, corresponding angles are the same.
- In similar figures, corresponding sides increase by the same number, or scale factor.

For each set of polygons, students should recognize that the two similar figures are similar because their corresponding angles are equal and their corresponding sides are related by the same scale factor. For example, in the rectangle set, we can multiply the side lengths of rectangle A by 4 to get the lengths of the corresponding sides of rectangle C. However, there is no number that we can multiply both the length and width of rectangle B by to get the dimensions of rectangle C. Another way of looking at this is that the number we multiply the width of rectangle A by to get its length would also work for rectangle C, but not for rectangle B. We can also look at ratios of corresponding sides, which are equal in similar figures.

If students have made sense of similar figures having equal corresponding angles and equal ratios of sides, you may want to assign each group to either the parallelogram set or the rectangle set to check how the areas of the two similar shapes are related.

3.2 • Building with Rep-tiles

This investigation is designed to help students focus on the relationship between the areas of similar figures.

Launch

Launch the activity by demonstrating what is meant by rep-tile, or repeating tile. A *rep-tile* is a shape that can be copied and put together to form a larger version of the same shape. Another way of looking at it is that the large shape can be covered with smaller, similar shapes. This is a different concept from a tessellation. For example, a regular hexagon will tessellate: copies of it can fit together without overlaps or gaps in a never-ending pattern. However, no larger regular hexagon can be found in the pattern formed by the small hexagons. The regular hexagon tessellates, but is not a rep-tile. If you put four squares together, however, you can form a large square that is similar to the small squares.

> Today we will investigate several shapes to see which of them are rep-tiles. I am going to show you two shapes; the first shape is a rep-tile and the second is not. Look at the shapes carefully, and tell me what you think a rep-tile is.

Show a square and a circle on the board or overhead projector. Some students may say that one tessellates or tiles, and one does not. Others may observe that the squares fit together without gaps, but the circles do not. Demonstrate this by adding copies of the square and the circle to your drawing.

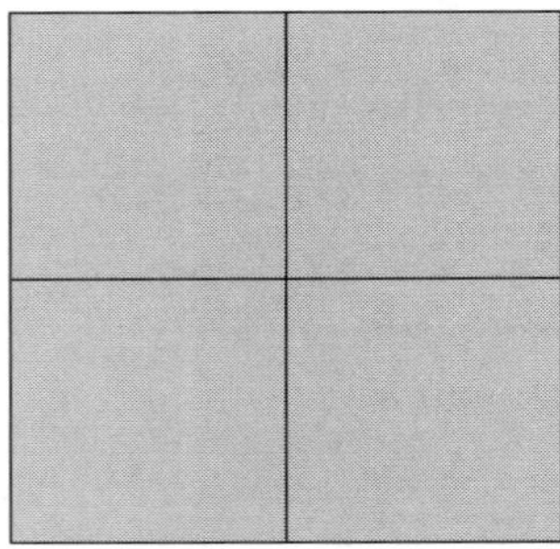

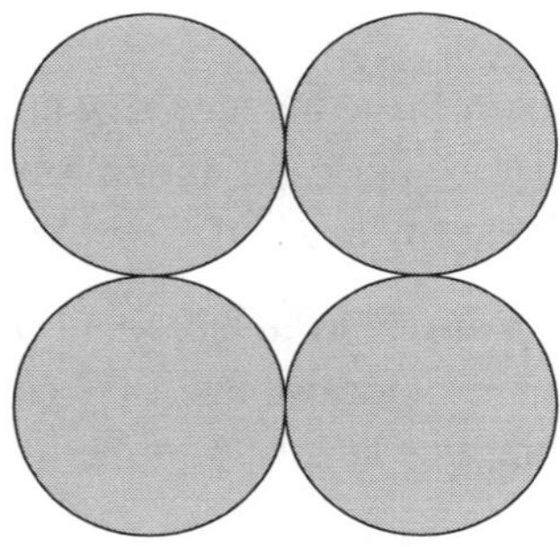

Show several copies of two more shapes, an equilateral triangle and a regular hexagon.

> Here are two more shapes. The triangle is a rep-tile, but the hexagon is not. Now what do you think a rep-tile is?

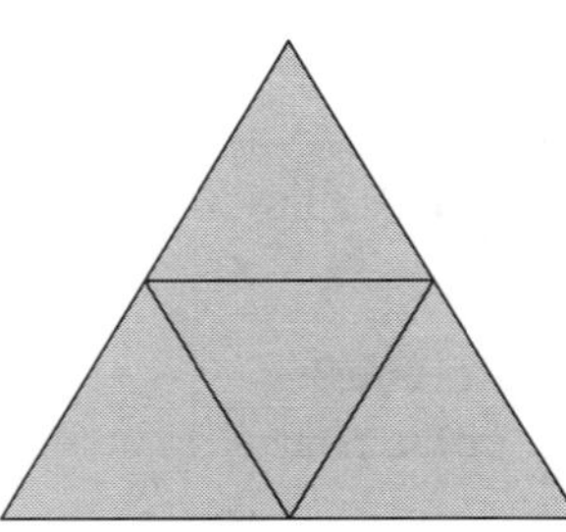

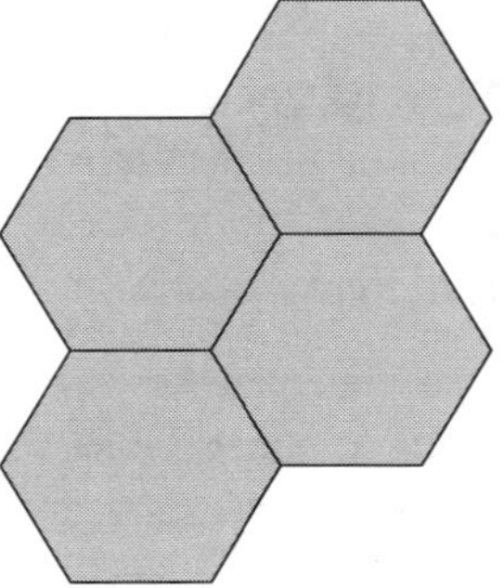

Continue to ask questions until students realize that the large shape made from the squares and from the triangles is similar to the original shape. This self-similar feature is what makes a figure a rep-tile.

> For each shape shown on page 30, your challenge is to see whether you can put together four identical copies of it to form a larger shape that is similar to the small shape. Some of the shapes are not rep-tiles, but many are—so don't give up until you are convinced that a shape is not a rep-tile. If you get stuck, check with students near you to see whether they have an idea that will help you.

Ask that as students discover which shapes are rep-tiles, they keep track of what they find in a table, recording the number of copies it took to make the larger shape and the scale factor between the rep-tile and the larger shape. Students need to make sketches of their arrangements so that they can recapture what they found.

Explore

Each student will need a ShapeSet or four copies of each shape cut from Labsheet 3.2.

Students with more developed spatial skills will find the rep-tiles more quickly. For students who are struggling, make suggestions about how they can systematically explore the possibilities. Point out that it is reasonable to assume that sides of the same length must be placed together and that corresponding angles must match. Also make sure they recognize that there are two ways to place two matching sides together, since one shape can be flipped over.

In part C, students are asked to try to make an even larger shape that is similar to the original shape. They will need to work in groups of four so that they have enough shapes to build the larger figures.

Summarize

Give students a chance to share what they found, perhaps by demonstrating their arrangements at the projector. Make a large table for the class in which you or students can record each rep-tile and its data.

Shape	Sketch of larger shape	Number of rep-tiles used	Scale factor from small to large
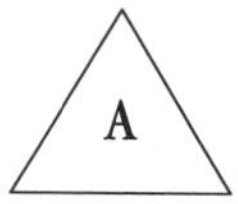 A	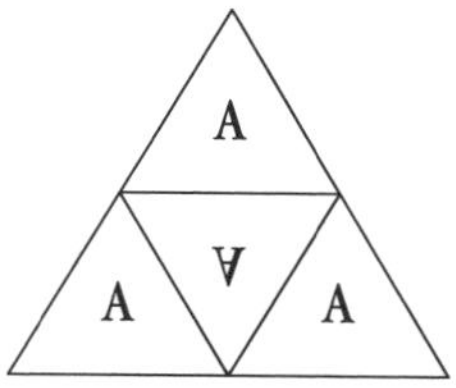 A A A A	4	2

Add a new column to the table to remind students that scale factors are associated with a direction of change—small to large, or large to small.

Shape	Sketch of larger shape	Number of rep-tiles used	Scale factor from small to large	Scale factor from large to small
A	A A A A	4	2	$\frac{1}{2}$

Students should be growing more comfortable with the idea that these scale factors are the inverse of each other. This is an opportunity to introduce the word *reciprocal*. Discuss the word, and offer several examples—such as that $\frac{1}{2}$ is the reciprocal of 2, 2 is the reciprocal of $\frac{1}{2}$, and $\frac{2}{3}$ is the reciprocal of $\frac{3}{2}$. You might demonstrate that the product of a number and its reciprocal is always 1. This makes sense, because if we use a scale of $\frac{1}{2}$ to shrink a figure, we must use a scale of 2 to return it to its original size. Some students might enjoy trying this.

After students have recorded all the shapes they found and you have helped to clean up the data by challenging any incorrect results, use the follow-up to focus the class on the relationship between scale factor and area. Question 1 uses the language of how many copies of a rep-tile are needed to make the larger figure. Question 2 relates the number of copies to a measure of area. (You could say that we are measuring area in units of rep-tiles or in units of small shapes.)

Take some time to focus on the triangle shapes that were investigated. Shapes A, I, P, and T are rep-tiles, because *every* triangle is a rep-tile. What is special about triangles is that the angles alone tell whether two triangles are similar. If corresponding angles are equal, the triangles have equal ratios for corresponding sides. One way to help students pull this concept from their experience with rep-tiles is to draw the following picture and have students do the same with a triangle of their choice.

Here is a large triangle. This isn't a special triangle; I just drew a triangle. I don't know its angle measures.

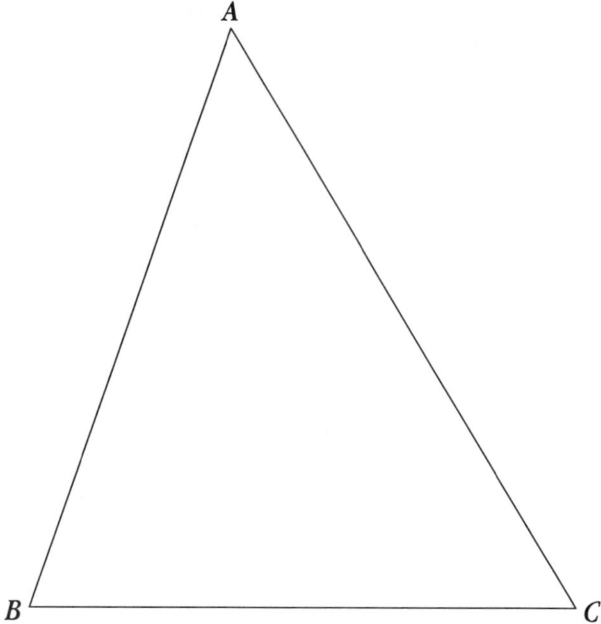

Now I will draw in some line segments that are parallel to the base of my triangle.

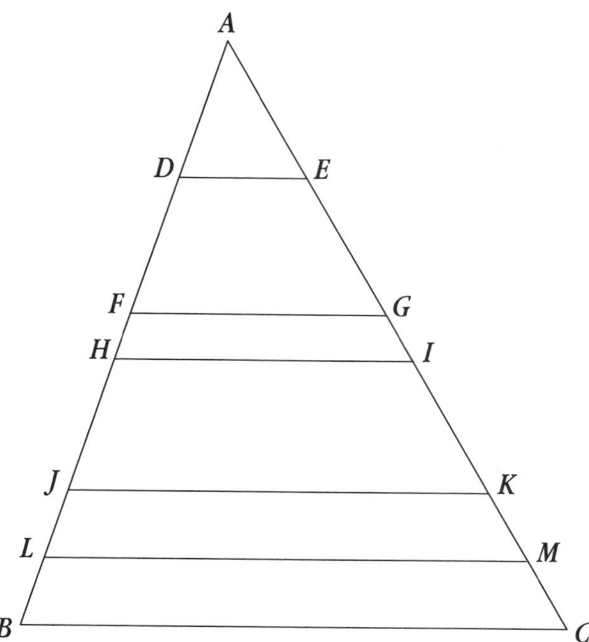

Name some triangles that you see in my drawing. *(ABC, ADE, AFG, AHI, AJK, ALM)* Are all of these triangles similar? How can we check to find out?

Students will probably say that the triangles look similar, but that we must check corresponding angles and whether corresponding side lengths grow by the same scale factor.

Which angles in this family of triangles are corresponding angles?

In this example, the angles within the triangles (starting from the top) at *E, G, I, K, M,* and *C* are corresponding and equal. Similarly, the angles at *D, F, H, J, L,* and *B* are corresponding and equal. Angle *A* is in every triangle. Therefore, every triangle in the family has equal corresponding angles. Students may need to measure these angles in order to be convinced.

Next, help the class check some pairs of corresponding sides to see whether the scale factor is the same for all pairs of sides.

We can check this by forming ratios of the side of one triangle to the corresponding side of another—as we did for the Wump family's rectangular noses.

In this example, the ratio between each side of triangle *ADE* and the corresponding side of triangle *AFG* is 1 to 2. The scale from the smaller to the larger is 2. Similarly, the ratio of the sides of triangles *ADE* and *AHI* is 3 to 7, so the scale factor from the smaller to the larger is $\frac{7}{3}$ or $2\frac{1}{3}$.

Now let's go the other way. If we create any two similar triangles, what do we see when we put one on top of the other with a pair of corresponding angles superimposed?

Demonstrate this idea with several pairs of triangles.

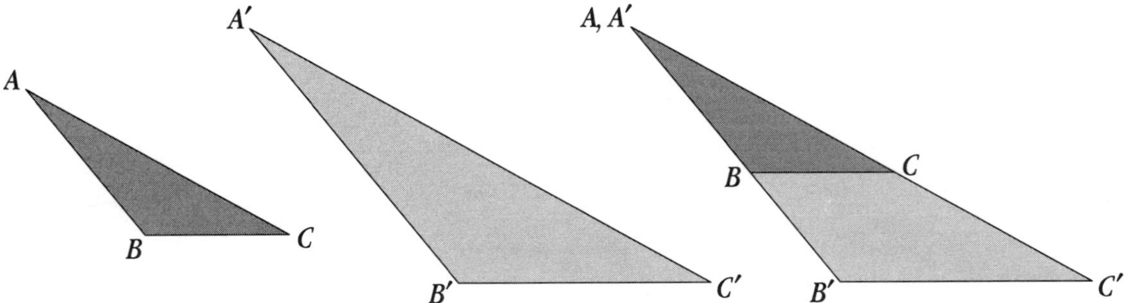

Students should begin to understand that *the angles in triangles have a special relationship: if the angles are equal, the triangles are automatically similar.* Triangles are special in this way. However, we must be careful with rectangles, because equal angles do not guarantee that two rectangles are similar.

Draw a few rectangles to help students understand this idea. For example, at first inspection, rectangles A, B, and C may all look similar, and their corresponding angles are obviously all similar. However, rectangle C is not similar to either of the other two.

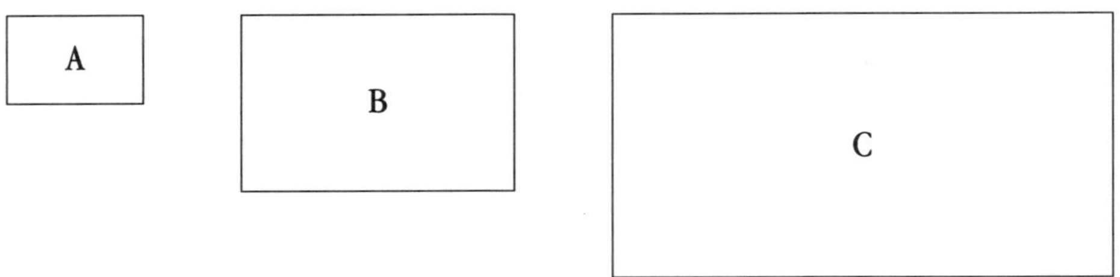

You may want to ask students to say what is special about triangles and what is special about rectangles, and then help them by re-stating and clarifying their ideas.

> Triangles are special, because we only have to check angles to determine whether two triangles are similar. Rectangles are special, because we only have to check that the ratio of each side of the image to the corresponding side of the original is the same for all sides to determine whether they are similar. For any other shapes, we must check corresponding angles *and* the ratios of corresponding sides to determine whether two shapes are similar.

3.3 • Subdividing to Find Rep-tiles

This problem has the same goals as Problem 3.2. In Problem 3.2, students built with rep-tiles to create larger, similar shapes. In this problem, they are challenged to work the other way—to subdivide a large shape into smaller, congruent shapes similar to the original.

Launch

Use the example in the student edition to explain the challenge. Distribute Labsheet 3.3 to each student. Have students work individually and then confer with a partner.

Explore

If a student is having difficulty, suggest that he or she cut out copies of the shape and build with them to see the pattern, then draw the small shapes inside the large shape.

As you see students finding good answers, you might ask them to copy their subdivided shapes onto a transparency of Labsheet 3.3 for sharing in the summary.

Summarize

As students share their findings, ask questions that focus on the scale factor and its relationship to the areas of the similar figures. You want students to understand and to be able to articulate that the *area grows by the square of the scale factor.* Their mental images of the arranged rep-tiles should help them intuitively understand this idea.

Review the follow-up questions as part of the summary.

Additional Answers

Answers to Problem 3.2

B. Shape J can be put together in two additional ways, because its short edge is half its long edge. (Note: The triangle shown on page 29 of the student edition works for the same reason: it is a right triangle, and its short leg is half its hypotenuse.) The other shapes can go together in only one way. The scale factors are all 2.

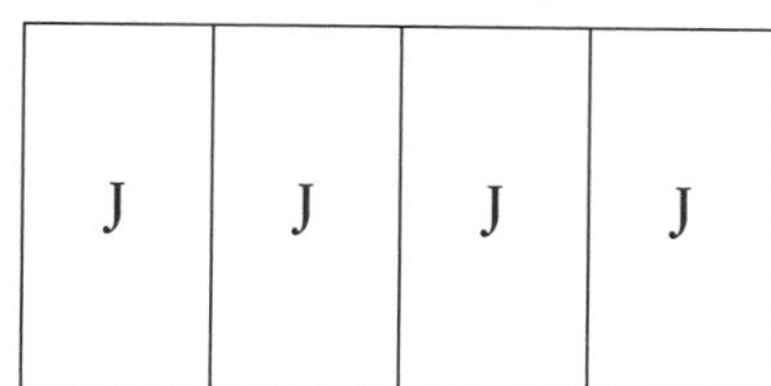

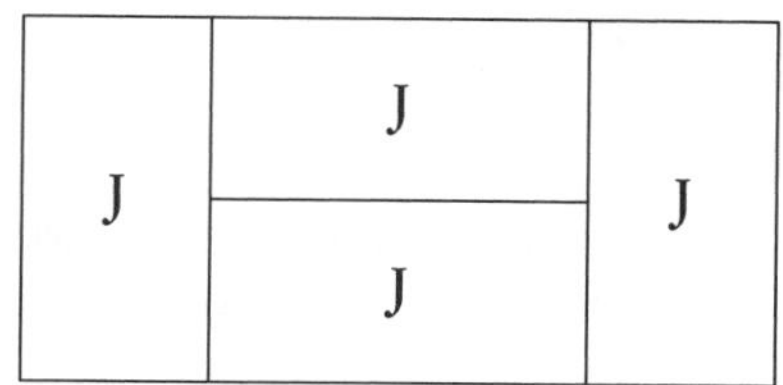

C. All of the rep-tiles can be arranged to form a larger figure consisting of 16 of the rep-tiles. For example:

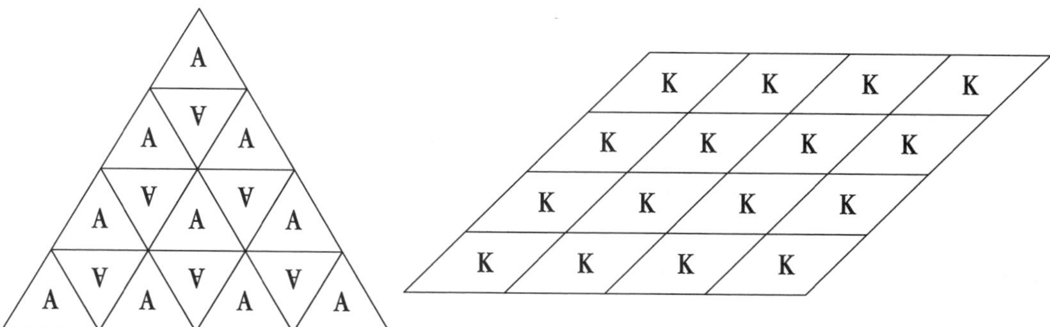

Some students may see that for any rep-tile, four 4-shape figures can be arranged to form a similar shape, giving a figure made of 16 rep-tiles with a scale factor of 4 from the 4-shape figure to the 16-shape figure. This same reasoning means that we can use 4 of these larger figures to create a super-large similar figure using $4 \times 4 \times 4$ or 64 of the original rep-tiles.

For the Teacher: Similar Triangles

Triangles are quite interesting, because we can add rows to the bottom of any triangle of rep-tiles to form a larger similar triangle. The pattern of how many rep-tiles we must add for each row is worth investigating. Moving from adding 3, then 5, then 7, we see that we add the next-largest odd number of triangles to form the bottom row. And each time we add a row, the total number of rep-tiles in the figure is a square number.

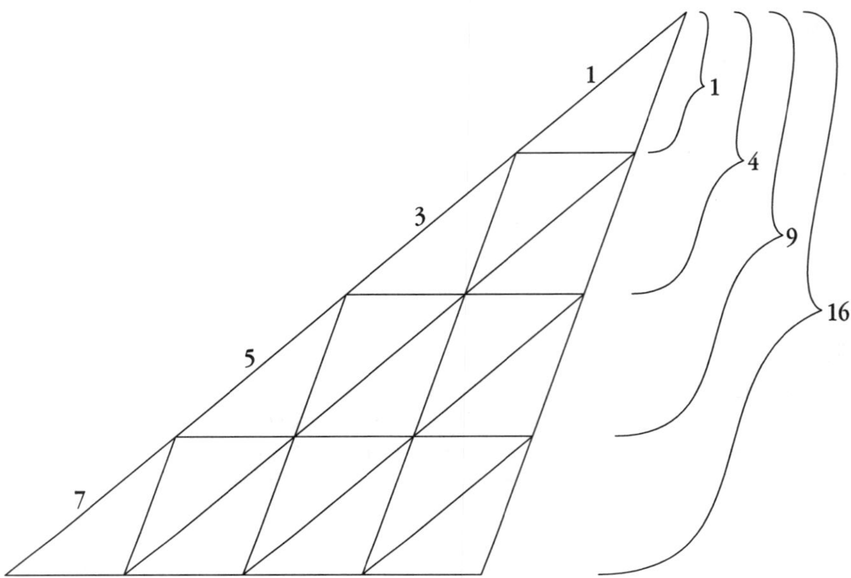

Why do these odd numbers add together to give the square numbers? The illustrations below help show what is happening. You could call this a visual proof.

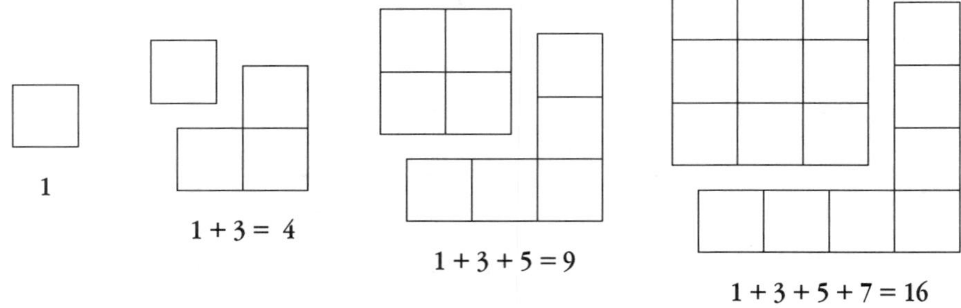

As with triangles, all parallelograms (including squares and rectangles) are rep-tiles. It's a little easier to see how parallelograms fit together in a 2×2 or 3×3 array than how triangles fit together.

Answers to Problem 3.2 Follow-Up

2. The number of copies of the original shape is a measure of the area of the new shape.

For the Teacher: Square Units

We can choose any kind of "covering" unit to measure area. We could call our unit of area the small shape and give the area of the larger shape in small-shape units. For a scale factor of 2, we just count and say the area is 4 "small shapes." However, students need to relate this to standard square units. If the area of a rep-tile is 23 square units and the scale factor is 2, then the area of the larger rep-tile pattern is $4 \times 23 = 92$ square units. Looking at the patterns of rep-tiles will make this concept more concrete.

Answers to Problem 3.3

For each shape, the scale factor from the small shapes to the original is 4.

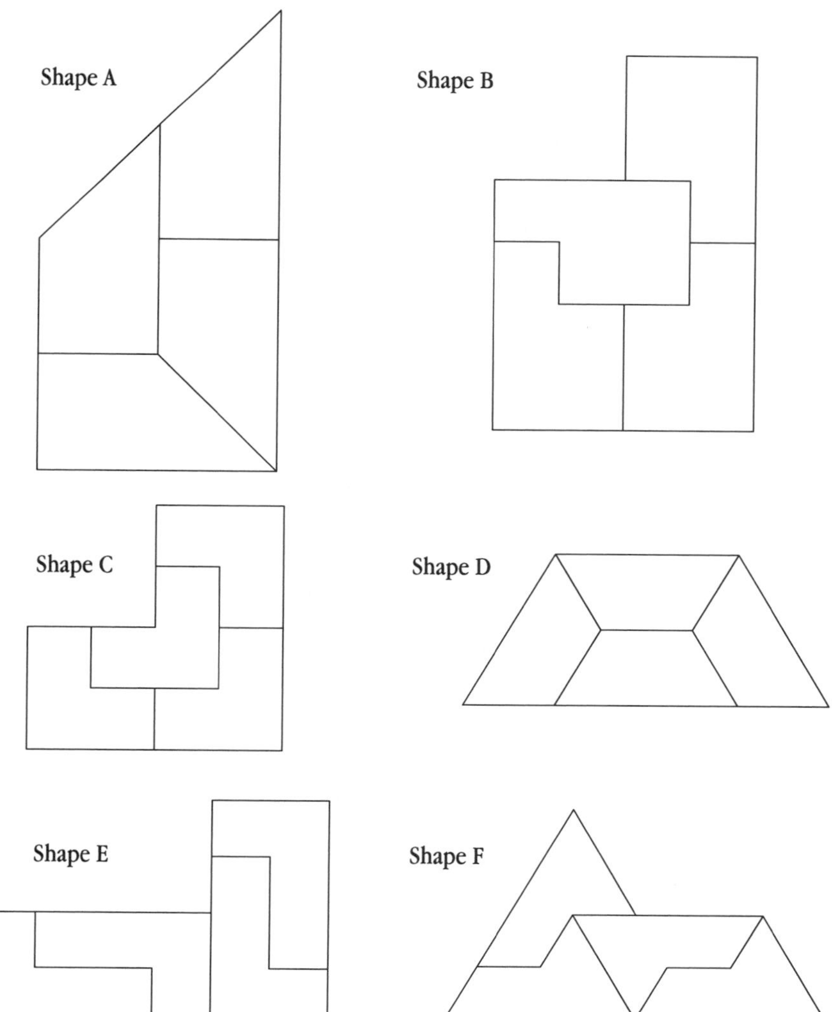

ACE Answers

Extensions

16. Yes, rectangles B and C are similar. Possible explanation: Since rectangle A is similar to rectangle B, the ratio of the short side of rectangle A to the long side of rectangle A is the same as the ratio of the short side of rectangle B to the long side of rectangle B. But since rectangle B is similar to rectangle C, the short side of rectangle C to the long side of rectangle C must equal this same ratio. This means the ratio between sides in rectangle C equals the ratio between sides in rectangle A, making rectangles C and A similar.

Using Similarity

Investigations 4 and 5 engage students in solving problems using the concepts and skills they have developed about similarity. In this investigation, the focus is on rectangles and the concept of scale factor as it relates to lengths and areas.

In Problem 4.1, Using Similarity to Solve a Mystery, students apply what they have learned to solve a real-world problem. Problem 4.2, Scaling Up, and Problem 4.3, Making Copies, are real-world scaling problems that require students to use the concept of scale factor. Problem 4.4, Using Map Scales, is a map-reading problem in which students must interpret a map's scale to determine actual distances and areas.

The ability to think about scaling up and down is a practical intellectual tool, and being able to solve real-world problems is the ultimate payoff for understanding the very powerful ideas of similarity and scale. In this unit, the contexts for this kind of reasoning are geometric. The *Comparing and Scaling* unit builds on these ideas in contexts that are more numeric.

Mathematical and Problem-Solving Goals

- ***To use the definition of similarity to recognize when figures are similar***
- ***To determine the scale factor between two similar figures***
- ***To use the scale factor between similar figures to find the lengths of corresponding sides***
- ***To find a missing measurement in a pair of similar figures***
- ***To use the relationship between scale factor and area to find the area of a figure that is similar to a figure of a known area***
- ***To solve problems that involve scaling up and down***

Materials

Problem	For students	For the teacher
All	Graphing calculators	Transparencies 4.1 to 4.4 (optional)
4.1	Rulers (1 per pair)	
4.2	Centimeter and half-centimeter grid paper (optional; provided as blackline masters)	
4.3		$8\frac{1}{2}$" by 11", 11" by 14", and 11" by 17" sheets of paper (optional)
4.4	Rulers (1 per group), state or local maps (optional; 1 per group)	
ACE	Centimeter grid paper (1 sheet per student)	

Student Pages 41–58 Teaching the Investigation 58a–58h

INVESTIGATION 4

Using Similarity

By now, you should have a good understanding of what it means for two figures to be similar. In the last investigation, you created similar figures by putting identical smaller figures together and by dividing a figure into identical smaller figures. You learned that the *scale factor* is the number that a figure's side lengths must be multiplied by to get the side lengths of a similar figure. By finding the number of figures it took to cover a larger, similar figure, you discovered the relationship between the scale factor and the areas of two similar figures. In this investigation, you will use all of your new knowledge to solve some interesting problems.

4.1 Using Similarity to Solve a Mystery

Many stores, particularly those that stay open late into the night, have surveillance cameras. One night the local Dusk to Dawn convenience store was robbed. The surveillance camera had taken several photographs during the robbery. By inspecting a picture of the robber standing in front of the cash register, police were able to determine the robber's height. How did they do it?

Did you know?

Measurement is used in investigatory and police work all the time. For example, some stores that have surveillance cameras mark a spot on the wall 6 feet from the floor so that, when a person is filmed standing near the wall, it is easier to estimate that person's height. Investigators take measurements of skid marks at the scene of auto accidents to help them determine the speed of the vehicles involved. Photographs and molds may be made of footprints at a crime scene to help determine the type of shoe and the weight of the person who made the prints. And measurements of holes and damage made by bullets can help investigators determine the type of gun that shot the bullet and the direction from which it was shot.

4.1 Using Similarity to Solve a Mystery

At a Glance

Grouping: small groups, then pairs

Launch

- Quickly review with the class what they have learned so far about similarity.
- Introduce the story of the robber and the photograph of the teacher.

Explore

- As groups work with the photograph, help students who are having trouble seeing similar figures.

Summarize

- Have groups share their strategies for finding the teacher's height.
- Assess students' understanding of similarity by discussing another photograph. *(optional)*

Tips for the Linguistically Diverse Classroom

Visual Enhancement The Visual Enhancement technique is described in detail in *Getting to Know Connected Mathematics*. It involves using real objects or pictures to make information more comprehensible. Example: While discussing the information presented in the "Did you know?" feature, you might show pictures of surveillance cameras, skid marks, footprints, and police officers investigating a crime scene.

Assignment Choices

ACE questions 1–7, 16–20, and unassigned choices from earlier problems

Problem 4.1

The teacher's guides for Connected Mathematics measure $8\frac{1}{2}$" by 11". Below is a photograph of a middle school teacher holding a teacher's guide.

A. Use the photograph to figure out how tall the teacher is. Explain your procedure.

B. How do you think the police determined the robber's height?

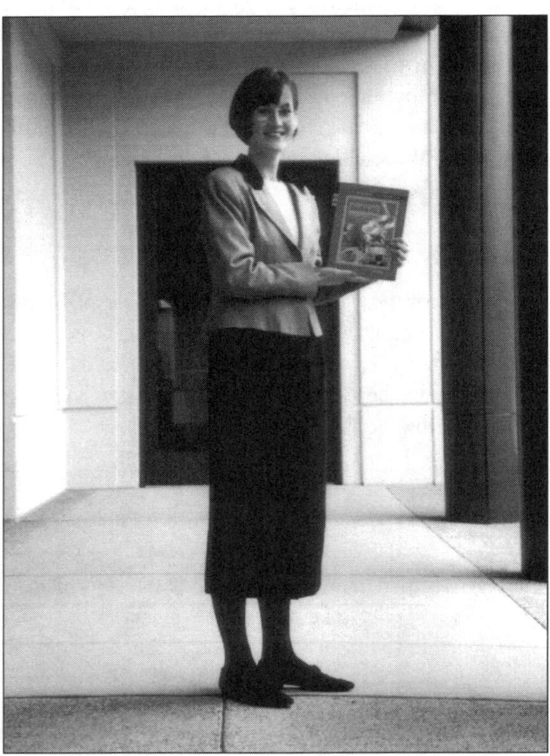

Problem 4.1 Follow-Up

1. Estimate the height of the door in the photograph.

2. Do you think your estimate in question 1 is an underestimate or an overestimate? Why?

Answers to Problem 4.1

A. The real book measures $8\frac{1}{2}$" by 11". The picture of the book is about $\frac{1}{2}$" by $\frac{5}{8}$". Since we must multiply $\frac{1}{2}$ by 17 to get $8\frac{1}{2}$, the scale factor between the picture and the real scene is 17. The teacher is about $4\frac{1}{4}$" tall in the picture, so we multiply her height by 17 to get $72\frac{1}{4}$", or about 6 ft.

B. The police probably measured the height of the real cash register, found the scale factor between the picture of the cash register and the real cash register, and multiplied the height of the robber in the picture by the scale factor to get the robber's real height.

Answers to Problem 4.1 Follow-Up

See page 58f.

4.2 Scaling Up

The concept of similarity has many practical applications. For example, designers often make a model of an object and then scale it up or down to make the real object. What kinds of models are likely to be smaller than the real objects? What kinds of models are likely to be larger than the real objects?

Problem 4.2

Raphael is closing his bookstore. He wants to place a full-page advertisement in the newspaper to announce his going-out-of-business sale. A full-page ad is 13" by 22", which allows for a white border around the ad.

Raphael used his computer to make an $8\frac{1}{2}$" by 11" model of the advertisement, but he wants the newspaper ad department to enlarge it to full-page size. Is this possible? Explain your reasoning.

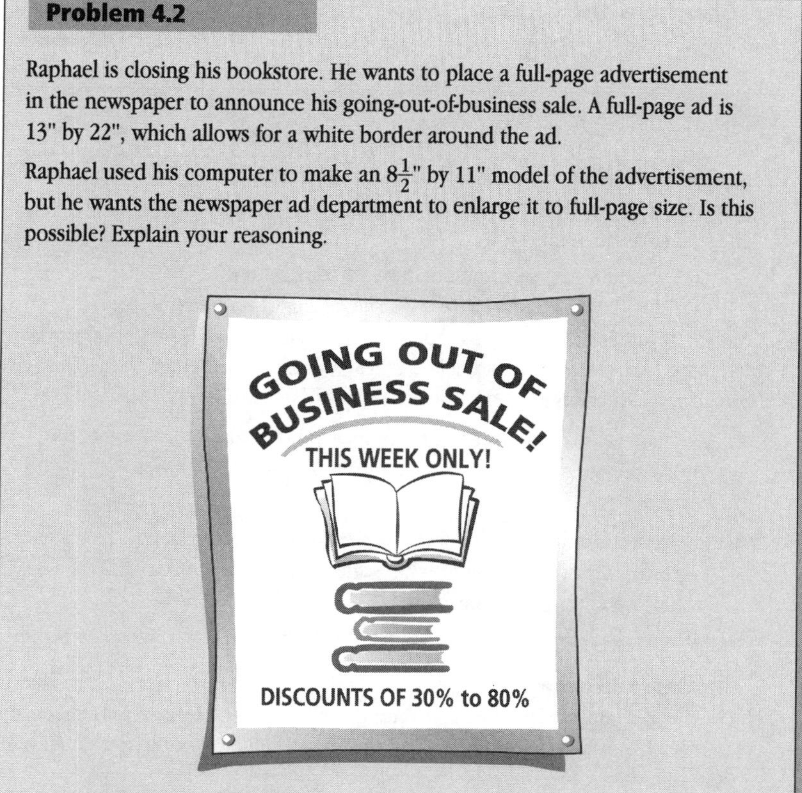

Problem 4.2 Follow-Up

What would you suggest Raphael say to the ad department about making a full-page, similar ad from his model?

4.2 Scaling Up

At a Glance

Grouping: small groups

Launch

- Read the problem and the follow-up with the class.
- Emphasize that the directions for the ad department must be clear and reasonable.

Explore

- Offer groups grid paper for sketching their ideas.
- For the follow-up, remind students that the ad must stay intact.
- As a challenge, ask for the dimensions of the largest possible similar ad. *(optional)*

Summarize

- As groups share their ideas, promote the discussion of different sets of directions.
- Ask questions to encourage students to show their understanding of similarity.

Answer to Problem 4.2

The scale between the length measurements of the model and the full-page ad is 2, but the scale between the width measurements is about 1.53. Since these are not equal, the ad cannot be enlarged to fit exactly on the whole page.

Answer to Problem 4.2 Follow-Up

Directions to the ad department will vary. Here are two suggestions students have given:

- Tell the ad department to enlarge the ad using a scale of 1.5. The full-page ad will have only a tiny margin at the sides, but 2.75" margins at the top and bottom.
- Tell the ad department to redraw the model so that it is 6.5" by 11" and then enlarge it by a scale factor of 2.

Assignment Choices

ACE questions 8, 9, 15, and unassigned choices from earlier problems

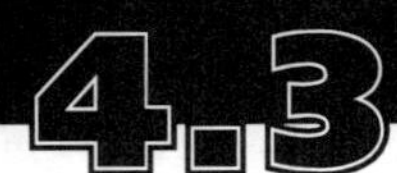

Making Copies

At a Glance

Grouping:* *groups of 4

Launch

- Talk about using copy machines to make enlargements and the three paper sizes.
- Discuss the relationship between a scale given as a percent and a scale factor.

Explore

- For the follow-up, students may want to draw figures to model what is happening.

Summarize

- Have groups share their answers.
- Help them generalize what they have learned.
- Talk about the follow-up, helping students understand the role of a scale factor in reductions of a figure.

4.3 Making Copies

When you use a copy machine to enlarge or reduce a document, you are dealing with similarity. On most copy machines, you indicate how much you want to enlarge or reduce something by entering a percent.

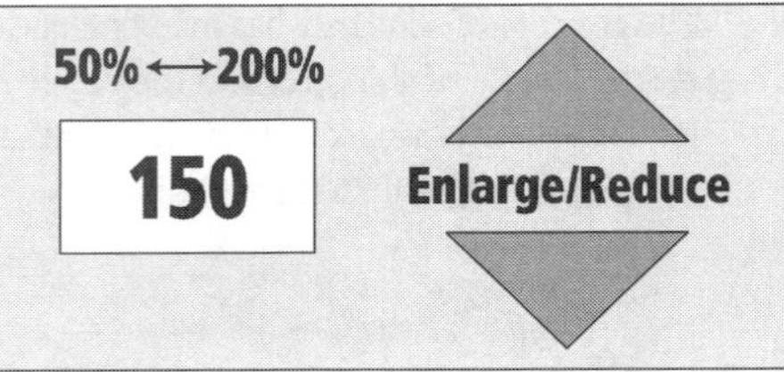

Problem 4.3

Raphael wants to make posters for his sale by enlarging his $8\frac{1}{2}$" by 11" ad. Raphael thinks big posters will get more attention, so he wants to enlarge his ad as much as possible.

The copy machines at the copy shop have cartridges for three paper sizes: $8\frac{1}{2}$" by 11", 11" by 14", and 11" by 17". The machines allow users to enlarge or reduce documents by specifying a percent between 50% and 200%. For example, to enlarge a document by a scale factor of 1.5, a user would enter 150%. This tells the machine to enlarge the document to 150% of its current size.

A. Can Raphael make a poster that is similar to his original ad on any of the three paper sizes—without having to trim off part of the paper? Why or why not?

B. If you were Raphael, what paper size would you use to make a larger, similar poster on the copy machine? What scale factor—expressed as a percent—would you enter into the machine?

Problem 4.3 Follow-Up

1. How would you use the copy machines described in the problem to reduce a drawing to 25% of its original size? Remember, the copy machines only accept values between 50% and 200%.
2. How would you use the copy machines to reduce a drawing to $12\frac{1}{2}$% of its original size?
3. How would you use the copy machines to reduce a drawing to 36% of its original size?

Assignment Choices

ACE questions 10–14 (14 requires centimeter grid paper), 21, 22, and unassigned choices from earlier problems

Answers to Problem 4.3

See page 58f.

Answers to Problem 4.3 Follow-Up

1. You would need to make a 50% reduction and then reduce the reduction by 50%.
2. You would need to reduce the second reduction in question 1 by 50% again, since $0.5 \times 0.5 \times 0.5 = 0.125$.
3. Two 60% reductions will give you an image that is 36% of the original, since $0.6 \times 0.6 = 0.36$. You might also reduce the original 50%, and then reduce the image 72% ($.5 \times .72 = .36$).

4.4 Using Map Scales

We use maps to help us find our way in unfamiliar places, to plan vacations, and to learn about other parts of the world. Maps are like scale drawings: they show a large area of land at a reduced size. To get a sense of the size of the place a map represents, you must know to what scale the map was drawn.

Arches National Park in Utah

Here is a map of the state of Utah. You can use the scale on the map to calculate distances.

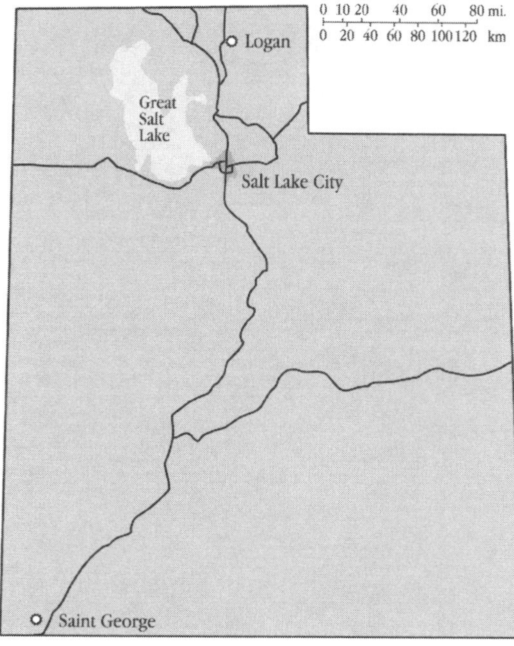

Using Map Scales

At a Glance

Grouping: small groups

Launch

- Let students examine and use the scales on several real maps. *(optional)*
- Introduce the map of Utah in the student edition.

Explore

- As groups work, make sure they understand how to use the map's scale.

Summarize

- Have groups share their methods and answers.
- Extend students' thinking by asking additional questions about areas and distances on the map. *(optional)*

Assignment Choices

ACE questions 23–31 and unassigned choices from earlier problems

Assessment

It is appropriate to use Quiz B after this problem.

Problem 4.4

A. How can you use the scale on the map to calculate the scale factor between the map and the real state? What is the scale factor?

B. How many miles of fencing would it take to surround the state of Utah?

C. Use the scale to estimate the area of Utah. Explain your work.

D. If you drove at a steady speed of 55 miles per hour, about how long would it take you to travel from Logan to Saint George?

Problem 4.4 Follow-Up

The total land and water area of the United States is about 3,717,522 square miles. What percent of this total area is the area of Utah?

Answers to Problem 4.4

A. On the map, 1 in represents 80 mi. Since 80 mi × 5280 $\frac{\text{ft}}{\text{mi}}$ × 12 $\frac{\text{in}}{\text{ft}}$ = 5,068,800 in, the scale factor from the map to the real state is 5,068,800.

B. The map has a perimeter of approximately $15\frac{1}{8}$ in. This means that Utah is about $15\frac{1}{8} \times 80 = 1210$ mi around, so you would need 1210 mi of fencing.

C. See page 58f.

D. It is about 5 in on the map from Logan to Saint George on the road shown. This means that the actual distance is about 5 × 80 = 400 mi. At 55 mph, it will take about 7 hrs and 15 min (7.27 hrs) to cover 400 miles.

Answers to Problem 4.4 Follow-Up

See page 58f.

Applications • Connections • Extensions

As you work on these ACE questions, use your calculator whenever you need it.

Applications

1. Find all the pairs of similar rectangles in the set below. For each pair you find, give the scale factor from one of the rectangles to the other.

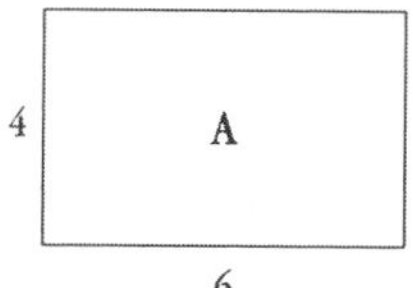

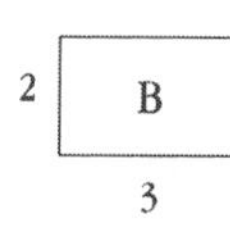

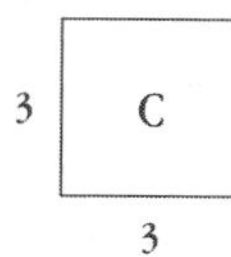

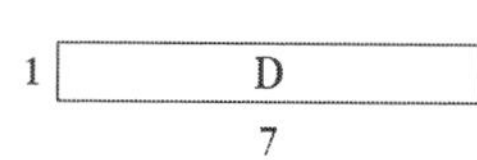

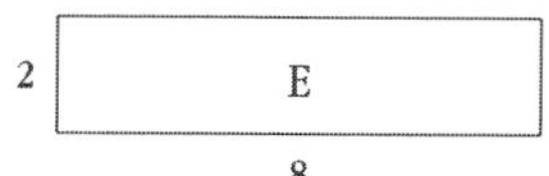

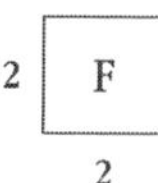

2. The rectangles below are similar.

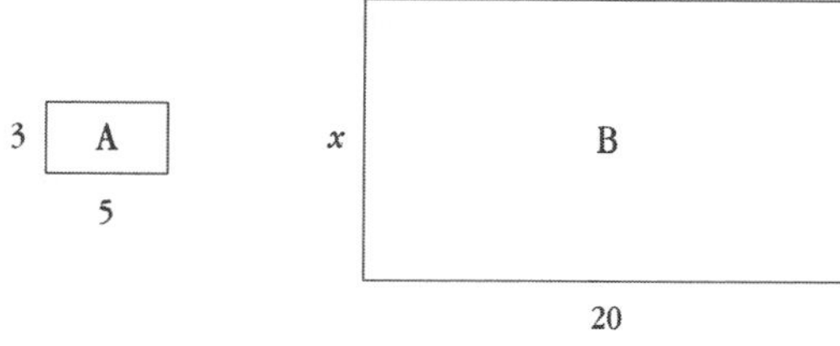

a. What is the value of x?

b. What is the scale factor from rectangle A to rectangle B?

c. Find the area of each rectangle.

d. What is the relationship of the area of rectangle A to the area of rectangle B?

Answers

Applications

1. Rectangles A and B are similar; the scale factor from rectangle A to B is $\frac{1}{2}$, and the scale factor from rectangle B to A is 2. Rectangles C and F are similar; the scale factor from rectangle C to F is $\frac{2}{3}$, and the scale factor from rectangle F to C is $\frac{3}{2}$.

2a. $x = 12$

2b. The scale factor from rectangle A to B is 4.

2c. Rectangle A has an area of 15 square units. Rectangle B has an area of 240 square units.

2d. The area of rectangle A is $\frac{1}{16}$ the area of rectangle B.

3a. $x = 2$

3b. The scale factor from rectangle C to D is $\frac{1}{2}$.

3c. Rectangle C has an area of 16 square units. Rectangle D has an area of 4 square units.

3d. The area of rectangle C is 4 times the area of rectangle D.

4a. $x = 6$

4b. The scale factor from rectangle E to F is $\frac{2}{3}$.

4c. Rectangle E has an area of 54 square units. Rectangle F has an area of 24 square units.

4d. The area of rectangle E is $\frac{9}{4}$ the area of rectangle F.

5a. $x = 6\frac{2}{3}$

5b. The scale factor from rectangle G to H is $\frac{5}{3}$.

5c. Rectangle G has an area of 12 square units. Rectangle H has an area of $33\frac{1}{3}$ square units.

5d. The area of rectangle G is $\frac{9}{25}$ the area of rectangle H.

3. The rectangles below are similar.

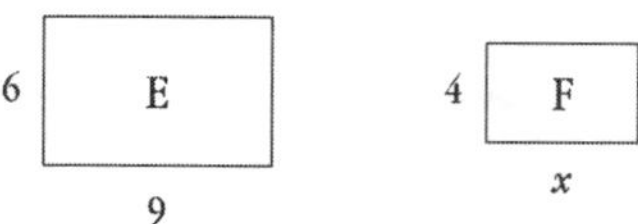

a. What is the value of x?

b. What is the scale factor from rectangle C to rectangle D?

c. Find the area of each rectangle.

d. What is the relationship of the area of rectangle C to the area of rectangle D?

4. The rectangles below are similar.

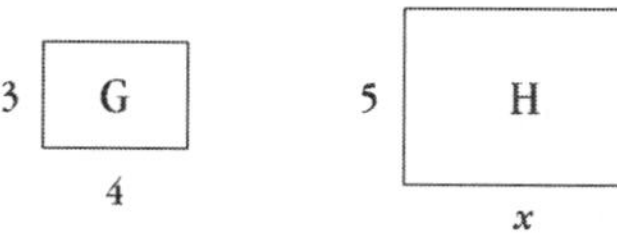

a. What is the value of x?

b. What is the scale factor from rectangle E to rectangle F?

c. Find the area of each rectangle.

d. What is the relationship of the area of rectangle E to the area of rectangle F?

5. The rectangles below are similar.

3 G 4 5 H x

a. What is the value of x?

b. What is the scale factor from rectangle G to rectangle H?

c. Find the area of each rectangle.

d. What is the relationship of the area of rectangle G to the area of rectangle H?

6. Sort the rectangles below into sets of similar rectangles. Describe the method you use.

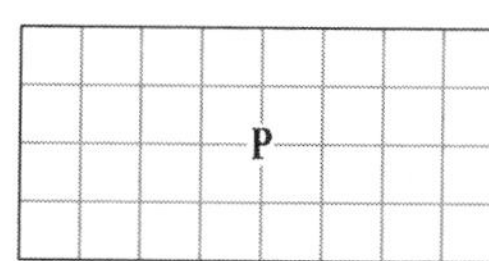

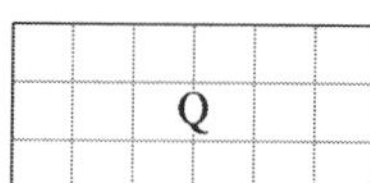

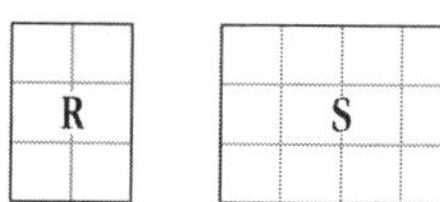

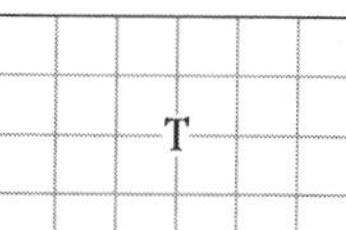

V

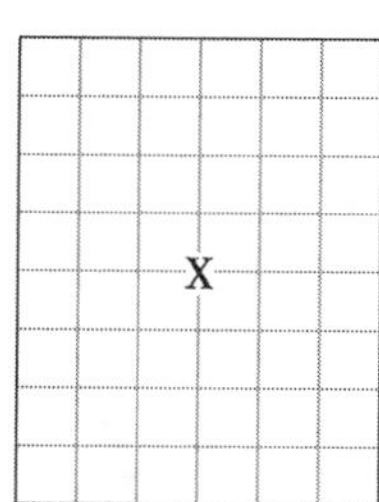

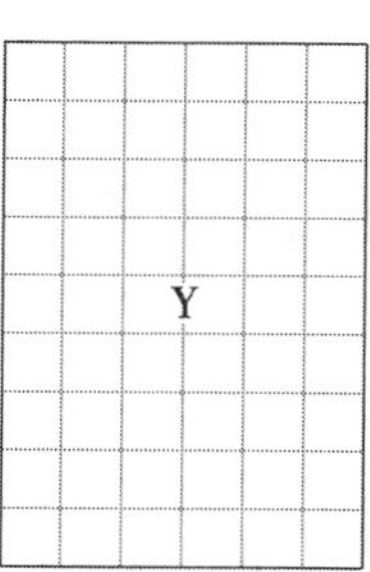

7. Ms. Auito wants to buy new carpeting for her bedroom. The bedroom floor is a rectangle, 9 feet by 12 feet. Carpeting is sold by the square yard.

a. How much carpeting does Ms. Auito need to buy?

b. If the carpeting costs $22 per square yard, how much will the carpet for the bedroom cost?

6. There are three families of rectangles (some of the rectangles must be rotated 90° to make the similarities clear):
Rectangles P and Q: The scale factor is $\frac{3}{4}$ from P to Q.
Rectangles R, T, V, and Y: The scale factor is 2 from R to T, 1 from R to V, and 3 from R to Y.
Rectangles S, U, and X: The scale factor is $\frac{1}{2}$ from S to U and 2 from S to X.

7a. Since carpeting is sold by the square yard, it is helpful to convert the dimensions of the room to yards. The room measures 3 yd by 4 yd, so Ms. Auito needs $3 \times 4 = 12$ yd^2 of carpeting.

7b. The carpeting will cost $12 \times 22 = \$264$.

8a. The library measures 22.5 ft by 30 ft (or 7.5 yd by 10 yd).

8b. She will need to buy $7.5 \times 10 = 75$ yd^2 of carpeting.

8c. The carpeting will cost $75 \times 22 = \$1650$.

9. Since the scale factor of $12\frac{1}{2}\% = \frac{1}{8}$, Duke is actually 8 times larger than the drawing.

9a. In the drawing, Duke measures about $5\frac{1}{2}$ in from his nose to the tip of his tail, so he is actually about $5\frac{1}{2} \times 8 = 44$ in long.

9b. Duke's height in the drawing is about $3\frac{1}{4}$ in, so he is actually about $3\frac{1}{4} \times 8 = 26$ in tall.

9c. Setting the copier at 200% (which acts as a scale factor of 2, doubling the dimensions) and successively copying three times will result in a full-size drawing. The original drawing is $12\frac{1}{2}\%$ of the actual dog. After the first copy, the drawing will be 25% of Duke. The second copy yields a drawing that is 50% of Duke's size, and the third copy takes the drawing up to 100% of Duke's size.

8. Ms. Auito (from question 7) really liked the carpet she bought for her bedroom, and she would like to buy the same carpet for her large library. The floor of her library is similar to the floor of her 9-foot-by-12-foot bedroom. The scale factor from the bedroom to the library is 2.5.

- **a.** What are the dimensions of the library?
- **b.** How much carpeting does Ms. Auito need for the library?
- **c.** How much will the carpet for the library cost?

9. Here is a drawing of Duke. The scale factor from Duke to the drawing is $12\frac{1}{2}\%$.

- **a.** How long is Duke from his nose to the tip of his tail?
- **b.** To build a doghouse for Duke, you would need to know his height so you could make a doorway to accommodate him. How tall is Duke?
- **c.** The local copy center has a machine that will print on poster-size paper. You can enlarge or reduce a document by specifying a setting between 50% and 200%. How could you use the machine to make a life-size picture of Duke?

10. Samantha drew triangle *ABC* on a grid, then applied a rule to make the triangle on the right.

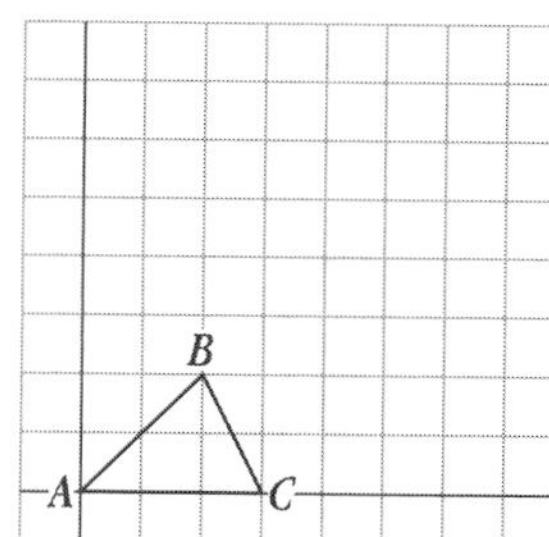

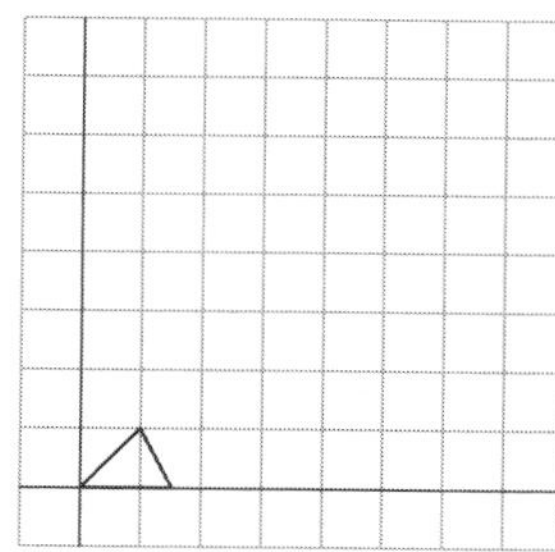

a. What rule did Samantha apply to make the new triangle?

b. Is the new triangle similar to triangle *ABC*? Explain. If the triangles are similar, give the scale factor from triangle *ABC* to the new triangle.

11. Samantha drew triangle *JKL* on a grid, then applied a rule to make the triangle on the right.

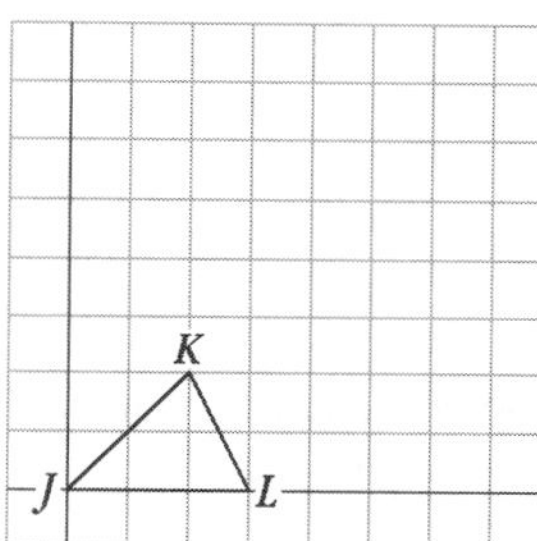

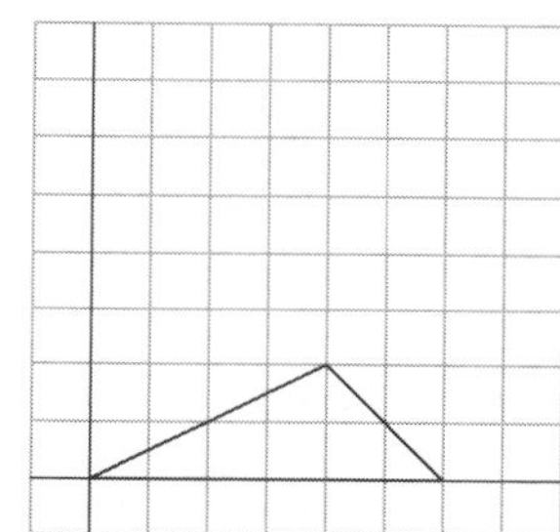

a. What rule did Samantha apply to make the new triangle?

b. Is the new triangle similar to triangle *JKL*? Explain. If the triangles are similar, give the scale factor from triangle *JKL* to the new triangle.

10a. $(0.5x, 0.5y)$

10b. Yes, they are similar, since they have the same shape—the coordinates were multiplied by 0.5. The scale factor from triangle *ABC* to the new triangle is 0.5.

11a. $(2x, y)$

11b. The triangles are not similar, because the scale factor from one length to the corresponding length is not constant.

12a. $(2.5x, 2.5y)$

12b. Yes, they are similar, since they have the same shape—the coordinates were both multiplied by 2.5. The scale factor from triangle *XYZ* to the new triangle is 2.5.

13a. See page 58g.

13b. The first triangle is similar to all of the larger triangles. The scale factors are 2, 3, 4, and so on.

12. Samantha drew triangle *XYZ* on a grid, then applied a rule to make the triangle on the right.

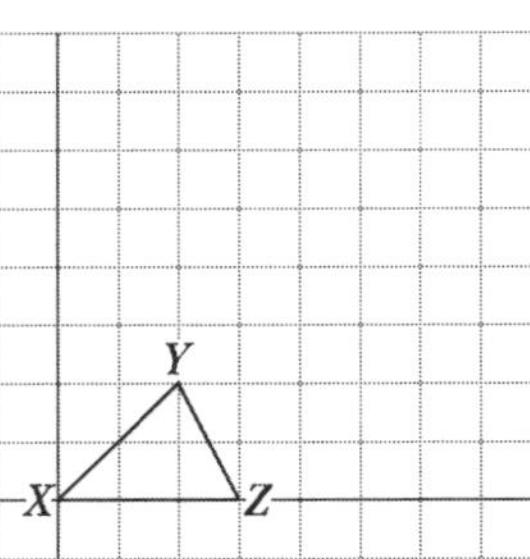

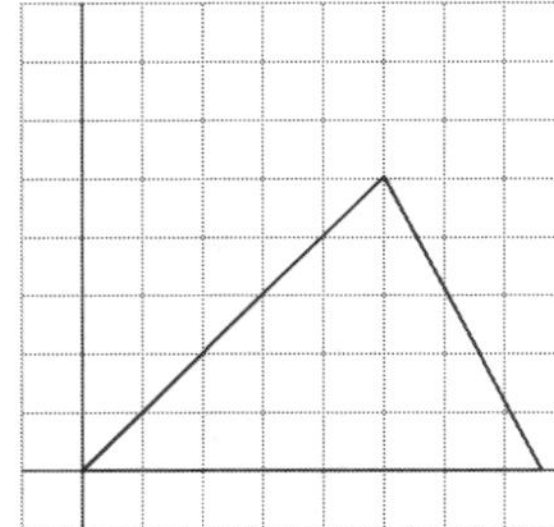

a. What rule did Samantha apply to make the new triangle?

b. Is the new triangle similar to triangle *XYZ*? Explain. If the triangles are similar, give the scale factor from triangle *XYZ* to the new triangle.

13. Examine the figures below.

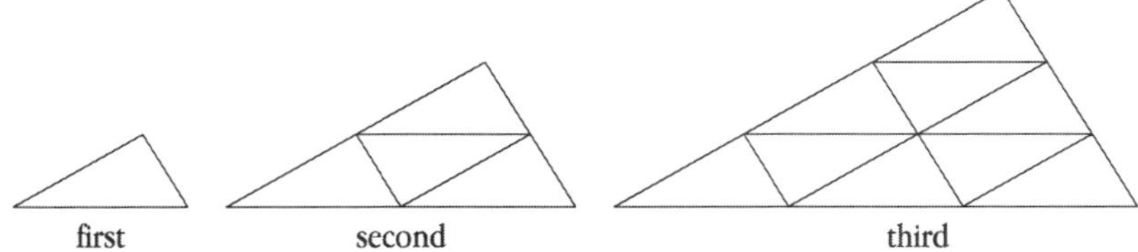

a. If the pattern continues, how many copies of the smallest triangle (the triangle labeled "first") will be in the fourth figure? The fifth figure? The tenth figure? Explain your reasoning.

b. Which of the larger figures is the first figure similar to? For any similar figures you find, give the scale factor from the first figure to the larger figure.

14. A rectangle has a perimeter of 20 centimeters and an area of 24 square centimeters.

a. Sketch the rectangle on centimeter grid paper.

b. Find the perimeter and area of the rectangle that is made by enlarging the rectangle you drew by a scale factor of 3.

c. Find the perimeter and area of the rectangle that is made by enlarging the original rectangle by a scale factor of 10.

d. Find the perimeter and area of the rectangle that is made by enlarging the original rectangle by a scale factor of $\frac{1}{2}$.

15. Rectangles B and C are similar to rectangle A.

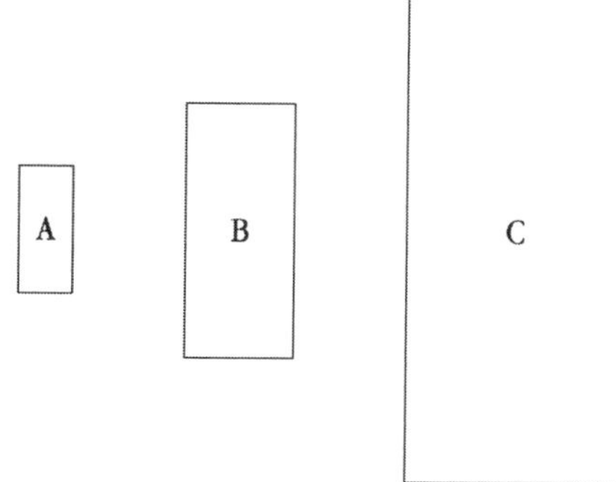

a. What is the scale factor from rectangle A to rectangle B?

b. What is the scale factor from rectangle A to rectangle C?

c. How many rectangle A's would it take to cover rectangle B?

d. How many rectangle A's would it take to cover rectangle C?

e. What is the scale factor from rectangle C to rectangle A?

f. What is the scale factor from rectangle C to rectangle B?

14a.

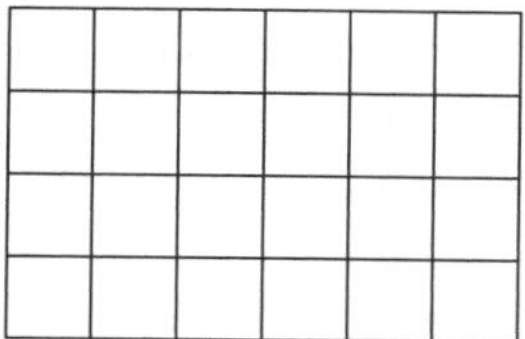

14b. The perimeter is $20 \times 3 = 60$ cm, and the area is $24 \times 9 = 216$ cm^2.

14c. The perimeter is $20 \times 10 = 200$ cm, and the area is $24 \times 100 = 2400$ cm^2.

14d. The perimeter is $20 \times \frac{1}{2} = 10$ cm, and the area is $24 \times \frac{1}{4} = 6$ cm^2.

15a. 2

15b. 4

15c. It would take 4 rectangle A's to cover rectangle B.

15d. It would take 16 rectangle A's to cover rectangle C.

15e. $\frac{1}{4}$

15f. $\frac{1}{2}$

Connections

16. They are similar. The scale factor from the small triangle to the large triangle is 3.

17. They are similar. The scale factor from the small triangle to the large triangle is 1.75.

18. They are not similar. (Note: Students may be confused by the fact that, although there is no constant scale factor from the small triangle to the large, a constant is added to each side.)

19. They are similar. The scale factor from the small triangle to the large triangle is 2. (Note: Students may have difficulty seeing this because of the triangles' orientation.)

20a. The ratio of a side length of the smaller triangle to the corresponding length in the larger triangle is 3 in question 16, 1.75 in question 17, and 2 in question 19.

20b. The ratio of the corresponding sides of two similar triangles equals the scale factor. (Note: You may want to explain that by using the same direction for each scale factor—for example, from small to large—and the same ratio—say, $\frac{\text{lengths of large}}{\text{lengths of small}}$—the relationships become clearer.)

Connections

In 16–19, tell whether the triangles are similar. If they are, give a scale factor.

16.

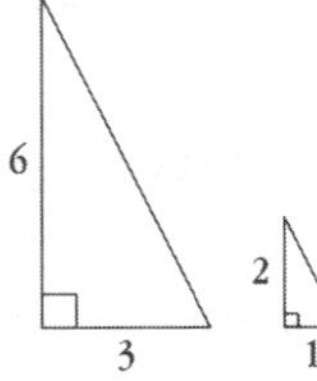

17.

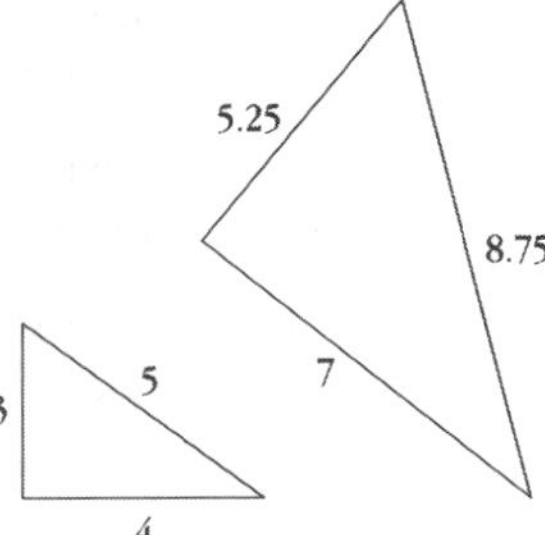

18.

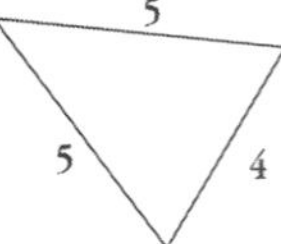

19.

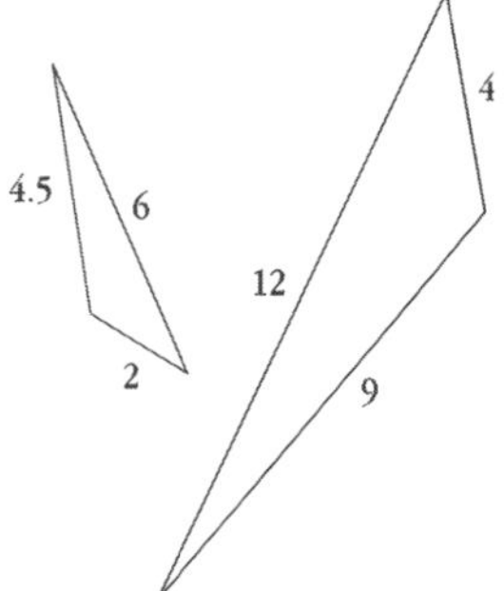

20. **a.** For each pair of similar triangles in questions 16–19, find the ratio of a side length of the larger triangle to the corresponding side length of the smaller triangle.

b. How does the ratio of a side length of a larger triangle to the corresponding side length of a smaller, similar triangle relate to the scale factor from the smaller triangle to the larger triangle?

21. On May 3, 1994, Nelson Mandela became the president of South Africa.

Nelson Mandela

A new flag was created as a symbol of unity. Here is a drawing of the new flag:

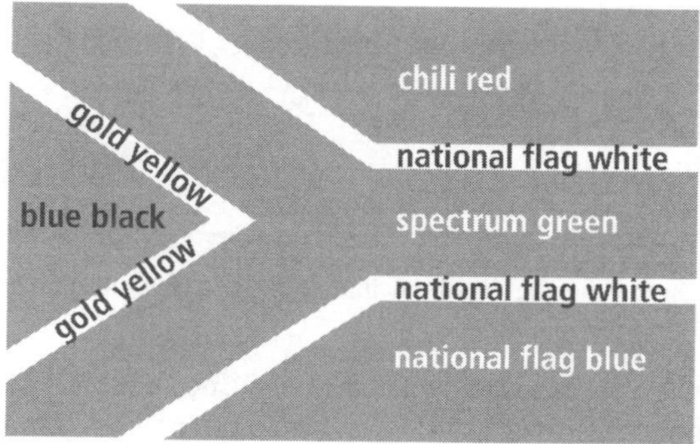

a. What is the area of the blue-black triangle in this drawing? ("Blue-black" is a shade of black.) Take whatever measurements you need to find the area.

b. What is the area of the chili-red section? Explain your reasoning.

c. Estimate the area of the spectrum-green section. Explain your reasoning.

21. Students can use a ruler or a transparent grid to measure the flag, which is drawn to scale.

21a. approximately $\frac{1}{2}(2.4 \times 3.4) = 4.1$ cm^2

21b. If we look at the section as a rectangle and a triangle, we can estimate the area as $1.7 \times 3.9 + \frac{1}{2}(1.7 \times 2.5) =$ 8.8 cm^2.

21c. The area is approximately 1.4×4.0 (the rectangle down the middle) + $2 \times 1.3 \times 4$ (estimating the two symmetric arms of the Y as two rectangles) = 16.0 cm^2.

22. The area from the drawing to Betsine's flag will increase by a factor of 100. The approximate amounts of material she will need are the following:

22a. 410 cm^2

22b. 880 cm^2

22c. 1600 cm^2

22d. 880 cm^2

23a. $12 \times 6\frac{2}{3} = 80$ m of fence

23b. $144 \times 0.25 = 36$ m^2 of carpeting

23c. $\frac{1}{20} \times 144 = 7.2$ cans

23d. $\frac{1}{12}$

23e. 4

22. Betsine Rosela would like to make a real flag from the drawing in question 21. She has decided that the scale factor from the drawing to her real flag will be 10.

a. How much blue-black material will Betsine need?

b. How much chili-red material will she need?

c. How much spectrum-green material will she need?

d. How much national-flag-blue material will she need?

23. An antique shop has a large dollhouse that is a model of a real house. The scale factor from the dollhouse to the real house is 12.

a. If there is $6\frac{2}{3}$ meters of fencing around the dollhouse, how long is the fence around the real house?

b. If the area of the living-room floor in the dollhouse is $\frac{1}{4}$ of a square meter, how much carpeting will be needed to cover the living-room floor in the real house?

c. If it takes $\frac{1}{20}$ of a can of paint to paint the outside of the dollhouse, how many cans would it take to paint the exterior of the real house?

d. What is the scale factor from the real house to the dollhouse?

e. If there are four windows on the front of the dollhouse, how many windows are on the front of the real house?

24. On grid paper, draw two triangles that are not similar, if possible. Explain how you know the triangles are not similar. If it is impossible to draw two such triangles, explain why.

25. On grid paper, draw two rectangles that are not similar, if possible. Explain how you know the rectangles are not similar. If it is impossible to draw two such rectangles, explain why.

26. On grid paper, draw two squares that are not similar, if possible. Explain how you know the squares are not similar. If it is impossible to draw two such squares, explain why.

27. On grid paper, draw two rectangles that are not similar but that have equal corresponding angles, if possible. Explain how you know the rectangles are not similar. If it is impossible to draw two such rectangles, explain why.

28. On grid paper, draw two triangles that are not similar but that have equal corresponding angles, if possible. Explain how you know the triangles are not similar. If it is impossible to draw two such triangles, explain why.

Extensions

29. a. Enlarge the drawing of the flag in question 21 by a scale factor of 3. Color your enlarged flag as closely as possible to the indicated colors.

b. What is the area of the blue-black section in your flag? The chili-red section? The spectrum-green section? Explain how you found your answers.

30. What happens if you enlarge a drawing by a scale factor of 1? Explain your answer. As part of your explanation, draw a picture of a figure and its enlargement by a scale factor of 1.

31. What is the relationship between the areas of two similar figures that are related by a scale factor of 1?

24. See page 58g.

25. See page 58g.

26. It is impossible to draw two squares that aren't similar, because every square is similar to every other square. They all have the same shape. Also, if you divide any two corresponding sides, you will get the scale factor between all pairs of corresponding sides, since a square's sides are all the same.

27. See the example in the answer to question 25.

28. See page 58h.

Extensions

29a. Since the original drawing is 5.6 cm $\times$ 8.5 cm, the new drawing should be 16.8 cm $\times$ 25.5 cm.

29b. Since area increases by the square of the scale factor, we can multiply our answers from question 21 by 9: the blue-black section is approximately $4.1 \times 9 = 36.9$ cm^2, the chili-red section is approximately $8.8 \times 9 = 79.2$ cm^2, and the spectrum-green section is approximately $16 \times 9 = 144$ cm^2.

30. Drawings show two identical figures. The enlargement is not only the same shape as the original, it is also the same size.

31. The areas are the same.

Mathematical Reflections

In this investigation, you used scale factors and their relationships to side lengths and areas in similar figures to solve real-world problems. These questions will help you summarize what you have learned:

1. How can you decide whether two figures are similar?
2. What does a scale factor between two similar figures tell you about the relationships between the length and area measures of the figures?
3. If the scale factor from a small figure to a large figure is given as a percent, how can you find the side lengths of the large figure from the side lengths of the small figure?
4. Decide whether each pair of rectangles below is similar. If the rectangles are similar, give the scale factor from the rectangle on the left to the rectangle on the right. If they aren't, explain why.

a.

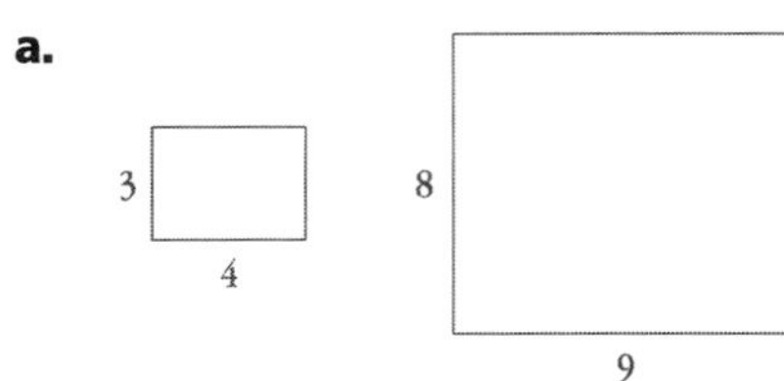

b.

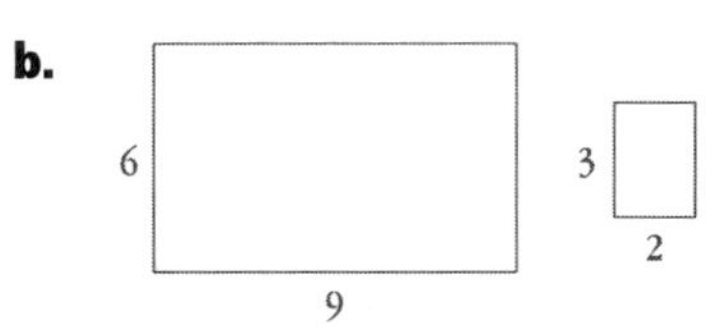

Think about your answers to these questions, discuss your ideas with other students and your teacher, and then write a summary of your findings in your journal.

Possible Answers

1. Corresponding angles must be equal, and the ratios of all corresponding sides must be the same (this number is called the scale factor). Triangles are special because if their corresponding angles are equal, their corresponding sides automatically have the same ratio. Rectangles are special because their angles are all 90°, but we still have to check whether all pairs of corresponding sides have the same ratio.

2. The length measures are related by the scale factor, and the area measures are related by the square of the scale factor. This means that if we know any length measures and the scale factor, we can compute the corresponding length measures. We can also compute the area of the image by multiplying the area of the original by the scale factor squared.

3. You can represent the scale factor as a fraction or a decimal, then multiply the side lengths of the small figure by this number to find the side lengths of the large figure.

4a. The rectangles are not similar, because the scale factor between the lengths is $\frac{9}{4}$, and the scale factor between the widths is $\frac{8}{3}$, which are not equivalent.

4b. See right.

4b. The rectangles are similar. The scale factor from the rectangle on the left to the rectangle on the right is $\frac{1}{3}$. (Note: This might confuse some students, since the rectangles are oriented differently. You may want to subdivide the larger rectangle to show how its area compares to the area of the smaller rectangle.)

TEACHING THE INVESTIGATION

4.1 • Using Similarity to Solve a Mystery

This is a good time to summarize what students know about similarity. Review the definition of similarity, how to determine whether two figures are similar, how to find the scale factor between two similar figures, and what the scale factor reveals about the side lengths and the areas of two similar figures. This review can lead directly to the Launch.

Launch

Begin by drawing the following rectangles. Then ask:

> **If these two rectangles are similar, what is the length of the large rectangle? What is the scale factor from the small rectangle to the large rectangle? How do their areas compare?**

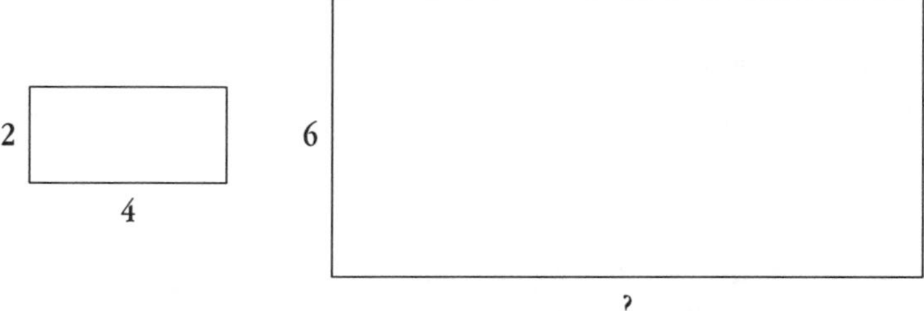

Introduce the problem, but don't go too far; leave the students on their own to figure out how they will get the information they need to solve the problem. Be sure students understand and can read the abbreviation for inches.

Explore

Have students work in groups of four to discuss strategies and then break into pairs to make whatever measurements they need. Pairs can come back together to compare answers and resolve any disagreements. Then, students can look at the follow-up.

Be on the lookout for students who are having trouble seeing any similar figures in the photograph. You might show them a real teacher's guide and ask what it could tell them about the scale of the photograph.

You might ask students to guess lengths before they measure them, which will help them build personal referents for lengths.

Summarize

Focus the summary on the students' strategies; their sharing of how they thought about the problem will broaden everyone's collection of intellectual tools. You and the class should expect some variation in answers, because all measurements are approximations. However, answers that are obviously unreasonable should be examined closely and efforts should be made to figure out why they are incorrect.

What would you expect the range of possible heights for the teacher to be? If an answer is over 7 feet, is that reasonable? What about an answer of under 4 feet?

How can police use this information to determine a robber's height from a photograph?

Talk about the follow-up questions. For a quick assessment, you could bring in another photograph (or a transparency of one) that contains an object for which the class can get an exact measurement. Students should be able to identify four measurements—three of which are known—then find the missing measurement by computing the scale factor and multiplying it by the corresponding measurement. Some students may use equivalent fractions to find the unknown measurement.

4.2 • Scaling Up

This is not an extensive problem, but along with the follow-up question, it is worthy of discussion in groups of two or three.

Launch

Read the problem setting and the follow-up with the class. Emphasize that students must give the ad department a reasonable set of directions for using Raphael's model to create the full-page ad.

Explore

Have students work in groups of three or four. Students may want to use grid paper to sketch their ideas. If a group is stuck, ask what the scale factor is between the length measures and between the width measures.

For the full-page ad to be similar to Raphael's model, what must be true?

As groups work on the follow-up, remind them to keep the ad intact as they figure out what directions to give the ad department. You might also want to ask groups to figure out the dimensions of the largest similar ad that would fit on a full page.

Summarize

Let groups share their ideas. Promote the discussion of different options for directing the ad department, helping the class examine each option to see whether it is reasonable and whether the mathematics makes sense.

Encourage students to explain their thinking about why their ideas will work. Look for mathematical ideas in their explanations, and ask questions that require them to demonstrate their understanding of similarity.

If we make a full-page ad that is similar to the original, are the parts of the ad (the pictures, the words, and so on) also similar to the original?

If we allow the margins to be different, or if we allow a slight distortion in the ad, can we make the ad fit on the page?

Yes; for example, the ad department could use the transformation $(1.5x, 2y)$ to make an ad that is not similar to but has the same information as the original. You may want to encourage students who suggest stretching the model ad more in one direction than the other to draw parts of the ad to see what they will look like. They should not cut off part of the ad. Also, the elements of the ad will now appear on a different scale from the model, and such distortion may not be acceptable to the person placing an ad.

4.3 • Making Copies

This problem gives scale in terms of percent, so you will need to quickly review the relationship between a scale given as a percent and a scale factor. For example, an enlargement of 150% is equivalent to a 1.5 scale factor.

Launch

In this problem, Raphael is trying to make a poster from his model ad that will fit on one of the paper sizes available.

If some students have had little experience with copy machines, help them understand the context and the options available on copy machines. You might make several enlargements of a picture on a photocopier to show the class. If you have the three paper sizes available, display them. If not, you may want to have students make models of the three paper sizes so that they have a sense of the possibilities.

Explore

Have students work in groups of four on the problem and the follow-up.

If students are having difficulty, help them to interpret the percent settings on the copy machines in terms of scale factor. For the follow-up, they may want to draw a small figure and experiment with shrinking it to look for a way to get a scale of $\frac{1}{4}$ when using a copy machine that has $\frac{1}{2}$ as its smallest scale. Drawing the figure on a grid will help some students.

Summarize

Let groups share their answers to the problem. After all their ideas have been discussed, ask them to think about a method that will *always* work to determine whether it is possible to enlarge or shrink a rectangle to fit another rectangle. Call on some students to share their ideas. In the discussion, help students to see that all problems of this sort can be solved by calculating the scale between the corresponding measures to see whether it is the same.

Talk about the follow-up questions, asking students for convincing arguments to support their answers. It may not be obvious to students that if, for example, you start with a length of

11 units and use a scale of 0.5, you will get a length of 5.5 units. If you reduce this new figure by a scale of 0.5, you now have length of 2.75 units, which is $\frac{1}{4}$ of the original length. Recognizing that $0.5 \times 0.5 = 0.25$, and translating this information into what you should do with the copy machine, is the heart of the follow-up. To make this concept clearer, you might go through an example such as the following:

> Suppose I take a piece of rope that is 12 meters long and reduce its length by a factor of 0.5 (or $\frac{1}{2}$). What would the new length of my rope be? *(6 meters)*
>
> Now suppose I reduced the new length of my rope by a factor of 0.5 again, what would the length of the rope be? *(3 meters)*
>
> What could you physically do to model what is happening to my rope? *(Cut a piece of rope 12 meters long or a strip of paper 12 inches long in half, and then cut one piece of it in half again.)*
>
> What factor of the original length of rope is the piece left after both reductions? *(The final piece is 3 meters and the original was 12 meters. Since it takes 4 lengths of 3 meters to equal 12 meters—$4 \times 3 = 12$—the final rope is $\frac{1}{4}$ the length of the original.)*
>
> Why does this make sense? *(Since $\frac{1}{2} \times \frac{1}{2} = \frac{1}{4}$, it makes sense that applying the scale factor $\frac{1}{2}$ to the original and then again to the image to get a new image would make the final image $\frac{1}{4}$ the length of the original.)*

For the Teacher: Multiplying by a Fraction

One of the things students often have difficulty with conceptually is that multiplying by a number smaller than 1 reduces the original; multiplication has been taught as a "makes larger" operation in the elementary grades. This concept makes the new world of rational numbers harder for students to enter.

4.4 • Using Map Scales

In this problem, students use a map's scale to determine distances. Maps are an important everyday use of scale. If the launch takes the better part of a class period, it will be time well spent.

Launch

Many students are not familiar enough with maps to know what to look for in the legend to figure out the map's scale. (You might ask the social studies teacher what experiences students have had with maps.) You may want to bring in several maps and have students work in groups to interpret the scales on the maps and perhaps locate landmarks and determine the distance between them.

Maps are an important everyday use of scale. If the launch takes the better part of a class period, it will be time well spent.

What does the scale on this map mean? How can you find distances on this map?

When you feel that students have some understanding of how to locate and use map scales, direct their attention to the Utah map in the student edition.

Explore

Have students work in groups of two or three, and assign the follow-up as part of the group work. As students work, you may need to ask questions to help groups that are struggling. The first hurdle is understanding the map's scale.

> Measure the length that is marked 80 miles. What is the actual length? *(It measures 1 inch.)* What does this mean? *(It means that 1 inch on the map is equal to 80 miles.)*

Help students to understand that this means the scale of the map is 80. We can measure distances on the map in inches and multiply by 80 to find the actual distances in miles.

Part C asks students to estimate the area of Utah using the map's scale. Some students may want to find the area of the map in square inches and then figure out what a square inch represents in terms of square miles. Some may need to draw a picture of a square that is 1 inch on a side, label the sides of the square as 80 miles, and figure out how many square miles this area represents.

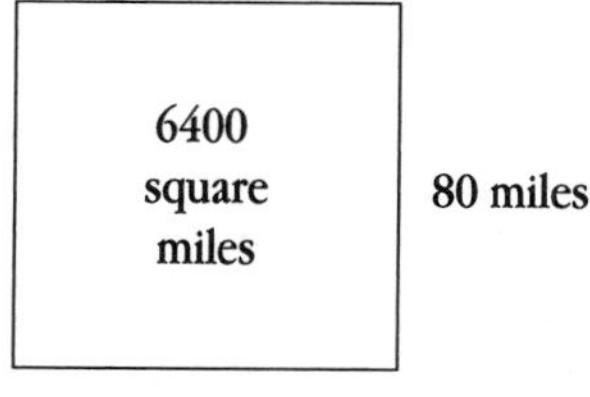

This will help them see that each square inch represents 6400 square miles. Others may want to label the sides of the state on the map in miles and calculate the area of the state from there.

Summarize

As groups report on their work, ask for mathematical explanations of their methods. If there are discrepancies in answers between groups, resolve them as a class. Spend time on parts B and C. Have groups give their answers and explain how they found their solutions. You might ask additional questions about the map of Utah to check students' understanding.

> How long is the state from the northwest corner to the southwest corner? How many miles is that?

How much area would you estimate is covered by the Great Salt Lake?

How is the map's scale different from a scale factor between two similar objects? *(The units—inches on the map and miles on the real state—are different.)*

How could we find the scale factor using the same units, inches? *(We would need to calculate how many inches are in a mile: 12 × 5280 = 63,360.)* So what is the scale factor? *(63,360 × 80 = 5,068,800)*

Why does the map's scale give accurate information, even though it compares two different units? *(Because it just changes the unit from inches to miles.)*

Additional Answers

Answers to Problem 4.1 Follow-Up

1. The door in the picture is $2\frac{1}{8}$" high. Using the scale factor of 22 (found in part A) makes the real door 46.75" high, or about 3 ft 11 in high.
2. An actual door is probably over 6 ft high, so my answer is an underestimate. The door is some distance behind the teacher, and the scale of the door should be determined using something that is the same distance from the camera as the door.

Answers to Problem 4.3

A. Raphael can make a 100% copy of his model onto 8.5" by 11" paper. This is a scale of 1 and gives a similar figure (in fact, a congruent figure). The other paper sizes are not similar to $8\frac{1}{2}$" by 11". For example, for the 11" by 14" size, we can compute $11 \div 8\frac{1}{2} = 1.29$ to find the scale for the smaller dimension. However, this scale does not work for the larger dimension, because 1.29 × 11 = 14.19, which is slightly more than 14. The scale for the larger dimension is 14 ÷ 11 = 1.27. Similarly, for the 11" by 17" size, the scale factor from $8\frac{1}{2}$ to 11 is still 1.29, but 14.19 is much less than 17. The scale for the 17" dimension is 17 ÷ 11 = 1.55.

B. Answers will vary. To get the largest possible poster, he could use the 11" by 17" paper. With a scale factor of 1.29 (or a 129% enlargement on the copy machine), he would get the largest width possible but would have to trim the extra length. This would give a poster that is 8.5 × 1.29 by 11 × 1.29, or about 11" by 14.2".

Answers to Problem 4.4

C. Possible answer: The state can be looked at as two rectangles—a small rectangle of about 0.875 in by 1.94 in, and a large rectangle of about 3.25 in by 3.5 in. These two rectangles have an area of 1.70 + 11.375 = 13.1 in^2. Multiplying by the scale factor of 6400 to get square miles gives about 84,000 mi^2 as the area of Utah.

Answers to Problem 4.4 Follow-Up

To find what fraction of the area of the United States the area of Utah occupies, we must divide 84,000 mi^2 (from part C in the problem) by 3,618,785 mi^2. This gives 0.023, so Utah is about 2.3% of the area of the United States.

ACE Answers

Applications

13a. 16, 25, 100; Explanations will vary. The pattern is that the number of triangles in the nth triangle is $n \times n$, or n^2. Another way to look at this is that the area is growing by the square of the scale factor from the original triangle to each new triangle. Some students may find it easier to form parallelograms from two of each triangle and then look at the patterns. Others may see that a diagonal row of triangles, containing two more triangles than the row before, can be added to each new triangle:

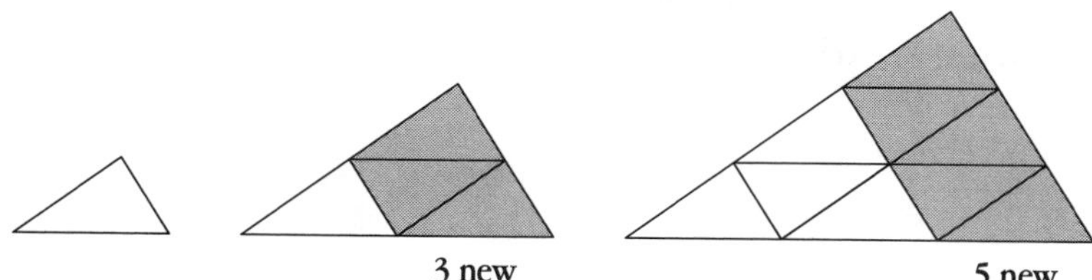

and that the difference between the square numbers increases by 2 each time:

Square numbers	1	4	9	16	25	36	49
Difference between the square numbers	3	5	7	9	11	13	. . .

Connections

24. Possible answer: These triangles are clearly not similar. One has a right angle, and the other doesn't. They are not the same shape. (Students may emphasize the "same shape" aspect of similarity or the need for a scale factor or equal angles.)

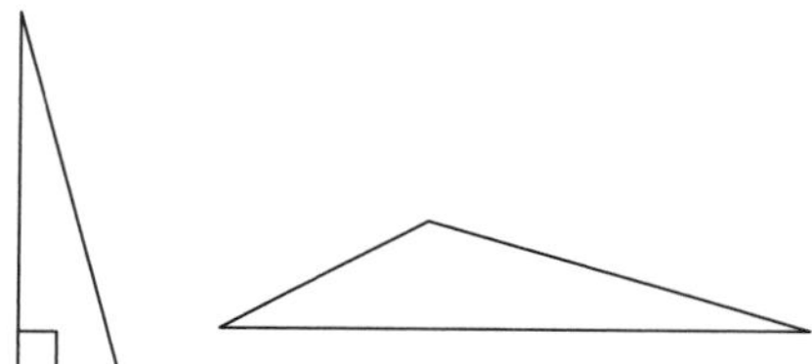

25. Possible answer: These rectangles are not similar, because they are not the same shape—one is skinny, while the other is shaped more like a square.

28. It is impossible to draw two such triangles. Any two triangles with equal corresponding angles are similar.

For the Teacher: Similar Triangles

The explanation for why it is impossible to draw two triangles that are not similar but that have equal corresponding angles is a stretch for students at this time. However, if they try to draw or build an example, they should realize that it is impossible. Nesting triangles is a good way to see this.

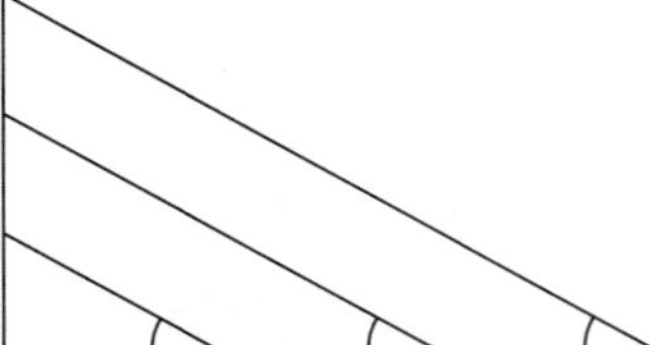

As we extend the sides of the angle we start with to make a new triangle, we decide how long we want the side, and when we make a copy of the second angle, the triangle is formed. Every new triangle has sides that are parallel and proportional to the original.

Similar Triangles

In this investigation, students will use their knowledge of similar triangles to find the height of a tall object (for example, the school building or a basketball hoop) and other inaccessible distances. Two methods are presented for measuring heights, the shadow method and the mirror method. A third method employs similar triangles to measure long distances. In each problem, students apply the special feature of triangles—that they are similar if their corresponding angles are equal. While students have not proved this, they should be convinced by now that it is a reasonable assumption.

In Problem 5.1, Using Shadows to Find Heights, students learn about the shadow method and apply it to estimate the height of a real-world object. In Problem 5.2, Using Mirrors to Find Heights, they learn about the mirror method and estimate the height of the object again. In Problem 5.3, Using Similar Triangles to Find Distances, students learn how similar triangles can be used to measure distances on the ground that cannot be measured directly, and then apply the method to a real-world measurement situation. Students make a line plot of their class's results using each estimation method and then compare them to see which method seems to give the most consistent results.

Mathematical and Problem-Solving Goals

- *To recognize similar figures in the real world*
- *To find a missing measurement in a pair of similar figures*
- *To apply what has been learned about similar figures to solve real-world problems*
- *To collect data, analyze it, and draw reasoned conclusions from it*

Materials		
Problem	**For students**	**For the teacher**
All	Graphing calculators, metersticks (1 per student or group), tools for measuring longer distances, such as tape measures, string, or sticks cut to 1 meter	Transparencies 5.1 to 5.3 (optional)
5.2	Mirrors (1 per student or group)	
5.3	Tools for measuring longer distances, such as tape measures, string, or sticks cut to 1 meter	

Student Pages 59–74 **Teaching the Investigation** 74a–74k

INVESTIGATION 5

Similar Triangles

How tall is your school building? You could find the answer to this question by climbing a ladder and measuring the building with a tape measure, but there are easier—and less dangerous!—ways to find the height of a building. In this investigation, you will see how you can use what you know about similar triangles to estimate heights and distances that are difficult or impossible to measure directly.

5.1 Using Shadows to Find Heights

If an object is outdoors, you can use shadows to help estimate its height. The diagram below illustrates how the method works.

On a sunny day, an object casts a shadow. If you hold a meterstick perpendicular to the ground, it will also cast a shadow. The diagram below shows two triangles. One is formed by an object, its shadow, and an imaginary line. The other is formed by a meterstick, its shadow, and an imaginary line. These two triangles are similar.

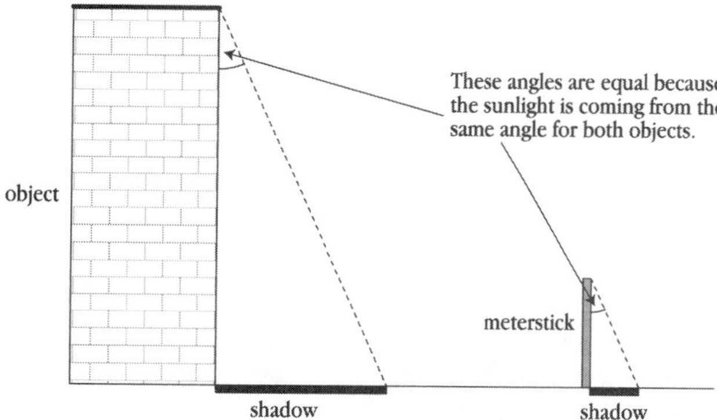
These angles are equal because the sunlight is coming from the same angle for both objects.
object
meterstick
shadow
shadow

To find the height of the object, you can measure the lengths of the two shadows and apply what you know about similar triangles.

5.1 Using Shadows to Find Heights

At a Glance

***Grouping:* groups of 4**

Launch

- Talk about the technique of using shadows to estimate an object's height.
- As a class, work through part A of the problem.
- Help the class choose an object to measure.

Explore

- Have groups go outside to make the necessary measurements.
- If students have only one meterstick per group, be sure they know how to use them to measure longer distances.

Summarize

- Help the class pool their data in a line plot.
- Ask questions to help students analyze the line plot.

Assignment Choices

ACE questions 1–4, 7, 13, and unassigned choices from earlier problems

Think about this!

Examine the diagram of the shadow method on the previous page. Can you explain why each angle of the large triangle is equal to the corresponding angle of the small triangle?

Problem 5.1

Mr. Anwar's class is using the shadow method to estimate the height of their school building. They have made the following measurements and sketch:

Length of the meterstick = 1 m
Length of the meterstick's shadow = 0.2 m
Length of the building's shadow = 7 m

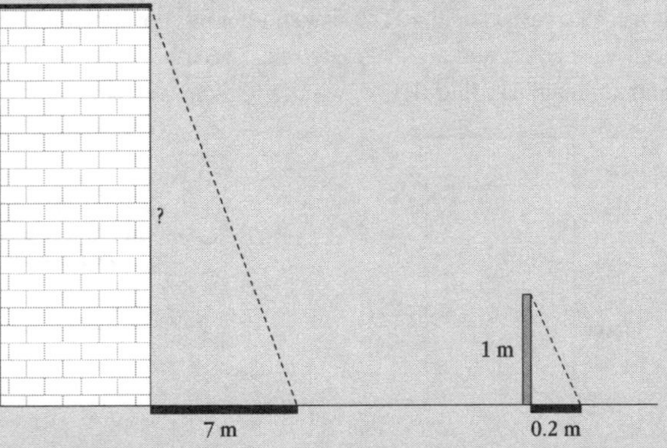

A. Use what you know about similar triangles to find the building's height from the given measurements. Explain your work.

B. With your class, choose a building or other tall object. Work with your group to estimate the object's height using the shadow method. In your answer, include the measurements your group made, and explain in words and drawings how you used these measurements to find the object's height.

Answers to Problem 5.1

A. The ratio of the meterstick's shadow to the meterstick is 5, because $0.2 \times 5 = 1$. Hence, the building is $7 \times 5 = 35$ m tall. Alternatively, the scale factor can be found by comparing the two shadows: $0.2 \times ? = 7$. The scale factor is thus 35, and the building is $1 \times 35 = 35$ m tall.

B. Answers will vary.

Problem 5.1 Follow-Up

Work with your teacher to pool the results from all the groups. Make a line plot of the data. What does your line plot tell you about the object's height? Save the line plot to use in Problem 5.2.

 Using Mirrors to Find Heights

The shadow method is useful for estimating heights, but it only works outdoors and on a sunny day. In this problem, you will use a mirror to help estimate heights. The mirror method works both indoors and outdoors. All you need is a level spot near the object whose height you want to estimate.

The mirror method is illustrated below. Place a mirror on a level spot at a convenient distance from the object. Back up from the mirror until you can see the top of the object in the center of the mirror. The two triangles shown in the diagram are similar.

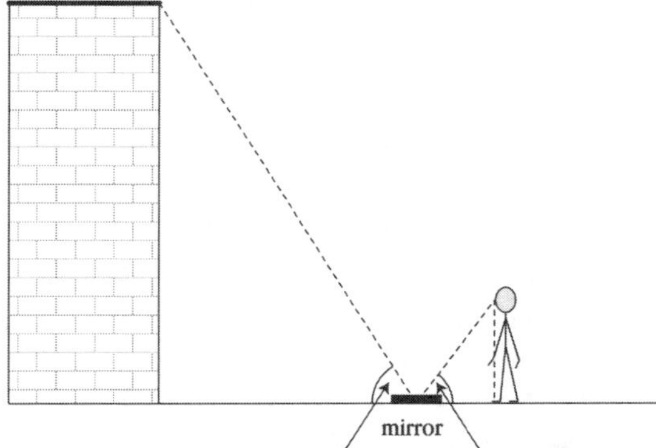

These angles are equal because light reflects off of a mirror at the same angle at which it hits the mirror.

To find the object's height, you need to measure three distances and then apply what you know about similar triangles.

Think about this!

Examine the diagram of the mirror method. Can you explain why each angle of the large triangle is equal to the corresponding angle of the small triangle?

Answer to Problem 5.1 Follow-Up

Here is a line plot of the measurements of a building taken in centimeters. Notice that the two outliers—250 cm and 342 cm—were included by using the notation "· · ·" to indicate where values were skipped.

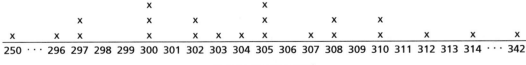

250	· · ·	296	297	298	299	300	301	302	303	304	305	306	307	308	309	310	311	312	313	314	· · ·	342
						x					x											
			x			x		x			x			x		x						
x		x	x			x		x	x	x	x		x	x		x		x		x		x

Height (centimeters)

5.2

Using Mirrors to Find Heights

At a Glance

Grouping: groups of 4

Launch

- Talk about the technique of using a mirror to estimate an object's height.
- Demonstrate the technique in the class.
- Have students work through part A.

Explore

- Have groups go outside to take the necessary measurements.
- Suggest that groups move the mirror and retake the measurements.

Summarize

- Pool the data, and analyze the resulting line plot.
- Help the class compare the line plots made from the two methods.
- Review how similar triangles make these estimates possible.

Assignment Choices

ACE questions 5, 6, 8, 10, 11, 12, 14, and unassigned choices from earlier problems

Problem 5.2

Jim and Qin-Zhong, students in Mr. Anwar's class, are using the mirror method to estimate the height of their school building. They have made the following measurements and sketch:

Height from the ground to Jim's eyes = 150 cm
Distance from the middle of the mirror to Jim = 100 cm
Distance from the middle of the mirror to the building = 600 cm

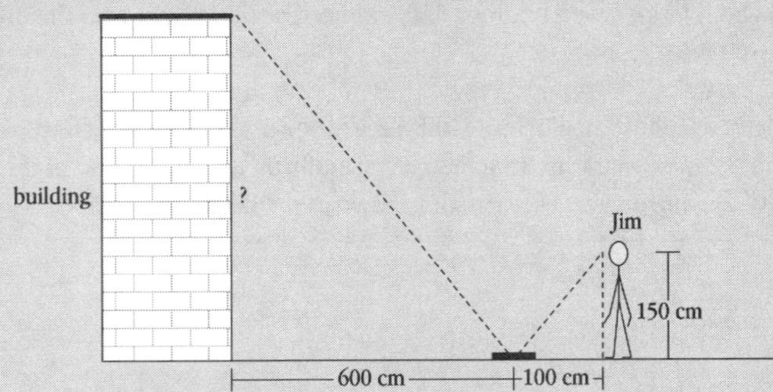

A. Use what you know about similar triangles to find the building's height from the given measurements. Explain your work.

B. With your group, use the mirror method to estimate the height of the same object or building you worked with in Problem 5.1. In your answer, include all the measurements your group made, and explain in words and drawings how you used the measurements to find the object's height.

C. How does the height estimate you made using the shadow method compare with the height estimate you made using the mirror method? Do you think your estimates for the object's height are reasonable? Why or why not?

Problem 5.2 Follow-Up

1. Work with your teacher to pool the results from all the groups. Make a line plot of the data.
2. Compare the line plot of the estimates you made using the mirror method to the line plot of the estimates you made using the shadow method (from Problem 5.1 Follow-Up). Which method seems to give more consistent results?

Answers to Problem 5.2

A. The bases of the triangles are corresponding sides. The scale factor from 100 to 600 is 6, so the height of the building is $150 \times 6 = 900$ cm.

B. Answers will vary.

C. Answers will vary.

Answers to Problem 5.2 Follow-Up

Answers will vary.

Using Similar Triangles to Find Distances

Mr. Anwar's class went to Bevort Pond for a picnic. Darnell, Angie, and Trevor wanted to find the distance across the pond. Darnell and Angie suggested that Trevor swim across with the end of a tape measure in his mouth. Trevor declined—the water was very cold! They decided to try to use what they had learned about similar triangles to find the distance across the pond. They drew a diagram and started making the necessary measurements.

Problem 5.3

Here is the diagram Darnell, Angie, and Trevor made, including their measurements.

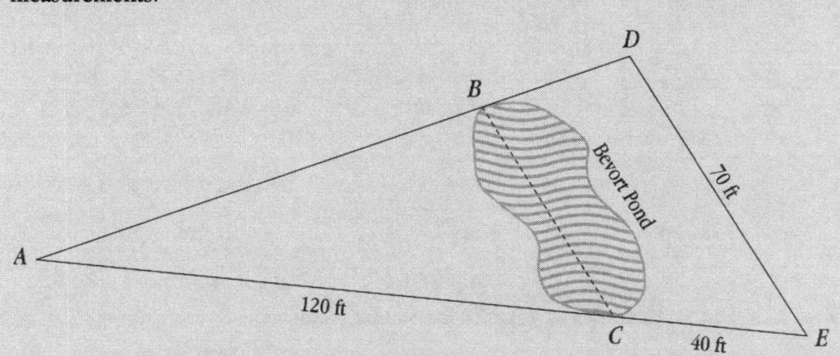

A. Name the two similar triangles in the diagram.

B. What is the scale factor from the large triangle to the small triangle?

C. What is the distance across the pond (measured along the dotted line)?

D. On your school grounds or in your neighborhood, find a pond or some other feature, such as a park, a playground, or a wooded area. Use the ideas in this problem to estimate the distance across the feature. Explain your work carefully.

Problem 5.3 Follow-Up

Is the large triangle Darnell, Angie, and Trevor measured the only one that will work to find the distance across the pond? If you think other triangles could be used, make a drawing of Bevort Pond showing another triangle that could be measured to determine the distance across the pond. If you think no other triangles would work, explain why not.

Using Similar Triangles to Find Distances

At a Glance

***Grouping:* groups of 4**

Launch

- Have students work on parts A–C of the problem.

Explore

- As a class, locate a physical feature to measure, and mark where the distance across will be estimated.
- Assist groups as they lay out their triangles and make their measurements.
- Ask groups to write about and make sketches of their findings.

Summarize

- As a class, make and analyze a line plot of the class data.

Answers to Problem 5.3

A. Triangles *ABC* and *ADE* are similar.

B. The scale factor from triangle *ADE* to triangle *ABC* is $\frac{120}{160}$, which is $\frac{3}{4}$ or 0.75.

C. The length of line *BC*, which is the distance across the pond, is $0.75 \times 70 = 52.5$ ft.

D. Answers will vary.

Answer to Problem 5.3 Follow-Up

See page 74h.

Assignment Choices

ACE questions 9, 15, 16, and unassigned choices from earlier problems

Answers

Applications

1a. sides *CD* and *XW*, sides *DE* and *WY*, and sides *CE* and *XY*

1b. ∠*CDE* and ∠*XWY*, ∠*CED* and ∠*XYW*, and ∠*ECD* and ∠*YXW*

2a. triangle *PQR* and triangle *PST*

2b. sides *PQ* and *PS*, sides *PR* and *PT*, and sides *QR* and *ST*

2c. ∠*PQR* and ∠*PST*, ∠*PRQ* and ∠*PTS*, and ∠*QPR* and ∠*SPT*

Applications • Connections • Extensions

As you work on these ACE questions, use your calculator whenever you need it.

Applications

1. The triangles below are similar.

a. Name all pairs of corresponding sides.

b. Name all pairs of corresponding angles.

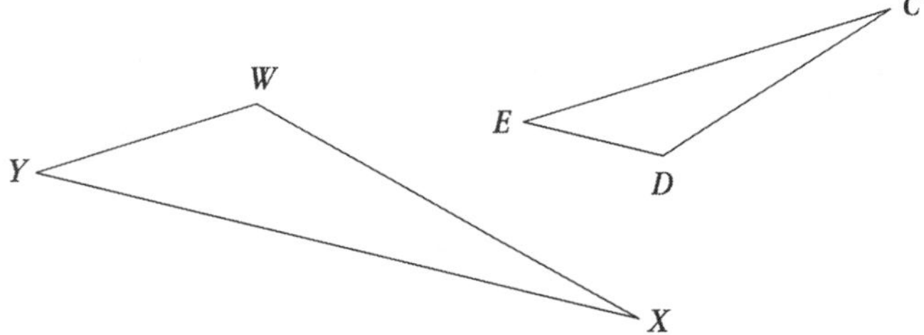

2. a. In the figure below, identify the similar triangles.

b. Name all pairs of corresponding sides for the similar triangles you found.

c. Name all pairs of corresponding angles for the similar triangles you found.

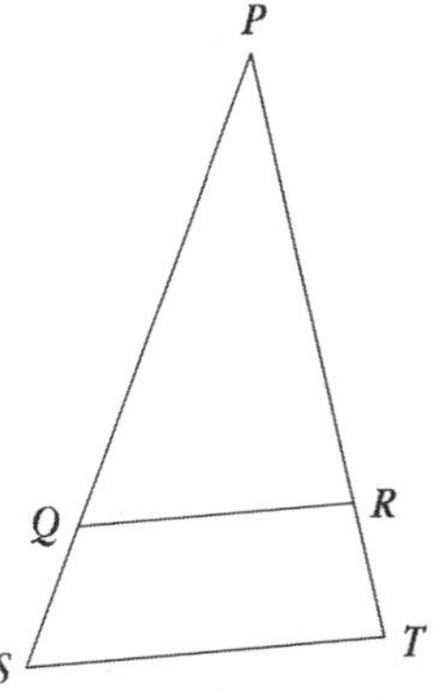

3. Daphne used the shadow method to estimate the height of the basketball backboard on the school playground. Here are the measurements she recorded. Use them to find the distance from the ground to the top of the backboard.

Length of meterstick = 1 m Length of meterstick's shadow = $\frac{1}{2}$ m
Length of backboard's shadow = $\frac{3}{2}$ m

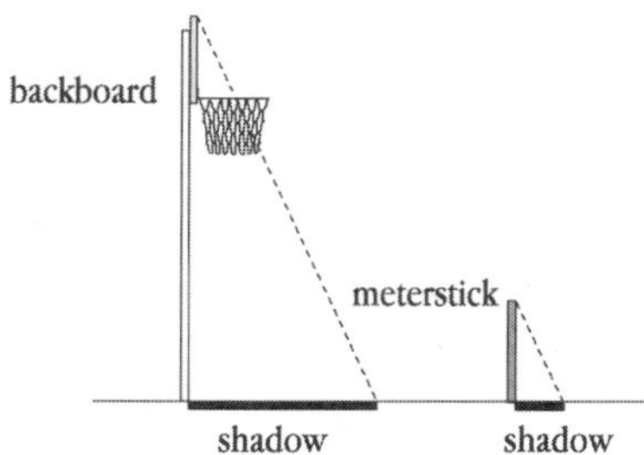

4. Darius used the shadow method to estimate the height of the flagpole in front of the city library. Here are the measurements he recorded. Use them to find the height of the flagpole.

Length of meterstick = 1 m Length of meterstick's shadow = 5 cm
Length of flagpole's shadow = 38 cm

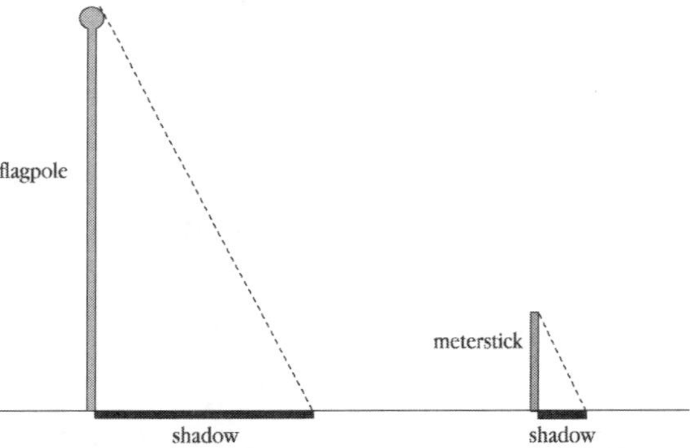

3. From the meterstick's shadow to the backboard's shadow, there is a scale factor of $\frac{3}{2} \div \frac{1}{2} = 3$. Therefore, the top of the backboard must be 3 times the height of the meterstick, or $3 \times 1 = 3$ m.

4. From the meterstick's shadow to the flagpole's shadow, there is a scale factor of $\frac{38}{5} = 7.6$. Therefore, the flagpole must be 7.6 times the height of the meterstick, or 7.6 m.

5. Since the distance from the mirror to Hank is twice Hank's height, the distance from the mirror to the principal should be twice the principal's height, so she must be $\frac{3.7}{2} = 1.85$ m tall. (Using scale factors is a bit more difficult. From the distance between the center of the mirror to Hank, to the distance from the center of the mirror to the principal, there is a scale factor of $3.7 \div 3 = 1.23$. Therefore, the principal's height is $1.5 \times 1.23 = 1.85$ m.)

6. The scale factor is $2.4 \div 1 = 2.4$, so the height of the classroom is $1.5 \times 2.4 = 3.6$ m.

5. The principal asked Hank to demonstrate what he was learning in math class. Hank decided to use the mirror method to estimate the principal's height. Here are the measurements Hank recorded. Use them to find the principal's height.

Height from the ground to Hank's eyes = 1.5 m
Distance from the center of the mirror to Hank = 3 m
Distance from the center of the mirror to the principal = 3.7 m

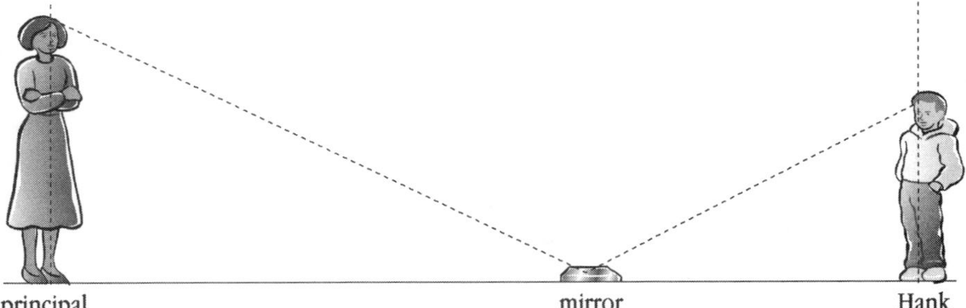

6. Stacia and Byron used the mirror method to estimate the height of their math classroom. Below are the measurements and sketch they made. Use them to find the height of the classroom.

Height from the ground to Stacia's eyes = 1.5 m
Distance from the center of the mirror to Stacia = 1 m
Distance from the center of the mirror to the classroom wall = 2.4 m

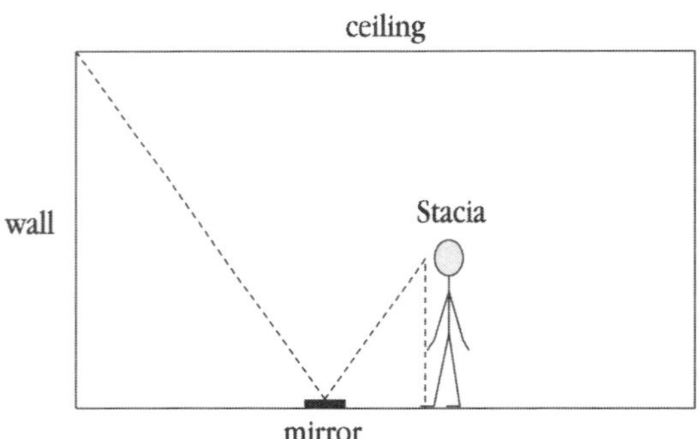

7. A stick 2 meters long casts a shadow 0.5 meters long. At the same time, the Washington Monument casts a shadow 42.25 meters long. How tall is the Washington Monument?

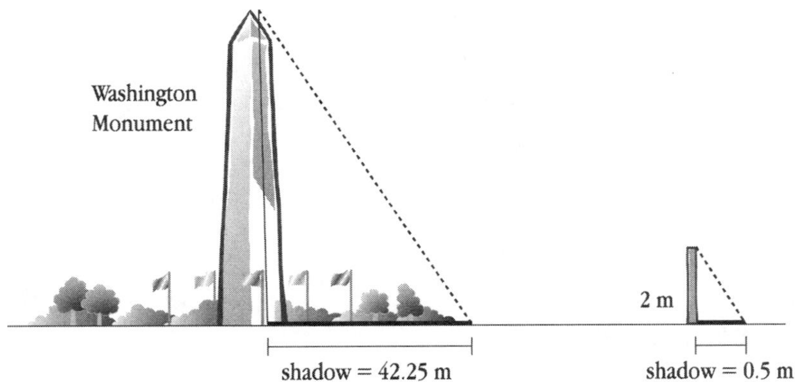

8. Joan used a mirror to estimate the height of a flagpole. Below are the measurements she recorded. What is the height of the flagpole?

Height from the ground to Joan's eyes = 5 feet
Distance from the center of the mirror to Joan = 2 feet
Distance from the center of the mirror to the flagpole = 9 feet

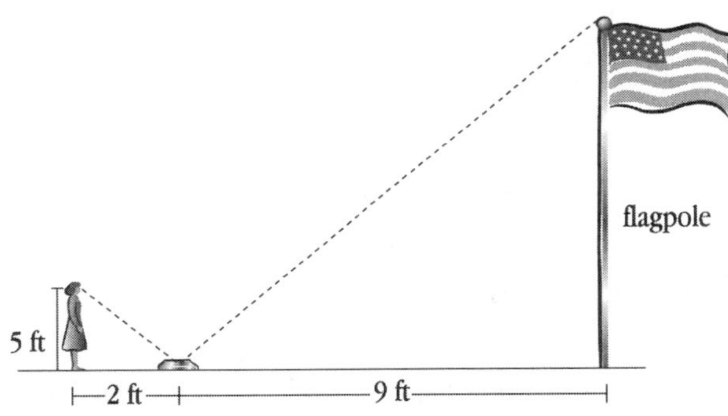

7. The scale factor from the stick's shadow to the monument's shadow is $42.25 \div 0.5 = 84.5$. Therefore, the monument is 84.5 times the height of the 2-meter stick, or 169 m.

8. The scale factor from the small triangle to the large triangle is $9 \div 2 = 4.5$, so the flagpole is $4.5 \times 5 = 22.5$ m tall.

9. The total length of 120 m on the large triangle corresponds to the length of 90 m on the small triangle, giving a scale factor of $\frac{3}{4}$ from the large triangle to the small. Therefore, the distance across the gravel pit is about $72 \times \frac{3}{4} = 54$ m.

Connections

10a. lines *DE, BF, FC,* and *BC;* lines *DF, EC, AE,* and *AC;* and lines *FE, BD, DA,* and *BA*

10b. Segment *BC* is twice as long as segment *DE,* because it is made from two lines that are both the length of segment *DE.*

9. What is the distance across the gravel pit shown in the drawing?

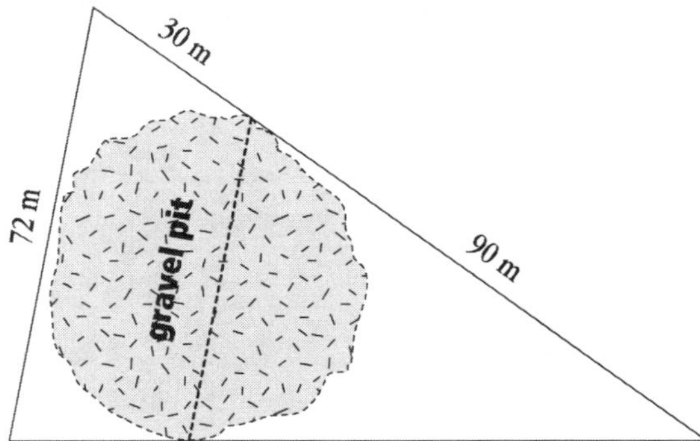

Connections

10. Look carefully at the figure below.

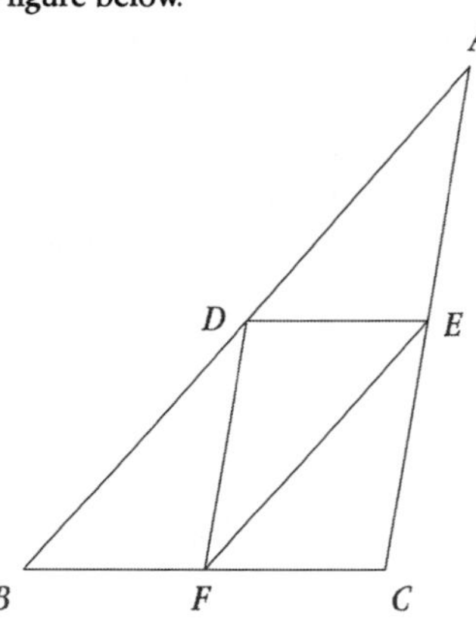

a. Which line segments look parallel?

b. Segment *DE* connects the midpoints of segments *AB* and *AC*. How does the length of segment *BC* compare to the length of segment *DE?* Explain.

11. Look carefully at the figure below.

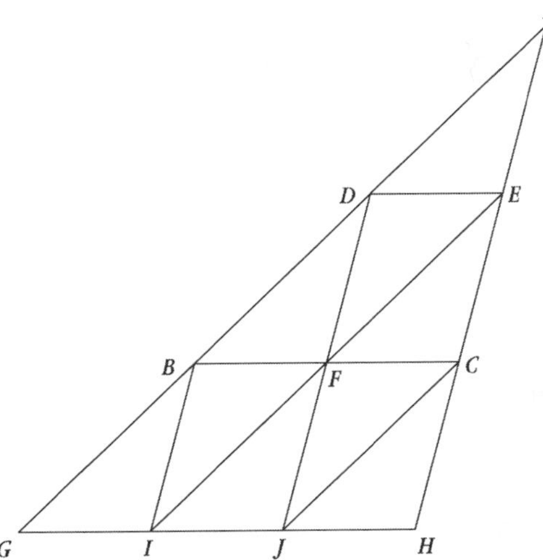

a. Which line segments look parallel?

b. How does this figure relate to the figure in question 10?

c. How does the length of segment *DE* compare to the length of segment *BC* and segment *GH*?

d. How are line segments *CJ*, *EI*, and *AG* related?

e. How are line segments *BI*, *DJ*, and *AH* related?

Extensions

12. Use the mirror method, the shadow method, or another method involving similar triangles to find the height of a telephone pole, a light pole, or a statue in your town. Report your results, and explain your method.

11a. Some of the parallel lines are lines *DE, BC,* and *GH;* lines *BI, DJ,* and *AH;* and lines *JC, IE,* and *GA.*

11b. This figure is the next largest similar figure that can be made with these rep-tiles.

11c. Segment *DE* is half the length of segment *BC* and one third the length of segment *GH.*

11d. There is a scale factor of 2 from segment *CJ* to *EI* and a scale factor of 3 from segment *CJ* to *AG.*

11e. There is a scale factor of 2 from segment *BI* to *DJ* and a scale factor of 3 from segment *BI* to *AH.*

Extensions

12. Answers will vary. It is important that students have an opportunity to try out these methods on real-world objects. They should begin to recognize some of the difficulties in collecting real-world data (for example, finding a flat area to place a mirror, or identifying the top point of a shadow that is cast by an irregularly shaped object such as a tree).

13a. See page 74i.

13b. From the similar triangles in the drawing, the scale factor is 900 ÷ 45 = 20. Hence, the building is 20 × 30 = 600 cm or 6 m tall.

14. See page 74j.

13. Tang plans to make some repairs on the roof of a building. He needs a ladder to reach the roof, but he's not sure how long the ladder should be. He thinks he has found a way to use similar triangles to find the height of the building. He stands 9 meters from the building and holds a 30-centimeter ruler in front of his eyes. The ruler is 45 centimeters from his eyes. He can just see the top and bottom of the building as he looks above and below the ruler.

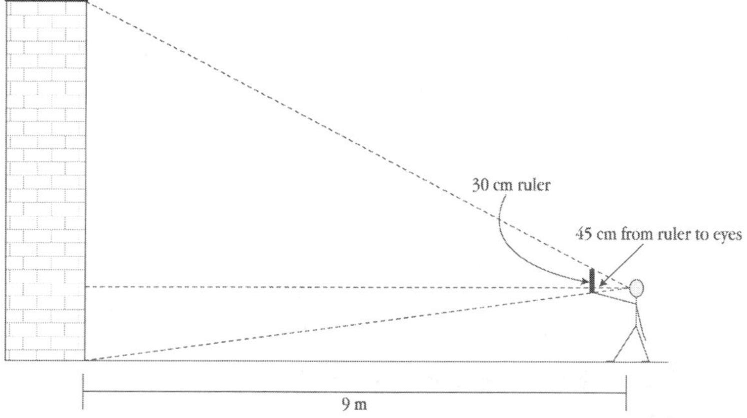

a. Do you see any similar triangles in the diagram that can help Tang figure out how tall the building is? Explain.

b. How tall is the building? Explain your reasoning.

14. In an *annular eclipse,* the Moon moves between the Earth and Sun, blocking part of the Sun's light for a few minutes. The Moon does not entirely cover the Sun; instead, a ring of light appears around the shadow of the Moon. In about 240 B.C., Aristarchus used eclipses to help correctly calculate the distances between the Earth, Moon, and Sun.

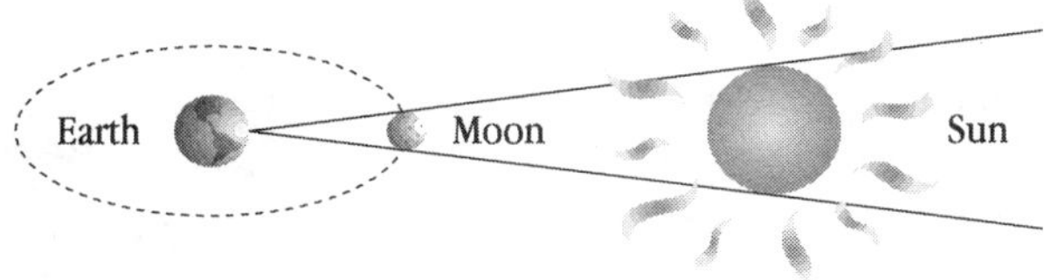

On May 10, 1994, there was an annular eclipse. Marquez's class decided to make some measurements they could use to calculate the distance from the Earth to the Moon. They constructed a viewing box like the one shown below.

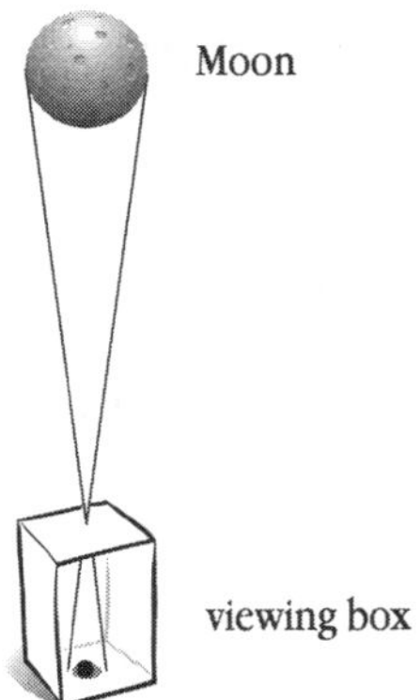

During the eclipse, the image of the Moon almost completely covered the Sun. The Moon's shadow and the ring of light surrounding it appeared on the bottom of the viewing box. The Moon's image was 1 meter from the hole and had a diameter of 0.9 centimeter. The class read in their science book that the actual diameter of the Moon is about 3500 kilometers. Use this data to find the distance to the Moon at the time of the eclipse.

ACE

15a. Answers will vary. Students should find that they need a friend to hold the coin.

15b. A dime, with a diameter of $\frac{11}{16}$ in, will need to be held about $\frac{238,000}{2160} \times \frac{11}{16} = 76$ in (6 ft 4 in) away. A penny, with a diameter of $\frac{3}{4}$ in, will need to be held about $\frac{238,000}{2160} \times \frac{3}{4} = 83$ in (6 ft 11 in) away. A nickel, with a diameter of $\frac{13}{16}$ in, will need to be held about $\frac{238,000}{2160} \times \frac{13}{16} = 90$ in (7 ft 6 in) away. A quarter, with a diameter of $\frac{15}{16}$ in, will need to be held about $\frac{238,000}{2160} \times \frac{15}{16} = 103$ in (8 ft 7 in) away. See illustration below right. (Note: The 238,000 miles from the Earth to the Moon is from *surface* to *surface.* These answers assume that the distance is from the Earth's surface to the center of the Moon.)

15. **a.** Some evening when you see a full moon, go outside with a friend and use a coin to exactly block the image of the moon. How far from your eyes do you have to hold the coin? Can you hold the coin yourself, or does your friend have to hold it for you?

b. The diameter of the Moon is about 2160 miles, and the distance from the Earth to the Moon is about 238,000 miles. Use these numbers, the diameter of your coin, and the concept of similar triangles to compute the distance you would have to hold the coin from your eye to just block the Moon. How does the distance you computed compare to the distance you measured in your experiment?

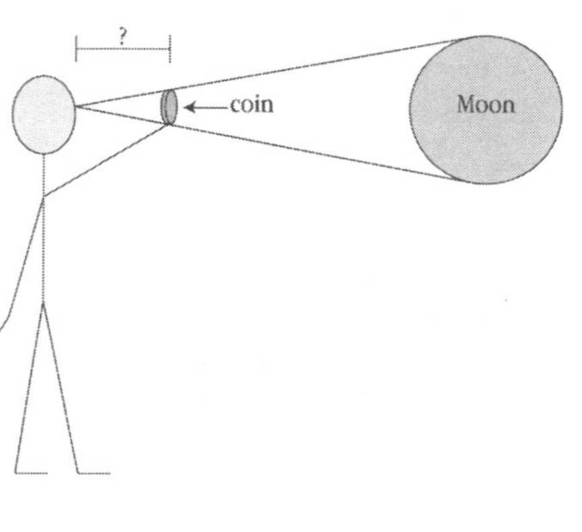

15b.

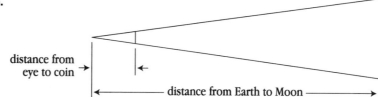

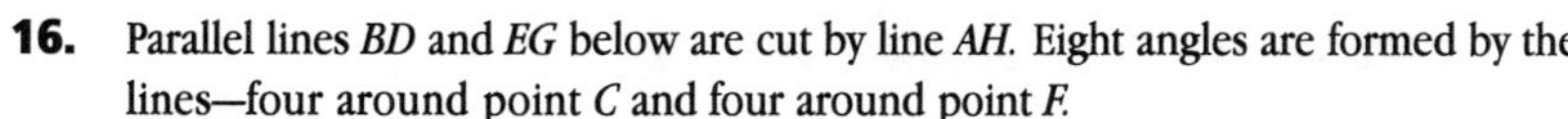

16. Parallel lines *BD* and *EG* below are cut by line *AH*. Eight angles are formed by the lines—four around point *C* and four around point *F*.

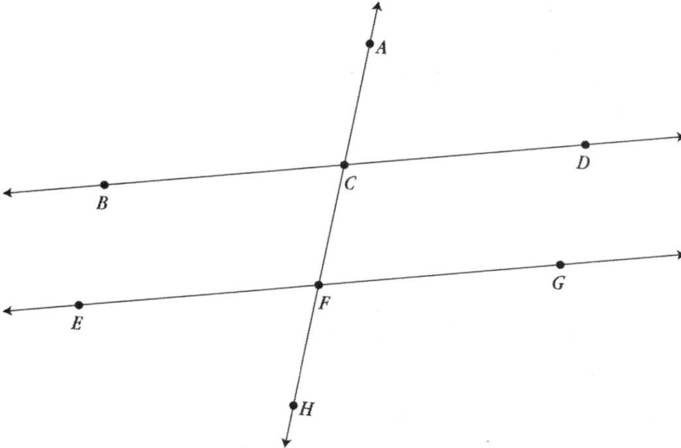

a. Find every angle that appears to be congruent to $\angle ACD$.

b. Find every angle that appears to be congruent to $\angle EFC$.

16a. $\angle BCF$, $\angle CFG$, and $\angle EFH$

16b. $\angle BCA$, $\angle DCF$, and $\angle GFH$

Possible Answers

1. See page 74k.

2. The fact that the ratios of corresponding sides in similar triangles are equal means we can use equivalent fractions to find the unknown length in a ratio that would make the triangles similar. The other useful property is that if the corresponding angles of two triangles are equal, the triangles are similar—which makes using triangles for estimating distances easier than using other figures.

3. The sides opposite the nested angles (point P in the illustration) are parallel and are related by the scale factor between the triangles.

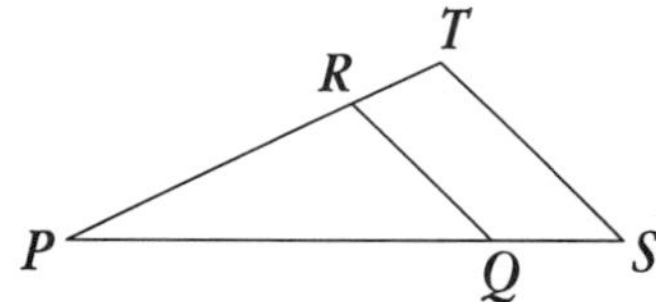

Mathematical Reflections

In this investigation, you used what you know about similar triangles to find heights of buildings and to estimate other inaccessible distances. These questions will help you summarize what you have learned:

1. Explain at least two ways you can use similar triangles to measure things in the real world. Illustrate your ideas with an example.
2. What properties of similar triangles are useful for estimating distances and heights?
3. If you take any two similar triangles and place the small triangle on top of the large triangle so that a pair of corresponding angles match, what can you say about the sides of the two triangles opposite these corresponding angles?

Think about your answers to these questions, discuss your ideas with other students and your teacher, and then write a summary of your findings in your journal.

Tips for the Linguistically Diverse Classroom

Diagram Code The Diagram Code technique is described in detail in *Getting to Know Connected Mathematics*. Students use a minimal number of words and drawings, diagrams, or symbols to respond to questions that require writing. Example: Question 2—A student might answer this question by writing the heading *Useful Because* and drawing two similar triangles; triangle *ABC*, with two sides labeled 3 and 4; and triangle *DEF*, with sides labeled 6, 8, and 10. Below this, the student might write $\angle ABC = \angle DEF$. Next to triangle *ABC*'s blank side, the student might write *side AC* = $\frac{1}{2}$ × *side DF*.

TEACHING THE INVESTIGATION

5.1 • Using Shadows to Find Heights

In this problem, students apply their knowledge of similarity to estimate the height of a tall object or building.

Launch

This is a good time to review the special cases of rectangles and triangles when determining similarity. Since all rectangles have equal angles and not all rectangles are similar, we must check ratios of corresponding sides (the scale factor) to verify that two rectangles are similar. With triangles, we only have to check the angles, because if the three corresponding angles are equal, the triangles have the same ratio of corresponding sides. If students are still struggling with this idea, refer to the work with triangle rep-tiles: *every* triangle is a rep-tile, and it is the angles that make this true.

You will need a sunny day to conduct part B of this activity. Introduce the situation to the class: When you want to make a fairly reasonable estimate of the height of a tower, a building, a pole, or another tall object, but there doesn't seem to be any easy way to measure it directly, what do you do?

> Our job is to find out how we can use mathematics to help us make such measurements. Today we are going to use the power of the sun to help us estimate the height of a tall object.
>
> When the sun shines on the earth, objects cast a shadow. From your experience, what can you say about the shadows that the sun casts?

Students may note that a shadow's length depends on the height of the object. They may know that shadows change length as the earth rotates on its axis. Shadows are longer when the sun is near the horizon—whether in the morning or evening—and very short in the middle of the day when the sun is more directly overhead.

> Let's think about the relationship between the length of a shadow and the height of an object. At any particular time of day, how will the shadows of two objects that are not the same height compare? *(The shadow of the taller object will be longer.)* This means that a shadow's length depends on the object's height.
>
> Imagine that you are looking at a tall pole. The sun is shining, and the pole is casting a shadow. In your mind, walk around the pole until you are standing so that you see the pole and its shadow from the side. Make a sketch of what you think this would look like.

You want students to mentally picture the two legs of the right triangle made by the pole and its shadow. Ask for a volunteer to share his or her sketch with the class, then ask:

> What do you think? Is your sketch somewhat like this one?

Ask students to add to their sketch a line to show the triangle formed by the pole, the shadow, and the line from the top of the pole to the tip of the shadow.

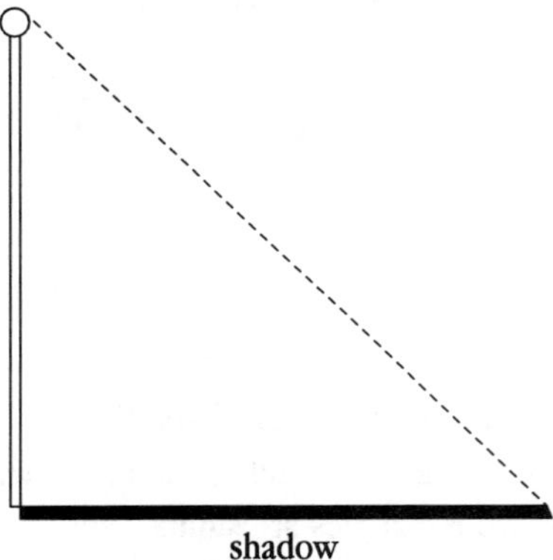

Students don't need to make completely accurate drawings at this stage. The exercise will increase their interest in the setting and start them visualizing such scenes.

> Suppose we took a meterstick outside and stood it on the ground. Picture an imaginary line (made by the sun's rays) from the top of the meterstick to the ground. Do you see the triangle formed by the meterstick, the light of the sun, and the shadow? Sketch this triangle.
>
> Suppose there is a tall object nearby, such as a flagpole or a tree. What do you think will be true about that object, its shadow, and the rays of the sun? Will they form a triangle?

The meterstick and the tall object both form triangles.

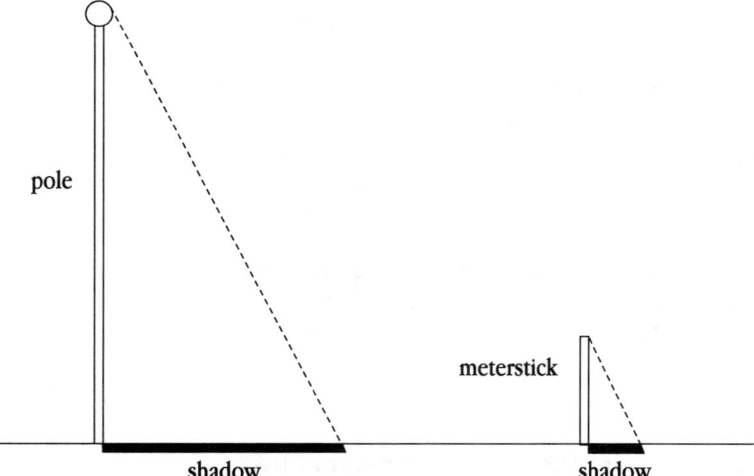

> Is the triangle similar to the one formed by the meterstick? Explain your reasoning.

The triangles are similar. Both triangles have a right angle. Since the sunlight is coming from the same angle toward both objects, the angles formed by the objects and their imaginary lines are equal. Since these two angles are equal, the remaining angles in the triangles are equal (since the angle sum of any triangle is 180°), which means the triangles are similar.

Now, propose the question of measuring the height of a real-world object—for example, the school building, a tree, a lamppost, or a flagpole.

> How might we use our meterstick and the sun to measure the height of our school? How could we find similar triangles? What measurements would we need to make?

After students have shared their ideas, refer to the illustration in the student edition, and talk about how to find the height of the building in Problem 5.1 using the information given.

When students are able to summarize how to use the sun and a meterstick to estimate an object's height, give the class directions for going outside to choose an object to measure.

Explore

Have students work in groups of four to take whatever measurements they need to estimate the chosen object's height.

Students may have had little opportunity to make measurements of distances greater than a meter, so some groups may need help getting started. An important goal of this problem is to give students these measuring experiences. Students could use a meterstick over and over to measure; they may need help marking where the ends fall and with accurately reading the last segment of the length. Students could also lay out the distances with string and then measure the string.

Summarize

Once groups have made their estimates, help the class pool the results and display the data in a line plot. Discuss the variations in the estimates and possible sources of error. All the measures will be estimates, so variation is expected. However, some students may have measured incorrectly, and others may have computed incorrectly with the scale factor.

> Based on our class data, what do you think the height of this object is? Why?

Students may suggest that the heights be averaged, which is a good suggestion.

> Who can describe exactly how his or her group used similar triangles to measure the object's height?
>
> Would we always be able to use this method to estimate the height of an object? Why or why not?

Save the line plot to compare with the one the class will make in Problem 5.2.

5.2 • Using Mirrors to Find Heights

We cannot always count on the sun to shine, and so we need other ways to estimate the height of tall objects. In this problem, students learn a technique that involves a mirror.

Launch

To introduce the mirror method, use a student to demonstrate the setup in the classroom. Place a mirror on the floor, with a clear area between the mirror and the chalkboard. Have the student stand straight and look into the mirror, then move forward or backward until the top of the chalkboard is reflected in the center of the mirror. Then, ask the student to stand still while the rest of the class inspects the setup.

Do you see any triangles formed in what you we have set up here?

One triangle is formed by the distance from the top of the board to the floor, the distance from the base of the wall to the reflection in the mirror, and the distance from the reflection to the top of the board. The second triangle is formed by the student's line of sight to the mirror, the height of the student (to eye level), and the distance from the student to the mirror.

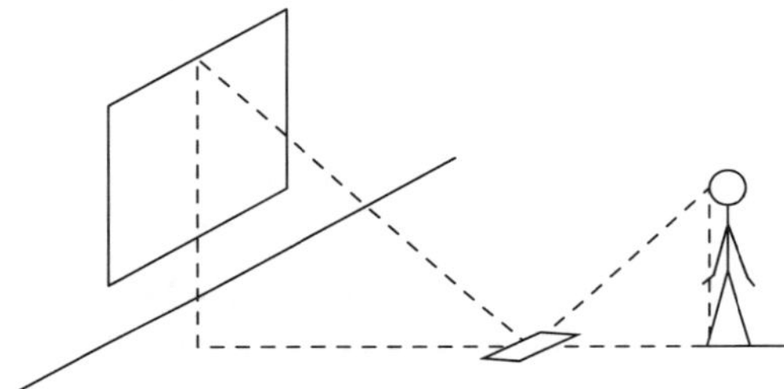

Sketch a picture of the setup, showing the two triangles. I will do a drawing too.

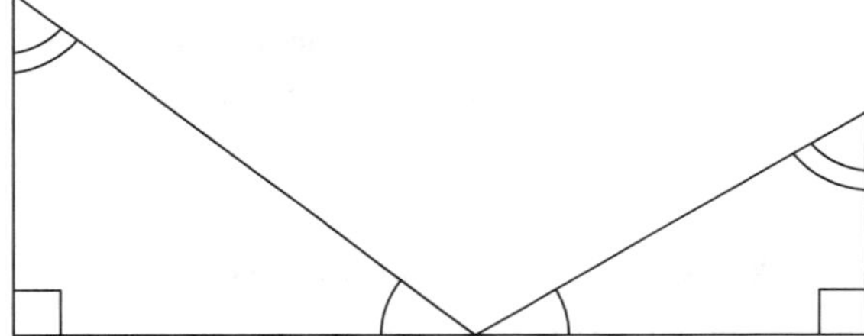

We want to mark corresponding angles on the sketch so that we can clearly see the two triangles and their orientation. Here is a way to mark the angles that many people use. A square is used to mark the right angles. One curved line is used to mark a pair of corresponding angles. Two curved lines are used to mark the other pair of corresponding angles.

Are these two triangles similar? Why or why not?

They are similar, because their corresponding angles are equal. This is a difficult corresponding angle problem, so you may need to help students explicitly identify which angles correspond. The triangles have corresponding right angles—one at the base of the wall, and one at the foot of the student. Also, the *angle of incidence* and *angle of reflection* are the same for the path of the light reflected in the mirror: light reflects off a mirror at the same angle at which it hits the mirror. This means that the two angles at the mirror—one formed by the lines from the mirror to the board, and one formed by the lines from the mirror to the student—are the same. And, if two of the angles in a pair of triangles are equal, the third pair of angles must be equal as well, since the angle sum of any triangle is 180°.

Point out that since groups will be choosing where to position their mirror, they may as well place it at a convenient distance from the base of the object, which will make the numbers easier to work with in the calculation.

> Let's move our mirror a convenient distance from the base of the wall. We'll measure a 3-meter distance to use as the position of the center of the mirror.

Once the mirror is in place, have the student again sight the top of the board in the center of the mirror.

> Observe how the triangles have changed. Is the student closer to or further from the board now? Why?

The eye's line of sight always makes the same angle with the floor as the line of reflection of the top of the board makes with the floor. As the mirror is moved further from the object, the person must move further from the mirror.

> What measurements must we make to use the similar triangles we see to estimate the board's height?

Make sure students understand that the necessary measurements are the distance from the student to the mirror, the distance from the center of the mirror to the base of wall (which was set by the placement of the mirror), and the distance from the floor to the student's eyes. These measurements will give us the scale, and the scale factor between the two triangles can then be used to find the missing side—which is the height being estimated.

> Let's have two volunteers make the measurements we need.

As a class, finish the calculations to estimate the board's height. Measure the board's height carefully. Discuss why the measurement and the estimate are not exactly equal. (All measurements are estimates, so there are bound to be small differences no matter how careful we are. Sloppy measuring will give larger differences.)

Read Problem 5.2 with the students, and have them complete part A individually. You may need to point out the right angles in the triangles to help students see that the height of the person corresponds to the height of the building.

Explore

Have students work in groups of four to use the mirror method to measure the height of the object they estimated with the shadow method.

Groups may want to try the mirror method more than once, using different students as the sighter. This will result in varying measurements, since people have different eye heights and sighting distances. They can also move the mirror and take the measurements again to test their estimates. Be prepared to help students make careful measurements.

Summarize

As a class, organize the group's data on a line plot. As before, talk about the variations in the estimates, possible sources of error, and the class's determination of the object's height based on the class data.

Display the line plot made for the shadow method, and discuss with the class how the estimates are alike and different.

> Describe the shape of each line plot. Given the data from the two methods, what do you think is the best estimate of the object's height?

If the two sets of data differ considerably, discuss possible reasons for the variation.

> In which method do you have the most confidence? Why?

There is no right answer to this question; you are just trying to get students to think about factors that affect the estimates, to remember that measurements are approximations, and to see that errors can be compounded through calculations made with imprecise measurements. The line plot with data clumped more tightly probably indicates the more consistent method.

Wrap up the summary by asking students once again to explain what triangles were formed and used in each procedure (the shadow and the mirror method), why the triangles are similar, and how the fact that they are similar allows us to estimate an object's height.

5.3 • Using Similar Triangles to Find Distances

This problem again uses similar triangles to estimate inaccessible distances—this time, the distance across a physical land feature rather than the height of an object.

Launch

If the class has done well on the first two problems, you may just want to read this problem with them and let them work on the example in groups before you discuss part D. If they are still trying to make sense of how to apply the ideas of similar triangles, go through the example with them, and then let groups of four do the outdoors activity.

Explore

Locate an area for the class to measure, such as a small pond, a park, a playground, or a wooded area. Or, have a group of students mark a boundary on the school grounds for a pretend pond (it does not have to be very large). Help the class clearly mark the two edges of the distance across the feature so that all groups will be estimating the same distance.

Have groups lay out their triangles and make the necessary measurements to estimate the distance across the feature. Each group should locate the vertices of the triangle they intend to use. You might want to check each group's triangle before they do the hard work of measuring the distances. Be sure the triangles are lined up so that one side of the triangle is parallel to the line of the distance across the feature (lines *DE* and *BC* in the example in the student edition). To do this, two students can stand on each side of the object at either end of the distance to be measured. Two other students can sight a side of the triangle parallel to the line between the two "marker" students.

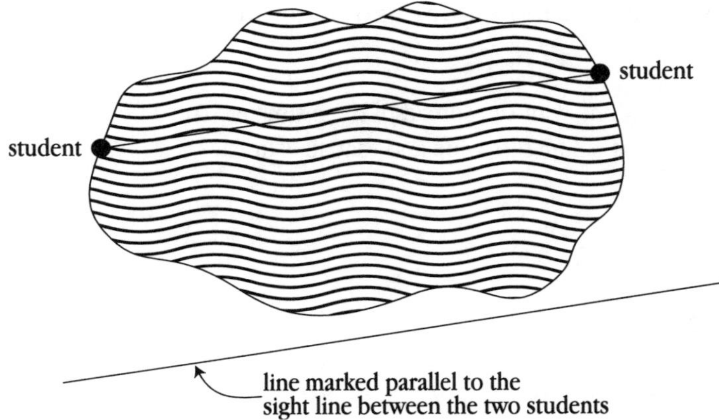

A second thing to watch for is that groups measure both the distance from a vertex of the triangle (point *A* in the drawing in the student edition) to the end of the line across the feature (point *C*), and the distance from this point to the other end of the same line segment (from point *C* to point *E*). Some students may measure the total distance *AE* and forget the measure of *AC*.

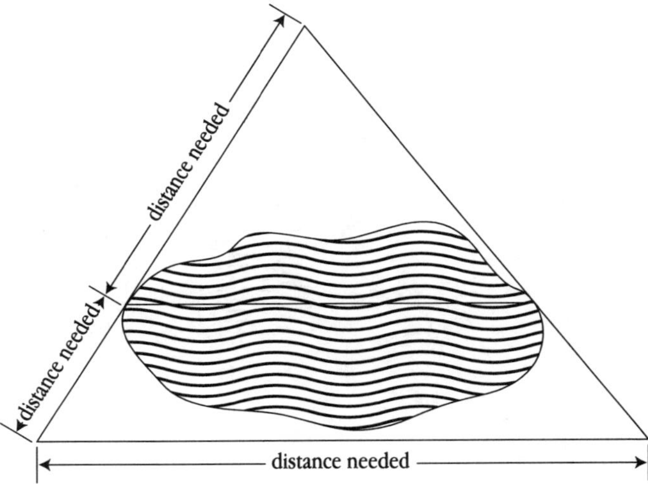

Some groups may want to use two different triangles and two sets of measurements to check their estimates.

Ask each group to write a report on how they did the problem, including a sketch or sketches with measurements.

Summarize

Give each group a chance to share their work. Make a line plot of all the estimates found.

> What would you estimate as the distance across the feature if you had to give one number to represent the work of our class?

Students will probably suggest that the estimates be averaged, which is a good suggestion.

> What else would you report if you could add more information about what the class found?

It is reasonable to give the average distance found, along with the spread of the estimates. For example, the class might report that their "pond" was 6.3 meters wide and that all estimates were between 5.5 and 7 meters.

Additional Answers

Answer to Problem 5.3 Follow-Up

The triangle that was staked out is only one of an infinite number of triangles that could be used. To measure the distance *BC*, each triangle must have a side parallel to *BC* (such as *DE* in the example), and two sides of the triangle must touch points *B* and *C*. The vertex *A* can be moved closer to or further from—and to the right or left of—where it is now. Below are several possibilities; you may want to show a similar diagram to the class.

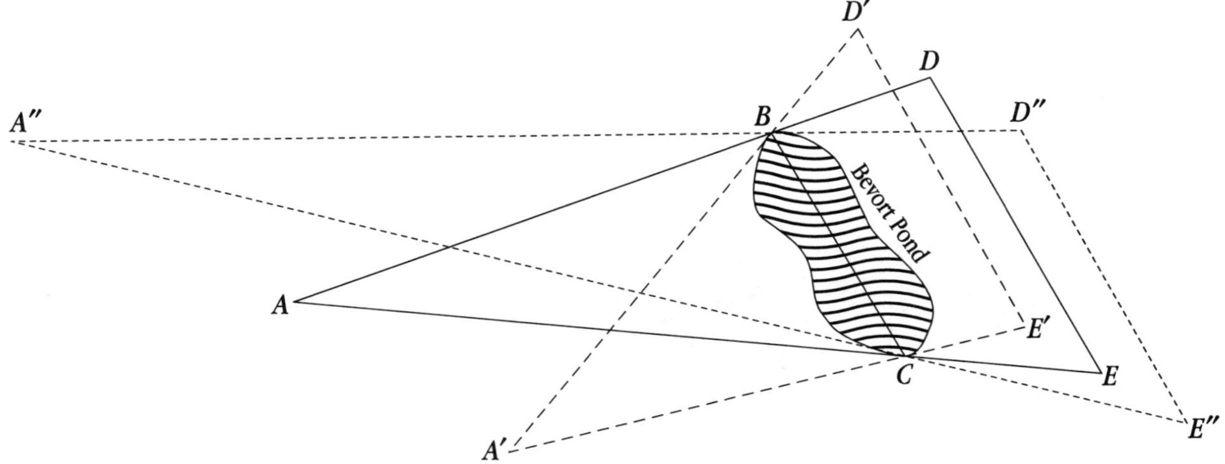

Triangle *ADE* may also be smaller than triangle *ABC.*

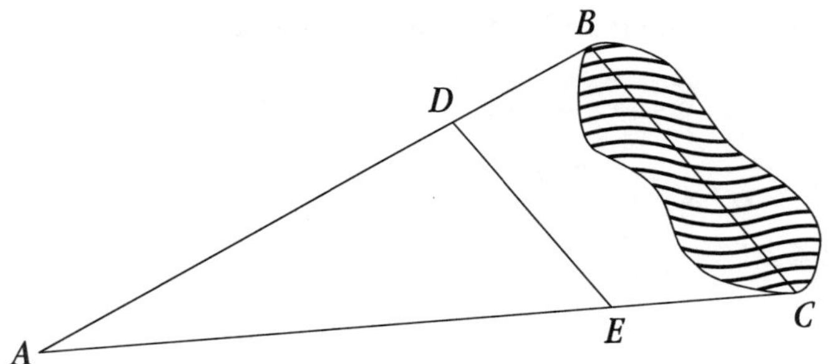

ACE Answers

Extensions

13a. The triangle made by Tang's vision is similar to the smaller triangle made by the ruler (see the two triangles indicated below). The 30-cm ruler corresponds with the height of the building, and the base of the large triangle (9 m or 900 cm) corresponds to the base of the small triangle (45 cm).

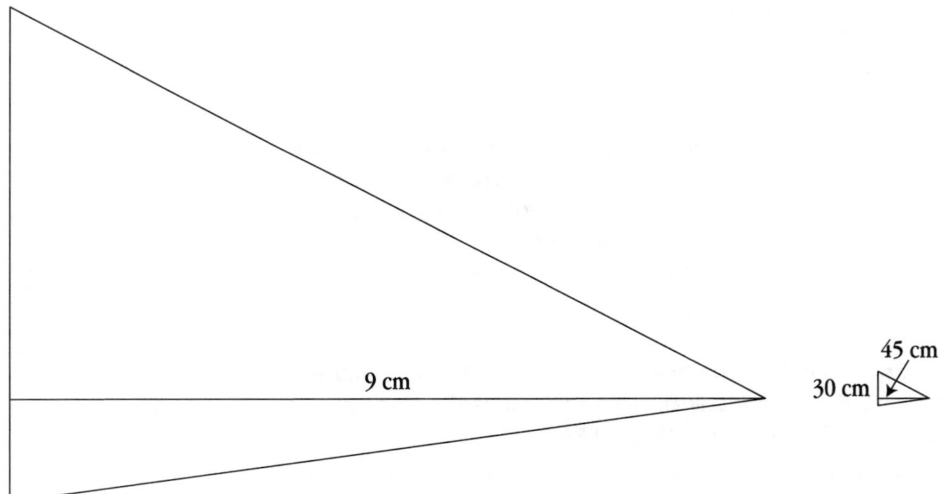

14. We can visualize the similar triangles as touching at their vertices. The distance from the top of the box to the center of the Moon corresponds to the distance from the top of the box to the bottom, where the image lies. The diameter of the image corresponds to the Moon's diameter.

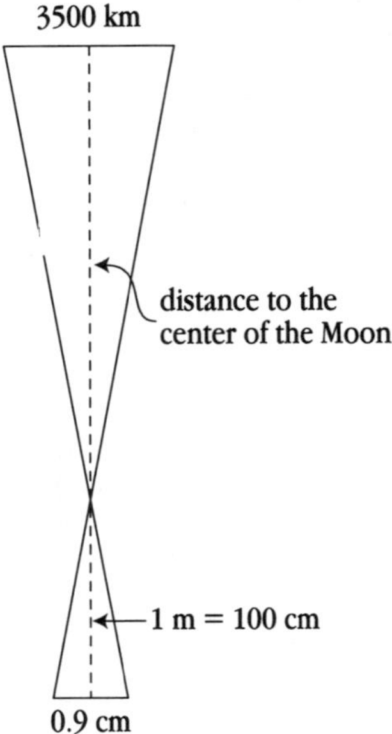

There are many ways to solve this problem; three are given here. Note that these solutions estimate the distance to the center of the Moon, not to the surface of the Moon. Also, students may add 1 meter to actually get to the ground, since they only found the distance from the center of the Moon to the top of the box. Of course, these measurements are all approximate, and the distance from the Earth to the Moon would vary far more than a meter, depending on such factors as the terrain of the Earth from which the measurements were made.

- Since the diameter of the image is 0.009 of the height of the small triangle (0.9 ÷ 100), we would expect that 3500 is 0.009 of the distance from the top of the box to the center of the Moon, which is 3500 ÷ 0.009 or about 390,000 km.
- The ratio of the height of the small triangle to its base is 100 ÷ 0.9 = 111. Therefore, the distance from the top of the box to the center of the Moon is about 3500 × 111 = 389,000 km (rounded to nearest 1000).
- The scale from the diameter of the image to the Moon's diameter is 3500 ÷ 0.9 = 3900, so the distance from the top of the box to the center of the Moon is about 3900 × 100 = 390,000 km. (Note: This method works, but it is important to recognize that the Moon's diameter is *not* 3900 times the diameter of the image, and that 3900 is *not* the scale factor. The true scale factor is found by dividing centimeters into centimeters or kilometers into kilometers, *not* centimeters into kilometers. The actual scale factor from the diameter of the image to the Moon's diameter is 3500 km ÷ 0.9 cm × 100,000 cm/km = 390,000,000. Also, the ratio of 0.9 **cm** to 3500 **km** only works when comparing 100 **cm** to *x* **km.** In other words, corresponding units must be the same.)

Mathematical Reflections

1. Answers will vary, but students should be able to discuss the shadow method, the mirror method, or the use of similar triangles (as in the pond problem). Possible answer: You can use similar triangles to find heights or distances that you can't measure directly. You have to find a way to make similar triangles with the length you want to measure as one of the sides of one of the triangles and a way to measure the corresponding side in the similar triangle. You must also be able to measure another pair of corresponding sides of the two triangles. These two sets of measures can be used to form the scale factor in two ways. These two are equivalent fractions. We know three of the numbers and just have to figure out the missing number, which is the length measure we are trying to find. The three pictures illustrate situations that summarize the kinds of pairs of triangles we used to solve problems in this investigation.

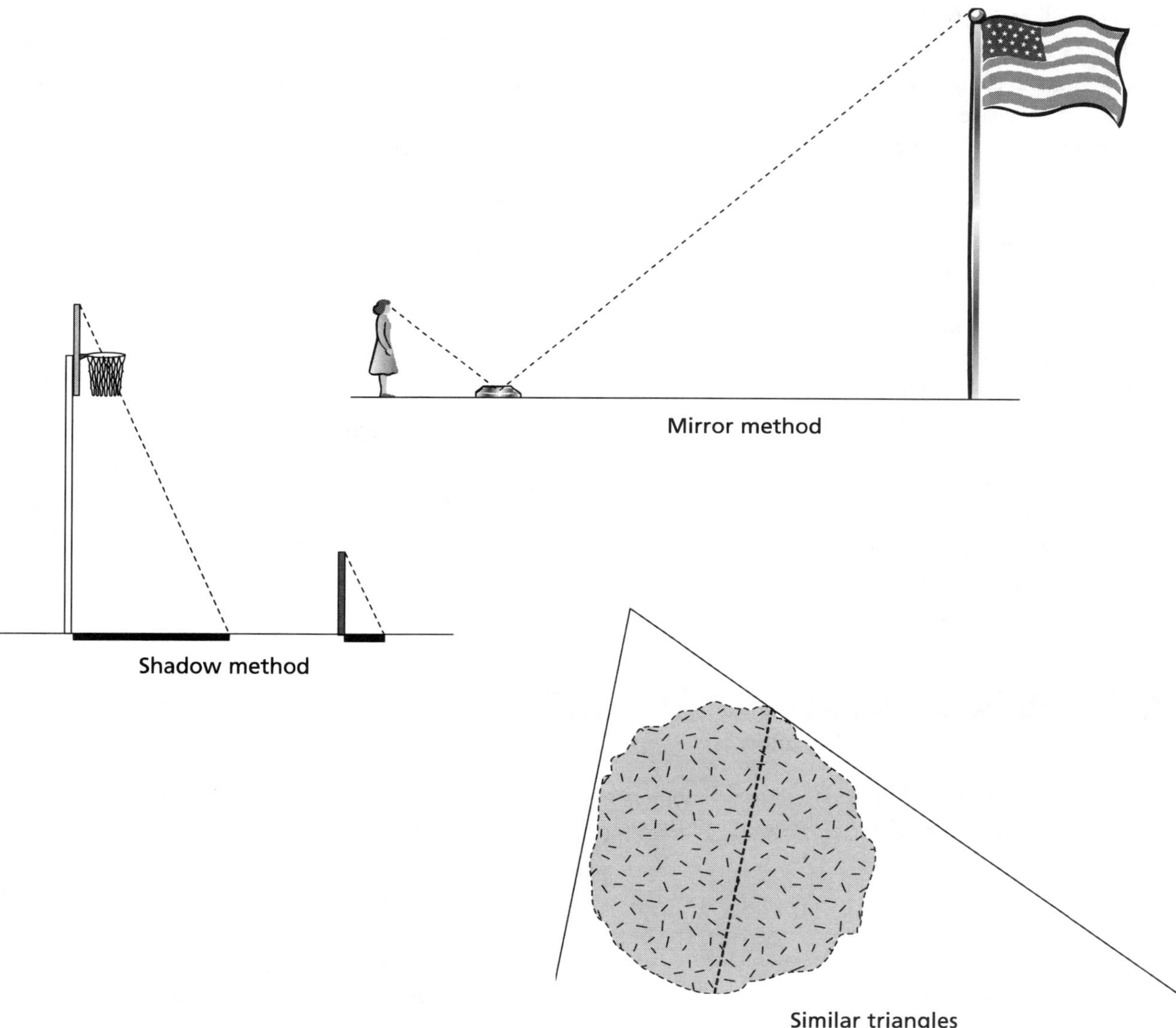

INVESTIGATION 6

Stretching and Shrinking with a Computer

This short investigation engages students in making enlargements and reductions of drawings on a computer. The activities visually reinforce the concepts students have worked with in earlier investigations. They also provide connections to other units: revisiting work with angles and the Logo computer language in the grade 6 unit *Shapes and Designs;* offering visual models of reflections to reinforce work done in the grade 6 unit *Ruins of Montarek;* and offering informal experience with negative numbers to help build the conceptual basis for the ideas students will encounter in *Accentuate the Negative.*

In Problem 6.1, Drawing Similar Figures with a Computer, students draw a simple figure and investigate how it can be altered by two *Turtle Math* tools, the Scale tool and the Change Shape tool. In Problem 6.2, Stretching and Shrinking Flags, students draw a simple flag, scale it up and down, and investigate the results. Although these problems will ideally be done with two to four students per computer, we encourage you to do this investigation even if you have only a single demonstration computer.

Mathematical and Problem-Solving Goals

- ***To continue to make decisions about whether figures are similar based upon constant angle measurements and ratios between two sides of the same figure***
- ***To continue to build understanding of angles as measures of rotation***
- ***To solve problems involving scaling and its effects on side lengths and area***
- ***To manipulate a figure visually by shrinking it to zero length and width and then changing its orientation (as the scale factor becomes negative)***

Materials

Problem	For students	For the teacher
All	Graphing calculators, Macintosh computers (optional; 1 per 2–4 students), *Turtle Math* software (optional)	Transparencies 6.1A to 6.2 (optional), Macintosh computer, preferably with an overhead display (optional), *Turtle Math* software (or other Logo software)
6.1	Angle rulers (1 per 2–4 students)	Note: To run *Turtle Math*, a Macintosh computer must be model LC or better with 4MB of RAM and System 7 or higher.
6.2	Grid paper (optional; provided as blackline masters), transparent grid paper (optional; copy the grids onto transparency film)	

Student Pages 75–84 | Teaching the Investigation 84a–84h

INVESTIGATION 6

Stretching and Shrinking with a Computer

In this investigation, you will use a computer program called *Turtle Math* to enlarge and reduce figures. You may already know how to use *Turtle Math* to draw figures. In this investigation, you will draw figures and then use tools to stretch and shrink them.

6.1 Drawing Similar Figures with a Computer

The problems in this investigation use only two commands: `fd` (forward) and `rt` (right turn).

When you begin a new *Turtle Math* session, you will see a turtle facing upward in the center of the Drawing window.

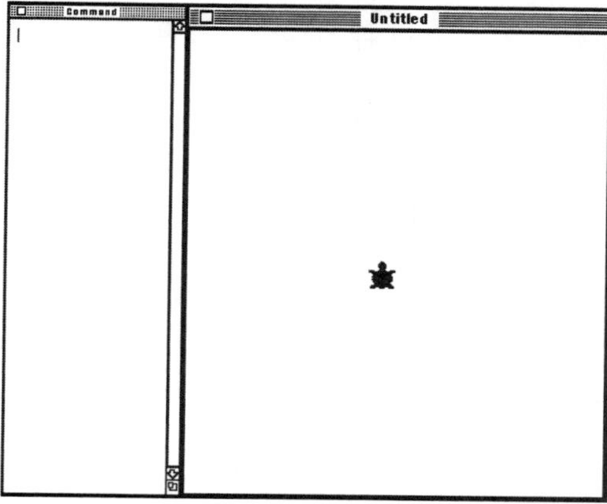

6.1

Drawing Similar Figures with a Computer

At a Glance

Grouping:* *small groups

Launch

- In advance, prepare how the class will do the computer work.
- If students have used *Turtle Math,* have them write commands for making other figures. *(optional)*

Explore

- Let students discover what the Scale and Change Shape tools do.
- If necessary, remind students to monitor the lengths and angle turns in the Command window.
- Remind students to press Return to see the turtle excute the command.

Summarize

- Review angle and side-length relationships. *(optional)*

Assignment Choices

ACE question 1 and unassigned choices from earlier problems

You tell the turtle how to move by typing commands in the Command window. Try telling the turtle to move forward: type `fd`, followed by a space, followed by a number. The number tells the turtle how many steps to take.

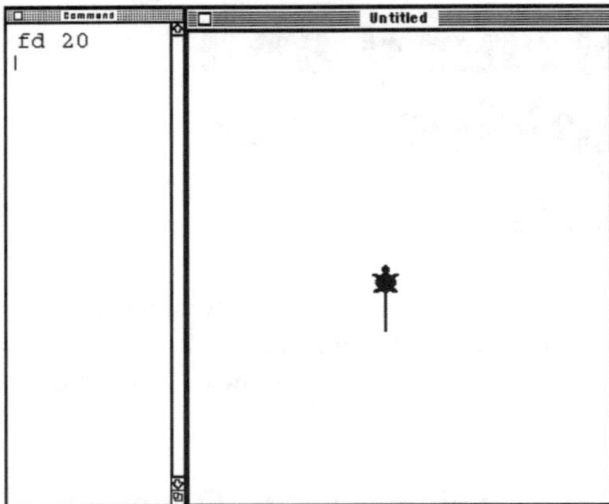

As the turtle moves, it leaves a track on the screen. Type another `fd` command to make the turtle go farther.

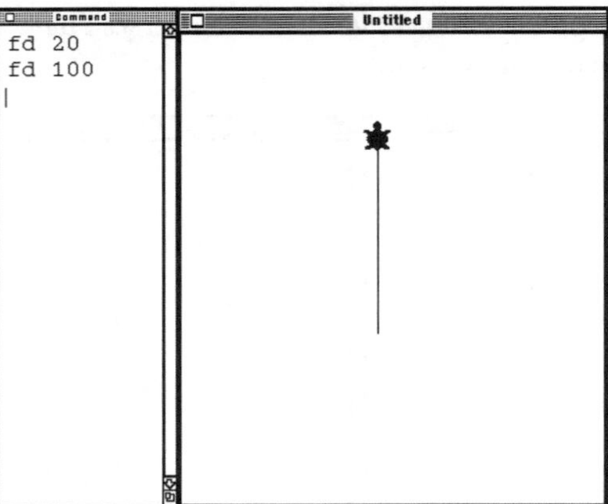

Now try making the turtle change direction: type the `rt` command, followed by a space, followed by a number. The number tells the turtle how many degrees to the right (clockwise) to turn.

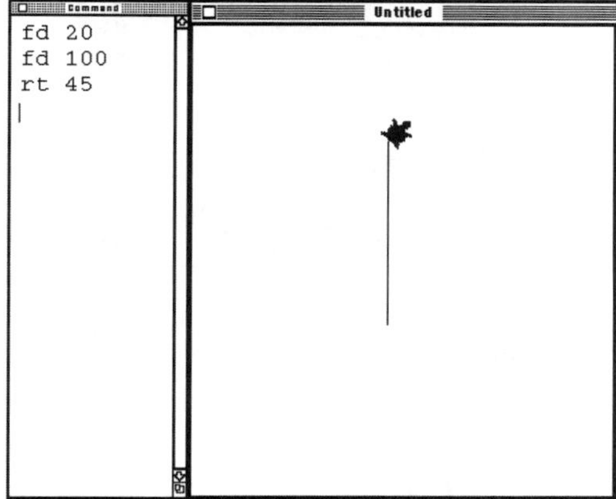

Notice that the turtle does not leave a track when you type a `rt` command. The `rt` command only tells the turtle to face a new direction. To continue drawing the track, type another `fd` command.

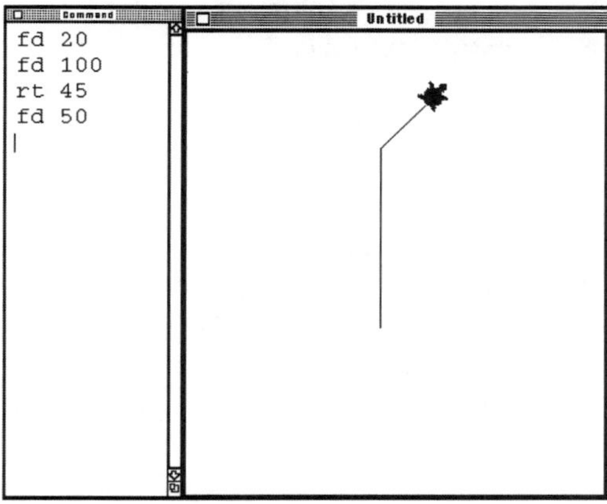

A selection of tools appears at the top of the *Turtle Math* screen. In this problem, you will use the Scale tool and the Change Shape tool. These tools let you change the size and shape of a figure.

Scale

Change Shape

Problem 6.1

Choose one of the figures below. Make the figure by typing the commands in the Command window.

Equilateral triangle	Rectangle	Right trapezoid
`fd 60`	`fd 30`	`fd 52`
`rt 120`	`rt 90`	`rt 90`
`fd 60`	`fd 70`	`fd 30`
`rt 120`	`rt 90`	`rt 60`
`fd 60`	`fd 30`	`fd 60`
	`rt 90`	`rt 120`
	`fd 70`	`fd 60`

After you've drawn the figure, save a copy of it on your computer. To save the drawing, select Save My Work from the File menu. Type a name for your drawing and then click on Save. After you've saved a copy of your drawing, experiment with using the Scale tool and Change Shape tool on your figure. Anytime you want to return to the original figure, just choose Open My Work from the File menu and select the name you chose for your drawing.

A. Which features of the original figure change when you use the Scale tool? Which features of the original figure change when you use the Change Shape tool? Be sure to discuss numbers of sides, side lengths, and angle measures.

B. Which features of the original figure stay the same when you use the Scale tool? Which features of the original figure stay the same when you use the Change Shape tool?

Problem 6.1 Follow-Up

Can either of the tools you investigated be used to create similar figures? To justify your answer, make sketches of what you see on the computer screen including side lengths and angle measures.

Answers to Problem 6.1

A. See page 84g.

B. As you use the Scale tool, the angles do not change, and the ratio between sides stays the same. For example, in a rectangle with adjacent sides of length 24 and 36, the ratio of the sides is 24 to 36, or 2 to 3. As the rectangle is changed with the Scale tool, the ratio of the sides remains 2 to 3. With the Change Shape tool, the lengths of sides that are not adjacent to the selected vertex are not changed, so the ratio of sides *does* change. Also, angles that are not adjacent to the sides that have changed will remain the same.

Answer to Problem 6.1 Follow-Up

See page 84g.

Stretching and Shrinking Flags

You have already studied how scale factors are related to lengths and areas of similar figures. *Turtle Math* is an excellent tool for investigating this concept further.

Problem 6.2

The set of commands below will draw a flag. Type in the commands exactly as they are shown; don't use any shortcuts. When you are finished, save a copy of your flag by using Save My Work from the File menu.

```
fd 80
rt 90
fd 50
rt 90
fd 30
rt 90
fd 50
```

Use the Scale tool to make enlargements and reductions of the flag. Make a chart like the one below, and fill in the missing information.

Scale factor	Sketch of figure	Height of flagpole	Length of flag	Width of flag	Area of flag
1	50, 30, 80	80 steps	50 steps	30 steps	1500 square steps
2					
0.5					
–1					

6.2 Stretching and Shrinking Flags

At a Glance

Grouping: small groups

Launch

- Ask questions that hint at the possibility of negative scale factors.
- Show students how to display whole numbers in the Command window.

Explore

- As students work, remind them to label their drawings.
- Offer students grid paper for their drawings.

Summarize

- Show students how to use the Grid tool.
- Have them share their ideas about negative scale factors and the effect changing dimensions has on area.
- Let students explore other figures. *(optional)*

Answers to Problem 6.2

See page 84h.

Assignment Choices

ACE questions 2, 3, and unassigned choices from earlier problems

■ **Problem 6.2 Follow-Up**

1. What happens to the flag when it is changed by a negative scale factor? Explain why you think this happens.

2. Which scale factors make a flag that is the same size as the original?

3. Which scale factors make a flag that is smaller than the original?

4. Which scale factors make a flag that is larger than the original?

Answers to Problem 6.2 Follow-Up

1. The `fd` command moves in a "negative" direction, so `fd 80` becomes `fd -80`. This means that the turtle backs up 80 steps. It then turns as normal, but once again goes forward by a negative amount, so it backs up. The result is that the figure changes its orientation. A figure of scale –1 is a 180° rotation of the original flag.
2. A scale factor of 1 or –1 will make a flag that is the same size as the original.
3. A scale factor of less than 1 and greater than –1, but not 0, will make a flag that is smaller than the original.
4. A scale factor of greater than 1 or less than –1 will make a flag that is larger than the original.

Applications • Connections • Extensions

As you work on these ACE questions, use your calculator whenever you need it.

Applications

1. Tonya wrote this *Turtle Math* program to draw a star.

```
rt 18
fd 80
rt 144
fd 80
rt 144
fd 80
rt 144
fd 80
rt 144
fd 80
```

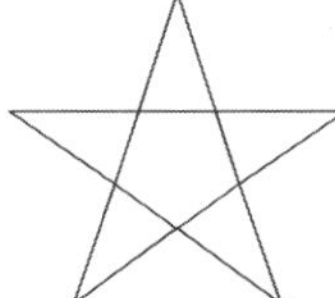

a. Change Tonya's program to draw a star that is similar to Tonya's but a different size.

b. What is the scale factor from Tonya'sx star to the star your prgram draws?

Answers

Applications

1a. Any program structured like Tonya's program, with five equal (all positive or all negative) `fd` or `bk` lines and five (all positive or all negative) `rt 144` or `lt 144` turns will produce a star similar to Tonya's.

1b. The scale factor will be the ratio of the number of steps moved forward (`fd`) in the image to the original forward motion, 80 steps. For example, if the new star has commands of `fd 40`, the scale is 40 to 80, or $\frac{1}{2}$.

Connections

2a. 100 to 40 = $\frac{100}{40}$ = 2.5

2b. 40 to 100 = $\frac{40}{100}$ = 0.4

Connections

2. Squares A and B were made using *Turtle Math.* The Grid tool was used to display a coordinate grid. You can use the grid to measure the size of each square in numbers of turtle steps.

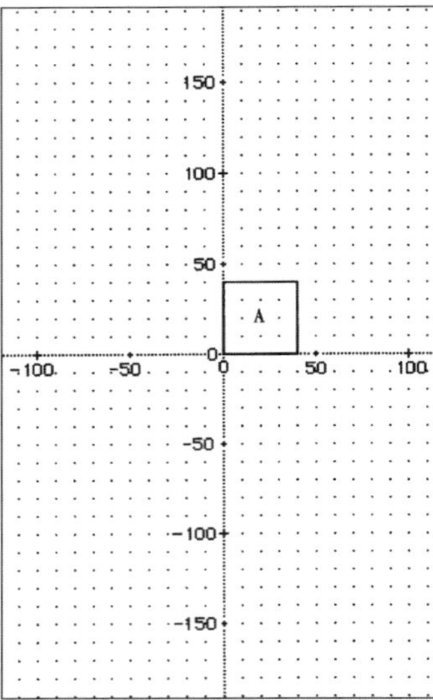

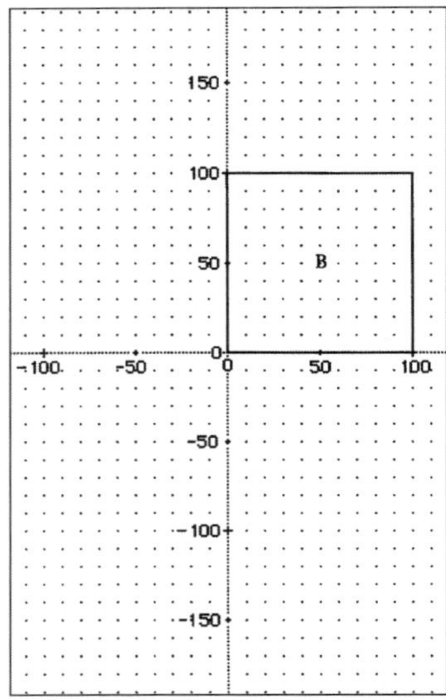

a. What is the scale factor from square A to square B?

b. What is the scale factor from square B to square A?

Extensions

3. The drawing below shows the Drawing window, with a grid, before any commands are entered.

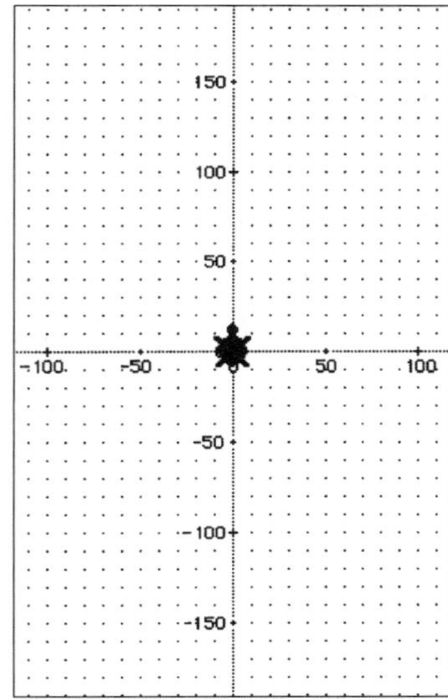

a. Jeff entered the commands below. Make a sketch that shows the turtle's new position.

```
fd -20
fd -35
fd 15
fd -70
fd 160
```

b. Jeff erased the commands to return the turtle to its starting point. Then, he entered each command *twice.* Make a sketch that shows the turtle's new position.

Extensions

3. See page 84h.

Possible Answers

1. If two figures are similar, corresponding angles are equal, and ratios of all corresponding sides are equal. This gives the scale factor between the figures. If the scale factor is 1 or –1, the two figures are congruent and therefore exactly the same. If the scale factor is a nonzero number other than 1 and –1, the figures will not have equal corresponding sides, but the ratios will still be the same. In fact, the ratios between any corresponding length measures will equal the scale factor.

2. The two figures may differ in size and orientation. This means that the lengths of corresponding sides may not be the same, but the ratio of corresponding sides must be the same.

3. The scale factor tells you the factor by which the sides and all other length measures between the two similar figures are related. If the scale factor between the figures is 1 or –1, the figures are congruent. If the scale factor is greater than 1 or less than –1, the image figure is greater than the original (it is stretched). If the scale factor is not 0 and is between –1 and 1 (excluding 1 and –1), the image figure is smaller than the original (it is shrunk).

Mathematical Reflections

In this unit, you have explored what the word *similar* means in mathematics. These questions will help you summarize what you have learned:

1. If two figures are similar, what characteristics of the figures are the same?
2. If two figures are similar, what characteristics of the figures may be different?
3. What does a scale factor tell you about two similar figures?

Think about your answers to these questions, discuss your ideas with other students and your teacher, and then write a summary of your findings in your journal.

Tips for the Linguistically Diverse Classroom

Original Rebus The Original Rebus technique is described in detail in *Getting to Know Connected Mathematics*. Students make a copy of the text before it is discussed. During the discussion, they generate their own rebuses for words they do not understand; the words are made comprehensible through pictures, objects, or demonstrations. Example: Question 1—key words for which students might make rebuses are *figures* (rectangles), *similar* ($\angle A = \angle G$; 1:2; _____ to __________), *characteristics* (angles; rectangle with an arrow pointing to a side).

6.1 • Drawing Similar Figures with a Computer

In this problem, students see changes in scale in a dynamic way. With the use of a computer, they stretch and shrink a figure, transforming it into a new, similar figure.

Launch

How you choose to launch this investigation will depend on computer availability and how much experience your students have had with *Turtle Math*. As you plan your launch, you may want to consider the following.

If you use a computer lab and your access to the lab is limited, plan carefully so students can finish their labwork in one class period. The day before, distribute angle rulers. Take time for a whole-class Logo refresher, then have students practice giving each other instructions using the `fd` and `rt` commands. They can prepare for Problem 6.2 by making their tables in advance.

If you have a small number of computers in your classroom, or students must go in small groups to another site to use computers, you may want some students to work with computers while the others remain at their desks. Here is a plan one teacher uses to accommodate this situation:

"Before the students begin working with computers, we spend time as a class reviewing simple Logo commands and general issues about how to turn on the computer and start the program. The media lab has an aide and enough computers to accommodate half my students. In the media lab, students are able to help each other and don't need my presence. The first day I send half the class to the lab, and the other half stays with me and works in small groups on ACE question 2 (students don't need computers for the ACE questions). We also discuss the Mathematical Reflections for Investigation 6, since these questions are about the entire unit, not just this investigation. The next day, the groups switch. Both groups have the same homework the second night, and we have a whole-class summary the third day. This is a little inefficient—as this investigation requires three days—but I find it useful to have smaller groups discussing this final reflection piece."

Transparencies 6.1B–6.1D give brief instructions for navigating the *Turtle Math* computer screen as it appears in the Macintosh version of the software. These transparencies may be used for classroom demonstrations if a display computer is unavailable. The teacher's guide for Investigation 6 of the *Shapes and Designs* unit offers a thorough introduction to the basics of *Turtle Math,* and you may want to read through it. Also, the teacher's resource guide that comes with the *Turtle Math* software has excellent instructions.

Once you have decided how students will do the computer work, read the introductory material to Problem 6.1, or have them read it on their own. Problem 6.1 gives sets of commands for drawing an equilateral triangle, a rectangle, and a right trapezoid. If your students are already familiar with Logo, you may want them to write their own sets of commands for drawing other figures. If so, remind them that the Scale and Change Shape tools work only with the right turn (`rt`) and the forward (`fd`) commands. An error message will appear if these tools are used with any other commands, such as `lt` or `repeat`.

We have deliberately said very little in the student edition about how the Scale and Change Shape tools work; most students will be able to use them without additional help. Clicking once on either tool causes the screen cursor to change into a picture of an open hand. Moving the hand to either a corner or a side of a figure, then clicking and holding down the mouse, causes the hand to close as it "grabs" the corner or side. The figure can then be dragged with the tool. Notice that you cannot drag the vertex where the turtle begins drawings.

The Change Shape tool stretches or shrinks the sides that are adjacent to the selected vertex or side. The Scale command changes the shape of the figure as it is dragged so that the figure remains similar to the original.

Before students begin, you may want to review saving and opening work.

Explore

Try to let students explore freely as they figure out what the Scale and Change Shape tools do. If their time with the computer is limited, encourage them to take brief notes about what they have discovered about the two tools and then move on to Problem 6.2.

If students have not had much Logo experience, you may wish to remind them that they can monitor changes in side lengths and angle turns by observing how the turtle instructions in the Command window change. (See the example shown in the answer to part A.)

Summarize

This is a good opportunity to review angle and side-length relationships. A common misconception students have is that the angle measures they see on their computer screen are the *internal* measures of the figures drawn. For example, the student edition gives these instructions for drawing an equilateral triangle:

```
fd 60
rt 120
fd 60
rt 120
fd 60
```

The equilateral triangle drawn will have side lengths of 60.

> How do we know that this set of Logo commands will draw an equilateral triangle? *(We know the triangle will be equilateral, because the sides are all the same length and the angle turns are all 120°.)*
>
> What is the measure of each angle in the triangle?

Students may need to measure the angles—by holding an angle ruler up to the computer screen or measuring on a picture of an equilateral triangle or a printout from the program—to answer this question. It is worth the time spent to help them understand that Logo commands tell the turtle how much to turn, *not* the measure of the internal angles.

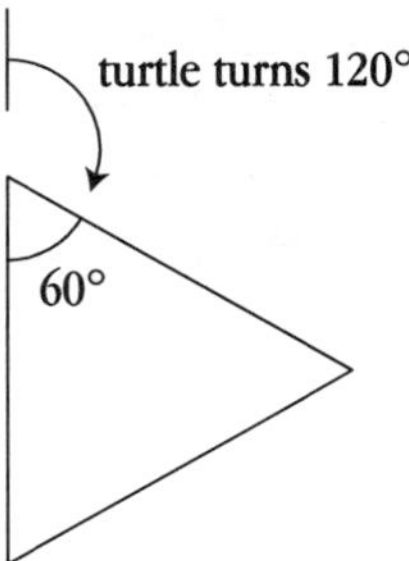

6.2 • Stretching and Shrinking Flags

In this lesson students continue to use *Turtle Math* to explore similarity.

Launch

An important new idea in this problem is the negative scale factor. In the *Accentuate the Negative* unit, students will do their first formal work with negative numbers. Problem 6.2 can help prepare them. Begin by asking:

> We have used the computer to shrink and enlarge figures. As we use the Scale tool, how can we tell what the scale factor is? *(We can watch the Command window and see how the dimensions of the picture change.)*
>
> What is the biggest possible scale factor we can use? *(It depends on the size of the original picture. We have a limited amount of space on the computer screen. The picture can only be enlarged until it reaches the top of the screen.)*
>
> What is the smallest possible scale factor?

Students may give examples of small fractions, such as $\frac{1}{4}$ or $\frac{1}{10}$. As you continue to probe, they may offer 0 or even negative numbers. At this point, leave the question of the smallest scale factor open, giving students a chance to use the computer to investigate the idea.

Introduce Problem 6.2, which asks students to draw a flag and then use the Scale tool to make enlargements and reductions of the flag.

> The scale factor from the original figure to itself is 1. As you complete the table for Problem 6.2, think about what the largest and smallest possible scale factors would be.

Explore

Students will find the task easier if they set the program to display whole numbers only. This is done by clicking the Options menu at the top of the screen and holding down the mouse button to see the menu choices. Continuing to hold down the mouse button, choose Decimal Places and then 0. Releasing the button changes the number of decimal places displayed to 0.

As they enlarge and reduce the flag, students will see the changes in length and width displayed in the Command window. They will have an easier time computing the flag's area if they write dimensions on their sketches. It will be helpful for them to sketch the flags on grid paper and to use the Grid tool on the computer, which superimposes a coordinate grid on the Drawing window (this is pictured on Transparency 6.1D).

Summarize

The two primary ideas in this problem are the effect of negative scale factors (which change the orientation of the object) and how changing a rectangle's dimensions changes its area (doubling the dimensions quadruples the area).

The computer activity offers students an informal conceptual model of extending the number line from positive to negative. Use this opportunity to ***informally*** discuss the idea of negative numbers being smaller than positive numbers (for example, $-1 < 1$) and negative numbers of greater absolute value being smaller (further from zero) than negative numbers of smaller absolute value. For example, even though the scale factor –2 flag is larger than the scale factor –1 flag, $-2 < -1$. However, avoid getting involved in an abstract discussion or bringing in the term ***absolute value***.

What did you discover about the largest and smallest scale factors?

Spend a few minutes letting students share their views, particularly about the smallest scale factor. At this point, it is fine to leave things unresolved. In the *Accentuate the Negative* unit, students will return to these questions when they have learned more about negative numbers.

For the Teacher: Projections

Students may bring up the issue of why, in their previous work, no matter what an image's orientation, scale factors were always positive. Now, however, a minus sign indicates a specific orientation. They may also wonder—since a scale factor of –1 means the flag is turned by 180°—what numbers might be assigned to other orientations. Complete answers to these questions require a discussion of *projections* (also called *dilations*) and *projection points* (or *dilation points*). At this stage, most students will not be ready to learn about projections. However, the following discussion might help you to answer these questions if they arise.

Scaling a figure on a grid is often done by making a transformation called a projection. Directions for scaling normally include not only the scale factor but the projection point. Following are three examples of changing a figure by a scale factor of –1. The three figures have different locations on the grid because the projection points (point *P* in each figure) differ.

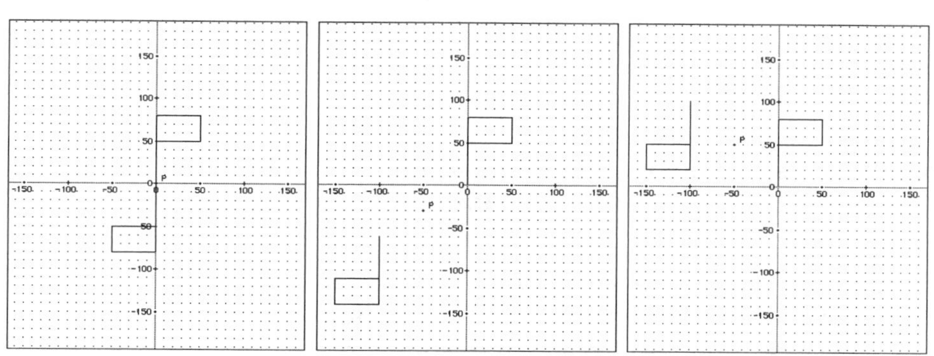

Below are three examples of figures that have been scaled by a factor of 2, with different projection points.

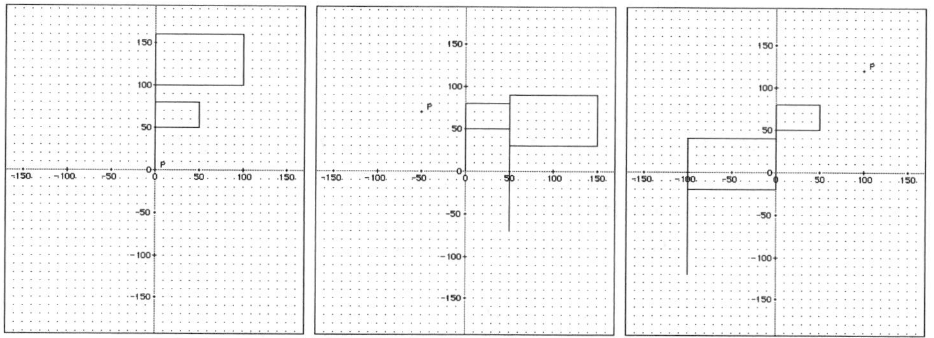

An important feature of a figure and its projection is that, if you draw lines between corresponding vertices of the two figures, all the lines will meet at a central point. This is the projection point.

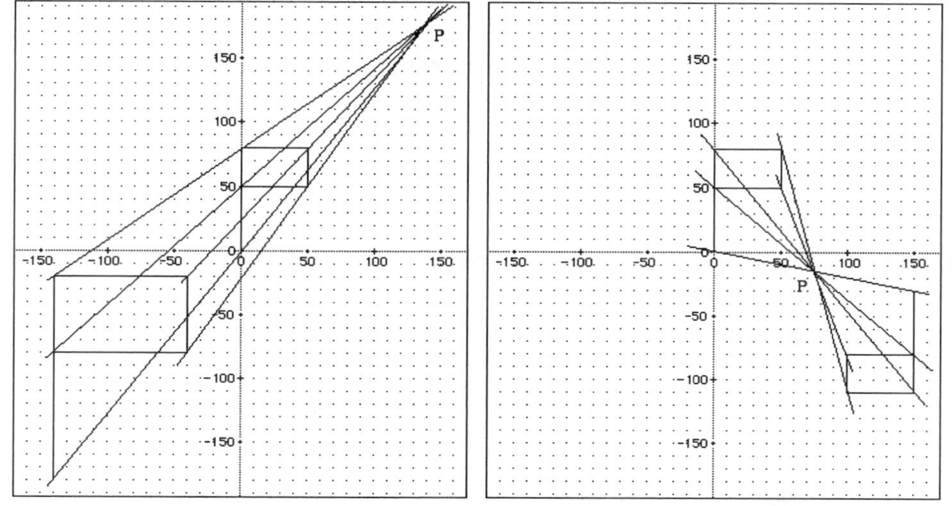

If the original figure and the projection are on the same side of the projection point, we say that the scale factor of the projection is positive. If the projection is on the opposite side, we say the scale factor is negative. The distance from the new figure to the projection point is related to the distance of the original figure from the projection point by the scale factor. In other words, if the new figure is twice as far from the projection point as the original figure, and they are on the same side of the projection point, we say that the new figure has a scale factor of 2. If the new figure is twice as far from the projection point as the original, and they are on opposite sides of the projection point, we say that the new figure has a scale factor of –2.

We use *Turtle Math* to demonstrate negative scale factors, because the turtle provides a nice visual model of moving in the same direction (for example, `fd 100`) when the scale factor is positive and in the opposite direction (`fd -100`) when it is negative.

A restriction of drawing similar figures with the Scale tool is that there are a limited number of locations that the stretched or shrunk figure can occupy. There are two reasons for this: *Turtle Math* stretches and shrinks figures only by doing projections, and it will scale figures from only one projection point, (0, 0).

The change in orientation that a figure undergoes as it is projected with a negative scale factor is a 180° rotation, a transformation that students will see again in the grade 8 unit *Maneuvering in the Plane*. The projection point that we use to specify the location of a similar figure can be compared to the center of a turn. While, in common language, we usually only talk about how *much* to turn, and in which direction, that does not tell the whole story. To be mathematically explicit, we must specify the location of the *center* of a turn as well as the direction and number of degrees turned. When we use the Scale tool to change the flag's orientation, we are transforming it in the same way as we would if we turned it about a centerpoint at (0, 0).

Some geometry software packages have a dilation or projection option. Students who are ready for an extra challenge may enjoy experimenting with one of those. You might also suggest that they try the transformations possible with the *Turtle Math* Motions menu.

If you have time, you may want students to experiment with changing the scale of other figures, such as those used in Problem 6.1. The equilateral triangle makes a nice demonstration.

> If we transform an equilateral triangle into another equilateral triangle by a scale factor of 2, how does the area change? *(The area increases by a factor of 4.)*

Transforming a figure by a scale factor of 3 is also an interesting question to explore. However, the flag in this problem is too large to expand to that size.

Can we transform the flag into a similar picture using a scale factor of 3? *(Yes, but not on the computer; the screen is not big enough to display it.)*

If we draw the flag, what would its dimensions be? *(height of flagpole, 240 steps; length of flag, 150 steps; width of flag, 90 steps)*

How would the area of the flag change? *(The area would be 9 times as great—13,500 square steps.)*

Additional Answers

Answers to Problem 6.1

A. The Scale tool changes all the side lengths in a figure. The Change Shape tool changes only the side lengths that are adjacent to the selected vertex or side. Neither tool affects the number of sides. The Change Shape tool also changes the angles measures in a figure, and it may change the turtle commands. In the example below, the original first command was `fd 100`. Selecting a line segment and dragging it with the Change Shape tool caused the first line the turtle drew to angle 22° to the right. This in turn caused the command `rt 22` to be added in the Command window.

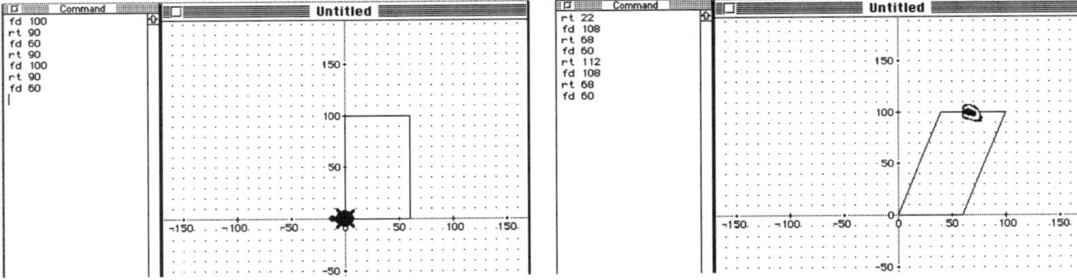

Answer to Problem 6.1 Follow-Up

The Scale tool transforms a figure into other, similar figures. We know that these figures are similar, because the angles and the ratios between the side lengths are both equal.

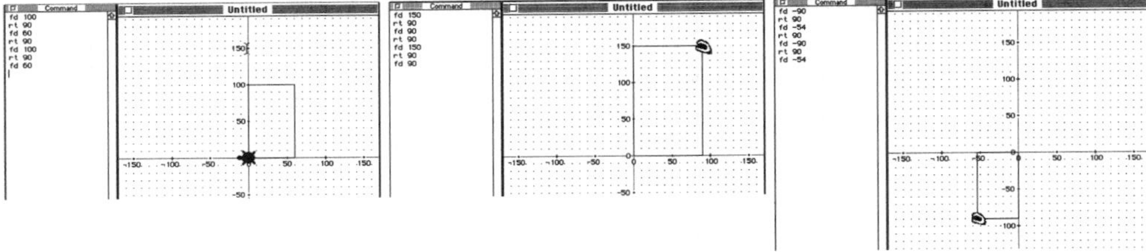

Answers to Problem 6.2

Scale factor	Sketch of figure	Height of flagpole	Length of flag	Width of flag	Area of flag
1	50, 30, 80	80 steps	50 steps	30 steps	1500 square steps
2	100, 60, 160	160 steps	100 steps	60 steps	6000 square steps
0.5	25, 15, 40	40 steps	25 steps	15 steps	375 square steps
–1	80, 30, 50	80 steps	50 steps	30 steps	1500 square steps

ACE Answers

Extensions

3a.

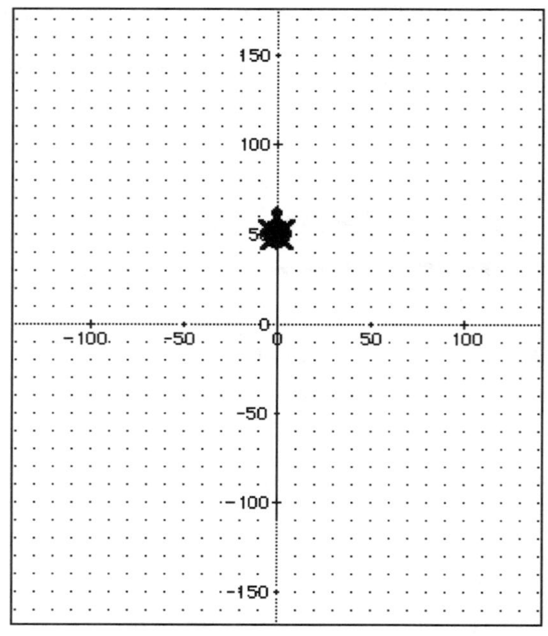

3b.

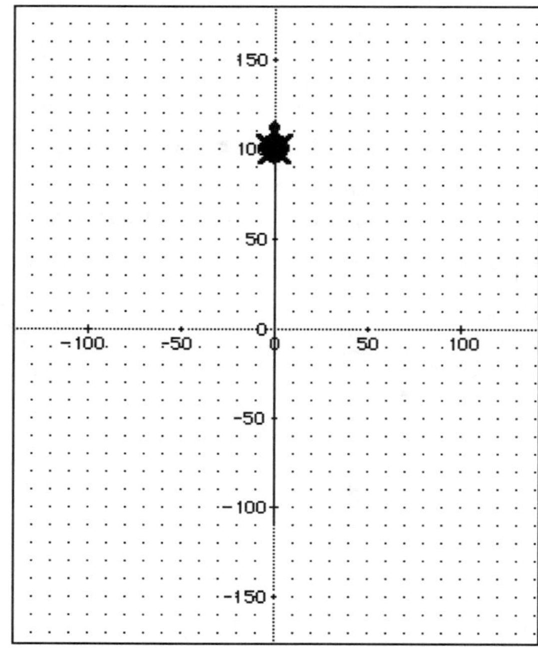

The Unit Project

All-Similar Shapes

Throughout this unit, you have worked with problems that helped you understand what it means for two shapes to be similar. You have learned that not all rectangles are similar. For example, an $8\frac{1}{2}$ by 11-inch sheet of paper is rectangular, and so is a business size envelope, but the envelope is long and narrow—not the same shape as the sheet of paper.

A group of students decided to look at rectangles that are square. They found that no matter what size square they drew, every square was similar to shape B in the ShapeSet and to all other squares. They concluded that *all squares are similar!* They decided to call a square an All-Similar shape.

The students wondered whether there were any other All-Similar shapes like the square. That is, are there any other groups of shapes called by the same name that are similar to all other shapes called by that name? Use your ShapeSet to investigate this question.

1. Make a list of the names of all the different types of shapes in the ShapeSet—squares, rectangles, triangles, equilateral triangles, circles, and regular hexagons.
2. For each type of shape, list the shapes (using their letter names) that belong in that group.
3. Sort the different types of shapes into two groups: All-Similar shapes (such as squares) and shapes that are not All-Similar (such as rectangles).
4. Describe the ways in which All-Similar shapes are alike.

Assigning the Unit Project

The unit project, All-Similar Shapes, helps students review what they have learned about similarity. A more detailed description of this project appears as a blackline master in the Assessment Resources section. You might assign the project as a take-home assignment for students to work on individually. Provide each student with copies of the blackline masters of the ShapeSet. Alternatively, you can give students a class period to work in groups on the project using the ShapeSet.

The categories of shapes students list may differ, but might include triangles, quadrilaterals, equilateral triangles, isosceles triangles, rectangles, trapezoids, squares, regular pentagons, rhombuses, regular hexagons, regular heptagons, regular octagons, and circles. Notice that these categories are not mutually exclusive. In addition to the shapes in the ShapeSet, you might encourage students to create their own shapes for each category.

The group of All-Similar shapes should include circles, squares, equilateral triangles, and the various regular polygons. Students should recognize that for all of these shapes, except for circles, all the side lengths and angle measures are equal.

Answers

Using Your Understanding of Similarity

1a. See page 86b.

b. Perimeter grows by the scale factor. For example, the perimeter of triangle J is 2.5 times the perimeter of triangle C.

The area grows by the square of the scale factor. For example, the area of triangle J is 2.5^2 or 6.25 times the area of triangle C.

Some students may try to subdivide triangle C into congruent copies of triangle J.

c. Triangles E and F are not similar to any of the triangles A, C, J, or G.

d. H and B are the only pair of similar parallelograms. The scale factor from H to B is 2.5; the scale factor from B to H is 0.4.

e. The perimeter of parallelogram B is 2.5 times the perimeter of H. The area of B is 2.5^2 or 6.25 times the area of parallelogram H.

f. Parallelograms D and I are not similar to each other or to parallelograms B or H.

Looking Back and Looking Ahead

Unit Reflections

Working on the problems in this unit helped you to understand the concept of *similarity* as it is applied to geometric shapes. You learned how to create similar shapes and how to determine whether two shapes are similar. You also discovered the relationships between the areas and perimeters of similar shapes and investigated applications using properties of similar shapes.

Using Your Understanding of Similarity— To test your understanding of similarity consider the following problems that ask you to recognize similar shapes and deduce their properties.

1. *The square has been subdivided into six triangles and four parallelograms. Some pairs of triangles and some pairs of parallelograms are similar.*

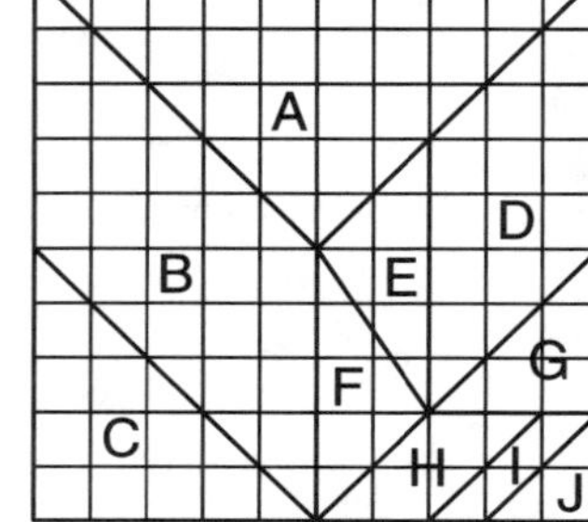

a. List two pairs of similar triangles in the figure. For each pair, give a scale factor that describes the size relationship of the two triangles.

b. Pick one pair of similar triangles and explain how their perimeters are related and how their areas are related.

c. List several pairs of triangles in the figure that are *not similar.*

d. List all pairs of similar parallelograms in the figure. For each pair, give a scale factor that describes the size relationship between the two parallelograms.

e. Pick two similar parallelograms and explain how their perimeters are related and how their areas are related.

f. List several pairs of parallelograms in the figure that are *not similar*.

How to Use
Looking Back and Looking Ahead: Unit Reflections

The first part of this section includes problems that allow students to demonstrate their mathematical understandings and skills. The second part gives them an opportunity to explain their reasoning. This section can be used as a review to help students stand back and reflect on the "big" ideas and connections in the unit. This section may be assigned as homework, followed up with class discussion the next day. Focus on the *Explaining Your Reasoning* section in the discussion. Encourage the students to refer to the problems to illustrate their reasoning.

2 *Suppose that a triangle is drawn on a coordinate grid.*

a. Which of the following rules will transform the given triangle into a similar triangle?

i. $(3x, 3y)$ **ii.** $(x + 3, y + 2)$ **iii.** $(2x, 4x)$

iv. $(2x, 2y + 1)$ **v.** $(1.5x, 1.5y)$

b. For each of the rules in part a that will produce a shape similar to the original triangle, give the scale factor from the original triangle to its image.

3 *The seventh-grade class photograph at Tierra del Sol Middle School measures 12 cm by 20 cm. The class officers want to enlarge the photo to fit on a large poster.*

a. Can the original photo be enlarged to 60 cm by 90 cm?

b. Can the original photo be enlarged to 42 cm by 70 cm?

Explaining Your Reasoning—To answer the questions in Problems 1–3, you had to use several basic properties of similar figures. You should be able to justify the answers you gave by applying those basic principles of similarity.

1. What condition(s) must be satisfied for two polygons to be called similar? What questions do you ask yourself when deciding whether two shapes are similar?
2. Suppose shape A is similar to shape B and the scale factor from A to B is a number k.
   - **a.** How will the perimeters of the two figures be related?
   - **b.** How will the areas of the two figures be related?
3. If two triangles are similar, what do you know about
   - **a.** the measures of sides in the two figures?
   - **b.** the measures of angles in the two figures?
4. Which of the following statements about similarity are true and which are false?
   - **a.** Any two equilateral triangles are similar.
   - **b.** Any two rectangles are similar.
   - **c.** Any two squares are similar.
   - **d.** Any two isosceles triangles are similar.

You will study and use ideas of similarity in several future *Connected Mathematics* units, especially when it is important to compare sizes and shapes of geometric figures. Basic principles of similarity are also used in a variety of practical and scientific problems when enlarging or shrinking of images is needed as in photography and photocopying.

2a. i. $(3x, 3y)$;
ii. $(x + 3, y + 2)$;
iv. $(2x, 2y + 1)$; and
v. $(1.5x, 1.5y)$

b. In Rule i the scale factor is 3;
in Rule ii the scale factor is 1;
in Rule iv the scale factor is 2;
in Rule v the scale factor is 1.5.

3a. No; the 12 cm by 20 cm photo is not similar to a photo that is 60 cm by 90 cm. Note that $\frac{12}{20}$ does not equal $\frac{60}{90}$.

b. The photo can be enlarged to a photo that is 42 cm by 70 cm. The scale factor from the small photo to the larger photo is 3.5.

Explaining Your Reasoning

1. The ratio of corresponding sides must be equal and the measures of corresponding angles must be equal.
Possible questions:
- Is the ratio of corresponding sides equal?
- Is there one number by which I can multiply each side length of one polygon to get the corresponding side lengths of the other polygon?
- Are the corresponding angles equal?

2a. The ratio of the perimeters is k or the perimeter of figure A is k times the perimeter of figure B.

b. The ratio of the areas is k^2, or the area of figure A is k^2 times the area of figure B, or k^2 copies of figure A will cover figure B. Students may say $k \times k$ rather than k^2.

3, 4. See page 86b.

Looking Back and Looking Ahead

Answers

Using Your Understanding of Similarity

1a. Triangles A, C, G, and J are all similar isosceles right triangles.
Triangles E and F are similar because they are congruent. They are not similar to the preceding set.

The lengths of some of the sides of the triangles are not rational numbers. To show that triangle J is similar to triangle C, note that the lengths of the legs of triangle C are 2.5 times the lengths of the legs of triangle J.

Students should be able to recognize that the length of the hypotenuse of triangle C is 2.5 times the length of the hypotenuse of triangle J. Note that the length of either hypotenuse is not a rational number, but each is the diagonal of a unit square. Thus, the hypotenuse of triangle C is 2.5 times the length of the hypotenuse of triangle J. Finding a scale factor from triangles C, G or J to triangle A may be more difficult, but students should be able to find the scale factor between pairs of triangles among C, G and J.

Note: The ≈ symbol is read "is approximately equal to."

Scale factors are:
From J to C: 2.5; C to J: $\frac{1}{2.5}$ or 0.4

From J to G: 1.5; G to J: $\frac{1}{1.5}$ or $\frac{2}{3} \approx 0.67$

From J to A: ≈ 3.5; A to J: $\frac{1}{3.5}$ or $\frac{2}{7} \approx 0.29$

From G to C: $\frac{5}{3}$; C to G: $\frac{3}{5}$ or 0.6

From G to A: $\frac{(5\sqrt{2})}{3} \approx 2.35$; A to G: $\frac{1}{2.35} \approx 0.43$;

From C to A: $\sqrt{2} \approx 1.4$; A to C: $\frac{1}{\sqrt{2}}$ or $\frac{5}{7} \approx 0.71$

From E to F or F to E: 1. These two triangles are congruent.

The scale factor going in the reverse direction is the reciprocal of the scale factor for the original order.

Explaining Your Reasoning

3a. The ratio of the measures of corresponding sides is equal. There is one number, the scale factor, which can be used to multiply each side of one triangle to get the corresponding measure of each side of the other triangle.

b. The measures of corresponding angles are equal.

4a. True. Since the lengths of the sides of an equilateral triangle are equal, the ratio of corresponding sides of any two equilateral triangles is the same. The measure of each corner angle of an equilateral triangle is 60°.

b. False. Two rectangles need not be similar. Consider a square whose side lengths are 5 cm and a rectangle whose length is 5 cm and width is 2 cm. They are not similar.

c. True. Any two squares are similar since each angle is 90° and the ratio of length to width in any square is 1. The ratios of corresponding side lengths are equal.

d. False. Isosceles triangles need not be similar. For example, a triangle with side lengths 3, 3 and 5 is not similar to a triangle with side lengths 3, 3 and 4.

Assessment Resources

Preparation Notes

Students are asked in several of the assessment pieces to decide whether two or more shapes are similar. Sometimes they are asked to draw the shapes to determine whether they are similar; sometimes they are given dimensions. With these types of problems, grid paper and dot paper can be very helpful. We recommend that students have access to either or both of these for all assessment pieces.

Quiz B

In Quiz B, students are asked to make a paper model of a television screen. This will require large rolls of paper (or smaller sheets of paper and tape), rulers, and scissors.

The Unit Test Take-Home Project

The Unit Test Take-Home Project gives students an opportunity to demonstrate their understanding of similarity concepts in a creative way. This activity is the capstone for the unit's theme of how the area of similar figures is related to their side lengths and an extension of the work students have done in class. Teachers have used this project for portfolio entries, mall displays, open houses, hallway bulletin boards, and school newspaper articles.

Students will first select a picture to enlarge or shrink. They will put a transparent grid over their picture (or draw their picture on a coordinate grid), determine ordered pairs, find new ordered pairs, and graph enough points to create a new image of the picture. In a report, they will elaborate on the techniques they used and describe how the image compares to the original. They are expected to verify or prove how the figure changed and how it remained the same by making comparisons between the original and the image.

A few days before assigning the project, have each student select a picture to use. You may want to supply coloring books (a good source for simple pictures), magazines, or comic sections of newspapers. In addition, have the following materials available:

large sheets of paper or newsprint
rulers
transparent grids
grid paper
angle rulers
glue sticks and tape
colored markers or pencils
tracing paper

Distribute the Unit Test Take-Home Project handout. We recommend that you use one class period to start the project, then allow students two to three days outside of class to work on the project. Use a second class period for students to receive feedback and make revisions as they complete their projects. They may need additional time outside of class to finalize their revisions.

Optional Unit Project

The optional Unit Project provides an opportunity for students to further develop their understanding of similarity. Students are asked to investigate several types of shapes and to determine whether all shapes of that type are similar (for example, *all* squares are similar) or not (for example, not all rectangles are similar). Shapes that do have this characteristic are dubbed "All-Similar" shapes.

Preparation Notes

Each student or small group will need a ShapeSet for this investigation. (If you do not have ShapeSet, you can make them by copying the blackline masters provided onto sheets of paper and cutting out the shapes.) They may also investigate additional shapes of their choice or design. Students will also need dot paper and centimeter or half-centimeter grid paper.

Because the task is a mathematical investigation that requires a great deal of time, it would be reasonable to have students work in groups of two or three. You may choose to have each group turn in one final report or have each member complete his or her own report.

Distribute the Unit Project handout. Read through the task with your students, making sure they understand (1) what it means to sort the shapes into different groups, (2) that shapes can be in more than one group, and (3) what it means to be an All-Similar shape.

We recommend that you use one class period to start the project, then give students two or three days outside of class to continue to work. In a second class period, students could compare findings and make revisions.

You may want to have groups or individuals share their results. It is not uncommon for some students to be able to identify some shapes that are an All-Similar shape—such as circles and equilateral triangles—but not be able to generalize that *all* regular-shaped figures are All-Similar shapes. Listing the All-Similar shape groups and describing the characteristics of these shapes may help students to see that they are all regular.

If your students have math portfolios, this project could be included in their portfolios. The students' drawings and written descriptions would serve as good indicators of what students have learned in this unit.

Name ______________________ Date ______________

Check-Up

1. A square and its image are shown on the grids below.

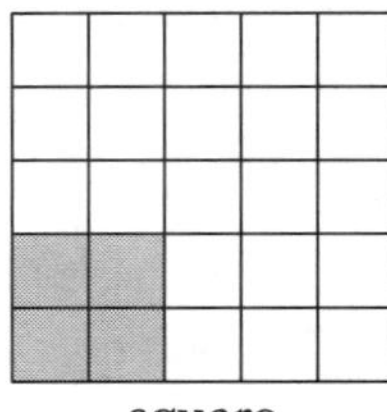
square

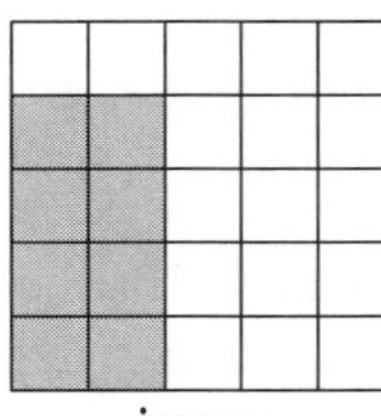
image

   a. Which of these rules was used to transform the square into the image?

   $(2x, 4y)$ $(2x, y)$ $(2x, 2y)$ $(x, 2y)$ $(x, 4y)$

   b. Are the square and its image mathematically similar? Explain.

2. Consider rectangle Z. Which of the other rectangles are similar to rectangle Z? For each rectangle you identify, explain why it is similar to rectangle Z.

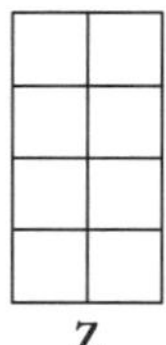
Z

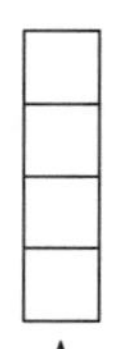
A

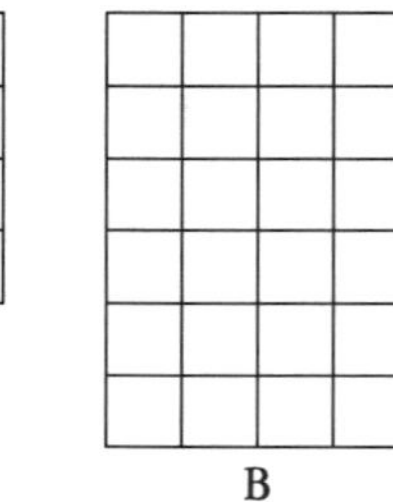
B

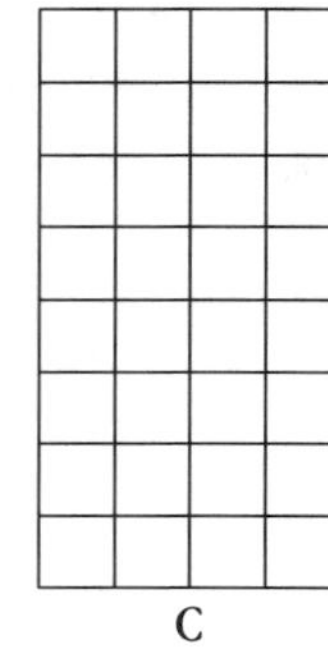
C

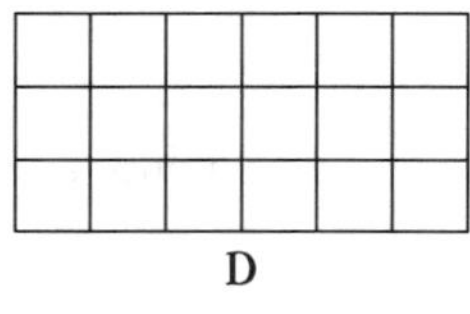
D

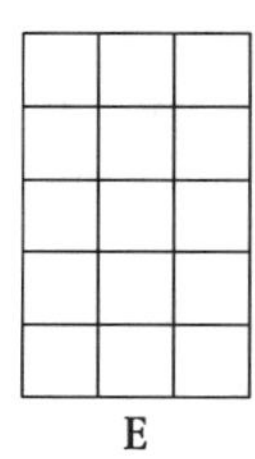
E

Name ______________________ Date ____________

Check-Up

3. These triangles are similar.

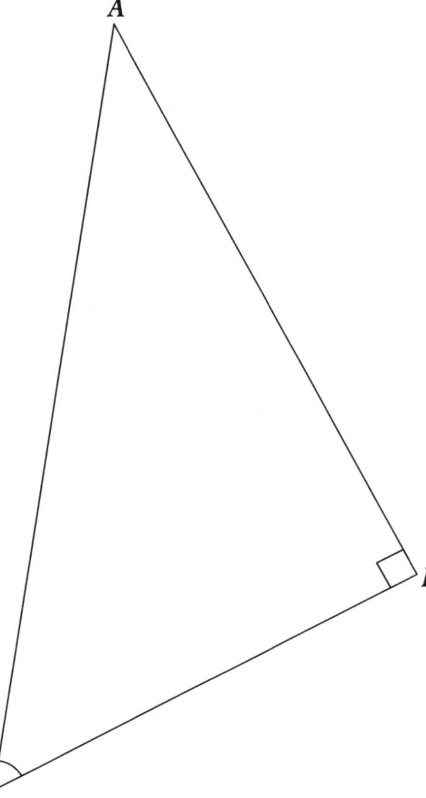

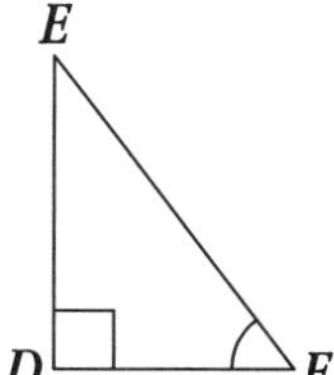

a. Name all the corresponding sides.

Side *AB* corresponds to side ______ .

Side *AC* corresponds to side ______ .

Side *BC* corresponds to side ______ .

b. Name all the corresponding angles.

$\angle D$ corresponds to $\angle$ ______ .

$\angle E$ corresponds to $\angle$ ______ .

$\angle F$ corresponds to $\angle$ ______ .

Name ______________________________ Date ______________

Check-Up

4. These triangles are similar.

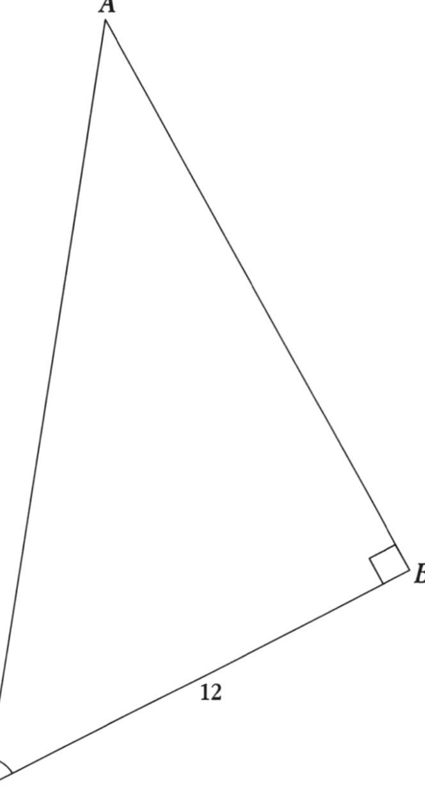

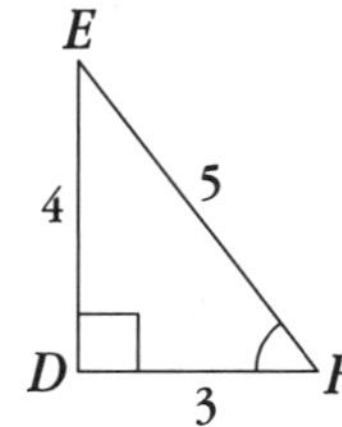

a. Using the side lengths of triangle *DEF* and the fact that the triangles are similar, what are the lengths of sides *AC* and *AB*?

side *AC* = ______ side *AB* = ______

b. What is the scale factor from triangle *DEF* to triangle *ABC*?

c. What is the scale factor from triangle *ABC* to triangle *DEF*?

d. How many times greater is the perimeter of triangle *ABC* than the perimeter of triangle *DEF*?

Names ______________________________ Date ______________

Quiz A

1. The triangles below are similar.

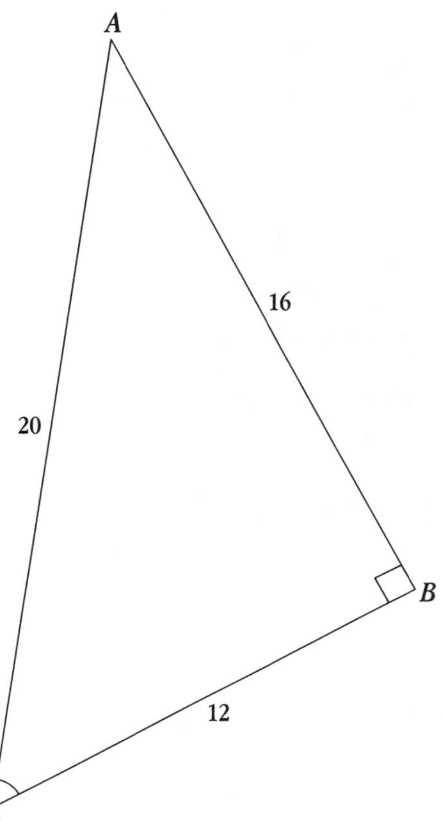

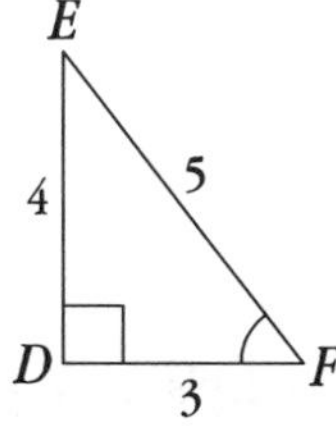

a. How many copies of triangle *DEF* would it take to cover triangle *ABC* with no overlaps or gaps?

b. Subdivide triangle *ABC* into smaller triangles congruent to triangle *DEF*, showing how the small triangles exactly cover the large triangle.

Names ____________________ Date ____________

Quiz A

2. Ryan drew a one-eyed triangle character on dot paper. Ashley used the rule $(3x, 3y)$ to enlarge Ryan's drawing, and she drew the character below.

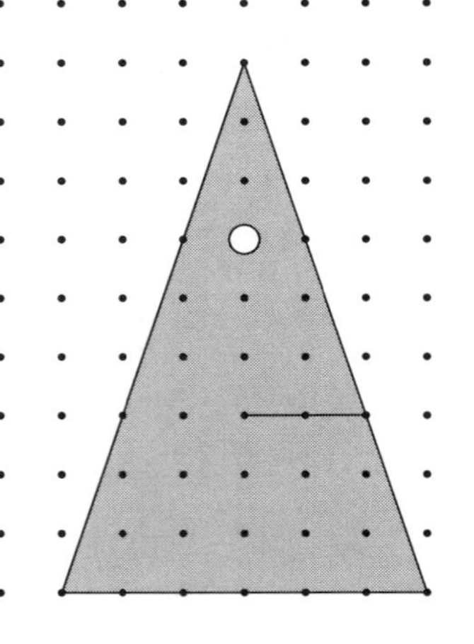

a. Simone saw Ashley's drawing and doubled all the lengths to create her own character. On the grids below, sketch Ryan's original character and Simone's new version of Ashley's character.

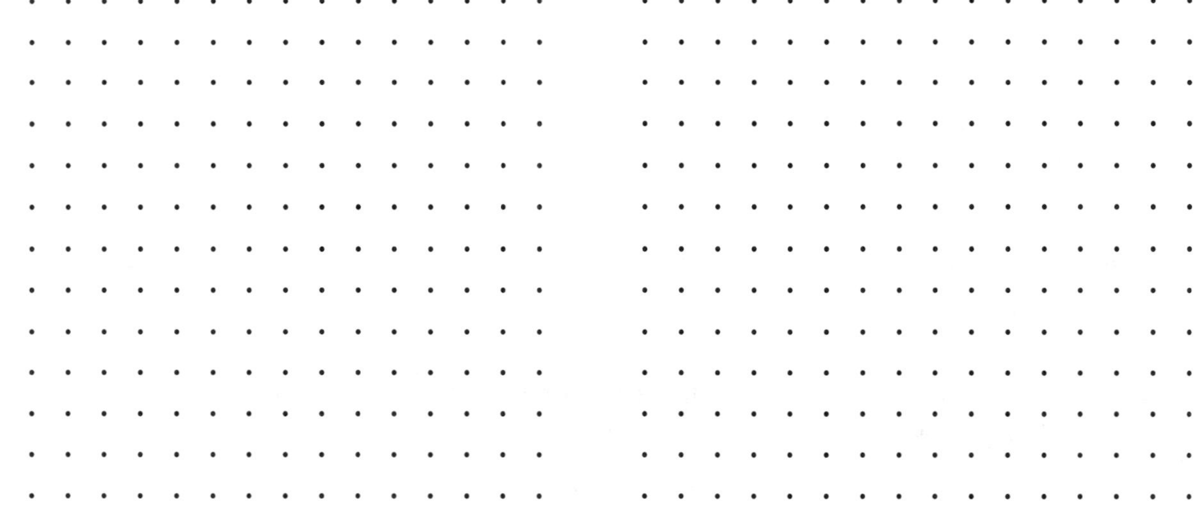

Ryan's one-eyed character

Simone's one-eyed character

Names ______________________________ Date ____________

Quiz A

b. Are Ryan's and Simone's characters similar? Explain.

c. Write a rule that would create Simone's character from Ryan's character.

3. a. Megan wanted to make a new video game character. Write a rule that would transform Mug (x, y) (see Problem 2.1 in your book) into Slug, who is very wide and not very tall.

b. Megan wanted Slug to move up (but not over) on the grid. What rule could do this for her?

c. Is Slug mathematically similar to Mug? Why or why not?

4. Are shapes A and B similar? Explain your answer.

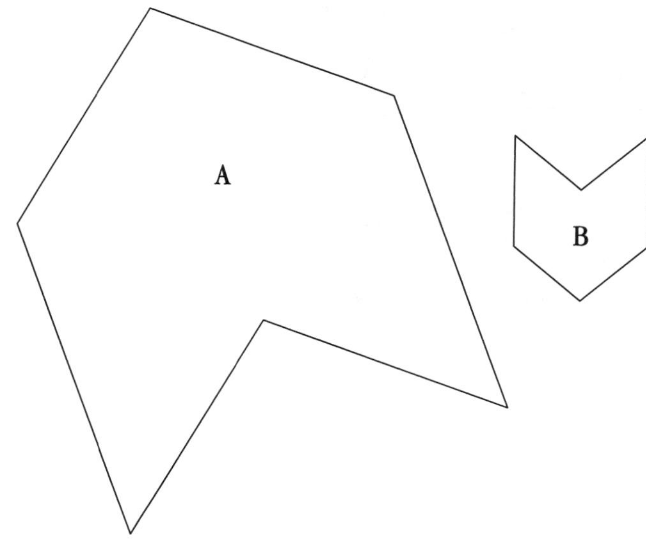

Names ____________________ Date ____________

Quiz B

1. The three triangles below are similar. Find the missing measurements.

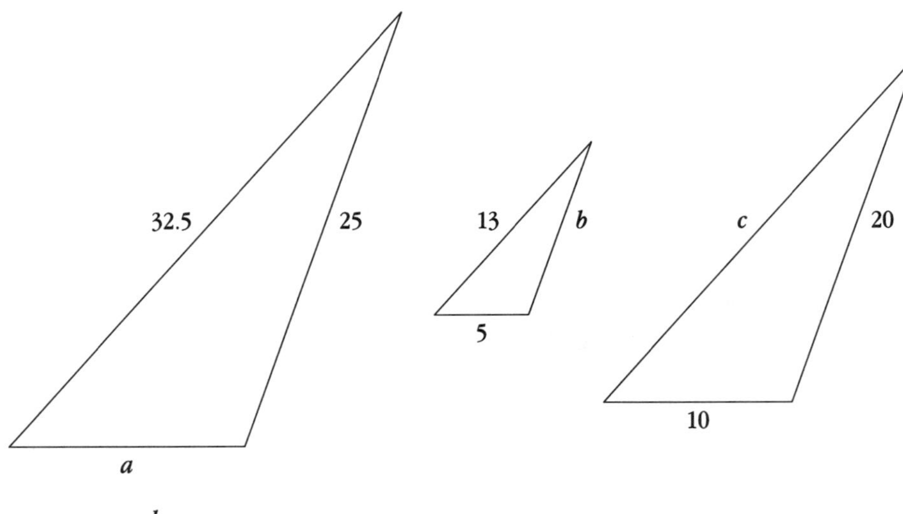

a = ____ *b* = ____ *c* = ____

In 2–5, use this information: Ken is an architect. He designed a house and made a model of it to show his client. This is an illustration of Ken's model.

Here are some of the measurements Ken knows:

	Model	Actual house
Height of door	10 cm	2 m
Height of building	40 cm	

Names ______________________________ Date ______________

Quiz B

2. What will the height of the actual house be? Show how you found your answer.

3. Ken used $\frac{1}{2}$ of a square yard of carpeting for six of the rooms in the model. How much carpeting will be needed in the actual house for the six rooms? Show how you found your answer.

4. If the model has two chimneys, how many chimneys will the actual house have? Explain your answer.

5. Ken used 11 centimeters of molding to frame a window of the model. How much molding will be needed to frame the same window of the actual house? Explain.

In 6–7, use this information: The dimensions of one picture frame on a reel of film are 1.6 cm by 2.2 cm. The dimensions of the television screen in Jin's bedroom are 18.8 cm by 24.5 cm.

6. Can one frame of a movie be enlarged to fill Jin's television screen completely, without eliminating any of the picture? Explain.

7. Jin's parents want to purchase a big-screen television for the family room. Jin wonders whether a frame of a movie could be enlarged to fit a big television screen.

   a. Give one set of dimensions for a television screen that could enlarge the frame of a movie without eliminating any of the picture.

Names ____________________ Date ____________

Quiz B

b. Use paper and tape to make a model showing the actual dimensions of your television screen from part a. Label the dimensions of your model.

c. Give the scale factor from the frame of a movie to your model television screen.

In 8–10, use this picture of a book, a meterstick, and a mitten.

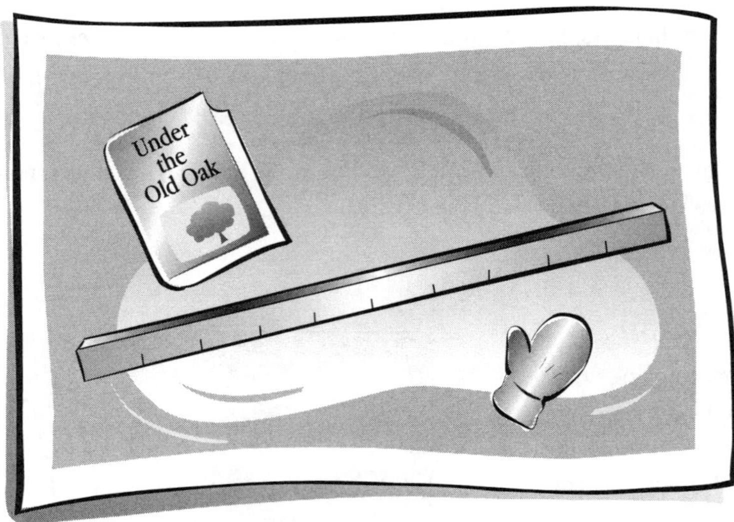

8. How do the three objects in the picture compare to their actual size? In other words, what is the approximate scale factor from the real objects to the objects in the picture? Explain how you determined the scale factor.

9. Use the picture to find the dimensions (the length and width) of the real book.

10. Find the length of the real mitten.

Assign these questions as additional homework, or use them as review, quiz, or test questions.

1. The ratio of the sides of a rectangle is $\frac{2}{3}$. Which of these could be the ratio of the sides of a similar rectangle?

   $\frac{4}{9}$ $\frac{4}{3}$ $\frac{2}{6}$ $\frac{4}{5}$ $\frac{6}{9}$

2. Which of the following rectangles is similar to a 10 by 15 rectangle?

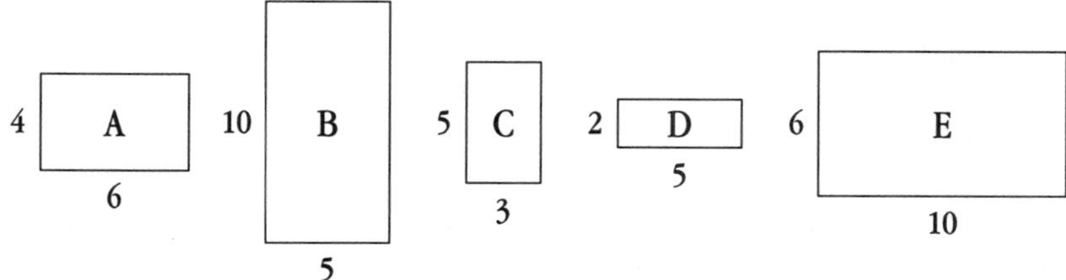

3. The Polygon Tool and Die company has created a new logo (a symbol for their company). They want to stamp their logo on small, medium, and large pieces of equipment. The size of the logo must match the size of the equipment, but the logos must all be similar. Design a logo for Polygon Tool and Die, and sketch three similar figures for the logo. Explain how you know they are similar.

4. In a–c, explain what would happen to a figure if you transformed it using the given rule.
   a. $(3x, 6y)$
   b. $(x + 2, y + 1)$
   c. $(2x, 2y + 5)$

5. The three rectangles below are similar. Find the missing measurements.

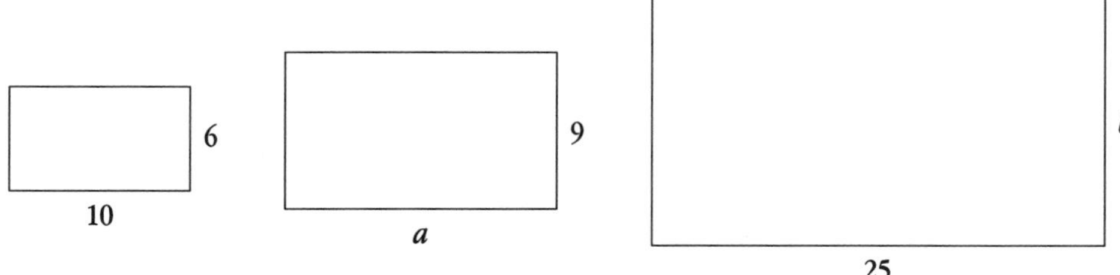

$a =$ ______ $b =$ ______

6. Complete the table below.

A 1
4

Rectangle	Scale factor	Short side	Long side	Perimeter	Area
A	1	1	4		
B	3				
C	10				
D	$\frac{1}{2}$				

7. If two figures are similar, which of the following ***might*** be different? Circle your answers, and explain each choice you make.

number of sides	size of angles
lengths of corresponding sides	ratio of corresponding sides
shape	area

8. A rectangle has dimensions of 1 and 6. Another rectangle was drawn from it using a scale factor of 1.5.
   a. The area of the large rectangle is how many times the area of the small rectangle?
   b. The perimeter of the large rectangle is how many times the perimeter of the small rectangle?

9. Gerald wanted to find the height of the flagpole at the entrance to his school. He used a mirror and recorded some measurements on a drawing. What is the height of the flagpole?

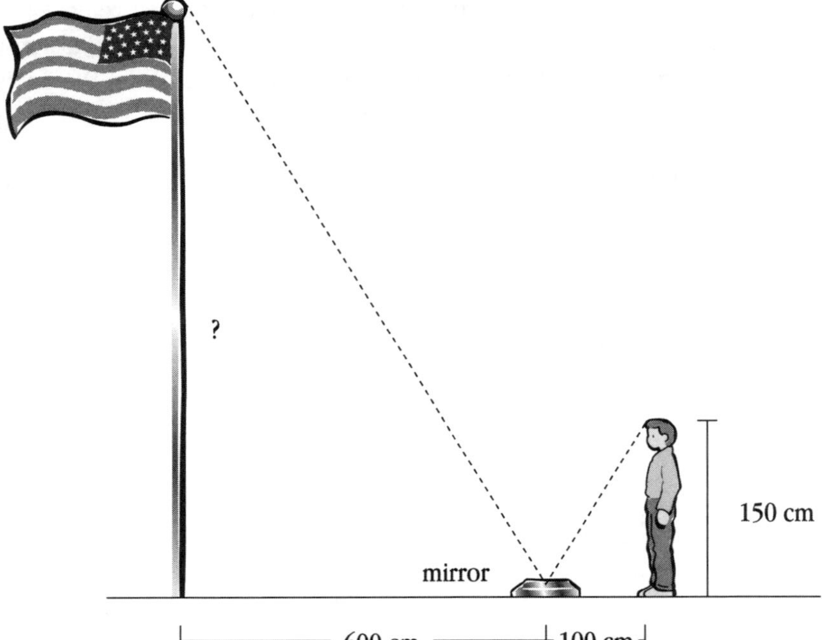

10. Below is a triangle and its image.

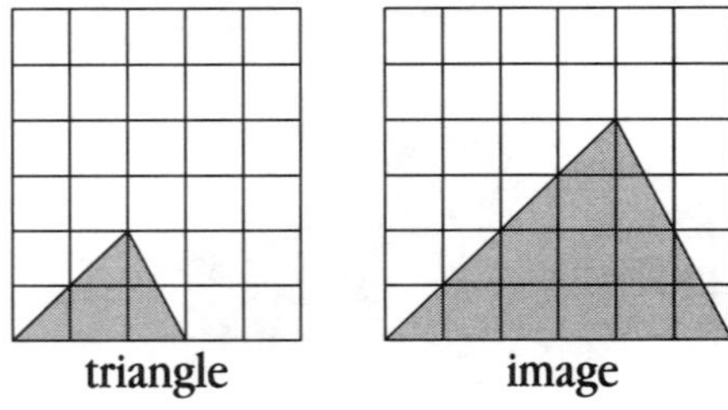

   a. Which of these rules was used to make the image?
   $(2x, 2y)$ $(x, 2y)$ $(2x, y)$ $(2x, 4y)$ $(4x, 2y)$
   b. Are the triangle and its image similar? Explain.

11. Mariella is a character in the Amusement Park video game. She is made according to these coordinates:

Body *(connect in order)*

A (4, 0)	*H* (2, 13)
B (5, 7)	*I* (2, 9)
C (7, 5)	*J* (3, 9)
D (8, 6)	*K* (0, 6)
E (5, 9)	*L* (1, 5)
F (6, 9)	*M* (3, 7) *(connect to A)*
G (6, 13)	

Eyes

Q (3, 12) *(make a small circle)*
R (5, 12) *(make a small circle)*

Mouth *(connect in order)*

S (3, 10)	*U* (5, 11)
T (3, 11)	*V* (5, 10)

a. Draw Mariella on grid paper.

b. Mariella is in the Fun House. When she passes through the Mystic Gateway, she undergoes an enlargement that is similar to the original Mariella. Write a rule that the producers of the video game could use to enlarge Mariella. (The new image must fit on a sheet of grid paper.)

c. Explain how you know that the enlargement is similar to the original Mariella.

d. When Mariella gets caught in the Distortion Room, she is no longer similar to the original Mariella. Write a rule that would transform Mariella when she is in the Distortion Room.

e. How do you know that the distorted figure is not similar to the original Mariella?

12. Gilligan belongs to the Model Sailboat Club. All club members have *similar* boats with *similar* sails. Find all the triangles below that could be used as sails by the club members. Explain your reasoning.

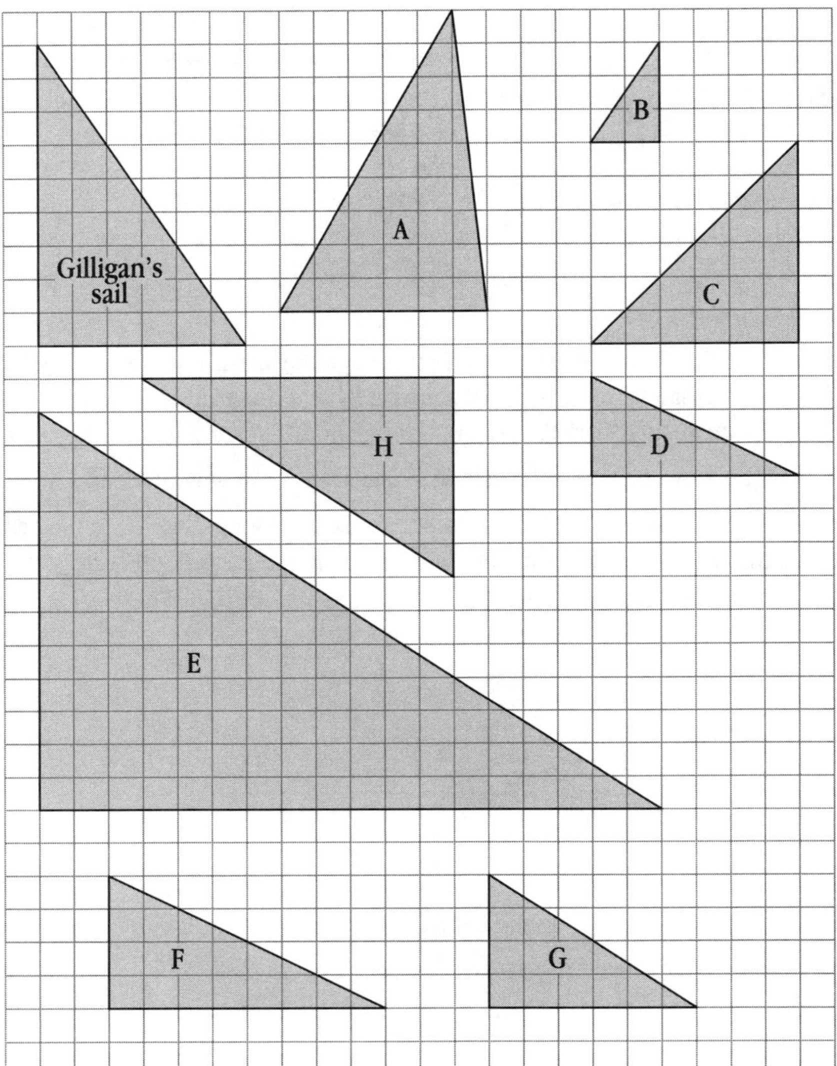

Name ______________________ Date ______________

Unit Test: In-Class Portion

1. The dimensions of six rectangles are given below.

Rectangle	Width	Length
A	18	21
B	15	24
C	24	28
D	$2\frac{1}{2}$	4
E	12	14
F	3	$\frac{1}{2}$

   a. Sort the rectangles into sets of similar rectangles. Tell which rectangles are in each set.

   b. Explain how you decided which rectangles were similar.

2. Triangles A and B are similar. The side lengths of triangle A are three times the side lengths of triangle B. In a and b, illustrate your answer by making a drawing.

   a. How many copies of triangle B will exactly fit into triangle A? ______

   b. How many times greater is the perimeter of triangle A than the perimeter of triangle B? ______

3. Catrina is using a photo-enlargement machine. She has a 3-inch-by-4 inch (3×4) photograph she wants to enlarge. The machine will makes enlargements in four sizes: 5×7, 8×10, 12×16, and 16×24. When Catrina tries to enlarge her photo to a couple of the sizes, the photo is not exactly similar—that is, some parts of the photo are cut off.

   a. If Catrina wants an enlargement that is similar to her original, what size(s) could she choose for the machine to make? Explain your answer.

   b. The costs of photos and their enlargements are based on the amount of photographic paper used. Catrina paid $0.30 for her 3×4 photo. How much would the enlarged photo(s) cost for the size(s) you gave in part a?

Name ______________________________ Date ____________

Unit Test: In-Class Portion

4. The two figures below are similar. Find the missing length.

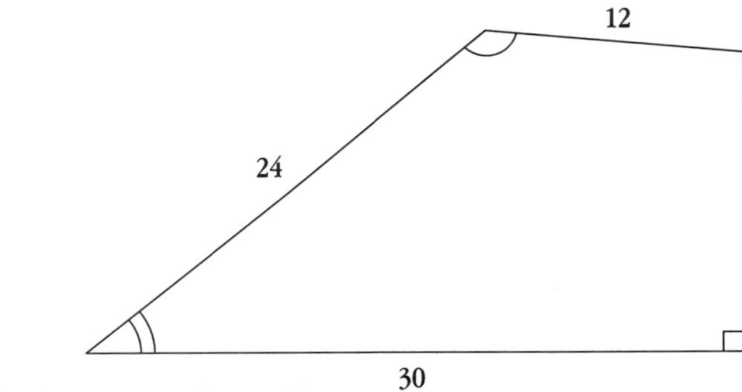

$a =$ ____

5. a. Draw two similar parallelograms on the grid below. Label your small parallelogram A and your large parallelogram B.

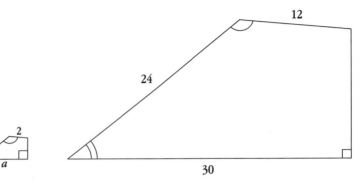

Name ______________________ Date ______________

Unit Test: In-Class Portion

b. How do you know your parallelograms are similar?

c. What is the scale factor from parallelogram A to parallelogram B?

d. How does the area of parallelogram A compare to the area of parallelogram B?

6. Henri's neighbor wants to cut down a dead tree that is in his yard. Henri is worried that when the tree is cut, it will fall on his garage, which is 42 feet from the tree. His neighbor decided to measure the height of the tree by using its shadow. The tree's shadow measured 47.25 feet. Henri put a yardstick next to the tree, and the yardstick cast a shadow of 3.5 feet.

a. How tall is the tree?

b. Will the tree hit Henri's garage if it falls the wrong way? Explain.

Name ______________________________ Date ______________

Unit Test Take-Home Project

This take-home project has two parts. First, you will draw a similar image of a picture by enlarging or shrinking it. Second, you will write a report on creating similar figures.

Part 1: Draw a Similar Image

Choose a picture or a cartoon to enlarge or shrink. Using a coordinate system, write a rule that would produce a similar image. If you enlarge your picture, the new image must have a scale factor of at least 4 times the original. If you shrink your picture, it must have a scale factor of no more than $\frac{1}{4}$ the original.

Your final project must be presented in a format that can be displayed for others to see. In your project, include the following:

1. Show the original picture and the image.
2. Identify the scale factor, and show how the lengths compare between the original and the image.
3. Identify two pairs of corresponding angles, and show how the angles between the original and the image compare.
4. Identify an area of the original and the corresponding area of the image, and compare them.

Part 2: Write a Report

Write a report describing how you created your similar figure. In your report, do the following things:

1. Describe the technique or method you used to create the image.
2. Describe the changes in the lengths, angles, and area between the original picture and the image.
3. Include a paragraph or more about other details you think would be interesting or would help the reader understand what they are seeing, such as a description of any problems or surprises you encountered while completing the project and the decisions you made as a result.

Name ______________________________ Date ______________

Optional Unit Project: All-Similar Shapes

Throughout the *Stretching and Shrinking* unit, you have worked with problems that helped you understand what it means for two shapes to be mathematically similar. You have learned that not all rectangles are similar. For example, rectangles G and H below (from the ShapeSet) are not similar. You might suspect this because the two rectangles do not appear to be the same shape, although their corresponding angles are equal (as they are all 90°).

G

H

A check shows that the ratios of the side lengths (short to long) within the figures and the ratios of the corresponding sides between the figures are not equal (although you only need to check one of these sets of ratios). Shape G has side lengths of 1 inch and 3 inches. Shape H has side lengths of 2 inches and 3 inches. The ratio between the sides is $\frac{1}{3}$ for shape G and $\frac{2}{3}$ for shape H. These ratios are not equivalent. The ratio of corresponding sides is $\frac{1}{2}$ for the short sides and $\frac{3}{3}$ for the long sides. Again, these ratios are not equal.

A group of students took a look at square rectangles. They found that no matter what size square they drew, every square was similar to shape B in the ShapeSet and to all other squares. They concluded that ***all squares are similar!*** They decided to call squares an All-Similar shape.

Shape B has side lengths of 1 inch. The other square below has side lengths of $2\frac{1}{2}$ inches. The ratios of the sides for shape B are $\frac{1}{1}$ and for the other square are $\frac{2.5}{2.5}$, which are equivalent ratios. The ratio of the corresponding sides between the rectangles is $\frac{1}{2.5}$ and $\frac{1}{2.5}$, which are also equivalent.

B

Name ______________________________ Date ______________

Optional Unit Project: All-Similar Shapes

The students wondered whether there were any other All-Similar shapes like the square—were there any other groups of shapes for which all shapes called by that name are similar to all other shapes called by that name?

Using your ShapeSet, investigate the students' question.

1. Make a list of the names of all of the different types of shapes in the ShapeSet. For example, there are rectangles, squares, triangles, equilateral triangles, circles, and regular hexagons.

2. For each type of shape, list which shapes (using their letter names) belong in that group.

3. Sort the different types of shapes into two groups: All-Similar shapes (for example, all squares are similar) and *not* All-Similar shapes (for example, all rectangles are not similar).

4. Describe the ways in which all the All-Similar shapes are alike.

Name ______________________________ Date ______________

Notebook Checklist

Journal Organization

_____ Problems and Mathematical Reflections are labeled and dated.

_____ Work is neat and is easy to find and follow.

Vocabulary

_____ All words are listed.

_____ All words are defined or described.

Check-Up and Quizzes

_____ Check-Up

_____ Quiz A

_____ Quiz B

Homework Assignments

_____ ______________________________

_____ ______________________________

_____ ______________________________

_____ ______________________________

_____ ______________________________

_____ ______________________________

_____ ______________________________

_____ ______________________________

_____ ______________________________

_____ ______________________________

_____ ______________________________

_____ ______________________________

_____ ______________________________

Name ______________________________ Date ______________

Self-Assessment

Vocabulary

Of the vocabulary words I defined or described in my journal, the word ______________ best demonstrates my ability to give a clear definition or description.

Of the vocabulary words I defined or described in my journal, the word ______________ best demonstrates my ability to use an example to help explain or describe an idea.

Mathematical Ideas

We hear the word *similar* often. People use it to talk about things that are alike in some way. In *Stretching and Shrinking,* I learned what the word *similar* means in the mathematical sense and how I can use the idea of similarity to think about some interesting problems.

1. a. I learned these things about mathematical similarity and what happens to lengths, areas, and angles when you enlarge or shrink figures:

b. Here are page numbers of journal entries that give evidence of what I have learned, along with descriptions of what each entry shows:

2. a. These are the mathematical ideas I am still struggling with:

b. This is why I think these ideas are difficult for me:

c. Here are page numbers of journal entries that give evidence of what I am struggling with, along with descriptions of what each entry shows:

Class Participation

I contributed to the class discussion and understanding of *Stretching and Shrinking* when I . . . (Give examples.)

Answers to the Check-Up

1. a. $(x, 2y)$

   b. They are not similar, because the sides have not grown proportionally. The width stayed the same, while the height doubled.

2. Rectangle C is similar to rectangle Z because there is a scale factor of 2 from rectangle Z to rectangle C. Rectangle D is similar to rectangle Z because there is a scale factor of 1.5 from rectangle Z to rectangle D.

3. a. side AB corresponds to side ED, side AC corresponds to side EF, side BC corresponds to side DF

   b. $\angle D$ corresponds to $\angle B$, $\angle E$ corresponds to $\angle A$, $\angle F$ corresponds to $\angle C$

4. a. side $AC = 20$, side $AB = 16$

   b. 4

   c. $\frac{1}{4}$

   d. The perimeter of triangle ABC is four times the perimeter of triangle DEF.

Answers to Quiz A

1. a. It would take 16 copies of triangle DEF to cover triangle ABC.

   b.

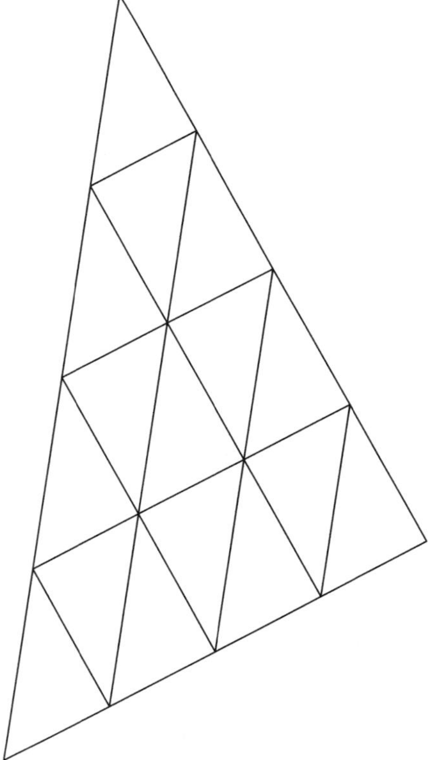

2. a.

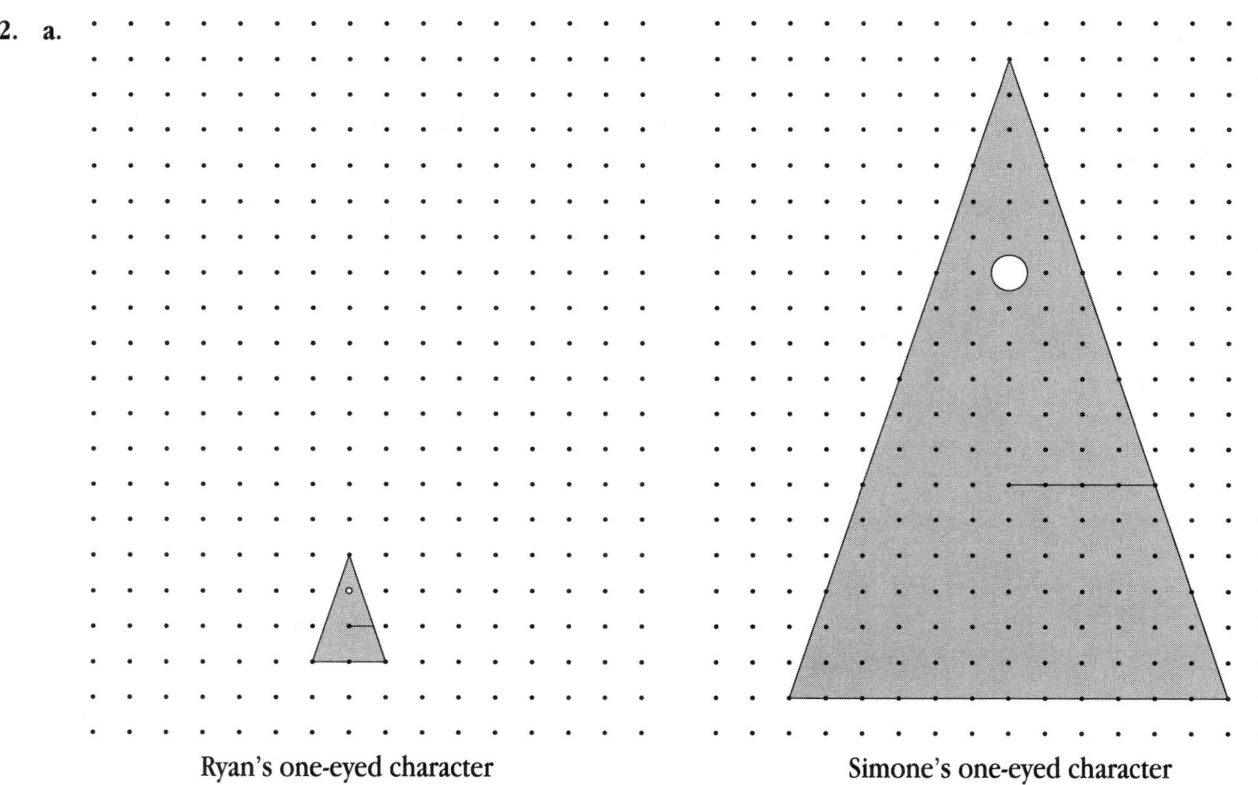

Ryan's one-eyed character

Simone's one-eyed character

b. Ryan's and Simone's characters are similar: the shapes are the same, corresponding angles are the same, and the sides are proportional. The scale factor from Ryan's character to Simone's character is 6. (Note: If students use the transitive property to answer this question—since Ryan's character is similar to Ashley's, and Ashley's is similar to Simone's, then Ryan's is similar to Simone's—you may want to ask them to support the answer with an explanation based on the properties of similar figures.)

c. $(6x, 6y)$

3. a. Any rule in which the coefficient of x is relatively large compared to the coefficient of y will work; for example, $(5x, 2y)$, $(3x, y)$, $(10x, \frac{1}{2}y)$.

b. Students should add some positive number to the second coordinate in their rule from part a; for example, $(5x, 2y + 4)$.

c. Slug is not similar to Mug, because Slug was stretched more horizontally than vertically. The figures have different shapes.

4. Shapes A and B are similar. They have the same basic shape, corresponding angles are equal, and the side lengths of shape A are 3 times the corresponding side lengths of shape B. (Note: Students may determine this by measuring or by cutting out the two shapes to compare their angles and sides.)

Answer Keys

Answers to Quiz B

1. $a = 12.5$, $b = 10$, $c = 26$
2. 8 m; Possible explanations: Multiplying the model's height by the scale factor of 20 (derived from the door's height going from 10 cm to 200 cm) gives 800 cm or 8 m. Or, finding the ratio of the door's height to the building's height on the model $(\frac{10}{40})$ and setting it equal to the ratio of the same measurements on the actual house $(\frac{2}{?})$ gives 8 m.
3. $\frac{1}{2} \times 20^2 = 200$ yd^2 of carpeting
4. 2 chimneys; Possible explanation: The number of items like windows, stories, rooms, and chimneys is the same on a model as it will be on the real object; only their size changes.
5. $11 \times 20 = 220$ cm or 2.2 m of molding
6. no; You can't multiply the dimensions of the picture frame by the same scale factor and get the television's dimensions. Comparing the smaller dimensions gives a factor of $18.8 \div 1.6 = 11.75$ from the picture frame to the television screen. Comparing the larger dimensions, however, gives a scale factor of $24.5 \div 2.2 =$ about 11.14. We cannot completely fill the television screen with the original picture without losing some of the image.
7. **a.** Some possible answers: 56 cm × 77 cm (scale factor of 35); 64 cm × 88 cm (scale factor of 40); 160 cm × 220 cm (scale factor of 100)

   b. Students' models should correspond with their answers and be labeled correctly. (Note: Making a model helps students to make sense of what measurements of a big-screen television would be appropriate. For example, using a scale factor of 10 to produce a screen measuring 16 cm × 22 cm would not produce something that could be considered a big-screen television.)

   c. Answers will vary.
8. The scale factor is 0.08 or $\frac{2}{25}$. In the picture, the meterstick measures 8 cm. Since a real meterstick measures 100 cm, the scale factor is $100 \div 8 = 0.08$.
9. The scale factor from the picture to the real objects is $\frac{25}{2}$ or 12.5, so the real book is about 26 cm by 20 cm.
10. The real mitten is about 21 cm long.

Answers to the Question Bank

1. $\frac{6}{9}$
2. rectangle A
3. Students can draw any shape in three similar versions (such as by using scale factors of 1, 2, and 3). Possible explanation: I know the shapes are similar, because there is a constant ratio between pairs of corresponding sides and because corresponding angles are equal.
4. **a.** The horizontal lengths would increase by a factor of 3, and the vertical lengths would increase by a factor of 6.

   b. The figure would stay the same size, but it would move to the right 2 units and up 1 unit.

   c. The figure would increase by a scale factor of 2 and would move up 5 units.
5. $a = 15$, $b = 15$

6.

Rectangle	Scale factor	Short side	Long side	Perimeter	Area
A	1	1	4	10	4
B	3	3	12	30	36
C	10	10	40	100	400
D	$\frac{1}{2}$	$\frac{1}{2}$	2	5	1

7. The following might be different: lengths of corresponding sides (if the scale factor is anything other than 1) and area (they will differ as the square of the scale factor).

8. **a.** The area is $1.5^2 = 2.25$ times as great.

   b. The perimeter is 1.5 times as great.

9. The flagpole measures $\frac{600}{100} \times 150 = 900$ cm.

10. **a.** $(2x, 2y)$

    b. They are similar, because all corresponding sides increased by a scale factor of 2 and corresponding angles are equal.

11. **a.**

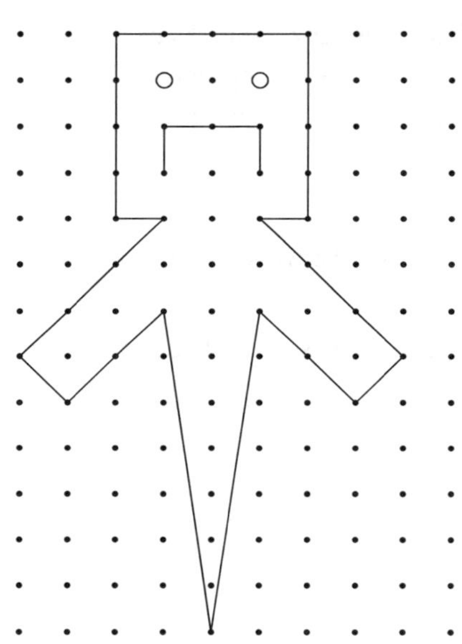

    b. The rule must be of the form (nx, ny), such as $(2x, 2y)$ or $(3x, 3y)$.

    c. Corresponding angles are equal and the ratios of corresponding sides are equal.

    d. The rule must be of the form (ax, by), where $a \neq b$, such as $(x, 3y)$ or $(2x, y)$.

    e. The lengths of corresponding sides are not the same ratio, corresponding angles are not equal, and the basic shape is not the same.

12. Sails B, E, G, and H are similar to Gilligan's sail. Possible explanation: The scale factor from Gilligan's sail to sail B is $\frac{1}{3}$, to sail E is 2, to sail G is 1.5, and to sail H is 1.

Answers to the Unit Test: In-Class Portion

1. a. *Set 1*—rectangles A, C, and E; *Set 2*—rectangles B and D; *Set 3*—rectangle F

   b. Possible explanation: For each rectangle, you can find the ratio of the shortest side to the longest side. Rectangles A, C, and E have a ratio of $\frac{6}{7}$; rectangles B and D have a ratio of $\frac{5}{8}$, and rectangle F has a ratio of $\frac{1}{6}$.

2. a. Nine copies will fit.

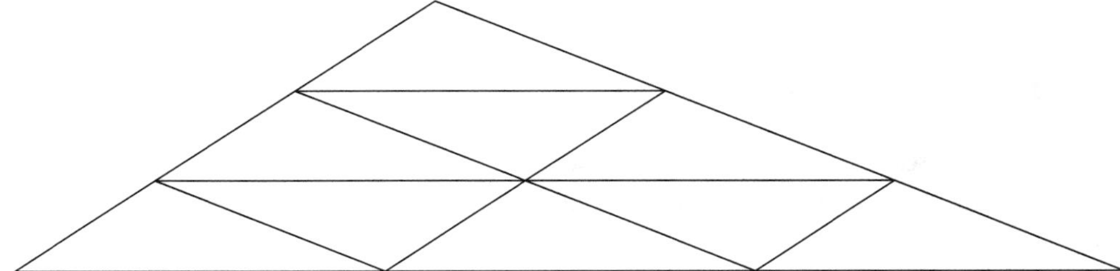

   b. The perimeter of the large triangle is $9 \div 3 = 3$ times greater.

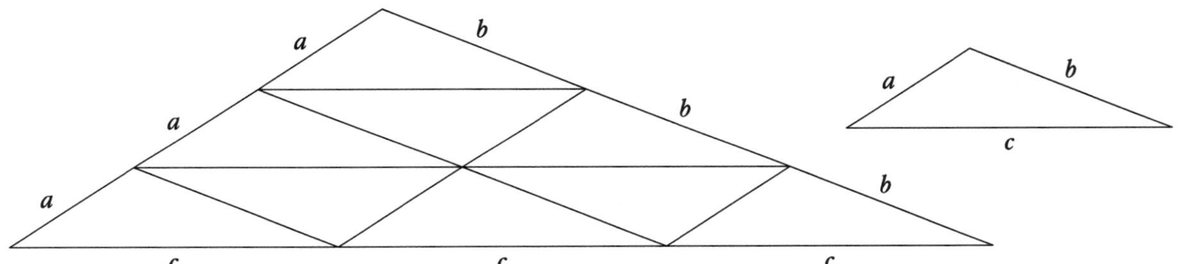

3. a. She could choose only 12×16, which would use a scale factor of 4. The other possibilities have different scale factors for the two dimensions.

   b. $0.30 \times 4^2 = 0.30 \times 16 = \$4.80$

4. $a = 5$

5. a. Possible drawing:

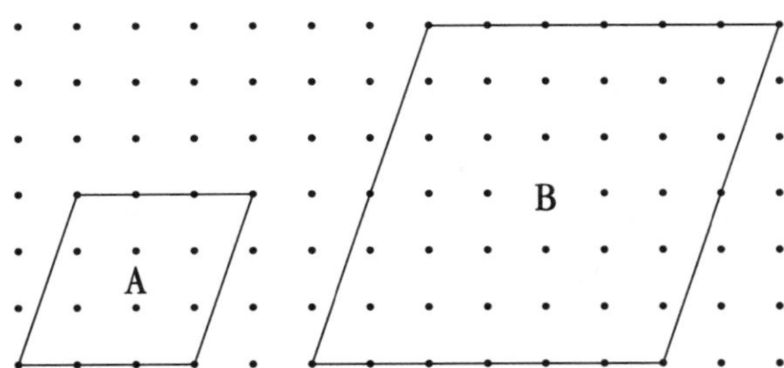

   b. Their corresponding angles are equal, all the lengths of parallelogram A grow by the same scale factor to give parallelogram B.

   c. Answers will depend on the drawings in part a.

   d. The area of parallelogram B is the square of the scale factor times the area of parallelogram A.

6. a. The scale factor from the yardstick's shadow to the tree's shadow is $47.25 \div 3.5 = 13.5$. Using this scale factor, the tree is $13.5 \times 1 = 13.5$ yd or 40.5 ft tall.

   b. no; If the tree fell toward the garage, there would be approximately $42 - 40.5 = 1.5$ ft of clearance.

Guide to the Unit Test Take-Home Project

The Unit Test Take-Home Project has two parts. First, students are asked to enlarge or shrink a picture using the coordinate graphing system and to identify their scale factor, compare two pairs of corresponding angles, and compare two corresponding areas within the drawings. Second, they are asked to write a report that describes the techniques they used and compares the original picture to its image. The blackline master for the project appears on page 104. Below is a general scoring rubric and specific guidelines for how the rubric can be applied to assessing the activity. A teacher's comments on one student's work follow the suggested rubric.

Suggested Scoring Rubric

This rubric employs a point scale from 0 to 4. Use the rubric as presented here, or modify it to fit your needs and your district's requirements for evaluating and reporting students' work and understanding.

4 **Complete Response**

- Complete, with clear, coherent work and written explanation
- Shows understanding of the mathematical concepts and procedures
- Satisfies all essential conditions of the project

3 **Reasonably Complete Response** *(work needs some revision)*

- Reasonably complete; may lack detail or clarity in work or written explanation
- Shows understanding of most of the mathematical concepts and procedures
- Satisfies most of the essential conditions of the project

2 **Partial Response** *(student needs some instruction to revise work)*

- Incomplete; work or written explanation is unclear or lacks detail
- Shows some understanding of the mathematical concepts and procedures
- Satisfies some of the essential conditions of the project

1 **Inadequate Response** *(student needs significant instruction to revise work)*

- Incomplete; work or written explanation is insufficient or not understandable
- Shows little understanding of the mathematical concepts and procedures
- Fails to address essential conditions of the project

0 **No Attempt**

- Irrelevant response
- Does not address the conditions of the project

Guide to the Unit Test Take-Home Project

Sample Student Project

As her project, one student enlarged a cartoon. Here is her report (her drawing could not be reproduced).

I used ordered pairs to enlarge my cartoon.
(coordinates on other sheet)
The scale factor for my drawing is 12.
The length of the bottom goes up by 12.
The length of Nancy's arm goes up by 12.
The length of the chair goes up by 12.
The corresponding angles stay the same.
90 on original & enlargement (chair)
(sleeve) 60° on both pictures
The area of the glass is 6 squares on the cartoon and the enlargements, however the squares on the enlargement are 12 times bigger. The glass on the enlargement is 144 times bigger (12^2).

(0, 3)
(7, 2)
Stop
(10, 2)
($10\frac{1}{2}$, 2)
Stop
(15, $1\frac{1}{2}$)
(16, $1\frac{2}{3}$)
Stop
($5\frac{1}{2}$, 3/4)
(11, 1)
($10\frac{1}{2}$, $1\frac{1}{2}$)
Stop ($10\frac{1}{2}$, $1\frac{1}{2}$)
($5\frac{1}{2}$, $\frac{3}{4}$)
(6, $1\frac{1}{4}$)
(7, $1\frac{1}{2}$)
Stop
(13, 0)
(13, 3)
(15, 3)
(15, 0)
Stop
draw food (it's too hard to plot)
($3\frac{1}{2}$, $1\frac{1}{4}$)
($3\frac{1}{4}$, $11\frac{1}{2}$)
make another line of same length
Stop
draw ∧ on chair
Stop
(3, $3\frac{1}{2}$)
(5, $3\frac{1}{2}$)
(5, 5)
(3, 5)
($3\frac{1}{2}$, $3\frac{1}{2}$)
Stop
draw Nancy using grids

A Teacher's Comments

Linda's drawing

Linda shows a good understanding of being able to create an enlarged similar drawing. What she doesn't do is create a drawing (display) that highlights the mathematics involved in the task. Nowhere on the drawing does she identify her scale factor or show how the lengths, angles, or areas of the figures in the two drawings compare. However, she does do this in her report. For that reason, Linda was given a 3 on her drawing. Her report shows that she does understand these ideas; she just did not demonstrate this understanding in the drawing. Linda needs to revise her drawing, but she does not need further instruction.

Linda's report

Linda's report is not very neat. However, if I look for the mathematics she is trying to communicate, I can find that she shows considerable understanding of similar figures. She states that her scale factor is 12 (which it is) and that the lengths change by the scale factor ("Nancy's arm goes up by 12"). She identifies corresponding angles and tells how they are equal, and she correctly gives the growth relationship between the areas (using the drinking glass in the picture to make her point). Linda states that she used ordered pairs to do the majority of the enlargement. She listed coordinates for many of the important points on the original drawing and then kept the same ordered pairs and used larger grids. This is very interesting, yet she doesn't really explain this aspect of her drawing in much detail. It is because of this that Linda was given a 3 for her report. Linda shows a clear understanding of the idea of similarity, and the majority of the mathematics needed for the report are there, but her report is incomplete. She lacks details, clarity, and did not write a paragraph that discussed what was interesting about making her drawing.

Guide to the Self-Assessment

Using the self-assessment in each unit, students can reflect on the mathematics in the unit and write about what they have made sense of, what they are still struggling with, and how they contributed to the class's understanding of the mathematics in the unit. The three student papers shown on pages 118–120, which came from a single class, are examples of how students might approach the self-assessment.

A Teacher's Comments

In reading the papers, the thing I was most struck by was how all three students wrote and listed what elements are needed for two figures to be similar but none of them explained *why* these are needed. They all list that corresponding angles must be equal, but none explains that if the angles were not, the shape of the figures would be different. They all write that ratios of corresponding sides must be equal (you have to read into Susy's and Stacy's papers to realize that this is what they mean), but again they don't explain why this is needed and how these ratios are linked to the scale factor between similar figures.

In writing about their class participation, the students again list but don't explain. They list the topics they felt they contributed to; Susy writes that she explained "why the mirror measuring and shadow measuring works," and Aimee writes that she contributed to the discussion on "what things change and what things stay the same in similar figures," but neither tells what she actually contributed.

Aimee's paper is the clearest and the most complete of the papers. Her drawing and labeled computational work help to show her understanding of scale factors and area relationships between similar figures. As stated above, though, her paper gives the elements of similar figures and how to find certain measures but does not explain why these procedures work or make sense. Aimee does not feel that she is struggling with any of the ideas in this unit. Her answer to part 1, her homework, her quizzes, and her participation in class conversations all support her statement. I have told my students that if part 1 is complete and supported by journal entries and other written work, it is OK for them to say that they are not struggling with any mathematical ideas from the unit.

Stacy's paper is interesting in that she writes that she is struggling with making sense of using mirrors and shadows to find heights: "I know how to find the height. But I'm not clear why it works." She says that the class did not discuss why the methods work. Both Aimee and Susy feel they do understand this idea; Susy writes of her class contribution: "I explained why the mirror measuring and shadow measuring works." Understanding how to use similar triangles to find the height of tall objects is a difficult concept for middle grades students. I'm not sure about the depth of understanding that Aimee and Susy have. Stacy's paper reminds us that one student's explanation does not mean that others have made sense of what was being said and internalized the idea.

Guide to the Self-Assessment

Susy's paper is typical of many students. She knows she is writing to the teacher, who has been in the class and heard all the conversation and knows the subject. Her writing is vague, and one needs to read into it. When she says "ratios are equivalent," I believe she is referring to ratios of corresponding sides. She writes that "area increases by multiplying scale factor by scale factor." Again, she expects the teacher to interpret that she is talking about the relationship between the areas of similar figures.

I know that it takes time for students to learn to communicate what they know in words. However, I also feel that my students don't really understand what I expect. Along with others, Susy's paper shows me that I need to help my students with this type of writing. After talking to the language arts teacher, I have decided that for the next couple of units I will concentrate on one section of the self-assessment tool at a time. For the next unit or two, I will work with my students on their writing about what mathematics they have learned. I will have them answer the whole self-assessment piece, but we will discuss this section in more detail. I will tell them that I am going to put more weight on this when I review their papers, and I will share some of the work with the language arts teacher and ask her for further suggestions to help me with my feedback to my students.

Susy

1. a.) What I learned about similar figures are the corresponding angles are the same, ratios are equivalent, the general shape stays the same. Area increases by multiplying scale factor by scale factor. Perimeter gets bigger or smaller. Corresponding sides increase by scale factor.

b.) #'s 26 and 27. These shows that I know what makes similar figures, similar figures.

2a.) The mathematical ideas I am still struggling with how on problem 5 on Inv. 5 ACE.

b.) These ideas were hard for me because I didn't see the two triangles untill Kristin showed me how.

c.) Evedence of this can be found on page 9. This shows that I didn't understand it, but I understand after Kristin explained it.

I contrbuted to classroom discutions while understanding Stretching and Shrinking Unit when I explained why the miror mesuring and shadow mesuring works. I also explained why aljebraic rules worked.

Aimee

1.a) After studying this unit I have learned how to tell if a figure is similar. If two figures are similar then the corresponding angles will be the same, so will the general shape. Also if two figures are similar the corresponding ratios will be equivalent. If they are similar then the corresponding sides increase by multiplying the same number which is called a scale factor. You can find the area of similar figures by multiplying the scale factor x scale factor Ex:

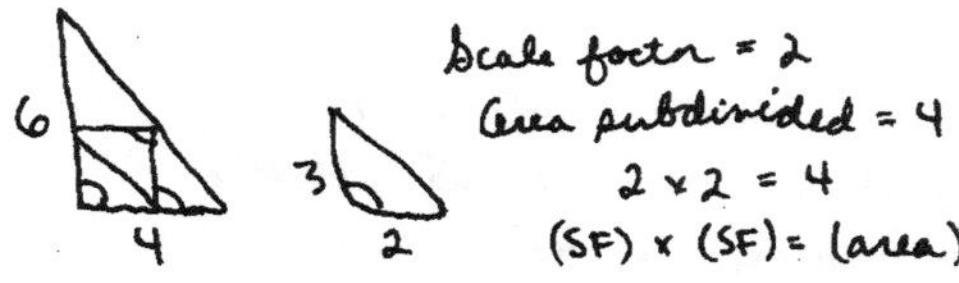

I also learned that to measure tall buildings or other tall things you can use similar ~~figures~~ triangles. Two methods are the shadow method and the mirror method For the shadow method you measure the shadows of two objects and find the scale factor of them. Then you multiply the scale factor x one of them - the objects (ex: meter stick) and that is the height of the taller building. For the mirror method you measure from yourself to your mirror, then from the mirror to the object, and you find the scale factor. Then measure from your eyes to the ground and multiply that by the scale factor.

b) Evidence of this can be found in my journal on pages 18, 24, 26, Sm chart, and 8-14. What these show is that I know how to find similar figures rectangles, and triangles. It also shows that I know how to find the height of taller objects such as the mirror and shadow method.

2.a) The mathematical idea that I am still struggling with is none.

Class Paticipation: I contributed to the classroom discussion and understanding of Stretching and Shrinking when we discussed what things change and what things stay the same in similar figures, and ~~wish~~ with what to put on the chart. I also contributed when we discussed what things grow by with similar triangles and how to enlarge them.

Guide to the Self-Assessment

Stacy

1). a) I leaned that simmilar figures have the same corresponding angle degrees, same general shape, same or eqivalent ratio's, the shape's sides all have the same scale factor. I also learned that the image can fit in the pre-image as many times as scale factor x scale factor = how many times. larger or smaller. the image is than the preimage I also learned the image's perimeter grew by the scale factor.

b) This journal page 3 shows what things simmilar have to or don't have to be simmilar.

2.a) A mathematical idea I'm still haveing trooble is the understanding of finding how tall large objects are by useing shadows & mirrors I know how to find the height. But I'm not clear ~~how~~ why it works.

b) I think this is difficult for me because we discussed how to do it, but not why it works. We never talked about why you measure from the mirror / shadow to your eyes, why don't you measure it from the top of your head to the mirror?

c) Evidence can be found on page 19, I jotted down questions I didn't know answers to, so I could ask them when we had time and I jotted them down also because I would try to use my knowlage of simmilar figures to answer my questions.

Class Participation

I participated in class in the disscussion of corresponding. I didn't exactly know what it was at first, but then I asked a question and then I knew what it was. I also participated when we made our charts about what simmilar figures did / didn't have in common. This unit I think I really did a good job of takeing notes on simmilarity because I knew I wasn't doing very well on check-ups and I knew my notes would be useful during check-ups. Also before in other units I felt lost sometimes because I wasn't paying attention. This unit payed attention more and I didn't feel lost. I actually learned something & understood it, with a few exceptions!

Blackline Masters

Labsheets

Transparencies

Additional Resources

Right-handed Version

P is the anchor point.

•
P

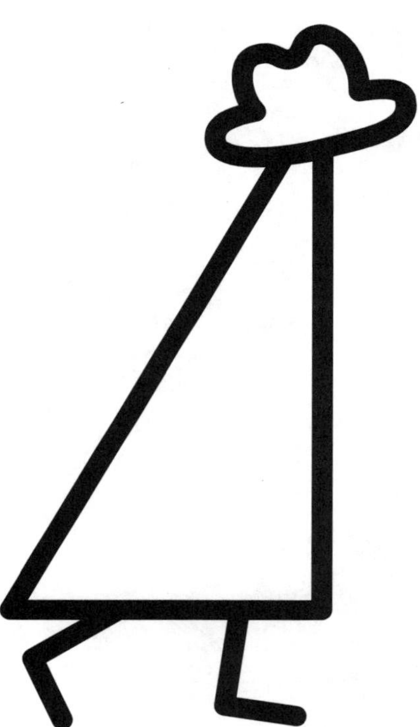

Left-handed Version

P is the anchor point.

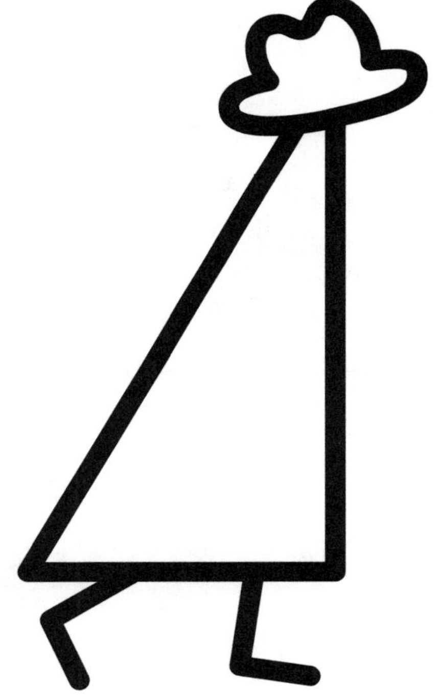

P

Labsheet 1.2A

Right-handed Version

P is the anchor point.

• *P*

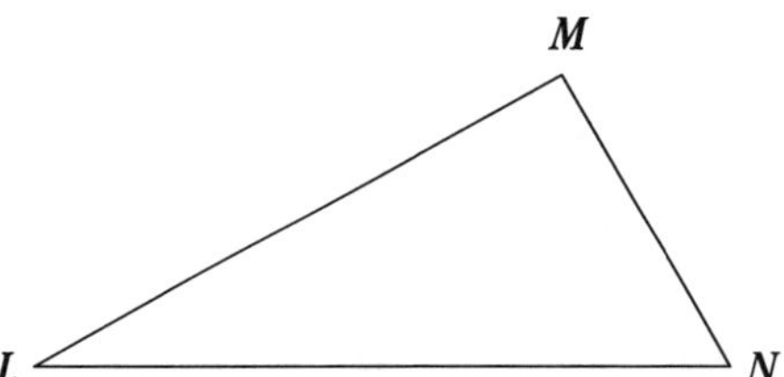

Labsheet 1.2B

Left-handed Version

P is the anchor point.

• *P*

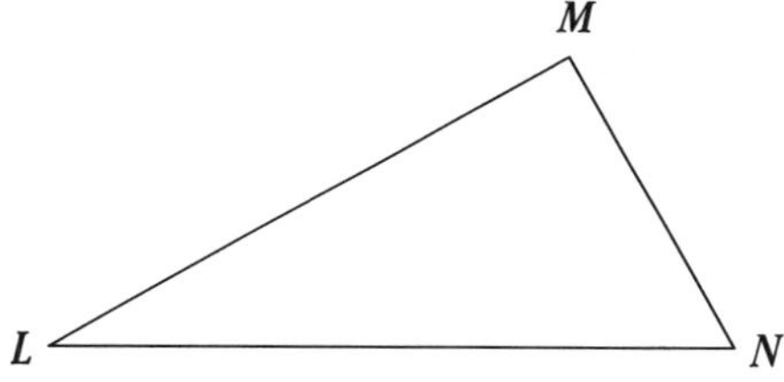

Labsheet 2.1A

The Wump Family

Plot each set of points separately. Connect the points in each set in order. Use the rules to complete the table. *Save your drawings for later problems!*

	Mug Wump	Zug	Lug	Bug	Thug
Rule	(x, y)	$(2x, 2y)$	$(3x, y)$	$(3x, 3y)$	$(x, 3y)$
Point	Set 1	Set 1	Set 1	Set 1	Set 1
A	(2, 0)	(4, 0)			
B	(2, 4)	(4, 8)			
C	(0, 4)				
D	(0, 5)				
E	(2, 5)				
F	(0, 8)				
G	(0, 12)				
H	(1, 15)				
I	(2, 12)				
J	(5, 12)				
K	(6, 15)				
L	(7, 12)				
M	(7, 8)				
N	(5, 5)				
O	(7, 5)				
P	(7, 4)				
Q	(5, 4)				
R	(5, 0)				
S	(4, 0)				
T	(4, 3)				
U	(3, 3)				
V	(3, 0) (connect *V* to *A*)				
	Set 2 (start over)	Set 2	Set 2	Set 2	Set 2
W	(1, 8)				
X	(2, 7)				
Y	(5, 7)				
Z	(6, 8)				
	Set 3 (start over)	Set 3	Set 3	Set 3	Set 3
AA	(3, 8)				
BB	(4, 8)				
CC	(4, 10)				
DD	(3, 10) (connect *DD* to *AA*)				
	Set 4 (start over)	Set 4	Set 4	Set 4	Set 4
EE	(2, 11) (make a dot)				
FF	(5, 11) (make a dot)				

Wump Grids

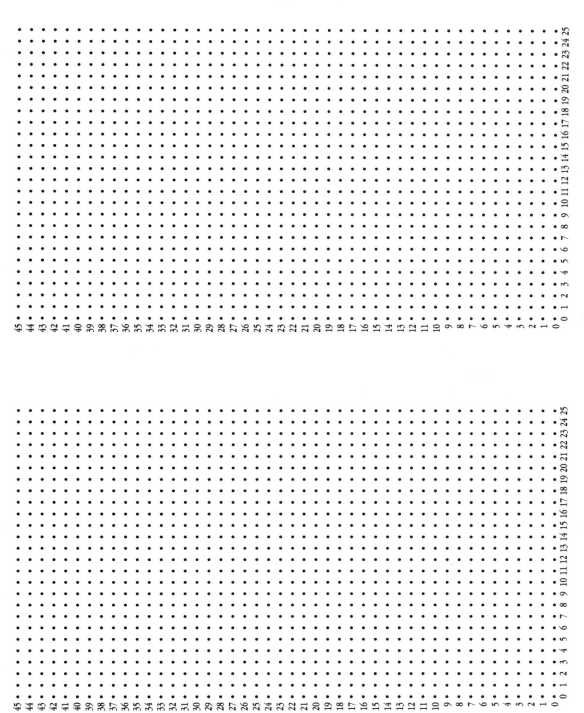

Labsheet 2.3A

Mug Wump's Hats

	Hat 1	Hat 2	Hat 3	Hat 4	Hat 5	Hat 6
Point	(x, y)	$(x + 2, y + 2)$	$(x + 3, y - 1)$	$(2x, y + 2)$	$(2x, 3y)$	$(0.5x, 0.5y)$
A	(0, 4)	(2, 6)	(3, 3)	(0, 6)	(0, 12)	(0, 2)
B	(0, 1)					
C	(6, 1)					
D	(4, 2)					
E	(4, 4)					
F	(3, 5)					
G	(1, 5)					
H	(0, 4)					

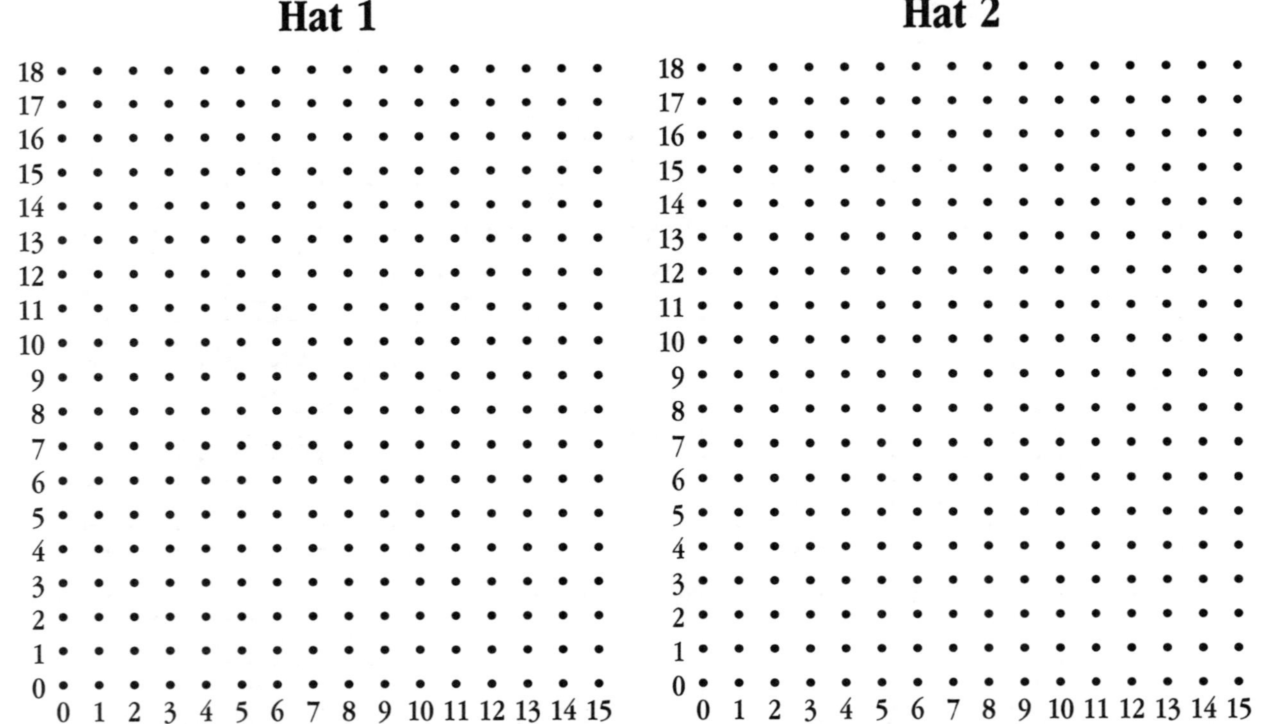

Hat Grids

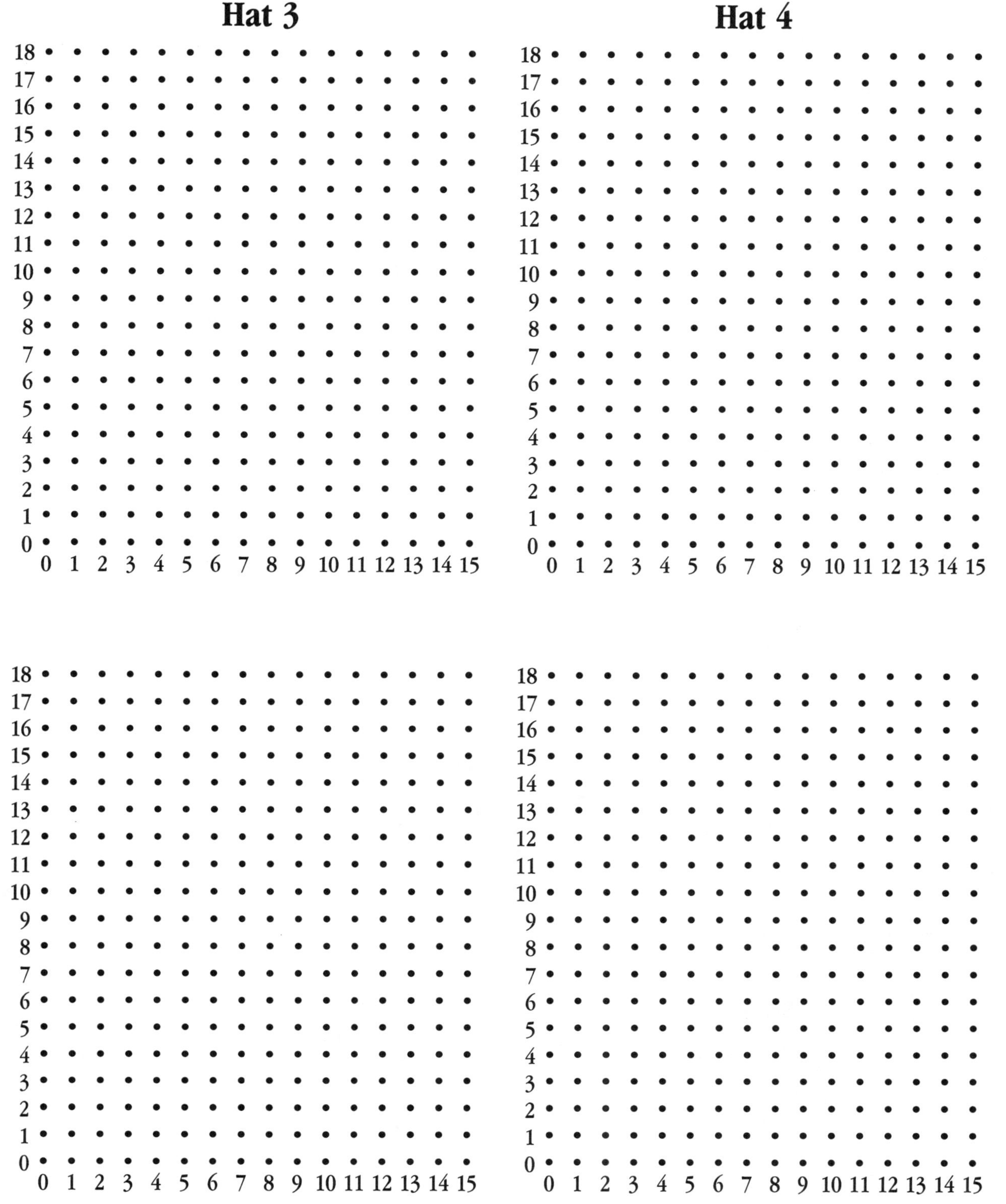
Hat 3
Hat 4
18
17
16
15
14
13
12
11
10
9
8
7
6
5
4
3
2
1
0
0 1 2 3 4 5 6 7 8 9 10 11 12 13 14 15

Polygon Sets

Rectangle set

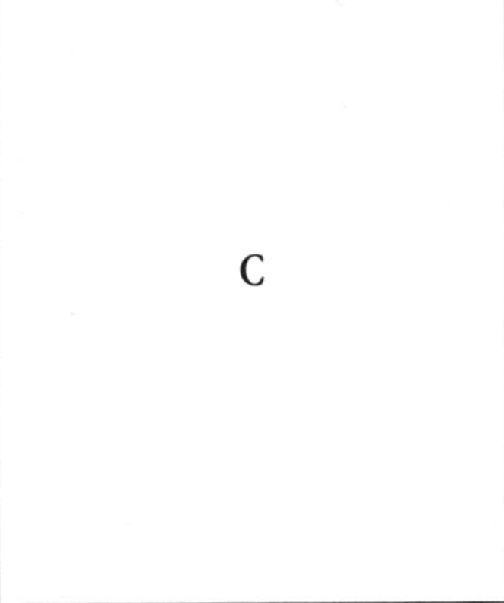

Parallelogram set

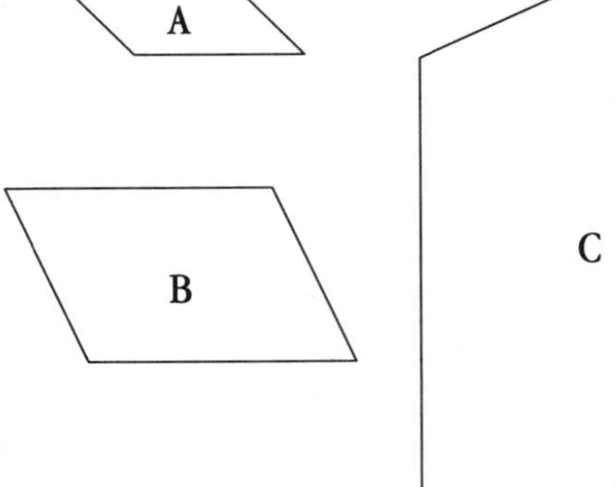

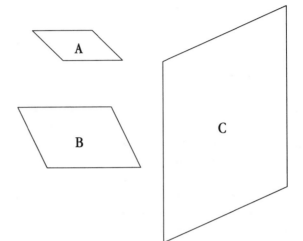

Decagon set

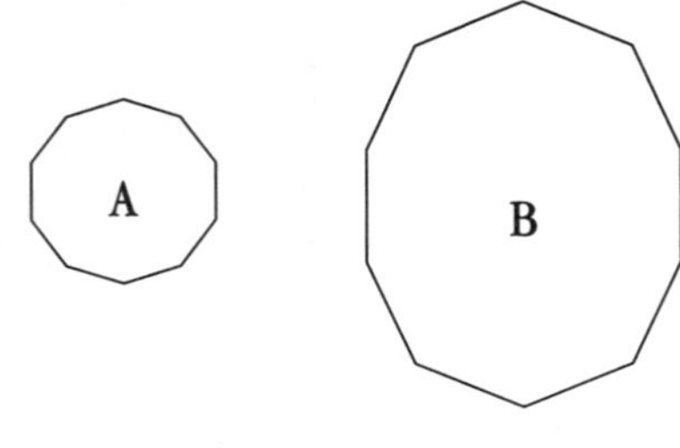

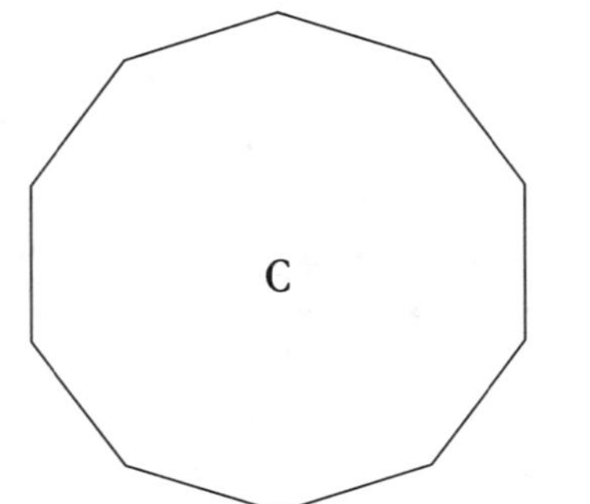

Star set

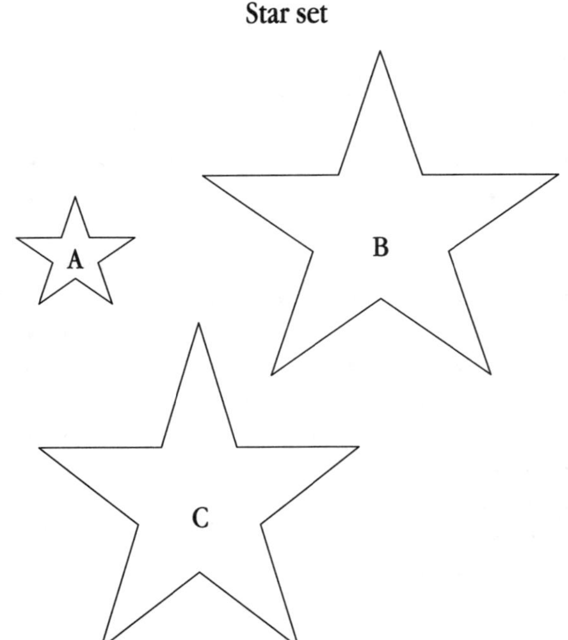

Shapes from the ShapeSet

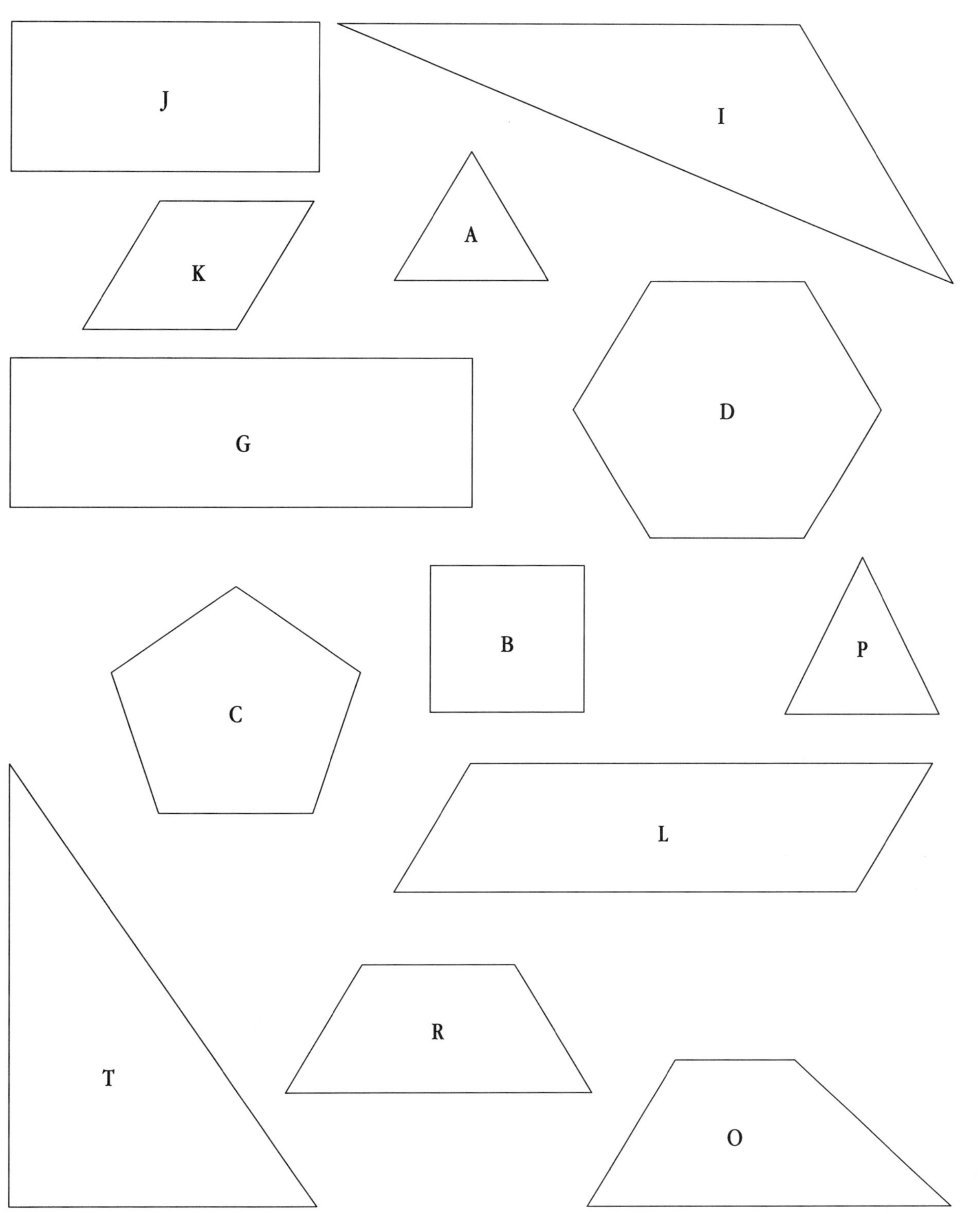

Labsheet 3.3

Shapes to Subdivide

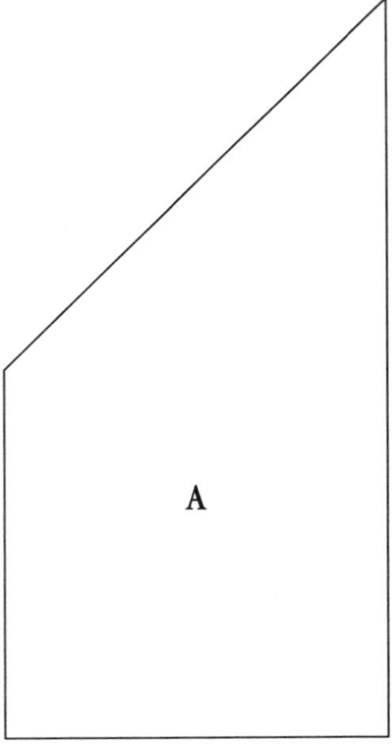

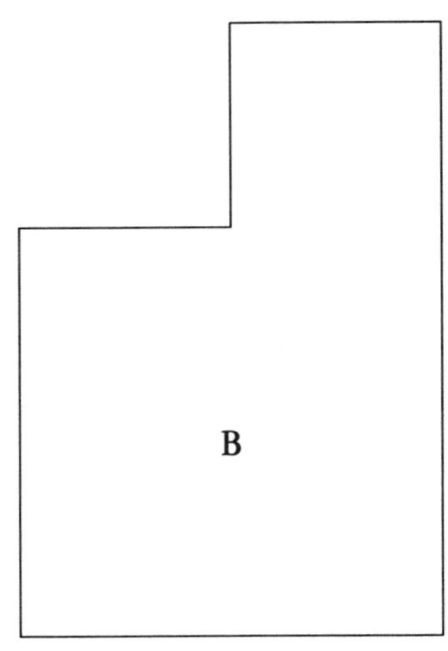

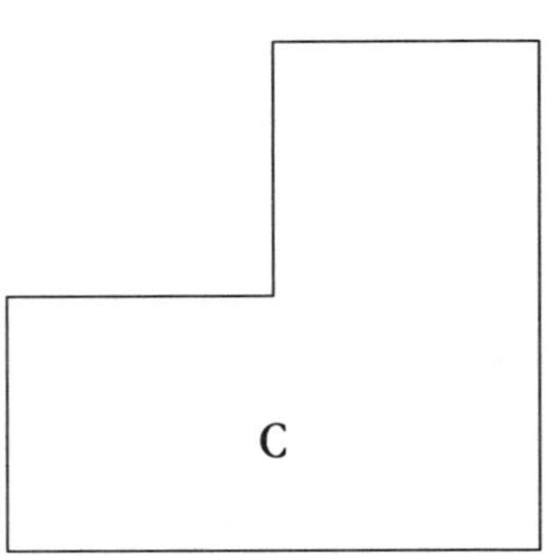

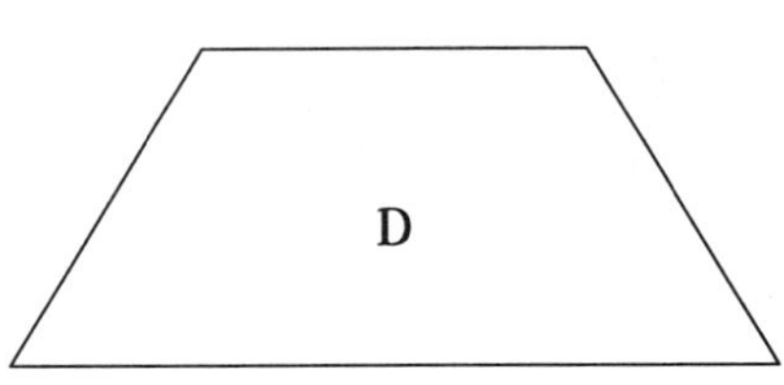

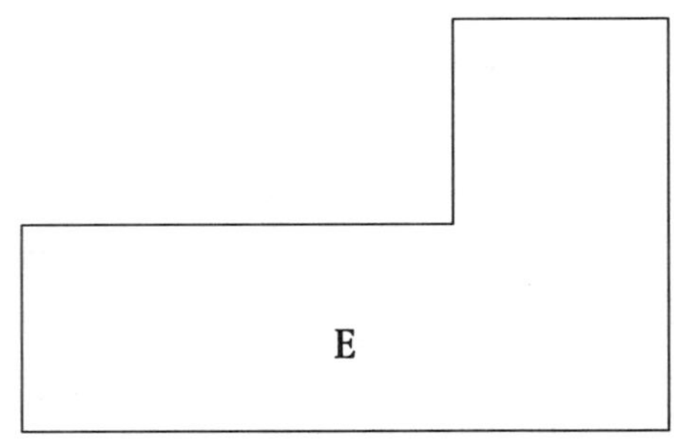

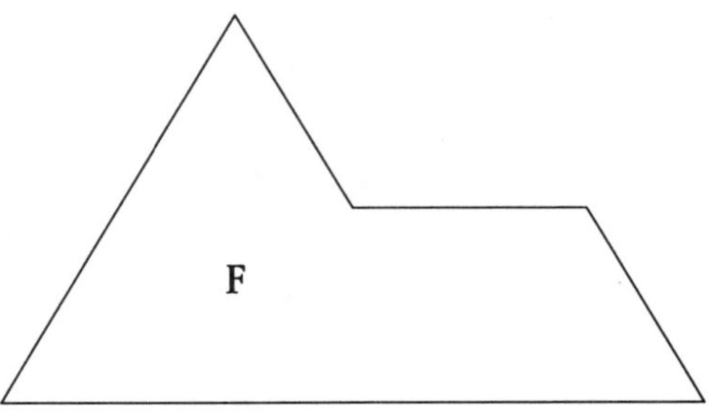

Transparency 1.1A

1. Make a "two-band stretcher" by tying the ends of two identical rubber bands together.
2. Tape the sheet with the picture you want to enlarge to your desk next to a blank sheet of paper. If you are right-handed, put the figure on the left. If you are left-handed, put it on the right.

Right-handed Setup

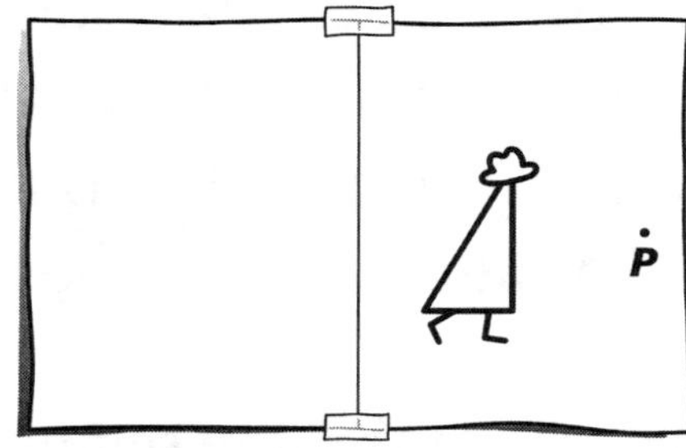

Left-handed Setup

3. With your finger, hold down one end of the stretcher on point *P*. Point *P* is called the *anchor point.*
4. Put a pencil in the other end of the stretcher. Stretch the rubber bands with your pencil until the knot is on the outline of your picture.
5. Guide the knot around the original picture, while your pencil traces out a new picture. (Don't allow any slack in the rubber bands.) This new drawing is the image of the original drawing.

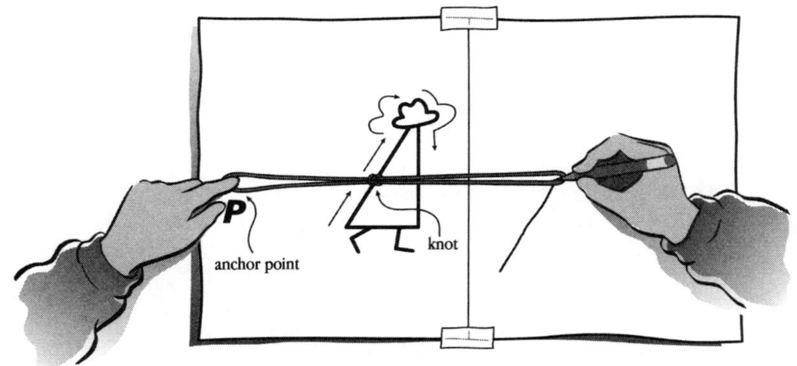

Transparency 1.1B

A. Use your stretcher to enlarge the figures on Labsheets 1.1 and 1.2.

B. Compare is an important word in mathematics. When you **compare** two figures, you look at what is the *same* and what is *different* about them. Compare each original figure to the enlarged image you made. Make a detailed list about what is the same and what is different about them. Be sure to consider

- the lengths of the line segments
- the areas
- the angles (for figures with angles)
- the general shape of the figure

Explain each comparison you make in detail. For example, rather than just saying that two lengths are different, tell exactly which lengths you are comparing and explain how they differ.

Lurking among the members of the Wump family are some impostors who, at first glance, look like the Wumps but are actually quite different.

A. Use the instructions for drawing Wumps to draw Mug Wump on the dot paper grid on Labsheet 2.1B. Describe Mug's shape.

B. Use Labsheet 2.1A and two more copies of Labsheet 2.1B to make Bug, Lug, Thug, and Zug. After drawing the characters, compare them to Mug. Which characters are the impostors?

C. Compare Mug to the other characters. What things are the same about Mug and Zug? Mug and Lug? Mug and Bug? Mug and Thug? What things are different? Think about the general shape, the lengths of sides, and the angles of each figure.

	Mug Wump	Zug	Lug	Bug	Thug
Rule	(x, y)	$(2x, 2y)$	$(3x, y)$	$(3x, 3y)$	$(x, 3y)$
Point	Set 1	Set 1	Set 1	Set 1	Set 1
A	(2, 0)	(4, 0)			
B	(2, 4)	(4, 8)			
C	(0, 4)				
D	(0, 5)				
E	(2, 5)				
F	(0, 8)				
G	(0, 12)				
H	(1, 15)				
I	(2, 12)				
J	(5, 12)				
K	(6, 15)				
L	(7, 12)				
M	(7, 8)				
N	(5, 5)				
O	(7, 5)				
P	(7, 4)				
Q	(5, 4)				
R	(5, 0)				
S	(4, 0)				
T	(4, 3)				
U	(3, 3)				
V	(3, 0) (connect *V* to *A*)				
	Set 2 (start over)	Set 2	Set 2	Set 2	Set 2
W	(1, 8)				
X	(2, 7)				
Y	(5, 7)				
Z	(6, 8)				
	Set 3 (start over)	Set 3	Set 3	Set 3	Set 3
AA	(3, 8)				
BB	(4, 8)				
CC	(4, 10)				
DD	(3, 10) (connect *DD* to *AA*)				
	Set 4 (start over)	Set 4	Set 4	Set 4	Set 4
EE	(2, 11) (make a dot)				
FF	(5, 11) (make a dot)				

Transparency 2.1C

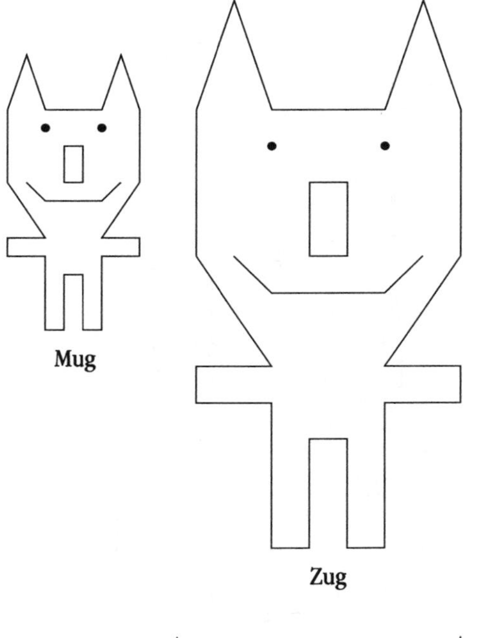

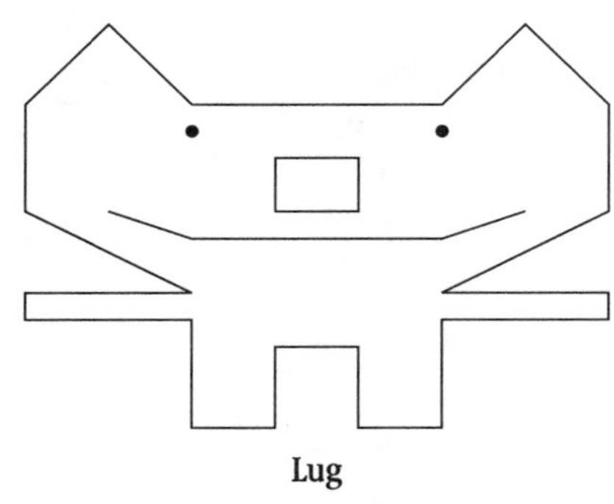

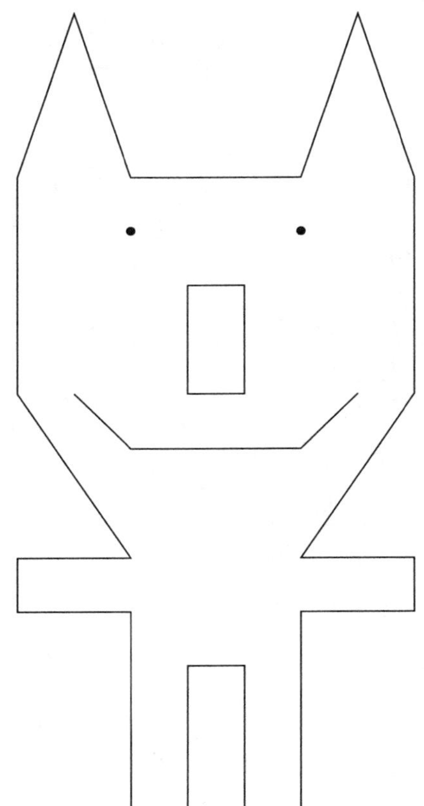

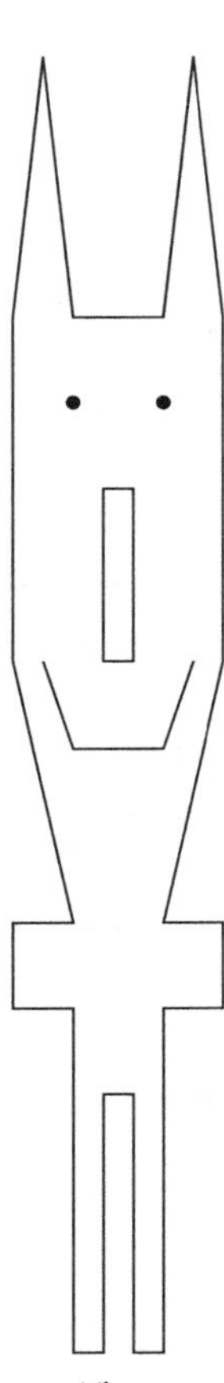

Transparency 2.1D

	Mug Wump	Zug	Lug	Bug	Thug
Rule	(x, y)	$(2x, 2y)$	$(3x, y)$	$(3x, 3y)$	$(x, 3y)$
Point	Set 1	Set 1	Set 1	Set 1	Set 1
A	(2, 0)	(4, 0)	(6, 0)	(6, 0)	(2, 0)
B	(2, 4)	(4, 8)	(6, 4)	(6, 12)	(2, 12)
C	(0, 4)	(0, 8)	(0, 4)	(0, 12)	(0, 12)
D	(0, 5)	(0, 10)	(0, 5)	(0, 15)	(0, 15)
E	(2, 5)	(4, 10)	(6, 5)	(6, 15)	(2, 15)
F	(0, 8)	(0, 16)	(0, 8)	(0, 24)	(0, 24)
G	(0, 12)	(0, 24)	(0, 12)	(0, 36)	(0, 36)
H	(1, 15)	(2, 30)	(3, 15)	(3, 45)	(1, 45)
I	(2, 12)	(4, 24)	(6, 12)	(6, 36)	(2, 36)
J	(5, 12)	(10, 24)	(15, 12)	(15, 36)	(5, 36)
K	(6, 15)	(12, 30)	(18, 15)	(18, 45)	(6, 45)
L	(7, 12)	(14, 24)	(21, 12)	(21, 36)	(7, 36)
M	(7, 8)	(14, 16)	(21, 8)	(21, 24)	(7, 24)
N	(5, 5)	(10, 10)	(15, 5)	(15, 15)	(5, 15)
O	(7, 5)	(14, 10)	(21, 5)	(21, 15)	(7, 15)
P	(7, 4)	(14, 8)	(21, 4)	(21, 12)	(7, 12)
Q	(5, 4)	(10, 8)	(15, 4)	(15, 12)	(5, 12)
R	(5, 0)	(10, 0)	(15, 0)	(15, 0)	(5, 0)
S	(4, 0)	(8, 0)	(12, 0)	(12, 0)	(4, 0)
T	(4, 3)	(8, 6)	(12, 3)	(12, 9)	(4, 9)
U	(3, 3)	(6, 6)	(9, 3)	(9, 9)	(3, 9)
V	(3, 0) (connect *V* to *A*)	(6, 0)	(9, 0)	(9, 0)	(3, 0)
	Set 2 (start over)	Set 2	Set 2	Set 2	Set 2
W	(1, 8)	(2, 16)	(3, 8)	(3, 24)	(1, 24)
X	(2, 7)	(4, 14)	(6, 7)	(6, 21)	(2, 21)
Y	(5, 7)	(10, 14)	(15, 7)	(15, 21)	(5, 21)
Z	(6, 8)	(12, 16)	(18, 8)	(18, 24)	(6, 24)
	Set 3 (start over)	Set 3	Set 3	Set 3	Set 3
AA	(3, 8)	(6, 16)	(9, 8)	(9, 24)	(3, 24)
BB	(4, 8)	(8, 16)	(12, 8)	(12, 24)	(4, 24)
CC	(4, 10)	(8, 20)	(12, 10)	(12, 30)	(4, 30)
DD	(3, 10) (connect *DD* to *AA*)	(6, 20)	(9, 10)	(9, 30)	(3, 30)
	Set 4 (start over)	Set 4	Set 4	Set 4	Set 4
EE	(2, 11) (make a dot)	(4, 22)	(6, 11)	(6, 33)	(2, 33)
FF	(5, 11) (make a dot)	(10, 22)	(15, 11)	(15, 33)	(5, 33)

Copy the chart. The Wumps in the chart are numbered according to their size. Mug is Wump 1. Since the segments that make up Zug are twice as long as the segments that make up Mug, Zug is Wump 2. Since the segments that make up Bug are three times as long as the segments that make up Mug, Bug is Wump 3. Since Lug and Thug are not similar to the Wumps, they are at the bottom of the chart.

A. Look carefully at the noses of Mug, Zug, Lug, Bug, and Thug. In your table, record the dimensions, the ratio of width to length ($\frac{\text{width}}{\text{length}}$), and the perimeter of each nose.

B. Look at the data you recorded for Mug, Zug, and Bug. What patterns do you see? Explain how the values in each column change as the Wumps get bigger. Look for relationships between the values in the different columns.

C. The rule for making Wump 4 is ($4x$, $4y$). The rule for making Wump 5 is ($5x$, $5y$). Add data to the chart for Wumps 4 and 5. Do their noses fit the patterns you noticed in part B?

D. Use the patterns you found to add data for Wumps 10, 20, and 100 to the chart. Explain your reasoning.

E. Do Lug's nose and Thug's nose seem to fit the patterns you found for the Wumps? If not, what makes them different?

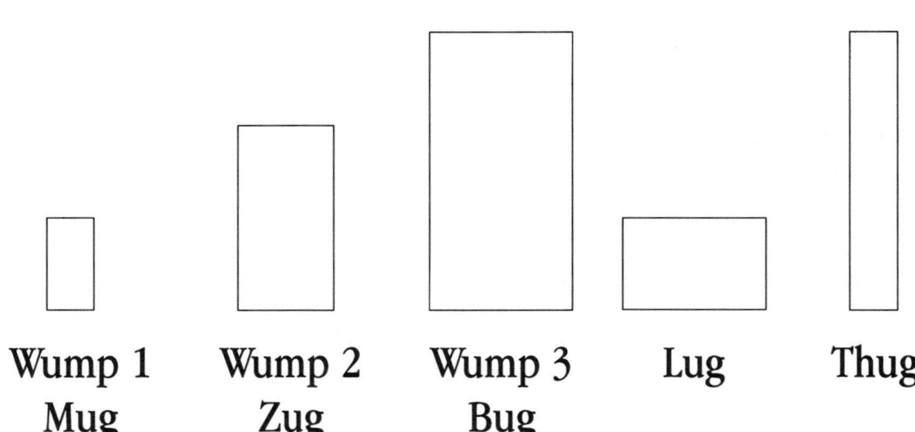

The Wump Noses (Plus Lug and Thug)

Wump	Width of nose	Length of nose	$\frac{\text{Width}}{\text{Length}}$	Perimeter
Wump 1 (Mug)	1	2	$\frac{1}{2}$	
Wump 2 (Zug)	2			
Wump 3 (Bug)	3			
Wump 4				
Wump 5				
⋮				
Wump 10				
Wump 20				
Wump 100				
Lug				
Thug				

Transparency 2.3A

Use the table and dot paper grids on Labsheets 2.3A and 2.3B.

- To make Mug's hat, plot points A–H from the Hat 1 column on the grid labeled Hat 1, connecting the points as you go.
- For Hats 2–6, use the rules in the table to fill in the coordinates for each column. Then, plot each hat on the appropriate grid, connecting the points as you go.

	Hat 1	Hat 2	Hat 3	Hat 4	Hat 5	Hat 6
Point	(x, y)	$(x + 2, y + 2)$	$(x + 3, y - 1)$	$(2x, y + 2)$	$(2x, 3y)$	$(0.5x, 0.5y)$
A	(0, 4)	(2, 6)	(3, 3)	(0, 6)	(0, 12)	(0, 2)
B	(0, 1)					
C	(6, 1)					
D	(4, 2)					
E	(4, 4)					
F	(3, 5)					
G	(1, 5)					
H	(0, 4)					

Hat 1

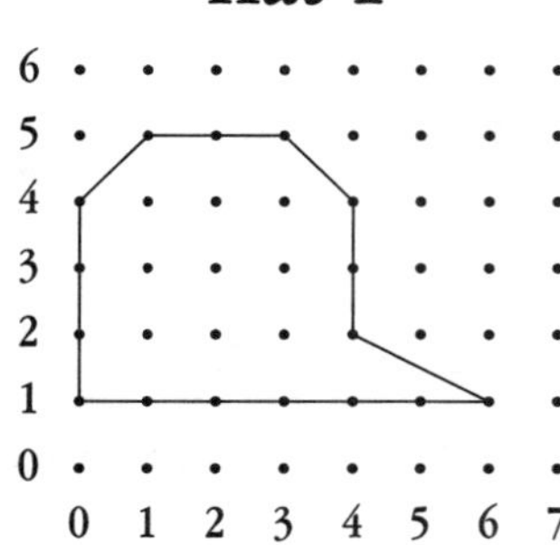

Hat 2

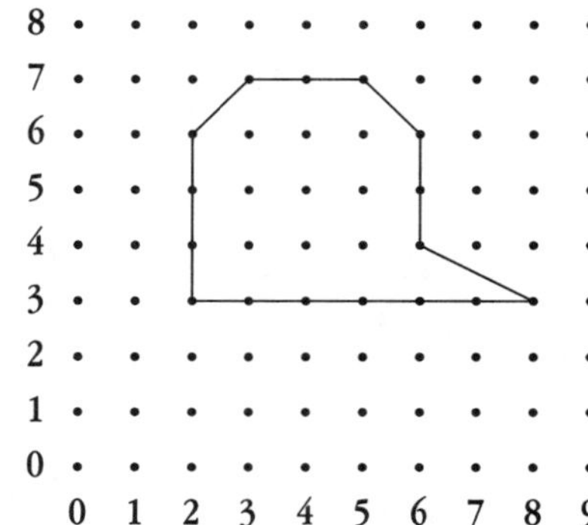

Hat 3

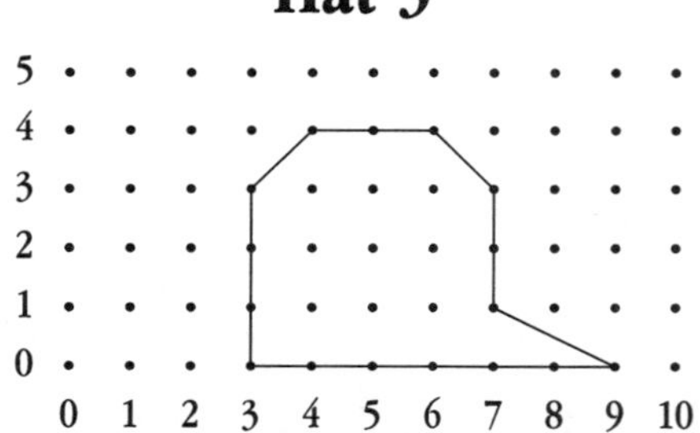

Hat 4

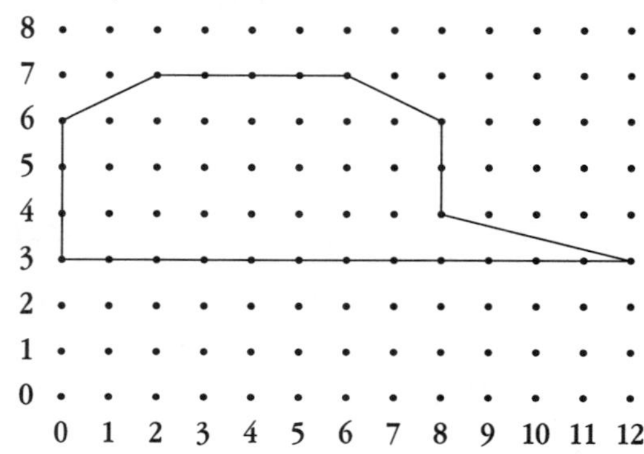

Hat 5

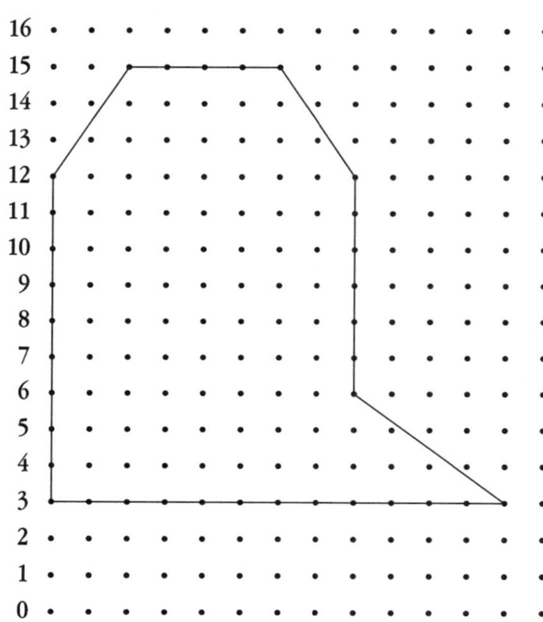

Hat 6

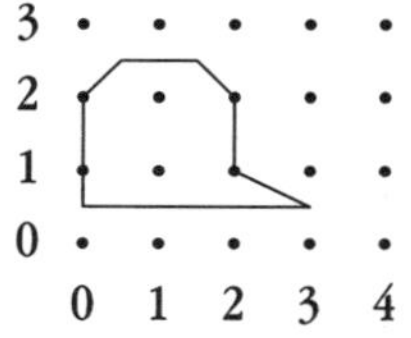

Examine the four sets of polygons. Two shapes in each set are similar, and the other is an impostor.

In each set, which polygons are similar? Explain your answers. You may cut out the polygons if it helps you think about the question.

Rectangle set

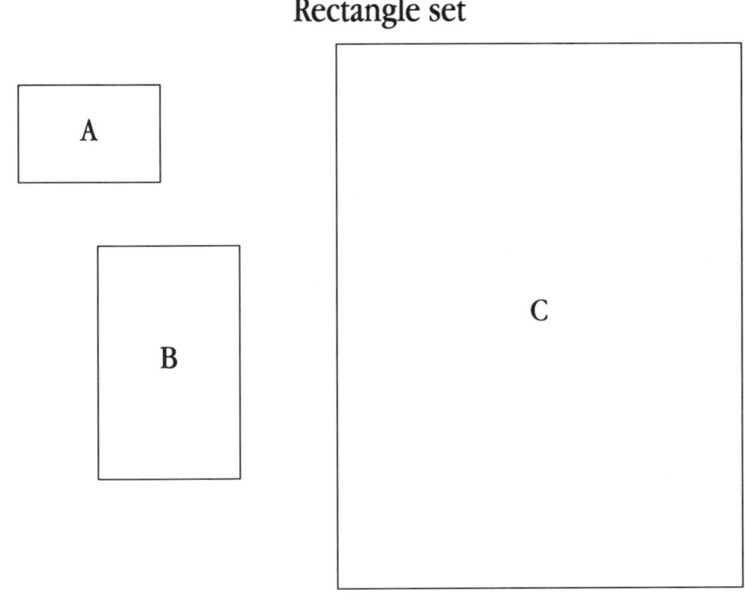

Star set

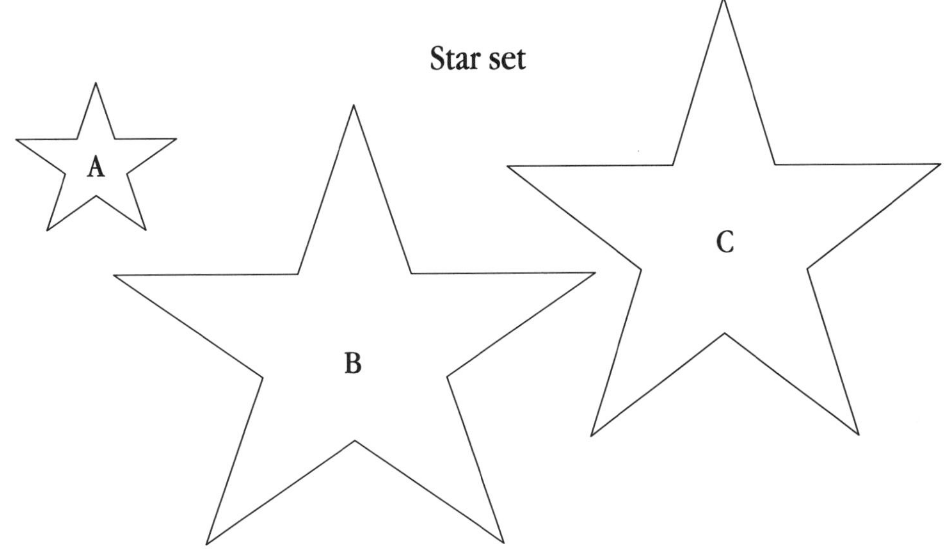

Transparency 3.1B

Polygon Sets

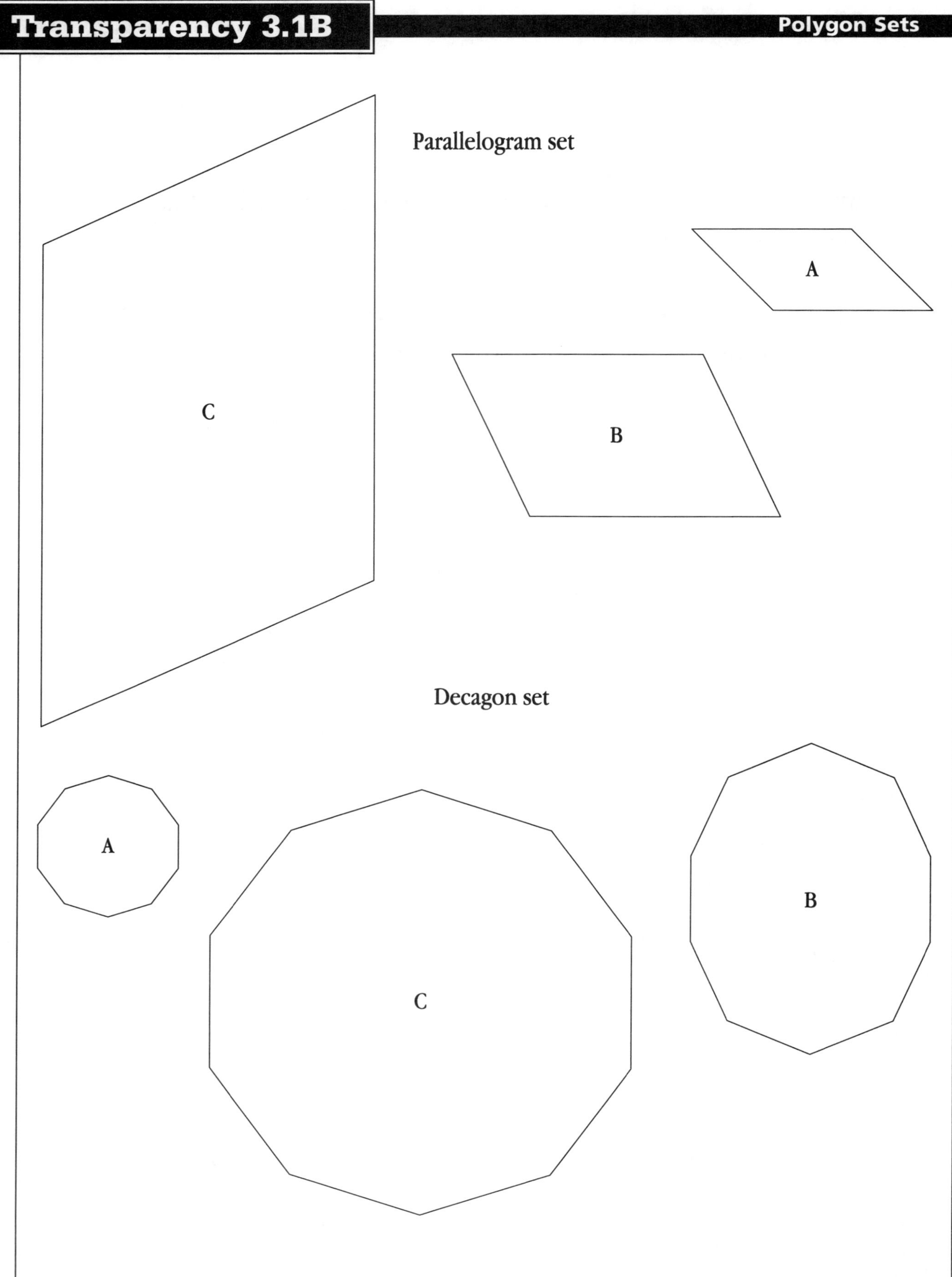

Use the shapes from your ShapeSet™, or cut out copies of the shapes from Labsheet 3.2.

A. Start with four copies of one of the shapes. Try to find a way to put the four copies together—with no overlap and no holes—to make a larger, similar shape. If you are successful, make a sketch showing how the four shapes (rep-tiles) fit together, and give the scale factor from the original shape to the new shape. Repeat this process with each shape.

B. For each rep-tile you found in part A, try to find a different way to arrange the copies to get a similar shape. Sketch each new arrangement. How does the scale factor of each new arrangement compare to the scale factor for the first arrangement?

C. Start with one of the rep-tiles you found in part A. Try to add copies of the rep-tile to this shape to make the next-largest similar shape. If you are successful, make a sketch showing how the copies fit together. Repeat this process with each rep-tile you found in part A.

Transparency 3.3

The shapes below appear on Labsheet 3.3. Try to find a way to divide each shape into four congruent, smaller shapes that are similar to the original shape. For each shape, give the scale factor from the smaller shape to the original shape.

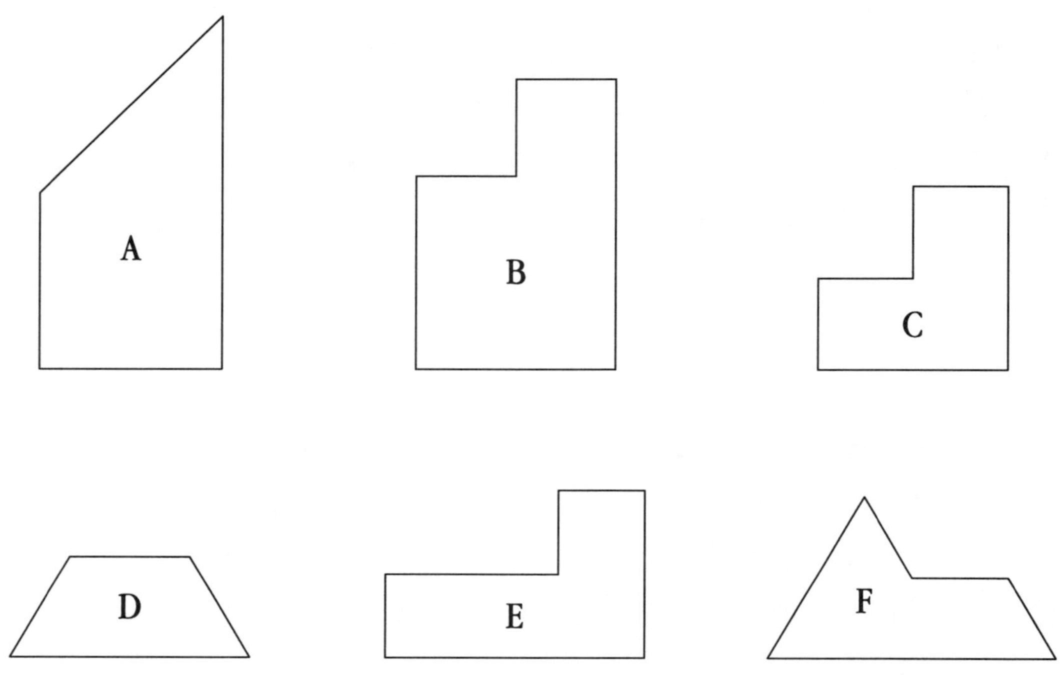

If you have trouble dividing a shape, experiment by cutting out copies of the shape and putting them together as you did in Problem 3.2.

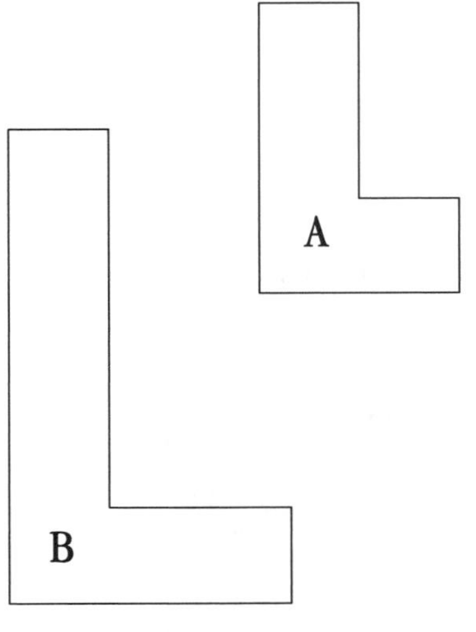
A
B

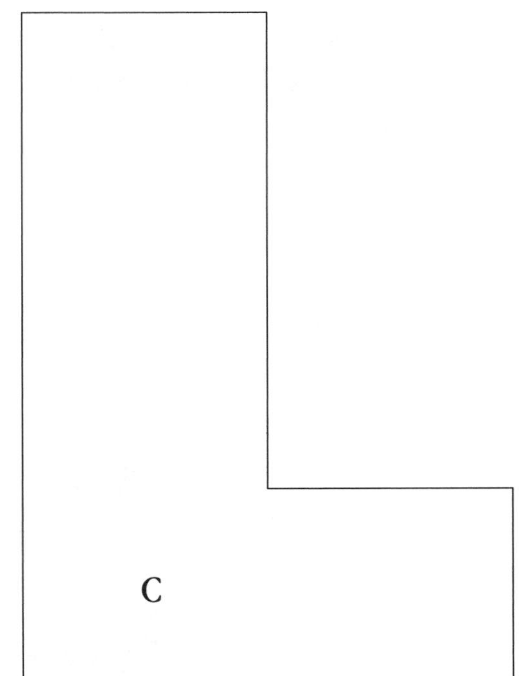
C

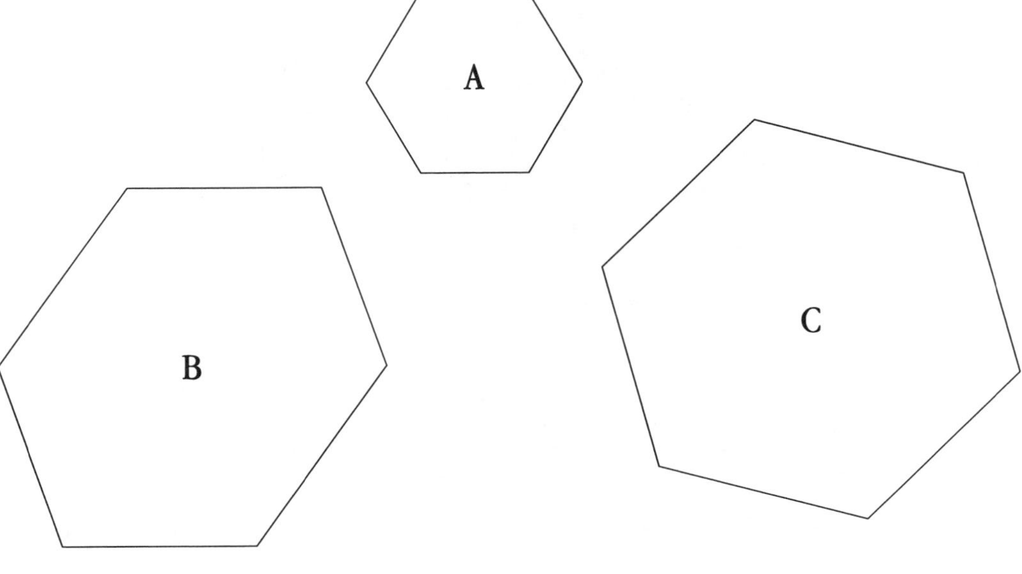
A
B
C

The teacher's guides for Connected Mathematics measure $8\frac{1}{2}$" by 11". Below is a photograph of a middle school teacher holding a teacher's guide.

A. Use the photograph to figure out how tall the teacher is. Explain your procedure.

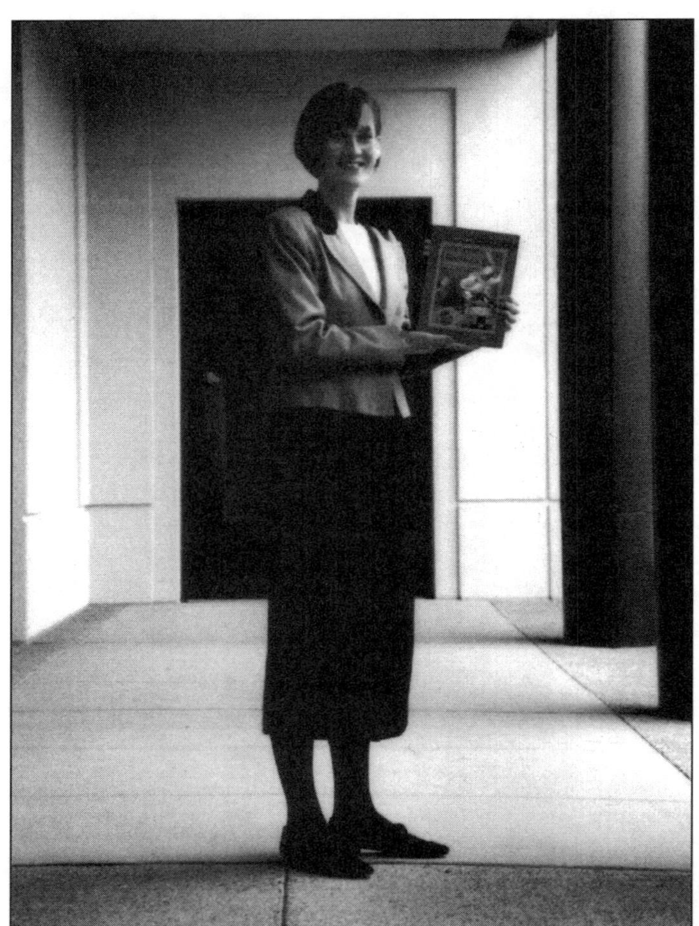

B. How do you think the police determined the robber's height?

Raphael is closing his bookstore. He wants to place a full-page advertisement in the newspaper to announce his going-out-of-business sale. A full-page ad is 13" by 22", which allows for a white border around the ad.

Raphael used his computer to make an $8\frac{1}{2}$"-by-11" model of the advertisement, but he wants the newspaper ad department to enlarge it to full-page size. Is this possible? Explain your reasoning.

Transparency 4.3

Raphael wants to make sale posters by enlarging his $8\frac{1}{2}$" by 11" ad. Raphael thinks big posters will get more attention, so he wants to enlarge his ad as much as possible.

The copy machines at the copy shop have cartridges for three paper sizes: $8\frac{1}{2}$" by 11", 11" by 14", and 11" by 17". The machines allow users to enlarge or reduce documents by specifying a percent between 50% and 200%. For example, to enlarge a document by a scale factor of 1.5, a user would enter 150%. This tells the machine to enlarge the document to 150% of its current size.

A. Can Raphael make a poster that is similar to his original ad on any of the three paper sizes—without having to trim off part of the paper? Why or why not?

B. If you were Raphael, what paper size would you use to make a larger, similar poster on the copy machine? What scale factor—expressed as a percent—would you enter into the machine?

Transparency 4.4

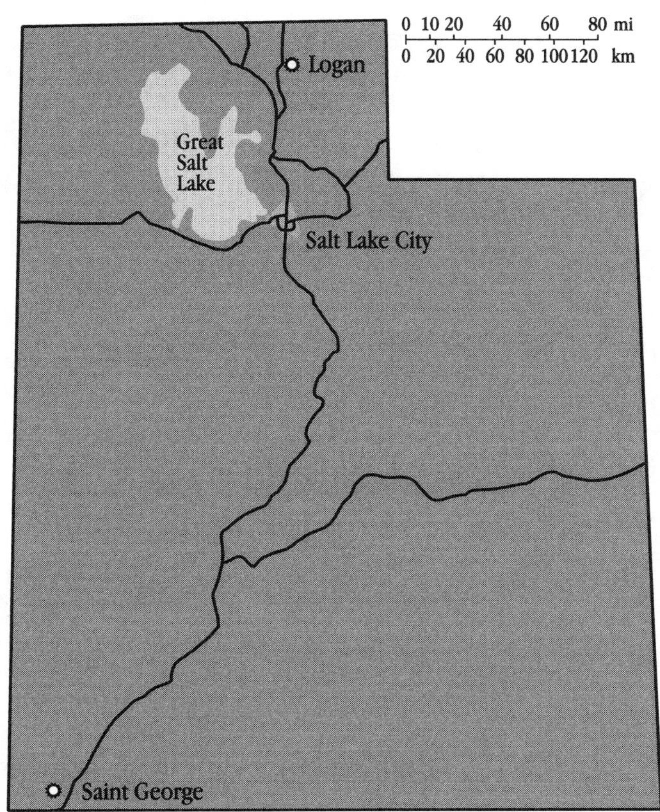

A. How can you use the scale on the map to calculate the scale factor between the map and the real state? What is the scale factor?

B. How many miles of fencing would it take to surround the state of Utah?

C. Use the scale to estimate the area of Utah. Explain your work.

D. If you drove at a steady speed of 55 miles per hour, about how long would it take you to travel from Logan to Saint George?

Mr. Anwar's class is using the shadow method to estimate the height of their school building. They have made the following measurements and sketch:

Length of the meterstick = 1 m
Length of the meterstick's shadow = 0.2 m
Length of the building's shadow = 7 m

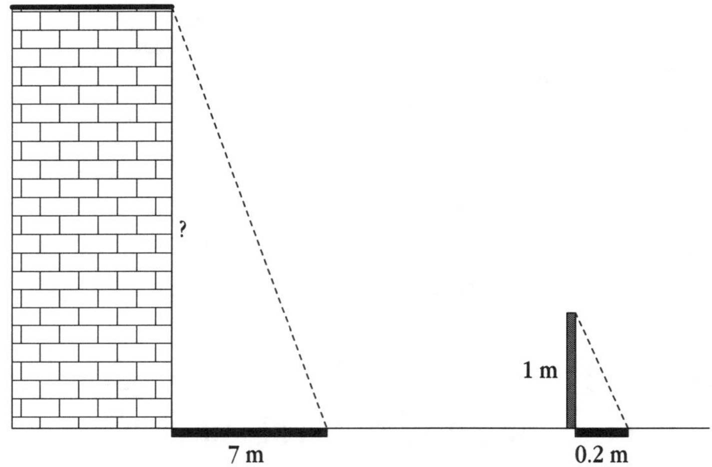

A. Use what you know about similar triangles to find the building's height from the given measurements. Explain your work.

B. With your class, choose a building or other tall object. Work with your group to estimate the object's height using the shadow method. In your answer, include the measurements your group made, and explain in words and drawings how you used these measurements to find the object's height.

Jim and Qin-Zhong, students in Mr. Anwar's class, are using the mirror method to estimate the height of their school building. They have made the following measurements and sketch:

Height from the ground to Jim's eyes = 150 cm
Distance from the middle of the mirror to Jim = 100 cm
Distance from the middle of the mirror to the building = 600 cm

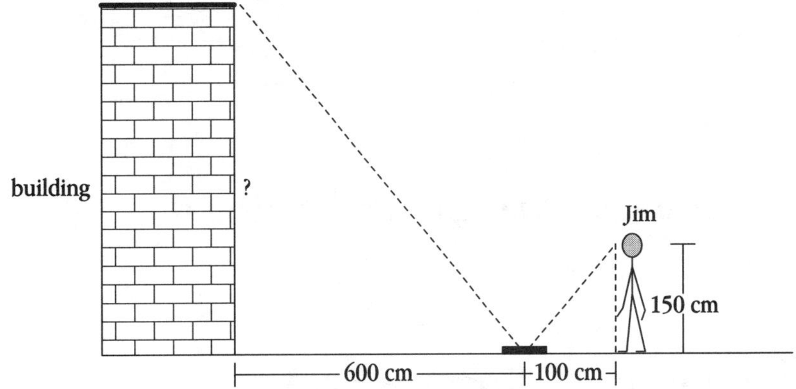

A. Use what you know about similar triangles to find the building's height from the given measurements. Explain your work.

B. With your group, use the mirror method to estimate the height of the same object or building you worked with in Problem 5.1. In your answer, include all the measurements your group made, and explain in words and drawings how you used the measurements to find the object's height.

C. How does the height estimate you made using the shadow method compare with the height estimate you made using the mirror method? Do you think your estimates for the object's height are reasonable? Why or why not?

Here is the diagram Darnell, Angie, and Trevor made, including their measurements.

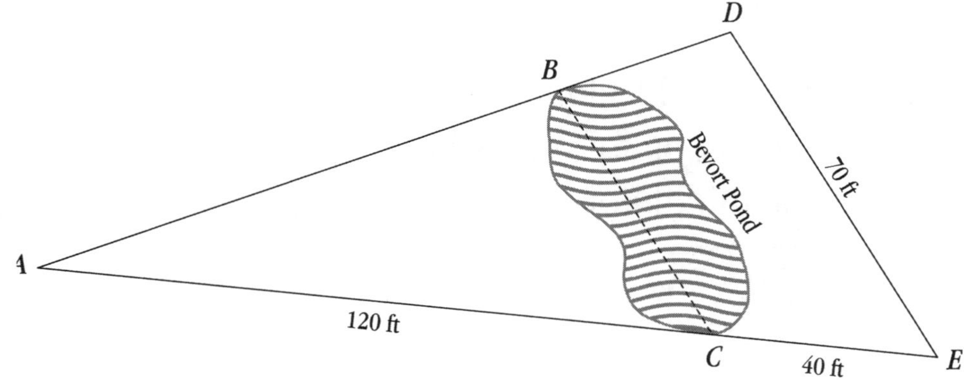

A. Name the two similar triangles in the diagram.

B. What is the scale factor from the large triangle to the small triangle?

C. What is the distance across the pond (measured along the dotted line)?

D. On your school grounds or in your neighborhood, find a pond or some other feature, such as a park, a playground, or a wooded area. Use the ideas in this problem to estimate the distance across the feature. Explain your work carefully.

Choose one of the figures below. Make the figure by typing the commands in the Command window.

Equilateral triangle	Rectangle	Right trapezoid
`fd 60`	`fd 30`	`fd 52`
`rt 120`	`rt 90`	`rt 90`
`fd 60`	`fd 70`	`fd 30`
`rt 120`	`rt 90`	`rt 60`
`fd 60`	`fd 30`	`fd 60`
	`rt 90`	`rt 120`
	`fd 70`	`fd 60`

After you've drawn the figure, save a copy of it on your computer.

A. Which features of the original figure change when you use the Scale tool? Which features of the original figure change when you use the Change Shape tool? Be sure to discuss numbers of sides, side lengths, and angle measures.

B. Which features of the original figure stay the same when you use the Scale tool? Which features of the original figure stay the same when you use the Change Shape tool?

This is the *Turtle Math* title screen. Click anywhere on the picture to move to the next screen.

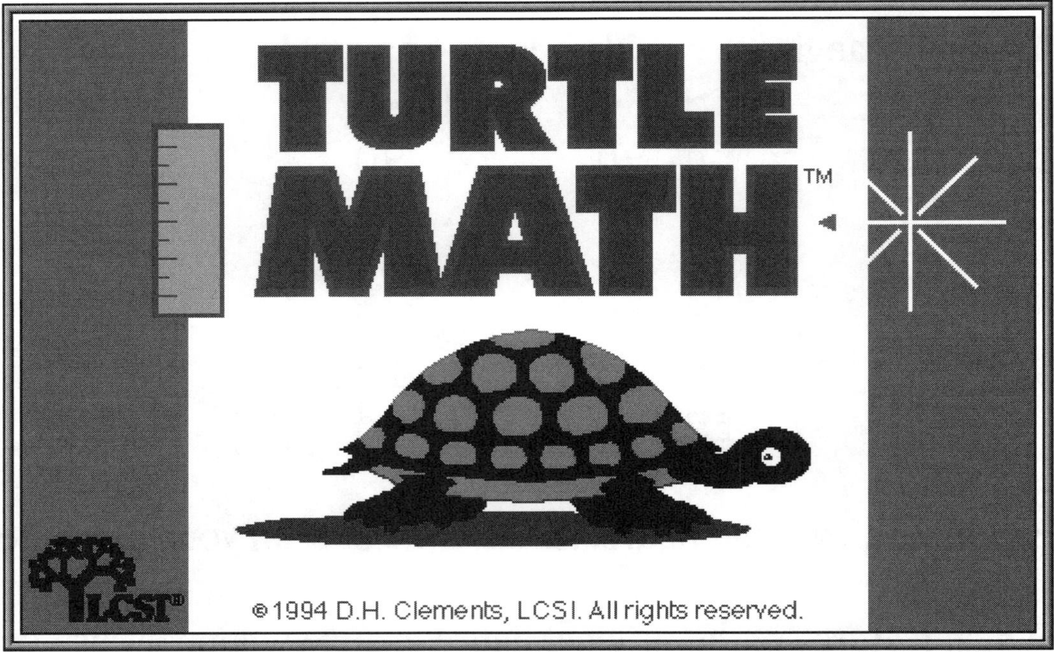

Click on Free Explore to get the Drawing window.

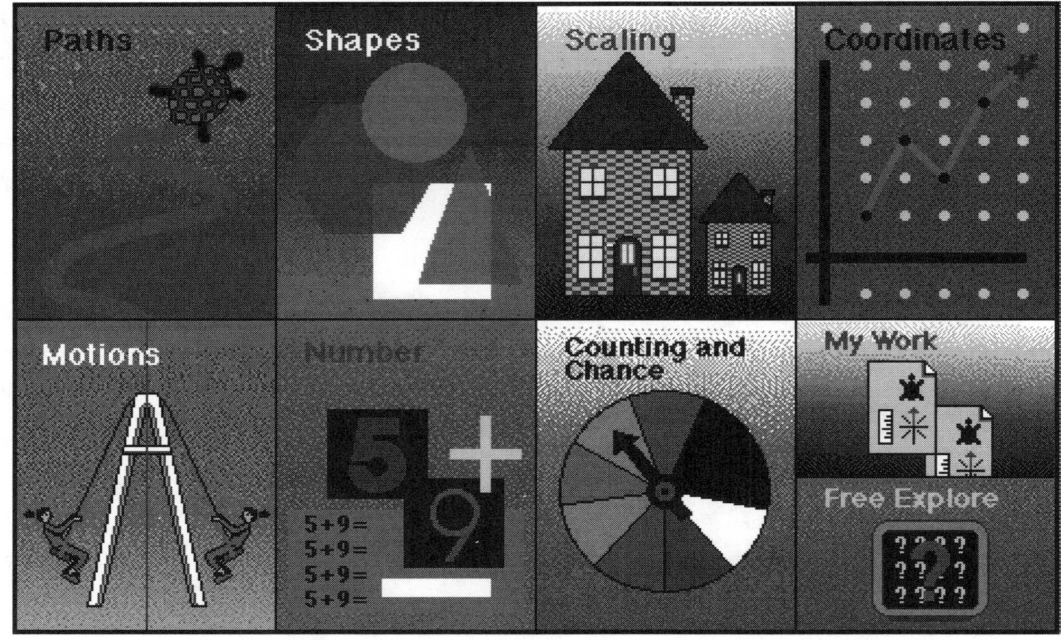

Type turtle instructions in the Command window. The turtle moves and draws in the Drawing window.

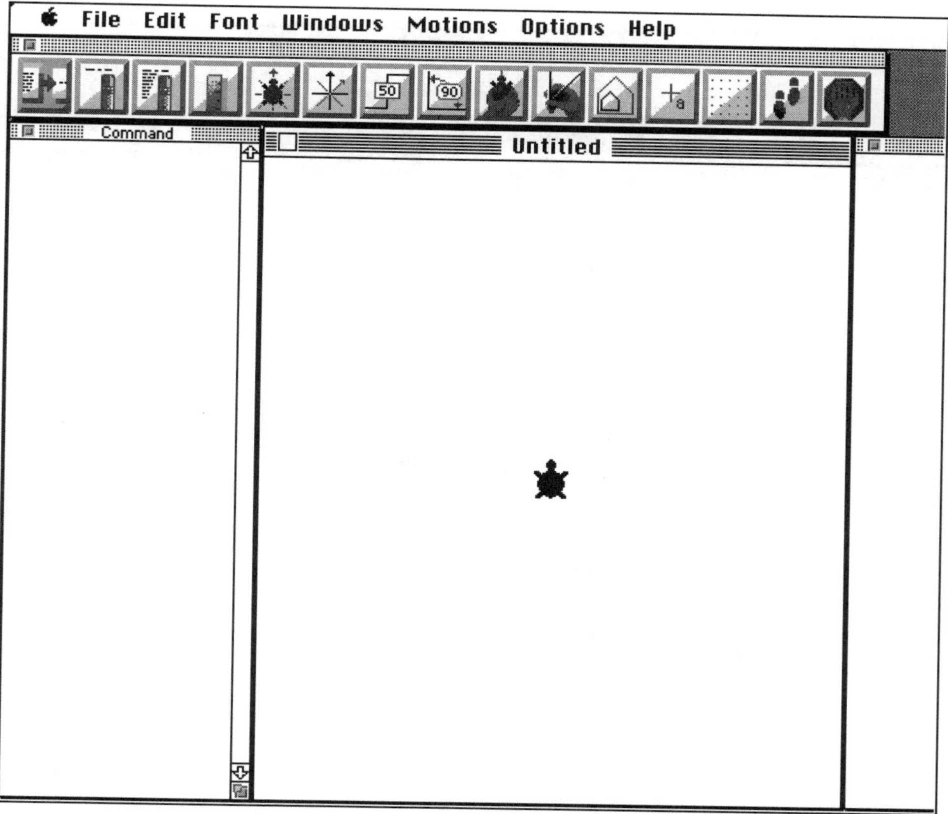

This is the *Turtle Math* tool bar.

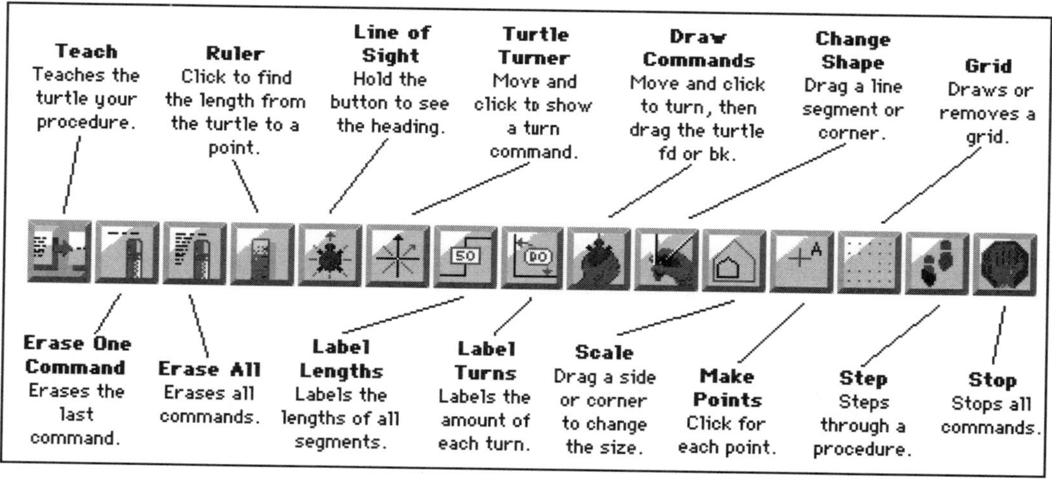

Transparency 6.1D

Click once on the Grid tool square to show a grid on the Drawing window. To remove the grid, click again.

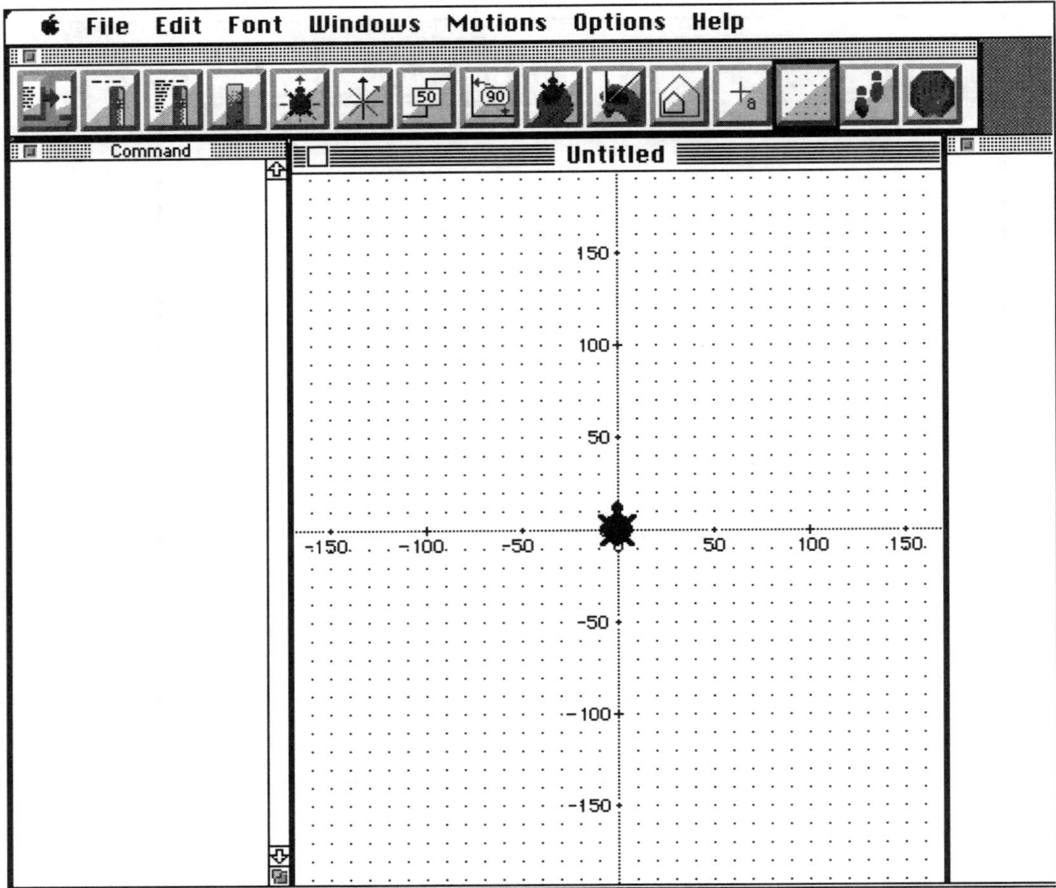

The set of commands below will draw a flag. Type in the commands exactly as they are shown; don't use any shortcuts. When you are finished, save a copy of your flag by using Save My Work from the File menu.

```
fd 80
rt 90
fd 50
rt 90
fd 30
rt 90
fd 50
```

Use the Scale tool to make enlargements and reductions of the flag. Make a chart like the one below, and fill in the missing information.

Scale factor	Sketch of figure	Height of flagpole	Length of flag	Width of flag	Area of flag
1	50, 30, 80	80 steps	50 steps	30 steps	1500 square steps
2					
0.5					
–1					

Family Letter (English)

Dear Family,

The next unit in your child's course of study in mathematics class this year is *Stretching and Shrinking.* Its focus is geometry, and it teaches students to understand and to use the concepts of similarity. Students look at what it means for figures or shapes to be mathematically similar. The goals of the unit include having students explore relationships among figures that have been stretched or shrunk, and the resulting changes in properties of the figures, such as area and perimeter.

In this unit, your child will use properties of similar figures to explore reductions and enlargements made on copy machines. Similarity will also be used to estimate the height of real objects (such as buildings and flagpoles) and the distance across large areas (such as ponds).

By the end of this unit, your child will know how to create similar figures, how to determine whether two figures are similar, and how to predict the growth of the lengths and areas between two similar figures.

You can help your child with the ideas in this unit in several ways:

- Talk with your child about any situations that are like those your child is encountering in the investigations—places in the real world where items are reduced or enlarged, such as models.
- Continue to have your child share his or her mathematics notebook with you, showing you the different ideas about similarity that have been recorded. Ask your child why these ideas are important, and try to share ways that reductions or enlargements help you in your work or hobbies.
- Look over your child's homework, and help your child make sure all questions have been answered and that all explanations are clear.

If you have any questions or concerns about geometry or your child's progress in the class, please feel free to call. We are interested in your child's success in mathematics and want to ensure that this year's mathematics experiences are enjoyable.

Sincerely,

Family Letter (Spanish)

Estimada familia,

La próxima unidad del programa de matemáticas de su hijo o hija para este curso se llama ***Stretching and Shrinking*** (Estiramientos y encogimientos). La misma trata principalmente sobre la geometría, y en ella los alumnos estudiarán y usarán conceptos sobre la semejanza. Además, examinarán el significado de la semejanza matemática entre figuras o formas. Los objetivos de esta unidad incluyen la exploración de las relaciones existentes entre figuras estiradas o encogidas y los cambios resultantes en las propiedades de las mismas como, por ejemplo, el área y el perímetro.

En esta unidad su hijo o hija aplicará propiedades de figuras semejantes para explorar las reducciones y las ampliaciones que realizan las fotocopiadoras. Se hará uso también de la semejanza para estimar la altura de objetos reales (como edificios y astas de banderas) y la distancia entre los extremos de zonas amplias (como lagitos).

Una vez finalizada la unidad, su hijo o hija será capaz de crear figuras semejantes, determinar si dos figuras son semejantes y predecir el aumento de las longitudes y de las áreas de dos figuras semejantes.

Para ayudar a su hijo o hija con las ideas de esta unidad, ustedes pueden hacer lo siguiente:

- Comenten con él o ella situaciones parecidas a las que va conociendo en las investigaciones, es decir, lugares del mundo real donde se reducen o amplían objetos como, por ejemplo, los modelos.

- Hagan que su hijo o hija continúe compartiendo con ustedes su cuaderno de matemáticas y que les enseñe sus anotaciones sobre la semejanza. Pídanle que les explique por qué éstas son importantes e intenten hablar de las diversas maneras en que las reducciones y las ampliaciones facilitan el trabajo o los pasatiempos.

- Repasen su tarea y comprueben juntos que todas las preguntas han sido contestadas y que todas las explicaciones han sido escritas con claridad.

Si ustedes necesitan más detalles o aclaraciones respecto a la geometría o sobre los progresos de su hijo o hija en esta clase, no duden en llamarnos. Nos interesa que su hijo o hija avance en el estudio de las matemáticas y queremos asegurarnos de que las experiencias matemáticas que tenga este año sean lo más amenas posibles.

Atentamente,

Half-Centimeter Grid Paper

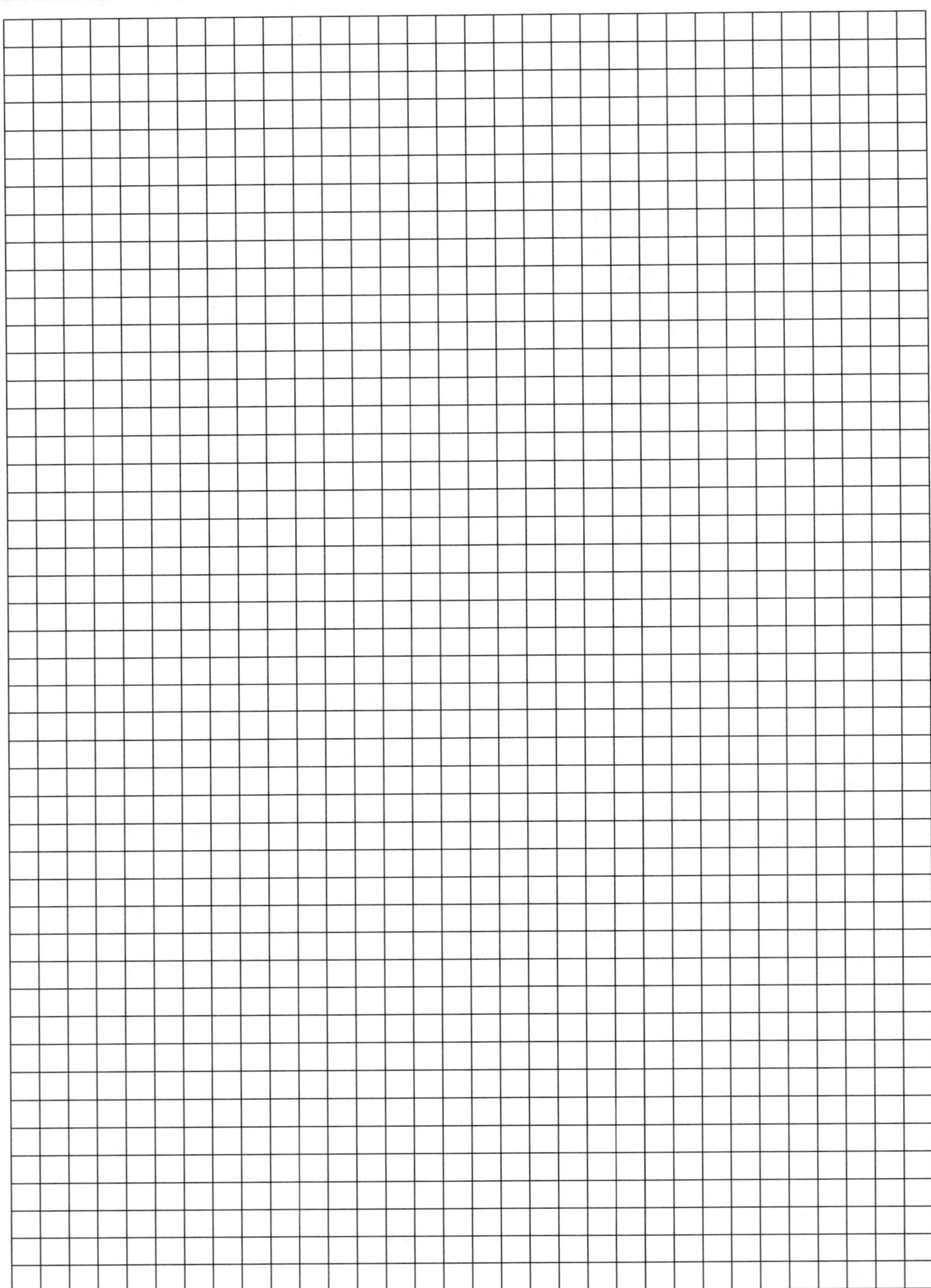

Centimeter Grid Paper

Dot Paper

ShapeSet

To make a complete ShapeSet, make eight copies of pages 1, 2, and 3.

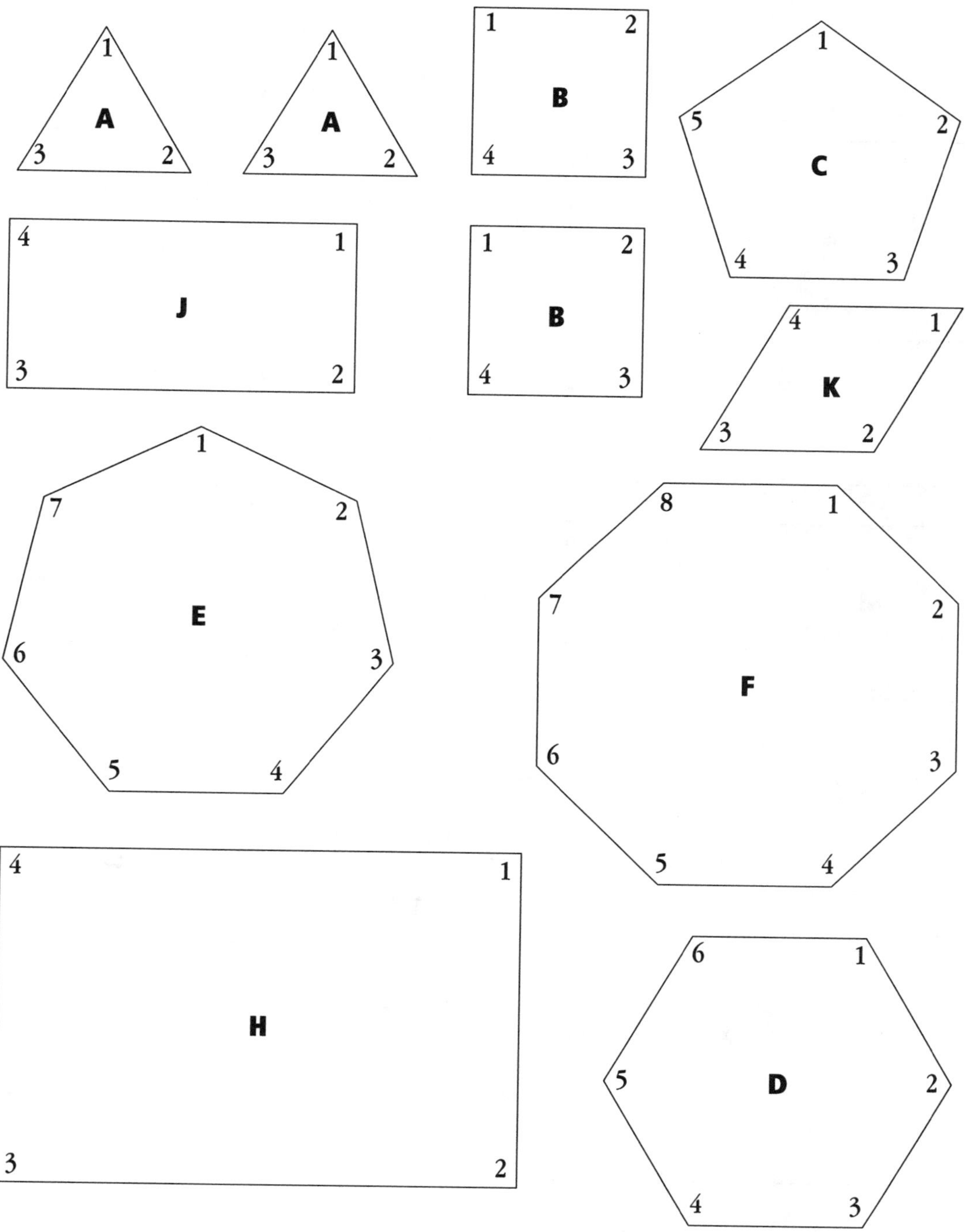

To make a complete ShapeSet, make eight copies of pages 1, 2, and 3.

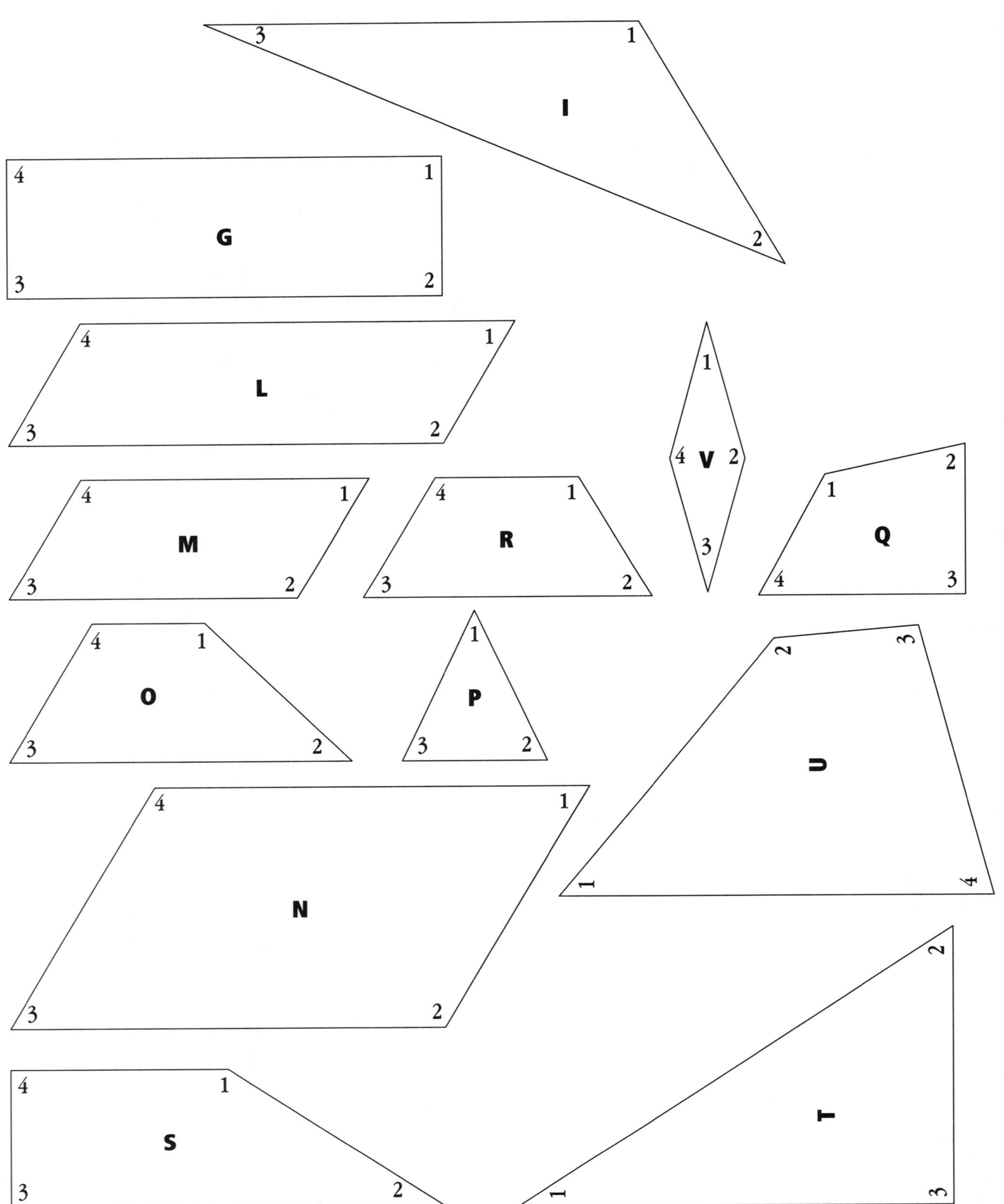

To make a complete ShapeSet, make eight copies of pages 1, 2, and 3.

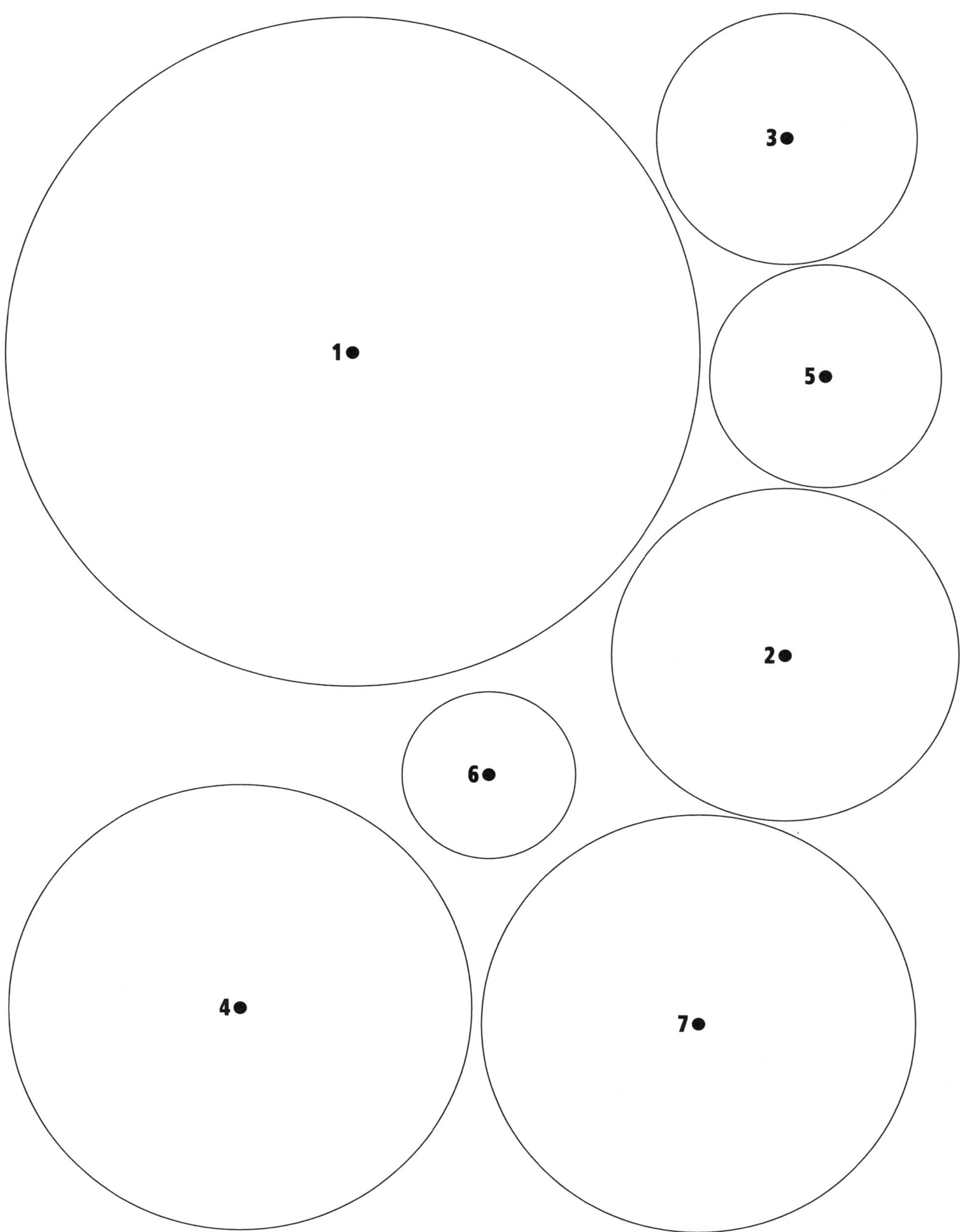

Additional Practice

Investigation 1

Use these problems for additional practice after Investigation 1.

1. Refer to the rectangle below to answer the following questions.

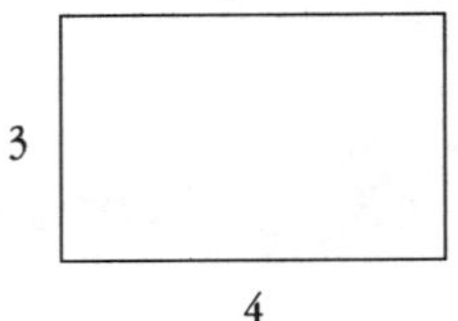

   a. Give the length and width of a rectangle that is an enlargement or a reduction of the above rectangle. Explain your reasoning.

   b. Give the length and width of a rectangle that is *not* an enlargement or a reduction of the above rectangle. Explain your reasoning.

2. Figure *VWXYZ* is an enlargement of figure *ABCDE*. Name all the pairs of corresponding sides and all the pairs of corresponding angles between the two figures.

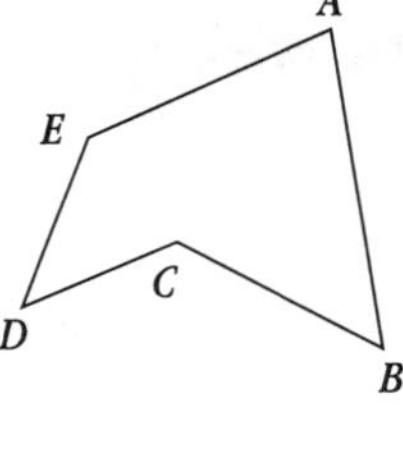

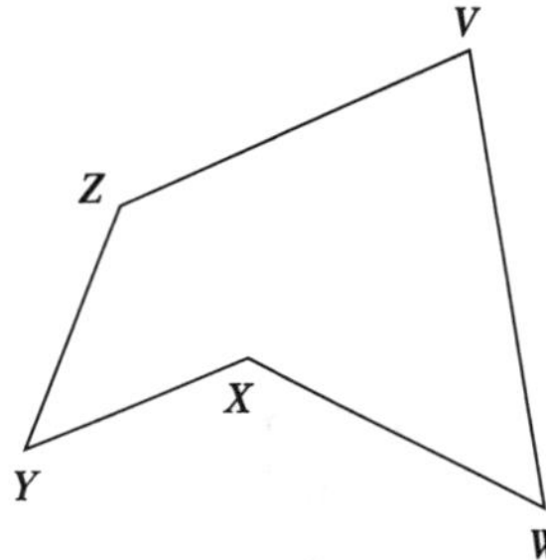

3. Draw a square. Then draw a square with a side length that is twice the side length of the original square.

   a. How many copies of the smaller square will fit inside the larger square?

   b. Will you get the same answer for part a no matter what side length you choose for the original square? Explain your reasoning.

4. Draw any rectangle that is not a square. Then draw a rectangle with side lengths that are twice the side lengths of the original rectangle.

   a. How many copies of the smaller rectangle will fit inside the larger rectangle?

   b. Will you get the same answer for part a no matter what side lengths you choose for the original rectangle?

Additional Practice

Investigation 2

Use these problems for additional practice after Investigation 2.

1. Draw any rectangle that is not a square. Draw a similar rectangle by applying a scale factor of 3 to the original rectangle.

   a. How many copies of the original rectangle will fit inside the new rectangle?

   b. Will you get the same answer for part a no matter what rectangle you use as the original rectangle? Explain your reasoning.

2. Make a figure by connecting the following sets of points:

   Set 1: (8, 5), (8, 8), (0, 8), (0, 5), (8, 5)

   Set 2: (4, 6), (8, 2), (0, 2), (4, 6)

   Set 3: (2, 6), (1, 6), (1, 7), (2, 7), (2, 6)

   Set 4: (6, 6), (7, 6), (7, 7), (6, 7), (6, 6)

   a. If you used the rule $(6x, 6y)$ to transform this figure into a new figure, how would the angles of the new figure compare with the angles of the original? How would the side lengths of the new figure compare with the side lengths of the original? How would the new figure's general shape compare with the general shape of the original?

   b. If you used the rule $(0.5x, 0.5y)$ to transform the original figure into a new figure, how would the angles of the new figure compare with the angles of the original figure? How would the side lengths of the new figure compare with the side lengths of the original? How would the new figure's general shape compare with the general shape of the original?

   c. If you used the rule $(3x + 1, 3y - 4)$ to transform the original figure into a new figure, how would the angles of the new figure compare with the angles of the original figure? How would the side lengths of the new figure compare with the side lengths of the original? How would the new figure's general shape compare with the general shape of the original?

3. If a figure on a grid is transformed by applying the rule $(2x, 3y)$, will the new figure be similar to the original? Explain your reasoning.

4. If a figure on a grid is transformed by applying the rule $(2x + 2, 2y - 2)$, will the new figure be similar to the original? Explain your reasoning.

Additional Practice

Investigation 3

Use these problems for additional practice after Investigation 3.

1. On grid paper, make a right triangle with legs of length 8 and 12.
   a. Give the leg lengths of two smaller right triangles that are similar to this right triangle and that have whole-number side lengths.
   b. Copies of each of the smaller right triangles can be put together to exactly match the original right triangle. How many of each smaller right triangle does it take to match the original right triangle?

2. On grid paper, make an isosceles triangle with base and height both equal to 6.
   a. Can isosceles triangles with base and height equal to 2 be put together to exactly match the original triangle? Is each smaller triangle similar to the original triangle?
   b. Can isosceles triangles with base and height equal to 4 be put together to exactly match the original triangle? Is each smaller triangle similar to the original triangle?

3. Find the missing values.
   a. $x = ?$

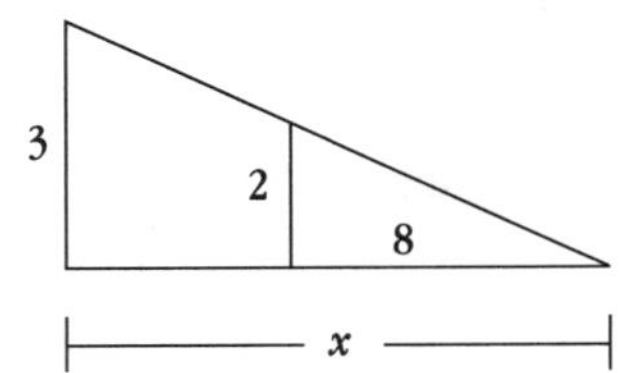

   b. $a = ?$

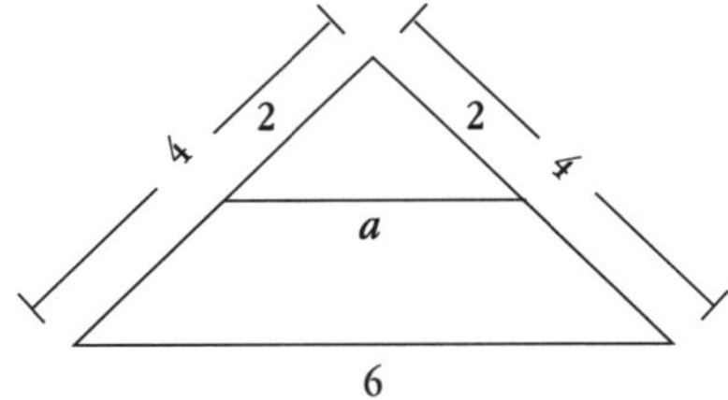

4. The drawing below shows how a square foot and a square yard compare.

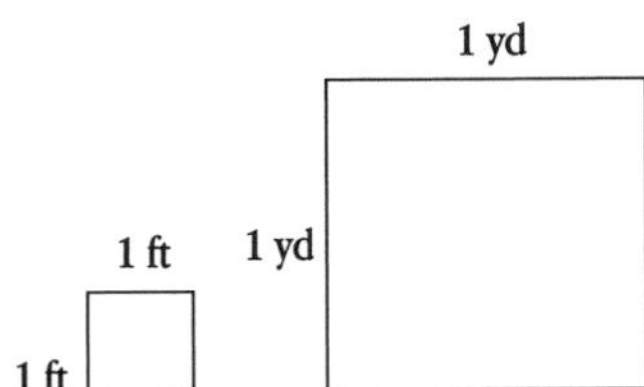

a. Are a square foot and a square yard similar? If so, what is the scale factor from a square foot to a square yard? What is the scale factor from a square yard to a square foot?

b. How many square feet are in a square yard? Explain your reasoning.

c. The area of a room is 28 square yards. What is the area of the room in square feet?

d. The area of a backyard is 1800 square feet. What is the area of the backyard in square yards?

e. Compare a square inch with a square foot and a square yard. What is the scale factor from a square inch to a square foot? What is the scale factor from a square inch to a square yard?

5. Area is often measured in square centimeters and square meters.

a. Are a square centimeter and a square meter similar? If so, what is the scale factor from a square centimeter to a square meter? What is the scale factor from a square meter to a square centimeter?

b. How many square centimeters are in a square meter? Explain your reasoning.

c. The area of a room is 28 square meters. What is the area of the room in square centimeters?

d. The area of a painting is 1800 square centimeters. What is the area of the painting in square meters?

Investigation 4

Use these problems for additional practice after Investigation 4.

1. Find all the pairs of similar rectangles below. For each pair you find, give the scale factor from the smaller rectangle to the larger rectangle.

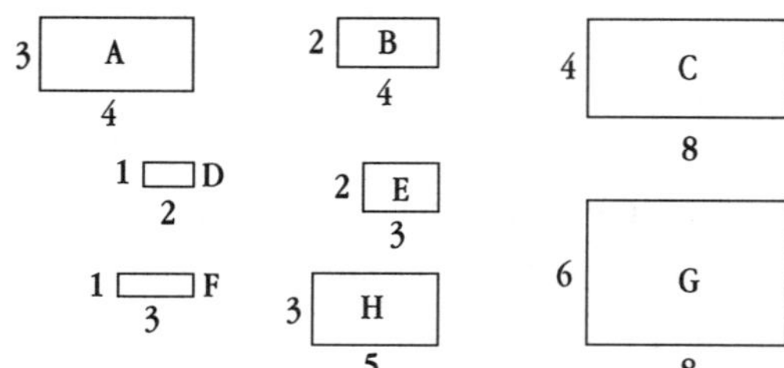

2. a. Draw two rectangles that are similar to rectangle B below. One of your rectangles should be smaller than rectangle B and the other should be larger than rectangle B.

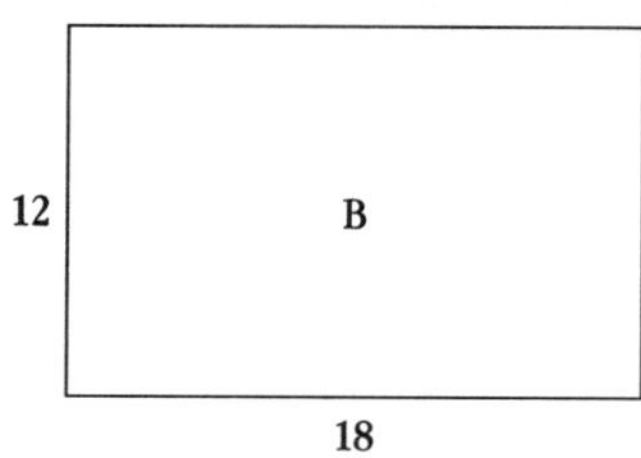

   b. What is the scale factor from rectangle B to each of your rectangles?

   c. Find the area of each of your rectangles.

   d. What is the relationship of the area of rectangle B to the area of each of your rectangles?

3. Use grid paper to help you complete this problem.

   a. Give the dimensions of all rectangles that have an area of 24 and whole-number side lengths.

   b. Give the dimensions of all rectangles that have an area of 6 and whole-number side lengths.

   c. Give the dimensions of all rectangles that have an area of 12 and whole-number side lengths.

   d. Which rectangles in parts a, b, and c are similar?

4. For each pair of figures, give the scale factor from figure A to figure B.

a.

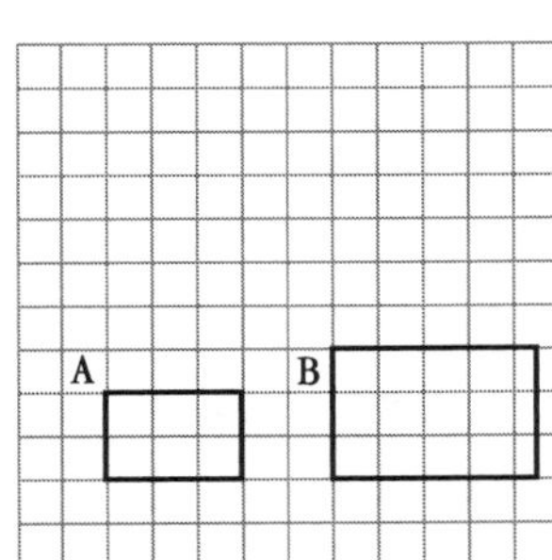

b.

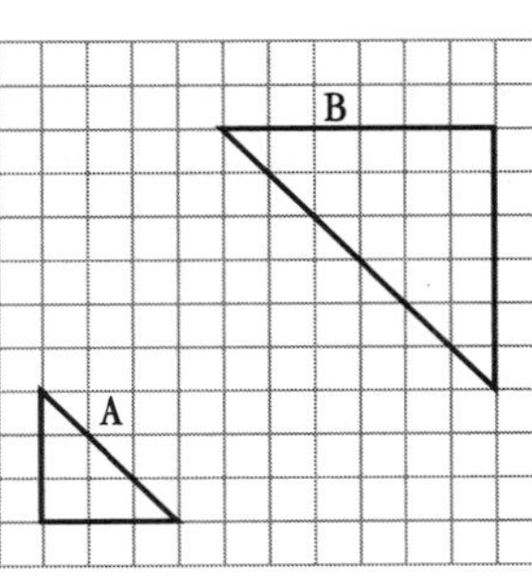

c.

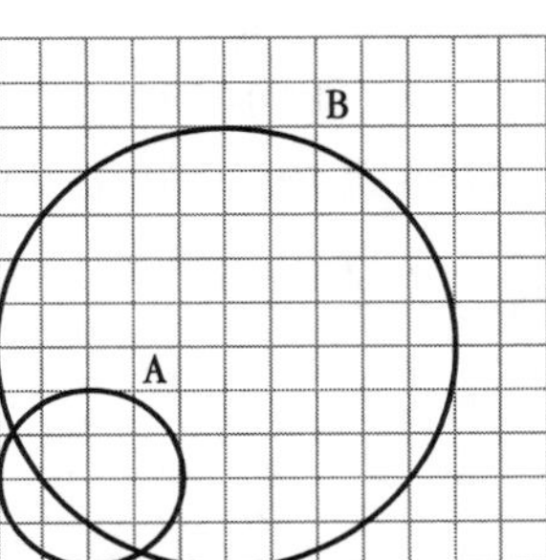

5. The parallelogram below has height 2 and base 3.

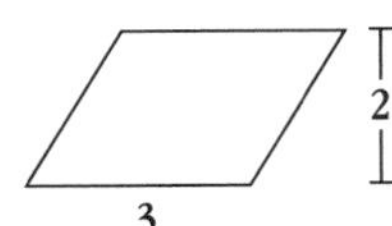

a. Using four copies of this parallelogram as rep-tiles, make a second parallelogram that is similar to the first. What are the base, height, and area of the new parallelogram?

b. How many copies of the original parallelogram would you need to make the next largest, similar parallelogram? What are the base, height, and area of this parallelogram?

c. If you continued making larger and larger parallelograms, how many copies of the original parallelogram would you need to make the fourth figure? The fifth figure? The tenth figure? What are the base, height, and area of each figure?

6. On grid paper, draw a rectangle with base 5 and area 30.

a. Find the base, height, and area of the rectangle made by enlarging the rectangle you drew by a scale factor of 3.

b. Find the base, height, and area of the rectangle made by enlarging the original rectangle by a scale factor of 10.

c. Find the base, height, and area of the rectangle made by reducing the original rectangle by a scale factor of $\frac{1}{2}$.

d. Find the base, height, and area of the rectangle made by reducing the original rectangle by a scale factor of 40%.

e. Draw a rectangle with a base of 3 and an area of 30. If you completed parts a, b, c, and d using this figure, how would the new measures (base, height, and area) compare with the measures you found with the first rectangle? Why do you think this is so?

7. A circle with circumference 6π and area 9π is enlarged by a scale factor of 3. What are the circumference and area of the enlarged circle? Explain your reasoning.

Investigation 5

Use these problems for additional practice after Investigation 5.

1. a. Identify the similar parallelograms in the figure below.
   b. Name all sets of corresponding sides for the similar parallelograms you found.
   c. Name all sets of corresponding angles for the similar parallelograms you found.

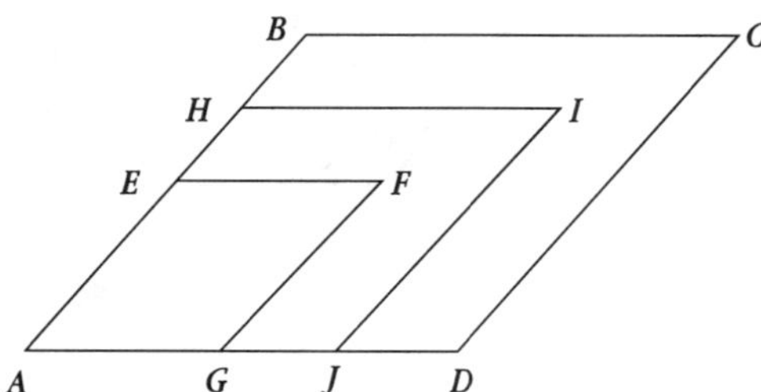

2. David is using the shadow method to estimate the heights of three trees in the school yard. For each set of data, make a diagram showing the tree, the meterstick, and the shadows, and then determine the missing information.

   a. Height of tree = ? — Length of shadow of tree = $\frac{9}{2}$
      Height of meterstick = 1 m — Length of meterstick's shadow = $\frac{1}{2}$
   b. Height of tree = 6.5 m — Length of shadow of tree = ?
      Height of meterstick = 1 m — Length of meterstick's shadow = $\frac{3}{4}$
   c. Height of tree = 7.2 m — Length of shadow of tree = 2.4 m
      Height of meterstick = 1 m — Length of meterstick's shadow = ?

3. Charlotte is using the mirror method to find the heights of objects. Here are some of the measurements she recorded. Make a diagram for each situation, and determine the missing information.

   a. Height from the ground to Charlotte's eyes = 1.5 m
      Distance from center of mirror to Charlotte = 1.5 m
      Distance from center of mirror to shed = 2.5 m
      Height of the roof of shed = ?
   b. Height from the ground to Charlotte's eyes = 1.5 m
      Distance from center of mirror to Charlotte = 0.5 m
      Distance from center of mirror to Charlotte's Great Dane = ?
      Height of the Charlotte's Great Dane = 1 m

4. Refer to the diagram below to answer the following questions.

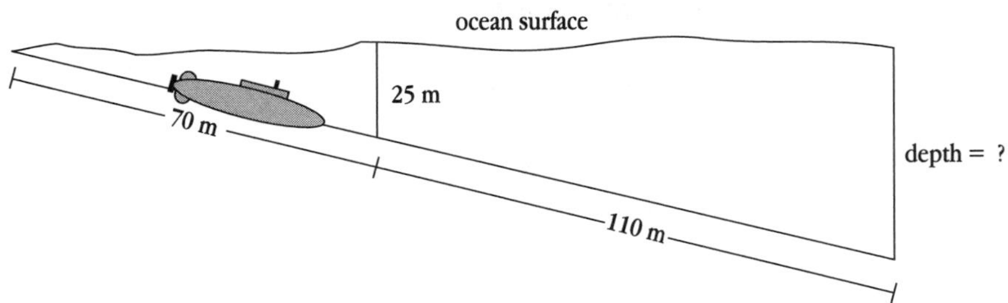

a. After traveling 70 m in its dive, the submarine is at a depth of 25 m. What will the submarine's depth be if it continues its dive for another 110 m?

b. If the submarine continues on its present course and travels a total of 300 m in its dive, what will the final depth of the submarine be?

Investigation 6

Use these problems for additional practice after Investigation 6.

1. Use the *Turtle Math* program below to answer the following questions.

```
fd 40
rt 90
fd 60
rt 90
fd 40
rt 90
fd 60
```

   a. Sketch the rectangle this program will create. Label the dimensions in turtle steps.

   b. Write a *Turtle Math* program that will draw a rectangle similar to the rectangle drawn with the above program so that the scale factor from the original rectangle to the new rectangle is 2.

   c. Write a *Turtle Math* program that will draw a rectangle similar to the rectangle drawn with the original program so that the scale factor from the original rectangle to the new rectangle is 75%.

   d. Write a *Turtle Math* program that will draw a rectangle similar to the rectangle drawn with the original program so that the scale factor from the original rectangle to the new rectangle is $\frac{1}{2}$.

   e. Write a *Turtle Math* program that will draw a rectangle similar to the rectangle drawn with the original program but with an area 9 times the original area. What is the scale factor from the orignial rectangle to the new rectangle? Explain your reasoning.

2. Use the *Turtle Math* program below to answer the following questions.

```
rt 120
fd 90
rt 120
fd 90
rt 120
fd 90
```

   a. Sketch the equilateral triangle this program will create. Label the dimensions in turtle steps.

   b. Write a *Turtle Math* program that will draw a triangle similar to the triangle drawn with the program above but with $\frac{1}{4}$ the original area.

   c. Write a *Turtle Math* program that will draw a triangle similar to the triangle drawn with the program above but with $\frac{1}{9}$ the original area.

Investigation 1

1. a. Answers will vary. Valid solutions are rectangles with width-to-length ratios of 3:4, such as 1.5×2 or 6×8.

   b. Answers will vary. Valid solutions are rectangles with width-to-length ratios that are not 3:4, such as 4×8.

2. Corresponding sides are *AB* and *VW*, *BC* and *WX*, *CD* and *XY*, *DE* and *YZ*, *EA* and *ZV*.

   Corresponding angles are *A* and *V*, *B* and *W*, *C* and *X*, *D* and *Y*, *E* and *Z*.

3. a. Four copies of the smaller square will fit inside the larger square.

   b. The answer to part a will be the same for any square. Possible explanation: The length and width are doubled no matter what size square you start with, so 2×2, or 4, smaller squares will always fit in the larger square.

4. a. Four copies of the smaller rectangle will fit inside the larger rectangle.

   b. The answer to part a will be the same for any rectangle.

Investigation 2

1. a. Nine copies of the original rectangle fit inside the new rectangle.

   b. The answer to part a will be the same for any rectangle. Possible explanation: The length and width are tripled no matter what size rectangle you start with, so 3×3, or 9, smaller rectangles will always fit in the larger rectangle.

2. The figure is a rectangle (set 1), a triangle (set 2), and two small squares (sets 3 and 4).

   a. The angles would have the same measure, and the sides would be six times as long as the corresponding sides of the original. The two drawings would be similar.

   b. The angles would have the same measure, and the sides would be half as long as the corresponding sides of the original. The two drawings would be similar.

   c. The angles would have the same measure, and the sides would be three times as long as the corresponding sides of the original. The two drawings would be similar. The larger drawing would sit to the right and down from the original.

3. no; To be similar the x- and y-coordinates need to be stretched or shrunk by the same scale factor. The rule $(2x, 3y)$ stretches the figure more in the y direction than in the x direction.

4. yes; In the new figure, the x- and y-coordinates are multiplied by the same number, so the resulting figure will be similar to the original.

Investigation 3

1. a. Possible answers: 4 and 6, or 2 and 3

   b. Possible answers: If the leg lengths are 4 and 6, then 4 copies of the right triangle can be put together to match the original right triangle. If the leg lengths are 2 and 3, then 16 copies of the right triangle can be put together to match the original right triangle.

2. a. yes; yes

   b. no; yes

3. a. $x = 12$

   b. $a = 3$

4. a. Yes, a square foot and a square yard are similar because all squares are similar. The scale factor from a square foot to a square yard is 3 and the scale factor from a square yard to a square foot is $\frac{1}{3}$.

   b. There are 9 square feet in 1 square yard. This is the square of the scale factor.

   c. The area of the room would be $28 \times 9 = 252$ square feet.

   d. $\frac{1800}{9} = 200$ square yards.

   e. The scale factor from a square inch to a square foot is 12. The scale factor from a square inch to a square yard is 36.

5. a. Yes, they are similar. The scale factor from a square centimeter to a square meter is 100. The scale factor from a square meter to a square centimeter is 0.01.

   b. 10,000 square centimeters = 1 square meter

   c. $28 \times 10{,}000 \text{ cm}^2 = 280{,}000 \text{ cm}^2$

   d. $1800 \text{ cm}^2 \div 10{,}000 \text{ cm}^2 = 0.18 \text{ m}^2$

Investigation 4

1. *B* and *C* (scale factor of 2); *D* and *B* (scale factor of 2); *A* and *G* (scale factor of 2); *D* and *C* (scale factor of 4)

2. a. Answers will vary.

   b. Answers will vary.

   c. Answers will vary.

   d. For all answers, the ratio of the areas will be the ratio of the squares of the scale factors.

3. a. 1×24, 2×12, 3×8, 4×6

   b. 1×6, 2×3

   c. 1×12, 2×6, 3×4

   d. 1×6 and 2×12 are similar (scale factor of 2); 2×3 and 4×6 are similar (scale factor of 2)

4. a. 1.5
   b. 2
   c. 2.5

5. a. base = 6, height = 4, area = 24
   b. 9 copies; base = 9, height = 6, area = 54
   c. 4th figure will need 16 copies; base = 12, height = 8, area = 96
   5th figure will need 25 copies; base = 15, height = 10, area = 150
   10th figure will need 100 copies; base = 30, height = 20, area = 600

6. a. base = 15, height = 18, area = 270
   b. base = 50, height = 60, area = 3000
   c. base = 2.5, height = 3, area = 7.5
   d. base = 2, height = 2.4, area = 4.8
   e. The original rectangle will be 3 by 10. The base and height measures would be different from those for the other rectangle, but the areas would be the same. This is because in each case, the area is multiplied by the square of the scale factor. Since the areas of the original rectangles were the same and because both rectangles are being multiplied by the same scale factors, the resulting area in each case will be the same.

7. The circumference is $3 \times 6\pi = 18\pi$, and the area is $(3)^2 \times 9\pi = 9 \times 9\pi = 81\pi$. The circumference increases by the scale factor, but the area increases by the square of the scale factor.

Investigation 5

1. a. Parallelograms *ABCD*, *AHIJ*, and *AEFG* are similar.
   b. *AB*, *AH*, and *AE*; *BC*, *HI*, and *EF*; *CD*, *IJ*, and *FG*; *DA*, *JA*, and *GA*
   c. *A*, *A*, and *A*; *E*, *H*, and *B*; *F*, *I*, and *C*; *D*, *J*, and *G*

2. a. 9 m
   b. $4\frac{7}{8}$ m
   c. $\frac{1}{3}$ m

3. a. 2.5 m
   b. $\frac{1}{3}$ m

4. a. The new depth will be $\frac{25}{70} \times 180$ m = 64.3 m.
   b. The new depth will be $\frac{25}{70} \times 300$ m = 107.1 m.

Investigation 6

1. a.

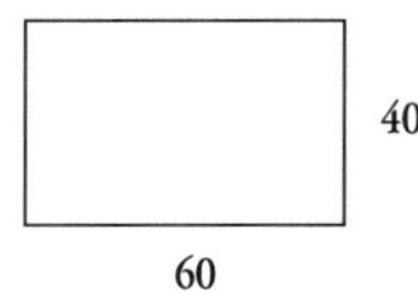

b.
```
fd 80
rt 90
fd 120
rt 90
fd 80
rt 90
fd 120
```

c.
```
fd 30
rt 90
fd 45
rt 90
fd 30
rt 90
fd 45
```

d.
```
fd 20
rt 90
fd 30
rt 90
fd 20
rt 90
fd 30
```

e. The scale factor from the original rectangle to the new rectangle is 3 because the area of the new rectangle is 3^2, or 9, times that of the original.
```
fd 120
rt 90
fd 180
rt 90
fd 120
rt 90
fd 180
```

2. a.

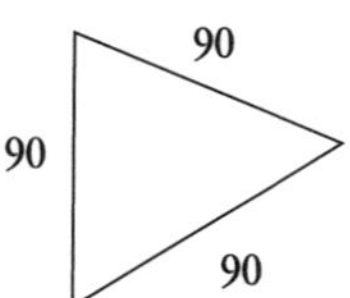

b.
```
rt 120
fd 45
rt 120
fd 45
rt 120
fd 45
```

c.
```
rt 120
fd 30
rt 120
fd 30
rt 120
fd 30
```

Descriptive Glossary

compare When we compare objects, we examine them to determine how they are alike and how they are different. We compare when we classify objects by size, color, weight, or shape. We compare when we decide that two figures have the same shape or that they are not similar.

congruent figures Congruent figures have corresponding angles that are equal and corresponding sides the same length.

coordinate graphing Coordinate graphing is making a graph using pairs of numbers—(x, y), called the x- and y-coordinates—to locate positions on a coordinate plane. The x-coordinate tells how far to move right or left (horizontally) from the origin, and the y-coordinate tells how far to move up or down (vertically). The combination of the two moves locates a point in the plane. For example, the pair of numbers $(3, {}^{-}0.5)$ indicates a unique point in the plane, 3 units to the right of the origin and down 0.5 units.

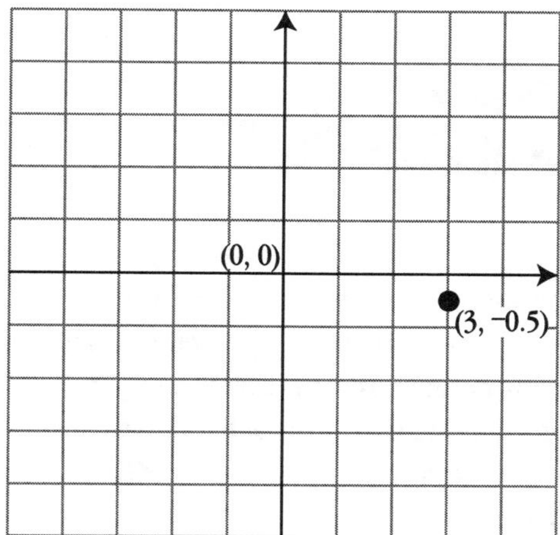

corresponds, corresponding Corresponding sides or angles have the same relative position in similar figures. In this pair of similar shapes, side AB corresponds to side $A'B'$, and $\angle BCD$ corresponds to $\angle B'C'D'$.

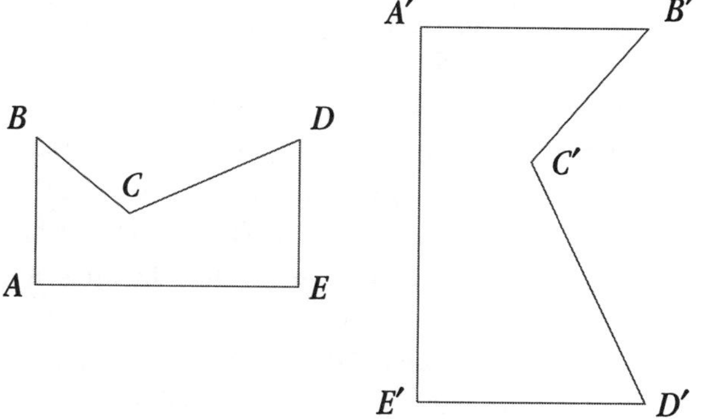

image An image is the figure that results from some transformation of a figure. It is often of interest to consider what is the same and what is different between a figure and its image.

ratio A ratio is a comparison of two quantities that tells the scale between them. Here are some examples of uses of ratios:

- In the similar figures above, suppose $AB = 2$ and $A'B' = 3$. Then the ratio of the length of AB to the length of $A'B'$ is $\frac{2}{3}$. The ratio of the length of $A'B'$ to AB is $\frac{3}{2}$.
- If a small figure is enlarged by a scale factor of 2, the ratio of the small figure's area to the large figure's area will be $\frac{1}{4}$. The ratio of the large figure's area to the small figure's area will be $\frac{4}{1}$, or 4.

Descriptive Glossary

scale factor The scale factor shows the ratio of the lengths of similar figures. If the scale factor is 3, all the length measures in the image are three times the corresponding measures in the original. If the scale factor is $\frac{2}{3}$, the image has length measures $\frac{2}{3}$ those of the original. The scale factor can be found by forming the ratio, or quotient, of the length of a side of the image to the length of the corresponding side in the original. The scale factor can be given as a fraction, a decimal, or a percent. If the scale factor is larger than 1, the image is larger than the original figure. If the scale factor is positive but less than 1, the image is smaller than the original figure. If the scale factor is 1, the original and the image are congruent. On a coordinate grid, it can be seen that scale factors less than 0 flip the figure over the x and y axes in addition to stretching or shrinking it. Scale factors between 0 and $^-1$ shrink the original; scale factors less than $^-1$ stretch the original, and a scale factor of $^-1$ produces an image congruent to the original but at a different place in the plane.

similar Similar figures have the same shape. Two figures are mathematically similar if and only if their corresponding angles are equal and the ratios of all pairs of corresponding sides are equal. This ratio, $\frac{\text{image length}}{\text{original length}}$, compares a side in the image to its corresponding side in the original. This means that there is a single scale by which all sides of the smaller figure "stretch" or "shrink" into the corresponding sides of the larger figure.

transform, transformation We transform a figure by changing the coordinates of the points in the figure by some rule that gives directions for adding an amount to a coordinate, or multiplying a coordinate by a number, or both. A transformation may change the figure in some way: it may be stretched or shrunk proportionally, it may maintain its shape and size and just be relocated in the plane, or it may be distorted.

Spanish Glossary

comparar Cuando comparamos objetos, los examinamos para determinar sus parecidos y diferencias. Cuando clasificamos objetos según su tamaño, color, peso o forma, estamos comparándolos. Al determinar que dos figuras tienen la misma forma o que no son semejantes, estamos haciendo una comparación.

corresponder, correspondientes Se dice que los lados o ángulos son correspondientes cuando tienen la misma posición relativa en figuras semejantes. En el siguiente par de figuras semejantes, el lado AB corresponde al lado $A'B'$ y $\angle BCD$ corresponde a $\angle B'C'D'$.

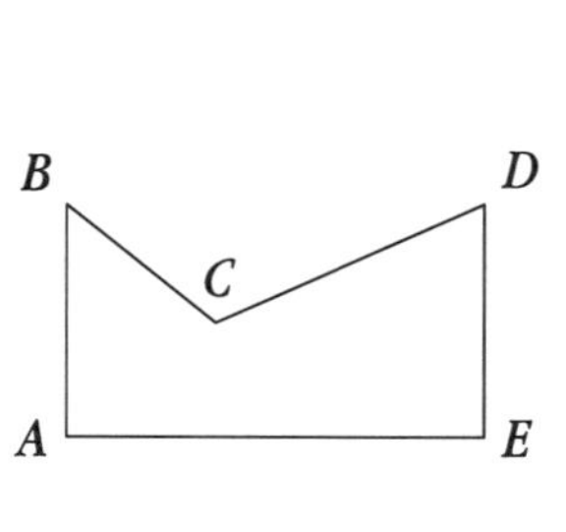

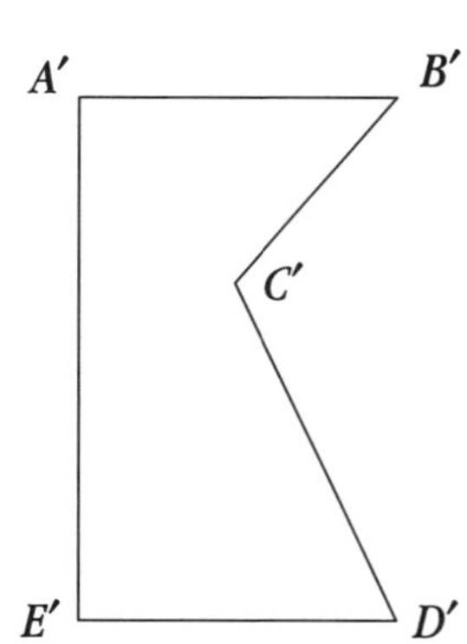

Spanish Glossary

factor de escala El número utilizado para multiplicar las coordenadas de una figura para ampliarla o reducirla. Si el factor de escala es 3, todas las longitudes de la imagen son tres veces las medidas correspondientes de la figura original. Si el factor de escala es $\frac{2}{3}$, las longitudes de la imagen son $\frac{2}{3}$ de las de la figura original. Para hallar el factor de escala se puede formar la razón, o cociente, entre la longitud de un lado de la imagen y la del lado correspondiente de la figura original. El factor de escala puede expresarse en forma de fracción, número decimal o porcentaje. Si el factor de escala es mayor que 1, la imagen es más grande que la figura original. Si el factor de escala es positivo pero menor que 1, la imagen es más pequeña que la figura original. Si el factor de escala es 1, la figura original y la imagen son congruentes. En una cuadrícula de coordenadas, es posible observar que los factores de escala menores que 0, además de estirar o encoger la figura, la invierten sobre los ejes de las x y de las y. Los factores de escala comprendidos entre 0 y $^{-}1$ encogen la figura original; los factores de escala menores de $^{-}1$ la estiran, y un factor de escala de $^{-}1$ produce una imagen congruente con la figura original pero en otro lugar del plano.

figuras semejantes Figuras que tienen la misma forma. Dos figuras son matemáticamente semejantes si y sólo si sus ángulos correspondientes son iguales y las razones entre todos los pares de lados correspondientes son iguales. La razón $\frac{\text{longitud de lado de la imagen}}{\text{longitud de lado original}}$ es la escala aplicada a todos los lados de la figura original para "estirar" o "encoger" cada lado para obtener los lados correspondientes en la imagen.

gráficas de coordenadas Las gráficas de coordenadas en las que se utilizan pares de números (x, y), llamados coordenadas x e y, para ubicar posiciones en un plano de coordenadas. La coordenada x indica a qué distancia moverse hacia la derecha o izquierda (horizontalmente) desde el punto de origen mientras que la coordenada y señala cuánto moverse hacia arriba o abajo (verticalmente). La combinación de los dos desplazamientos permite ubicar un punto único en el plano. Por ejemplo, el par de números (3, –0.5) indica un punto situado 3 unidades a la derecha del punto de origen y 0.5 unidades hacia abajo.

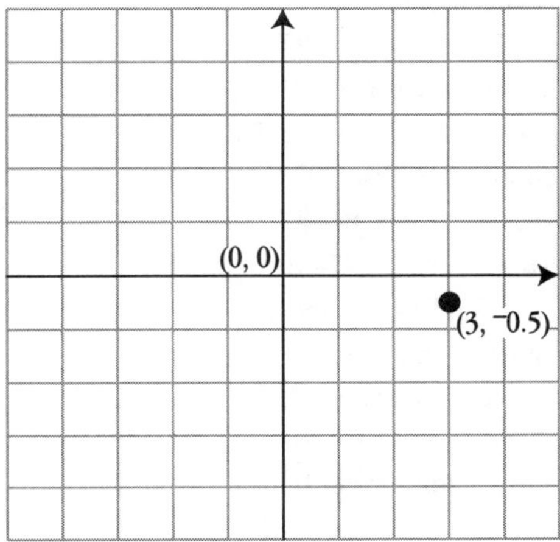

imagen La figura que resulta al realizar la transformación de otra figura. A menudo es interesante tener en cuenta en qué se parecen y en qué se diferencian una figura y su imagen.

razón Una comparación de dos cantidades que indica la escala existente entre ellas. He aquí algunos ejemplos de los usos de razones:

- En el par de figuras semejantes que aparece en la página 88, imagina que $AB = 2$ y $A'B' = 3$. La razón entre la longitud de AB y $A'B'$ es $\frac{2}{3}$. La razón de la longitud de $A'B'$ con respecto a AB es $\frac{3}{2}$.
- Si una figura pequeña se amplía a un factor de escala 2, la razón entre el área de la figura pequeña y la de la figura grande será $\frac{1}{4}$. La razón del área de la figura grande con respecto a la figura pequeña será $\frac{4}{1}$, o sea 4.

Index

Index

Index